Kitāb Laṭā'if al-Minan fī Manāqib Abī al-ᶜAbbās al-Mursī wa Shaykhihi Abī al-Ḥasan

The Subtle Blessings in the Saintly Lives of Abū al-ᶜAbbās al-Mursī and his master Abū al-Ḥasan al-Shādhilī

The Founders of the Shādhilī Order

Laṭā'if al-Minan

The Subtle Blessings in the Saintly Lives of Abū al-ʿAbbās al-Mursī and his master Abū al-Ḥasan al-Shādhilī

The Founders of the Shādhilī Order

TRANSLATED FROM THE ARABIC

WITH A PREFACE AND NOTES BY

Nancy Roberts

FONS VITAE

First published in 2005 by
Fons Vitae
49 Mockingbird Valley Drive
Louisville, KY 40207
http://www.fonsvitae.com

Library of Congress Control Number: 2005927163

ISBN 1-887752-61-7

This book was typeset by Neville Blakemore, Jr.

Printed in Canada

Contents

Translator's Preface

The present translation of *Laṭā'if al-Minan* is based on the edition prepared by Shaykh Khālid ᶜAbd al-Raḥmān al-ᶜAkk (Damascus: Dār al-Bashā'ir, 1992), as well as an edition reviewed and introduced by ᶜAbd al-Raḥmān Ḥasan Maḥmūd, Second Printing (Cairo: ᶜĀlam al-Fikr, 1992), in which some errors and omissions found in the former edition are corrected. When translating the extensive poetry sections in Chapter 9 and the Conclusion, I compared al-ᶜAkk's edition with four other editions of the book to ensure that the reading I was working from was reliable.

Of the editor's footnotes, I have translated only those which deal directly with the documentation of prophetic traditions; hence, I have not included those which either go into alternative versions of given traditions or which serve simply to explain specific terms or expressions which appear in the text, since such explanations are incorporated into the English translation. Consequently, all footnotes which appear are my own explanatory notes with the exception of those identified specifically as editor's notes.

For a detailed and scholarly overview of Ibn ᶜAṭā' Allāh's literary corpus, as well as additional biographical information on Ibn ᶜAṭā' Allāh, Shaykh Abū al-Abbās al-Mursdī, and Shaykh Abū al-Ḥasan al-Shādhilī, please see the Translator's Introduction to Dr. Mary Ann Koury Danner's *The Key to Salvation and the Lamp of Souls*, a translation into English of Ibn ᶜAṭā' Allāh's *Miftāḥ al-Falāḥ wa Miṣbāḥ al-Arwāḥ* (Cambridge: The Islamic Texts Society, 1996).

I am greatly indebted to Dr. William Chittick's *The Sufi Path of Knowledge: Ibn al-ᶜArabī's Metaphysics of Imagination* (Albany: State University of New York Press, 1989) for definitions of Sufi terminology, for which Chittick provides clarification through his translations of passages out of Ibn al-ᶜArabī's *Meccan Revelations*. I want to extend special thanks to Gray Henry-Blakemore of Fons Vitae Publications for entrusting me with this work, and to Dr. Mary Ann [Danner] Fadae, who put in the word of confidence which brought my path together with Gray's. And more than perhaps any other person on earth, I owe thanks to my husband, Dr. Amin Odeh, whose understanding of the Sufi path in its various manifestations on both the intellectual and experiential levels, as well as his infinite patience and wonderful ability to rephrase Ibn ᶜAṭā' Allāh's words in such a way that a novice like myself could grasp what he has to say with sufficient clarity to render it into English, gave me the courage to take on this blessed task.

I would not be exaggerating if I said that the translation of this book felt like entering into a sacrament, day after day after day. From my first reading of its opening pages, I knew it had something profoundly special to offer me, and that I would be a fortunate woman indeed if I could convey it in English to others with a spiritual hunger in their hearts. For those who seek a better understanding of what it means to walk the Sufi path, Ibn ᶜAṭā Allāh offers a marvelous entry, not by giving them a list of how-tos but, rather, simply by introducing his readers to his beloved shaykh, Abū al-ᶜAbbās al-Mursī and his shaykh's shaykh, Abū al-Ḥasan al-Shādhilī. As I entered their world—their actions, their words, and the formative influence they exerted on the author—I felt myself unwittingly receiving their blessing and wanting more than ever to experience something of the immediacy of the Divine which was so vivid for them. For those who struggle with crippling guilt, Ibn ᶜAṭā Allāh brings assurance of the depth of the Divine mercy, and for those complacent in their righteousness, a reminder that even the most virtuous of our actions are nothing but gifts of grace. Whether in commenting on words from the Qur'ān or prophetic hadiths, relating incidents from his life and the lives of his spiritual masters, or transmitting the words of their prayers and spiritual litanies, this man of faith has a way of addressing spiritual truths to his reader's situation and infusing life with a sense of hope and Divine purpose, sometimes with a touch of humor, sometimes in a way that forces one to stop and puzzle, but never without the profoundest compassion and wisdom. Whoever reads Ibn ᶜAṭā' Allāh's words with an open heart will find both challenge and solace, a mirror reflecting his or her own frailties and a potion that offers renewed strength for the journey.

Laṭā'if al-Minan

The Subtle Blessings in the Saintly Lives of Abū al-ᶜAbbās al-Mursī and his master Abū al-Ḥasan al-Shādhilī

The Founders of the Shādhilī Order

Introduction

In the name of God, the Most Gracious,
The Dispenser of Grace

May God's blessings and peace rest upon our master Muḥammad, and upon his household and companions.

Praise be to God, who opens the door of His love to His friends (*awliyā'*).[1] He enlivens their souls, [delivering them] from the bonds of alienation and leading them to offer Him the service which is His due. He imparts His light to their minds, thereby enabling them to see for themselves the marvels of His power. He guards their hearts from all that is other than He, and cleanses them of all manner of [worldly] effects until they attain the knowledge of Him!

He reveals to their spirits the holiness of His perfection and the attributes of His majesty until they are captives to His presence.

He grants their innermost beings the joy of nearness to Him and sudden stirrings of [the divine] attraction until they attain realization through the vision of His unity. He takes them from themselves and consumes them so utterly that they are no longer present to themselves, causing them to drown in the sea of His being.

He scatters the armies of separation with the battalions of union for His elect, guarding the sanctuary of their innermost beings with [spiritual] lights lest it be a manifestation of anything other than His utter incomparability!

He has launched the stars of the sciences in the heavens of understanding, thereby to guide travelers into the presence of His divinity. He has illumined the moon of divine oneness in the expanse of [His] incomparability, while [created] beings vanish in the presence of His pre-eternity. After all, what existed with Him in His pre-eternity such that it will be with Him in his post-eternity? Rather, He is the First and the Last [in and of Himself], not together with His creation, and He is the Manifest and the Hidden. What is the entire universe when compared with His utter holiness?!

I praise Him, for praise is due to Him for His attributes of majesty and greatness.

I thank Him, for thanksgiving is due to Him for the wealth of His blessings.

I bring my supplications before Him, and how could I do otherwise, when He is the One who has encompassed everything with His mercy, and when He has showered His servants in the realms of the seen and the unseen with His abundant graces?

I confess to Him that I have been remiss in fulfilling my duties toward Him as the one and only Sovereign,[2] and I know that no one can fully comprehend Him either in His essence or in His attributes.

The servant possesses nothing of God but that which He has graciously bestowed upon him, nor may he attain additional merits or advantages except those which God has added unto him or be victorious in the realm of earthly causes and effects but by total reliance upon Him.

[He is] the Almighty, the all-Powerful, the Truly Wise, the One who holds sway [over all His creatures], the Observer of the action of everyone who acts, and the glance of everyone who looks. Nothing within our consciences is concealed from Him, nor do the hidden recesses of our hearts escape His knowledge!

Through his royal dominion He has revealed His wisdom, and through His kingdom, His power. He has made

Himself known to everything, and nothing denies His lordship: "Oh verily, His is all creation and all command. Hallowed is God, the Sustainer of all the worlds" {Al-Aᶜrāf [The Faculty of Discernment] 7: 54}.

I bear witness that there is no god but God alone, who has no partner, while everything bears witness to His unity in His divinity. I bear witness that Muḥammad is His servant and His messenger, chosen from among all other creatures, who is renowned in the worlds of the seen and the unseen for the perfection of his elected status, and the one who demonstrated perfect loyalty to his Master in his station as a servant. May God's everlasting blessings and abundant peace rest upon him and upon his household and companions.

* * *

My intention in writing this book has been to mention a number of the virtues of our master and companion, the pole of gnostics,[3] the signpost of the rightly guided, the supreme apologist for Sufism, the travelers' guide, the rescuer of the perishing, he who brings together the science[s] of names, letters and circles,[4] he who speaks by the light of his flawless spiritual insight into [people's] secret thoughts, the "cave" of those with perfect certainty, the elite of those who have arrived, he who unveils the suns of knowledge after they have set and the secrets of subtle intimations after they have departed, he who has arrived in God and who assists others in doing the same: Shihāb al-Dīn, i.e., Abū al-ᶜAbbās Ibn ᶜUmar al-Anṣārī al-Mursī.

God caused him to dwell in His paradise[5] and granted him, throughout the hours, the bliss of His intimate companionship. I mention his shaykh from whom he received instruction as well as the battles in which he was reported to have engaged[6] or about which he [al-Mursī] heard from him [i.e., al-Mursī's shaykh], as well as his miracles, his sciences, his secrets, his dealings with God, may He be praised and exalted, the commentaries which he offered on verses from the Book of God Almighty, his explication of the meaning of this or that report which had been passed down on the authority of the Messenger of God ﷺ, or statements which he made on this or that truth (which had been passed down on the authority of some follower of the [Sufi] path) the meaning of which had not been understood. I mention, in addition, what he passed down on the authority of his shaykh, Abū al-Ḥasan al-Shādhilī, may God be pleased with him, poetry which was either composed by him or recited in his presence, or poetry which was composed and recited about him and which contained mention of the path and its followers.[7] I have recorded those traditions concerning him which are susceptible of confirmation, be they many or few.

The companions[8] of the shaykh, imam and pole Abū al-Ḥasan (may God hallow his spirit) recorded a number of his sayings, although he (may God be pleased with him) never composed a book. It was reported to me that he was once asked, "O master, why do you not compose books on the evidence for God Almighty and the Sufi sciences?" To which he (may God be pleased with him) replied, "My books are my companions!"

Nor did our shaykh Abū al-ᶜAbbās (may God be pleased with him) write any book on such subjects. The reason for this is that the sciences of this community are the sciences of spiritual realization, which people's minds cannot bear.

I once heard our shaykh, Abū al-ᶜAbbās (may God be pleased with him) say, "All that is contained in the books of the people amounts to [nothing more than] teardrops from the shores of the sea of realization!"

Not knowing whether any of the companions of our shaykh, Abū al-ᶜAbbās (may God be pleased with him) had undertaken to compile his words and to record his virtuous traits and deeds and the secrets of his sciences and marvels, I was spurred to write this book. However, I only undertook to do so after having sought guidance from God Almighty and asked Him for help (for He is the best of all helpers) as well as for direction to the clear path.

I have divided the book into an introduction, ten chapters and a conclusion. As for the introduction, it contains evidence which demonstrates that our Prophet Muḥammad ﷺ is superior to all other descendents of Adam, that is, to all other human beings, and indeed, to all other creatures. In each section, I present evidence from the Book of God Almighty and from the Sunnah of His Prophet ﷺ. I make clear that the friends of God (saints) receive their sustenance from the "Muḥammadan reality," and that they are none other than the manifestations of the lights of prophethood and the points of ascent for their radiances. I have also come to realize that the lights of friendship with God (sainthood) are ever constant due to the necessary perpetuity of the lights of prophethood.

I make mention of the difference between messengerhood, prophethood, and sainthood, or friendship with God. In addition, I make clear who is most worthy of the inheritance spoken of in the saying of the Prophet ﷺ, "Scholars are the heirs of the prophets."[9]

I explain what the knowledge is which God praises in this fashion, and who those scholars are who are most worthy of being drawn near to Him.

I discuss the fact that the friends of God who appear in times of deep darkness are the most worthy to have God increase their light and grant them such abundant certainty that their victory is assured, thereby enabling them to drive back the deep darkness of the times and to defeat the armies of heedlessness with their hosts of light.

I make mention of the various types of friendship with God, i.e., sainthood, the rarity of the saint's value, the excellence of his rank and the purity of his station based on the contents of the Qur'an and the prophetic traditions, in order to prepare you to believe the traditions which have been passed down concerning God's friends and the miracles of those whose hearts He has purified.

As for the ten chapters of this book, their contents may be summarized as follows:

Chapter One introduces his [al-Mursī's] shaykh from whom he received this rank and a testimony from the eminent scholars who were his contemporaries that he was the pole of his era and the one who served as the standard bearer of his time for those who have experienced a vision of the divine reality.

Chapter Two presents the shaykh's testimony that he was heir to the station of sainthood and the one who held the position of unquestioned preeminence. It contains his own testimony to the copious blessings which God had bestowed upon him, and the testimony of the friends of God that through his arrival at the knowledge of God, he had attained the utmost one could possibly desire.

Chapter Three deals with his trials and battles and what his companions experienced with him, as well as his "unveilings" (*mukāshafāt*).

Chapter Four deals with his knowledge and asceticism, his piety and high aspirations, his magnanimity and patient endurance, and the rightness of his path.

Chapter Five concerns itself with verses from the Book of God Almighty whose meaning he clarified and whose content he disclosed.

Chapter Six presents the prophetic traditions which he commented upon, divulging secrets contained therein based on the teachings of "the elect" (*ahl al-khuṣūṣiyah*).

Chapter Seven presents his explanations of problematic statements made by those who have experienced the divine realities (*ahl al-ḥaqā'iq*), and his interpretation thereof based on the most beautiful of paths.

Chapter Eight presents his statements on the [divine] realities and mystical stations, and his clarification of certain enigmas in this connection.

Chapter Nine presents poetry which he composed and recited himself or which was composed and recited in his presence, as well as verses which were recited about him and which contain mention of his singular traits.

Chapter Ten presents the phrases of divine remembrance (*dhikr*) and the prayer of supplication with which he used to conclude his speech. It also presents the *ḥizb*[10] which he composed for those who had become recipients of his knowledge and understanding, as well as additions from the *dhikr* and the *ḥizb* employed by his shaykh, Abū al-Ḥasan, which were required in order for others to join his path.

As for the Conclusion, it deals with the ongoing nature of our link with him and his admonitions in both prose and poetry, which awaken one to God and gather one to Him.

* * *

Not everything which I heard from the shaykh (may God be pleased with him) was I able to recall as I was composing this book, nor was I able to confirm everything I recalled. However, in writing this work, my intention has been to benefit my readers in general, and this community[11] in particular. It is my hope that, through this book, those to whom God has apportioned a share of grace and in whose hearts He has placed the light of guidance might believe in the [mystical] states of this community; that those who have disbelieved will return to the acknowledgment [of the truth of what I present] and those who have been arrogant and contemptuous, to an attitude of fairness and impartiality; that we might experience love for those whom God has willed to receive guidance; that it might stand as evidence calling for a response from those who have not [yet] been aided by God's providence; and that those who have believed in this community might, through their belief, enjoy a share of friendship with God and of greater nearness to His providential care.

Al-Junayd (may God be pleased with him) said, "Belief in this knowledge of ours is friendship with God. If you have failed to receive the grace within yourself, then fail not to believe in the grace which others have received." [As God Almighty declares,] "...and if no rainstorm smites it, then soft rain" {Al-Baqarah [The Cow] 2: 265}. A certain gnostic once said, "Belief in an 'opening' (*fatḥ*) [on someone else's part] can only come about through an 'opening' [on the part of the person believing]." Support for what this gnostic said may be found in the words of God Almighty, "...for he to whom God gives no light, no light whatever has he!" {Al-Nūr [The Light] 24: 40}.

God says, "...yet go on reminding [all who would listen]: for verily, such a reminder will profit the believers" {Al-Dhāriyāt [The Dust-Scattering Winds] 51: 55}; and, "In this, behold, there is indeed a reminder for everyone whose heart is wide awake, that is, [everyone who] lends ear with a conscious mind" {Qāf 50: 37}; and, "Only they who are endowed with insight keep this in mind!" {Al-Zumar [The Throngs] 39: 9}.

If God wills good for any of His servants, He causes them to believe in His saints and in what they have brought. Someone's intellect might fail to accept these things; however, on what basis can he claim that God must only give His saints that which can be comprehended by people's minds? It has been said: It is feared that those who disbelieve in them [God's saints] will meet an undesirable end.

Abū Turāb al-Nakhshabī once said, "Whoever does not believe in these miracles has renounced his faith"; in other words, the matter has been concealed from him, which prevents him from seeing the power of God Almighty.[12] God has caused us and you to be among those who acknowledge His bounty to His servants, and who believe in the signs of His providence in those who know His love; He is the One who holds such matters in His hands, and He is capable of bringing them to pass.

I have not refrained from speaking in this book about problematic matters, resolving difficult questions, drawing attention to matters of great import, or disclosing the secrets of those who, in their fccblc-sightedness, have not believed in this community. After all, God—may He be praised and exalted—renders such discussion a tool which serves His ends alone in perfect sincerity. He uses it to deliver us from the sloughs of alienation in order that He might, in His abundant grace, grant us truthfulness in our words, deeds and states, usher us into the ranks of those who know Him both now and in the hereafter, and graciously enable us to understand what is revealed on His authority and to listen well to what He says. He is indeed the All-

Powerful Divinity who is worthy of our full-hearted response.

I have entitled this book *Laṭā'if al-Minan fī Manāqib al-Shaykh Abī al-ᶜAbbās wa Shaykhihi Abī al-Ḥasan* ("Subtle Graces [as Revealed] in the Virtuous Traits and Deeds of Shaykh Abū al-ᶜAbbās and His Shaykh, Abū al-Ḥasan"). The time has now come for me to set about doing what I have intended and to make clear what I hope to accomplish. To God, exalted be He, do I turn for aid, upon Him do I rely, and Him do I beseech through the rank of glory and honor bestowed upon Muḥammad, the master of all God's messengers ﷺ.[13] God is our sufficiency, and a most excellent Guardian!

In introduction, we say: Know that God, may He be praised and exalted, inasmuch as He wished to complete His grace toward us and to pour out His mercy in unlimited abundance, and given that His consummate bounty moved Him to bestow the knowledge of Himself upon His servants (despite His awareness that the minds of the vast majority of them would be incapable of comprehending His divinity), has given His prophets and messengers the perfect ability to accept His divinity and that for which it calls[14] and to receive [this understanding] from Him by virtue of the secret of His uniqueness which He has placed within them. God's prophets and messengers teach others on His authority in order that others may likewise be gathered together on the basis of His divine oneness. As such, they are the *barzakhs* of lights,[15] the treasure-troves of secrets, a mercy given, a grace purified, whose innermost beings He guarded in His pre-eternity from servitude to any being other than He, preserving them in His providence from dependence upon [earthly, finite] effects.

They love nothing and no one but Him and they worship Him alone. He casts the Spirit by His command upon them and continues supplying them [with spiritual riches] through His support and aid. The celestial sphere of prophethood and messengerhood continued in its orbit until it had returned to its point of origin, then to be sealed by the one who possessed the perfection of chosenness, that is, by our Prophet, Muḥammad ﷺ, the flawless master, the opener and the sealer, the light of lights, the secret of secrets, the one revered both in this abode and the abode to come, the one whose minaret shines out over all other creatures, and whose glory is more radiant than any other's.

This is made evident by the Qur'an, where God declares, "And [thus, O Prophet,] We have sent thee as [an evidence of Our] grace[16] towards all the worlds" {Al-Anbiyā' [The Prophets] 21: 107}. He through whom others have received mercy is superior to others; as for the meaning of "world," it refers to all entities other than God, may He be exalted.

God's setting of the Prophet ﷺ above all other human beings is reflected in his words, "I was a prophet when Adam was [still] between water and clay."[17] [He ﷺ also stated,] "I am the master of Adam's son[s], which I say without boasting."[18] As for God's having set him ﷺ above Adam himself (may peace be upon him), he ﷺ indicates this in his statement, "On the Day of Resurrection, Adam and the prophets who succeeded him will be beneath my banner. I am the first intercessor, the first intercessor whose pleas will be granted by God, and I will be the first one to be revealed when the earth is split asunder."[19]

The well-known tradition of intercession (*ḥadīth al-shafāᶜah*) was passed down to us by the shaykh, imam, preserver of the Qur'an[20] and chief *ḥadīth* scholar of his day, Sharaf al-Dīn Abū Muḥammad ᶜAbd al-Mu'min Ibn Khalaf

Ibn Abī al-Ḥasan al-Dumyāṭī, after which I either recited it back to him, or someone else recited it back to him in my hearing. He said: We were told by the two shaykhs, Imam Fakhr al-Quḍāh Abū al-Faḍl Aḥmad Ibn Muḥammad Ibn ᶜAbd al-ᶜAzīz Ibn al-Ḥubāb al-Tamīmī and Abū al-Taqī Ṣāliḥ Ibn Shujāᶜ Ibn Sayyidihim al-Mudlajī al-Kinānī, on the authority of the *sharīf*[21] Abū al-Mafākhir Saᶜīd Ibn al-Ḥusayn Ibn Muḥammad Ibn Saᶜīd al-ᶜAbbāsī al-Ma'mūnī, on the authority of Abū ᶜAbd Allāh al-Fazārī, on the authority of ᶜAbd al-Ghāfir al-Fārisī, on the authority of Abū Aḥmad Muḥammad Ibn ᶜIsā Ibn ᶜAmmūriyah al-Jalūdī, on the authority of Abū Isḥāq Ibrāhīm Ibn Muḥammad Ibn Sufyān the scholar of jurisprudence, on the authority of Abū al-Ḥusayn Muslim Ibn al-Ḥajjāj Ibn Muslim al-Qushayrī al-Nīsābūrī, on the authority of Abū al-Rabīᶜ al-ᶜAtakī, on the authority of Ḥammād Ibn Zayd, on the authority of Maᶜbad Ibn Hilāl al-ᶜAnzī, on the authority of Saᶜīd Ibn Manṣūr, who said (the following wording being his):

> We were told by Ḥammād Ibn Zayd, who was told by Maᶜbad Ibn Ṭalāl: We set out to visit Anas Ibn Mālik and sought a hearing with him through Thābit's good offices. When we arrived, he was performing the mid-morning prayer. Thābit requested his permission for us to see him, and we entered. He seated Thābit with him on his bed and Thābit said to him, "Abū Ḥamzah, your brethren from Baṣrah would like to ask you to relate the tradition of intercession to them."
>
> And he said, "We were told by Muḥammad ﷺ: On the Day of Resurrection, people will surge forward like the waves of the sea, one after another. They will come to Adam, upon him be peace, and say to him, 'Intercede for your descendants.' But

he will say, 'I am not worthy to do so. Rather, you must ask Abraham, upon him be peace, since he was God's beloved friend.'

"They will then approach Abraham, upon him be peace, [with the same request] and he will say, 'I am not worthy to do so. Rather, you must ask Moses, upon him be peace, since he spoke directly with God.'

"They will then come to Moses, upon him be peace, and he will say, 'I am not worthy to do so. Rather, you must ask Jesus, upon him be peace, since he is the word of God, and His spirit.'

"Hence, they will go to Jesus, upon him be peace, and he will say, 'I am not worthy to do so. Rather, you must ask Muḥammad, may God's blessings and peace be upon him!'

"Thereupon I will be brought forward and I will say, 'I am worthy to do so.' I then set out and request my Lord's permission [to make intercession], and permission is granted. I stand before Him, praising Him with encomia which, were not God Almighty Himself to inspire me therewith, I would be unable to bring forth on my own, and I fall down in prostration before Him.

"I am told, 'O Muḥammad, lift your head. Speak and you will be heard. Ask and you will receive. Make intercession and your request will be granted.'

"I say, 'O Lord, my nation, my nation!'[22]

"I am told, 'Set forth, and if anyone has faith in his heart the weight of a grain of wheat or barley, release him from it [the hellfire].'

"So I set forth and do as I have been instructed, after which I return to my Lord and praise Him as I did before. Then I fall down before Him in prostration and I am told, 'O Muḥammad, lift your head. Speak and you will be heard. Ask and you will receive. Make intercession and your request will be granted.'

"I say, 'O Lord, my nation, my nation!'

"I am told, 'Set forth, and if anyone has in his heart a mustard seed's weight of faith, release him from it.'

"So I set forth and do as I have been instructed, after which I return to my Lord and praise Him as I did before and fall down in prostration before Him. I am told, O Muḥammad, lift your head. Speak and you will be heard. Ask and you will receive. Make intercession and your request will be granted.'

"I say, 'O Lord, my nation, my nation!'

"I am told, 'Set forth, and if anyone has in his heart a mustard seed's weight of faith, release him from it.'

"So I set forth and do as I have been instructed, after which I return to my Lord and praise Him as I did before and fall down in prostration before Him. I am told, 'O Muḥammad, lift your head. Speak and you will be heard. Ask and you will receive. Make intercession and your request will be granted.'

"I say, 'O Lord, my nation, my nation!'

"I am told, 'Set forth, and if anyone has in his heart less than, less than, less than a mustard seed's weight of faith, release him from the hellfire.'

"So I set forth and do as I have been instructed."

This is the tradition which Anas related to us. We departed, and when we had reached Ẓahr al-Jubān we said, "Let us pass by and greet al-Ḥasan, who is in hiding in the home of Abū Khalīfah."

When we entered the house, we said, "Abū Saᶜīd, we have just come from visiting your brother, Abū Ḥamzah, who related to us a tradition—the tradition of intercession—the likes of which we have never heard before."

"Let me hear it!" he replied. And we related the tradition to him.

"Tell me the rest of it," he said.

"That's all he told us," we replied.

He said, "He [Anas Ibn Mālik] related this tradition to us twenty years ago as a young man, when his memory was still sharp. He left something out [this time], though I don't know whether he forgot to mention it, or whether he [simply] did not wish to speak to you about it, lest you grow complacent."

"Tell us what it is," we said.

Laughing, he replied, "Man is a creature of haste..."[23] [Then he added,] "I do intend to tell you, though!"

[He then related the following part of the tradition:]

> Then I return to my Lord a fourth time and I praise Him as I did before, then fall down in prostration before Him. I am told, "O Muḥammad, lift your head. Speak and you will be heard. Ask and you will receive. Make intercession and your request will be granted."
>
> I say, "O Lord, grant me permission [to release from the hellfire] those who say, 'There is no god but God.'"
>
> He says to me, "This is not for you to do. However, [I swear] by My glorious might, My majesty and My greatness, I will most surely release from

> the hellfire whoever says, 'There is no god but God.'"

And he said, "I testify of al-Ḥasan that he related this to us based on his having heard Anas Ibn Mālik relate it to him about twenty years earlier as a young man with his memory still sharp."

Note, then, may God have mercy on you, how this tradition reveals the eminence of his station ﷺ and the loftiness of his authority, in that not even the greatest of God's messengers and prophets vied with him ﷺ for this rank which belongs exclusively to him, namely, that of interceding on behalf of everyone who is gathered on the Day of Resurrection.

If you were to say: Why is it, then, that Moses directed his petitioners to Noah in one tradition, and to Abraham in this one, after which Noah yielded to Abraham, and Abraham to Moses, and Moses to Jesus, and Jesus to Muḥammad ﷺ? In other words, why were they not directed to Muḥammad ﷺ from the very beginning?

[In answer to such a question, I say,] if Muḥammad ﷺ had been identified as their intercessor from the very start, it would not be clear from this tradition that none other than he has been given this rank. The Truth, may He be praised, willed that each prophet should point to the one who had succeeded him and that each of them should say, "I am not worthy to do so," thereby relinquishing this rank and making no claim thereto until they came to Jesus, who pointed them to the Messenger of God ﷺ, who said, "I am worthy to do so."

This tradition contains a number of truths, for example, that faith is capable of increase or decrease. Another such truth is that the gnostic sciences[24] have no limit. This may be understood from the Prophet's saying, "Were not God

Almighty Himself to inspire me therewith, I would be unable to bring them forth on my own." It is likewise supported by his ﷺ saying, "I offer You boundless praise, for Yours are all the praiseworthy attributes with which You have described Yourself." This truth is likewise reflected in the words of God, may He be praised and exalted, "...they cannot encompass Him with their knowledge" {Ṭā Ḥā [O Man] 20: 110}.[25] The tradition of intercession contains other truths as well, of course; however, were we to discuss all of them, we would go beyond the purpose of this book.

I once heard our shaykh, Abū al-Abbās (may God be pleased with him) say, "All of God's prophets were created from mercy; however, our prophet ﷺ is mercy itself." God, may He be praised and exalted, declares, "And [thus, O Prophet,] We have sent thee as [an evidence of Our] grace[26] towards all the worlds" (Al-Anbiyā' [The Prophets] 21: 107}.

May God's blessings and peace rest upon him and his household, may he attain honor and nobility, glory and might. For he invited others to God with clear spiritual vision, indisputable evidence, discernment born of nearness to God, and the most manifest of paths. He exhorted others to tread the path of right guidance and to shun the path of destruction. There is nothing capable of drawing one nearer to God but that he invited others to embrace it, no courtesy which it is fitting for the servant to observe with God but that he urged others to adopt it, nothing which would distract God's servants from Him but that he warned them against it, nor any action which would alienate them from God but that he drew them away from it. He spared no effort or counsel to deliver God's servants from the morasses of alienation and places of peril until the night of polytheism and its effects had passed and the daylight of faith had appeared. He ﷺ raised the banner of religion and completed its law, defining its obligations and rulings and making clear what it would allow and prohibit. Moreover, just as he elucidated laws for us, he likewise opened to us the door of understanding, thereby leading one narrator to say: The Messenger of God ﷺ has left us; yet indeed, the birds move through the sky and through them we gain knowledge. As God, may He be praised, has said, "There shall be no coercion in matters of faith. Distinct has now become the right way from the way of error" {Al-Baqarah [The Cow] 2: 256}. He has also said, "Today have I perfected your religious law for you, and have bestowed upon you the full measure of My blessing, and willed that self-surrender to Me shall be Your religion" {Al-Mā'idah [The Repast] 5: 3}.

He ﷺ said, "I have left it white and pure."[27] May God grant him the most abundant reward which has ever been bestowed upon a prophet on behalf of his nation.

When he ﷺ had completed his explication of the path of right guidance and had revealed to God's servants those paths which lead unto Him, God took him to that abode which is better for him and more worthy after he had been given a choice [between what this world has to offer, and what lies with God] and he had chosen the Supreme Companion. It was then that the Truth, may He be praised, established the invitation to God as a perpetual mission of his ﷺ nation based upon what they had inherited from him and received on his authority. The Truth has testified to them concerning this, rendering them worthy of the tasks which this mission entails. God, may He be praised, says, "Say [O Prophet]: 'This is my way: Resting upon conscious insight accessible to reason, I am calling [you all] unto God—I and they who follow me" {Yūsuf [Joseph] 12: 108}.

[In explanation of this verse,] Shaykh Abū al-ᶜAbbās says, "that is, based on a direct personal perception: He ﷺ saw with his own [spiritual] eyes the path which was best suited to each of his followers and, having seen it, urged him to follow it." Evidence in support of the shaykh's interpretation (may God be pleased with him) may be seen in the fact that the instructions which he ﷺ gave to his companions varied in accordance with their respective paths. He ﷺ said to Bilāl, for example, "Spend [out of your wealth], O Bilāl, and have no fear that the One enthroned on high will fail to provide for you in abundance."[28] By contrast, however, he ﷺ told another man who wished to give up his wealth, "Keep your money. To leave your heirs wealthy is better for you than to leave them dependent and forced to beg from others."[29] A man once said to him ﷺ, "Advise me [what to do]." To which he ﷺ replied, "Be diffident before God the way you would be in the presence of a righteous man of your tribe."[30] When another man came to him ﷺ with the same request, he replied, "Do not become angry."[31]

I once heard our shaykh, Abū al-ᶜAbbās (may God be pleased with him) say, "In his words, 'I and they who follow me,' the Truth was opening the door of personal insight to the [the Prophet's] followers." In other words, the meaning of God's words, "Say [O Prophet]: 'This is my way: Resting upon conscious insight accessible to reason, I am calling [you all] unto God—I and they who follow me" {Yūsuf [Joseph] 12: 108} is that "those who follow me invite others to God based on personal insight and understanding." This interpretation is consistent with the requirements of the Arabic language. Hence, if you were to say, "Zayd calls [others] to [support] the sultan based on words of counsel, he and his followers," this would mean that his followers likewise issue the call concerned based on words of counsel.

If this interpretation is correct, then we may say that the Apostle ﷺ called others to God based on the perfect insight [given to him by virtue of his] mission, while the friends of God, or saints, call others to God based on their own respective insights, in their capacities as poles, as persons of righteousness and veracity, and as friends of God.

The Prophet ﷺ said, "Scholars are the heirs of the prophets."[32] He ﷺ also said, "Indeed, the prophets bequeathed neither dinars nor dirhams; rather, they bequeathed knowledge;"[33] and, "The scholars of my nation are like the prophets [*anbiyā'*] of the children of Israel."[34] A point to note here is that he ﷺ did not say, "The scholars of my nation are like the *messengers* (*rusul*) of the children of Israel." There are those who suppose that a prophet (*nabī*) is someone who has been given a revelation only for himself, whereas a messenger (*rasūl*) is someone who has been sent to others; however, this distinction is not valid; if it were, then we would have to ask why he ﷺ mentions only the prophets, and not the messengers, in his statement, "The scholars of my nation are like the prophets [*anbiyā'*] of the children of Israel." Further evidence for the invalidity of this distinction is found in the words of God, may He be praised, "Yet whenever We sent forth any apostle or prophet before thee, and he was hoping [that his warnings would be heeded], Satan would cast an aspersion on his innermost aims: but God renders null and void whatever aspersion Satan may cast, and God makes His messages clear in and by themselves, for God is all-knowing, wise" {Al-Ḥajj [The Pilgrimage] 22: 52}, which shows that both the prophet and the messenger are sent by God.

What distinguishes a prophet from a messenger, as has been noted by certain scholars, is that the prophet does not bring a new law, but rather, comes to confirm the law which was brought by those before him. An example of a prophet was Joshua son of Nun, who came to confirm the law of Moses and to command that the contents of the Torah be carried out; however, he did not bring a new law. The role of messenger, by contrast, is exemplified in Moses, upon him be peace, who came with a new law, namely, that which was contained in the Torah. He ﷺ thus said, "The scholars of my nation are like the prophets of the sons of Israel," not in the sense that they bring a new law but rather, in the sense that they come to confirm what has already been revealed and to command that it be carried out.

Consider, now, the following statements:

> "Scholars are the heirs of the prophets."

> "The scholars of my nation are like the prophets of the children of Israel."

> "Indeed, the prophets bequeathed neither dinars nor dirhams; rather, they bequeathed knowledge."

> "Indeed, the [earthly] world is cursed, cursed is everything therein excepting the remembrance of God and whatever is consistent therewith, as well as the scholar and the student."[35]

> "Indeed, the angels lower their wings before the seeker of knowledge."[36]

> "God [Himself] proffers evidence—and [so do] the angels and all who are endowed with knowledge—that there is no deity save Him, the Upholder of Equity..." {Āl ᶜImrān [The House of ᶜImrān] 3: 18}.

> "...God will exalt by degrees those of you who have attained to faith and, [above all,] such as have been vouchsafed knowledge..." {Al-Mujādalah [The Pleading] 58: 11}.

> "Nay, but this [divine writ] consists of messages clear to the hearts of all who are gifted with knowledge..." {Al-ᶜAnkabūt [The Spider] 29: 49}.

When knowledge (*ᶜilm*) is mentioned in the Qur'an or in the statements of the Messenger of God ﷺ, it refers to that knowledge which is beneficial, which subdues passionate craving and suppresses [earthly desires], and which is attended by reverent fear and repentance. God, may He be praised, declares, "of all His servants, only such as are endowed with knowledge stand in awe of God..." {Al-Fāṭir [The Originator] 35: 28}.[37]

Hence, He does not consider the knowledge of those who do not stand in awe of Him to be true knowledge. David, upon him be peace, said, "O Lord, whoever does not stand in true awe of You has no knowledge, and whoever fails to obey Your commands does not stand in true awe of You." Thus, the evidence of that knowledge which God seeks is reverent fear, while the evidence of the presence of reverent fear is obedience to God's commands. As for knowledge which is attended by the desire for this temporal life, self-serving flattery of those who possess earthly advantage, striving for worldly gain, collecting and amassing [wealth], vainglory and the constant demand for more, the pursuit of longevity and forgetfulness of the afterlife: how far is someone who possesses this type of knowledge from being an heir of the prophets! After all, is it possible for that which is inherited to be passed on to its heir with qualities other than those which characterized it when it was in the possession of the one who bequeathed it?

Scholars [i.e., possessors of knowledge] who are characterized by the traits just described may be likened to a candle which provides light for others while burning itself down.[38] God has caused the knowledge of those who fit this description to stand as evidence against them and as cause for them to suffer severe chastisement. Be not deceived by the fact that such knowledge may offer benefits to people, be they in outlying desert regions or in metropolises. As the Prophet ﷺ declared, "Truly, God upholds this religion [even] through the immoral man."[39]

Someone who acquires knowledge in order to gain this world and to achieve status therein may be likened to someone who picks up excrement with a sapphire spoon. How noble the means, and how ignoble the end sought! Similarly, someone who spends forty or fifty years in the pursuit of knowledge, yet without acting on what he has learned, may be likened to someone who spends the same period of time performing ritual ablutions over and over again in the pursuit of ritual purity, yet without performing a single prayer. After all, the purpose of knowledge is action, just as the purpose of ritual purity is the performance of prayer. A man once asked al-Ḥasan al-Baṣrī (may God be pleased with him) about a particular matter and al-Ḥasan issued him a legal ruling on the matter in question. The man then said to al-Ḥasan, "The jurisprudents disagree with you." In reply, al-Ḥasan rebuked the man, saying, "Woe be to you! And have you ever seen a [true] jurisprudent? The true jurisprudent has come to understand, on God's authority, what He commands and what He prohibits!"

I once heard our shaykh, Abū al-ᶜAbbās (may God be pleased with him) say, "The true jurisprudent is one for whom the veil on his heart's eyes has been rent and who has seen the kingdom of his Lord!" Given the fact that the call to God continues in perpetuity, you should know likewise that the lights which are manifest in the friends of God derive from none other than the radiance of the lights of prophethood [which shine] upon them. The Muḥammadan reality is like the sun, while the hearts of the saints are like moons; the moon shines due to its facing the sun and the appearance of the sun's light upon it. Thus, the sun sheds its light both by day and by night due to the appearance of its light in the moon and, as a consequence, it never really sets. You may understand from this that it is necessary for the lights of the saints to shine continuously due to the continuous manifestation of the light of the Messenger of God ﷺ within them. The saints are God's "signs" which He recites to His servants by disclosing them one after another. [As God Almighty declares,] "These messages of God do We convey unto thee, setting forth the truth" {Al-Jāthiyah [Kneeling Down] 45: 6}.[40] Commenting on the words of God, almighty and majestic is He, "Any message which We annul or consign to oblivion, we replace it with a better or a similar one" {Al-Baqarah [The Cow] 2: 106}, I once heard our shaykh, Abū al-ᶜAbbās (may God be pleased with him) say, "In other words: Never do We cause a saint to depart but that we replace him with a better or similar one."

A certain gnostic was once asked about the "saints of sustenance" (*awliyā' al-madad*): Are their numbers ever reduced by one? He replied, "If their numbers were reduced by [even] one, the heavens would not send down their rain, nor would the earth bring forth its vegetation. The corruption of a given era is not due to their being fewer in number, nor to their providing less [spiritual] sustenance. However, if a given era is corrupt, God (may He be praised) wills that they be hidden while continuing to be present. Thus, if the people of this or that era are turning away from

God and showing preference for that which is other than He; if words of exhortation are lost upon them and reminders fail to incline their hearts toward God, they will not be worthy of the appearance of God's friends in their midst. It is for this reason that they have said, "God's friends are brides, and brides are not seen by criminals." The Prophet ﷺ said, "Give not wisdom to those who are unworthy thereof lest you do it an injustice, and forbid it not to those who are worthy thereof lest you do an injustice to them."[41] If God, may He be praised, has instructed us through the words of His Messenger ﷺ not to give wisdom to those who are unworthy of it, then who is worthier than we are of this lovely creation? He ﷺ said, "If you find earthly passions being obeyed, niggardliness holding sway, this temporal world being given preference, and everyone admiring his own opinion, you should keep to your own private affairs."[42] Having heard the Messenger of God's counsel, they [i.e., the saints] chose to go into hiding; indeed, God Himself chose this for them despite the necessity of there being, during the same era, imams [spiritual leaders] from among them who remain visible, standing as evidence of the truth and traveling the path of righteousness based on the words of the Prophet ﷺ, "There will continue to be a community belonging to my nation who are manifest witnesses to the truth, and who will not be harmed by those who oppose them until the Day of Judgment."[43]

ᶜAlī Ibn Abī Ṭālib (may God be pleased with him) once said to Kumayl Ibn Ziyād, "O God, leave not the earth bereft of those who will stand as evidence of Your truth, those who, though small in number, enjoy the highest standing with God, whose hearts cling to the loftiest abode, and who are God's vicegerents among His servants and in His land. Ah, how I long to see them!" In his book entitled *Khatm al-Awliyā'*, the lordly imam Muḥammad Ibn ʿAlī al-Tirmidhī (may God be pleased with him) narrates the following tradition with a chain of transmission which he traces back to Ibn ʿUmar (may God be pleased with him), who said, "The Messenger of God ﷺ said, 'My nation is like the rain; one doesn't know whether the first rain is the best, or the last.'"[44] He [al-Tirmidhī] also narrates the following with a chain of transmission which he traces back to Abū al-Dardā', who said, "The Prophet ﷺ said, 'The best of my nation are those who live at its beginning and at its end, while those who live in the time intervening are vexed and troubled.'"[45] He [al-Tirmidhī] also narrates on the authority of ʿAbd Al-Raḥmān Ibn Samurah that, "I once came bearing good tidings from the Battle of Mu'tah. But when I mentioned the deaths of Jaʿfar, Zayd and Ibn Rawāḥah, the Messenger of God's companions wept. He ﷺ asked them, 'What makes you weep?' They replied, 'And how could we but weep when the best, the most honorable, and the most gracious of us have been slain?' 'Weep not,' he ﷺ told them. 'My nation is like a garden whose owner collected the off-shoots of its palm-trees, prepared its pathways, and trimmed the trees' leaves, after which it produced a crop for one year, then for another. However, its later crops might well include the best dates and the longest stalks. By the One who sent me with the truth, the son of Mary will most surely find among my nation [those who are worthy to be] successors to his disciples."

With a chain of transmission which he [al-Tirmidhī] traces back to Sahl Ibn Saʿd, he narrates that "he ﷺ said, 'Indeed, among the descendents of the descendents of the descendents of men who are my companions there are men and women who will enter Paradise [wherein they shall be blessed with good] beyond all reckoning.'[46] He then recited, 'and [to cause this message to spread] from them unto other people as soon as they come into contact with them, for He alone is almighty, truly wise! Such is God's bounty: He grants it to anyone who is willing [to receive it], for God is limitless in His great bounty' {Al-Jumᶜah [The Congregation] 62: 3-4}."[47]

With a chain of transmission which he traces back to the Prophet ﷺ himself, he narrates, "In every generation of my nation there will be those who outrun all others [in doing good]."[48]

Know—may God cause you to be among the elect of His servants and introduce you to the subtle intimations of His love—that be they manifest or hidden, the just and veracious or the friends of God, the corruption of the time will neither obscure their light nor diminish their standing. After all, they are not with time,[49] but rather, with the Appointer of the times; those who are with the Appointer of times will not change with the changes of time, whereas those who are with time will change with the changes of time and will be vexed by time's vexations.[50]

Imam Abū ᶜAbd Allāh al-Tirmidhī (may God be pleased with him) said, "People belong to one of two groups. The first group consists of God's laborers, who worship Him in righteousness and godly fear and who are in need of the most prosperous of times, the upward turn of fortune, and the reign of truth and justice, since it is from this that they derive their sustenance. As for the second group, it consists of those who have been endowed with clear certainty and, as a consequence, worship the Truth out of loyalty to His oneness through the removal of the veil[51] and disengagement from worldly causes. Those who belong to this group have no concern for the vicissitudes of time, and ill-fortune causes them no harm. As the Prophet ﷺ said, 'God has servants whom He nourishes with His mercy and whom He revives in good health, while trials pass them by without harming them like the passing of a dark night.'"[52]

He ﷺ also said, "My nation will pass through trials which no one will survive but those to whom God has granted life through knowledge."[53] Commenting on this tradition, al-Tirmidhī states, "that is, through the knowledge of God, or so it seems to us."

I once heard our shaykh, Abū al-ᶜAbbās (may God be pleased with him) say, "Men of the night are the [true] men, and the saints are supported at such a [dark] time by two things, namely, wealth and certainty: with wealth, given people's widespread bankruptcy, and with certainty, given people's many doubts." A gnostic once said, "God has servants who, the greater the darkness of the time, the more brilliant the lights of their hearts become. After all, they are like the stars: The darker the night, the more brightly they shine. And what are the lights of the stars by comparison with the lights of His friends' hearts? The lights of the stars grow dim; as for the lights of His friends' hearts, no dimming do they know. The lights of the stars guide in the world, to the world, while the lights of His friends' hearts guide to God, exalted be He."

This same message is conveyed by the following lines:

While the stars ascend in the heavens,
The stars on earth are of greater splendor.

For the former shine for a time, then are hidden,
While the latter are not obscured by hiddenness.

The former guide in the darkness of the nights,
While the latter guide by removing the veil.

A Sufi once said in the presence of a jurisprudent, "God has servants who live through times of severe tribulation, but the tribulations do them no harm." The jurisprudent replied, saying, "This is something I cannot understand." I will give you an example of this very thing: The angels who are placed in charge of the hellfire are in the fire, but the fire harms them not.

I heard our shaykh, Abū al-^{c}Abbās (may God be pleased with him) say, "This world may be likened to the hellfire saying to the believer, 'pass on quickly, O believer, for your light has extinguished my blaze.'"

Know that the saints and sainthood (friendship with God) are of the most momentous significance. As evidence of this, it will suffice you to know what was narrated to us by the noble shaykh who provided the chain of transmission for this tradition, Shihāb al-Dīn Abū al-Ma^{c}ālī Aḥmad Ibn Isḥāq Ibn Muḥammad Ibn al-Mu'ayyad al-Abarqūhī (may God have mercy upon him). He said, "In the year 619, Abū Bakr ^{c}Abd Allāh Ibn Muḥammad Ibn Sābūr al-Qalānisī al-Shīrāzī said to us, 'In the year 503, Imam Abū al-Mubārak ^{c}Abd al-^{c}Azīz Ibn Manṣūr al-Shīrāzi al-Adamī told us (it was recited back to him as I listened), "The shaykh and imam Abū Muḥammad Rizq Allāh Ibn ^{c}Abd al-Wahhāb Ibn ^{c}Abd al-^{c}Azīz Ibn al-Ḥārith Ibn Asad al-Tamīmī al-Ḥanbalī (it was dictated to me on Saturday, the 16th of Ṣafar in the year 483 in Isfahan) told us, 'We were told by Abū ^{c}Umar ^{c}Abd al-Wāḥid Ibn Muḥammad Ibn ^{c}Abd Allāh Ibn Mahdī al-Fārisī, on the authority of Abū ^{c}Abd Allāh Muḥammad Ibn Makhlad Ibn Ḥafṣ al-^{c}Aṭṭār al-Khaṭīb al-Dūrī, on the authority of Muḥammad Ibn ^{c}Uthmān Ibn Karāmah, on the authority of Khālid Ibn Makhlad, on the authority of Sulaymān Ibn Bilāl, on the authority of Shurayk Ibn Abī Namir, on the authority of ^{c}Aṭā', on the authority of Abū Hurayrah, who said: The Messenger of God ﷺ said, "God, almighty and majestic is He, declared, 'Whoever shows enmity to any of My friends has declared war upon Me.[54] No servant of mine has drawn near to Me by anything dearer to Me than those obligations which I have required of him. Moreover, my servant never ceases drawing near to Me through supererogatory acts of worship until I love him. And if I love him, I become the hearing by which he hears, the sight by which he sees, the hand by which he strikes and the foot on which he walks. If he should ask anything of Me, I will most surely grant it, and if he seeks refuge in Me, I will most surely protect him. There is no act in the face of which I hesitate as I do in the face of [taking] the soul of a believer who abhors death, for I [myself] abhor causing him anguish despite the fact that it [death] is something from which there is no escape.'"

The above tradition is narrated by al-Bukhārī (may God be pleased with him) in his *Ṣaḥīḥ*. It has also been narrated based on another chain of transmission, where it reads, "And if I love him, I become for him hearing, sight, a tongue, a heart, a mind, a hand, and a support."

Lend a close ear, then—may God be gracious unto you—to what this tradition conveys about the abundance of the saint's power and the eminence of the rank which the Truth has granted him. The Prophet ﷺ declared, "Whoever shows enmity to any of My friends has declared war upon Me." For the friend of God has gone from disposing of his own affairs to relying upon God's disposal thereof; from defending himself to allowing God to defend him; and from [trusting in his own] power and strength to [trusting in God's] by his sincere reliance on God. As God, may He be praised, declares, "for everyone who places his trust in God, He [alone] is enough" {Al-Ṭalāq [Divorce] 65: 3}.

He likewise declares, "...for We had willed it upon Ourselves to succor the believers" {Al-Rūm [The Byzantines] 30: 47}. This [distinction] was theirs because they had made God their ultimate concern, as a result of which He drove back from them all that was other than He, fulfilling the obligation which He had set for Himself to come to their defense.

I was told by Shaykh Shihāb al-Dīn al-Abarqūhī, "I went in to see Shaykh Abū al-Ḥasan al-Shādhilī (may God be pleased with him) and heard him say, 'God, almighty and majestic is He, says, "O My servant, make Me your supreme concern and I will guard you from that which causes you concern. O My servant, so long as you belong to yourself, you are in the place of remoteness, and so long as you live through Me, you are in the place of nearness. So choose for yourself."'"

Another tradition states, "Whoever is so busy with the remembrance of Me that he has no time to ask Me [for what he desires], I will give him the best of what I give to those who ask."[55] Hence, if the Truth, may He be praised, wishes them to be so occupied with His remembrance that they have no leisure to make requests of Him, how could He but wish them to be so occupied with remembering and praising Him that they have no leisure to defend themselves?

When someone has come to know God, the door to his self-defense is closed. After all, the gnostic is required by his knowledge not to bear witness in action to anyone but the One whom he has known. How can anyone defend [himself] when he sees God sovereignly at work among human beings? And how can God deprive his friends of His succor when they have cast themselves upon His mercy, in submission and surrender to whatever verdict He wills to hand down? He, in the strongholds of His mighty power and beneath the pavilions of His majesty, preserves them from everything but the remembrance of Him, severing them from everything but His love and keeping them from everything but the presence of His nearness. His remembrance and praise are ever on their tongues, while His light fills their hearts with gladness. He has given them a homeland in His presence, their hearts kneel before Him, and their secret longings are fulfilled through the vision of His oneness.

I once heard our shaykh, Abū al-ᶜAbbās (may God be pleased with him) say, "The saint is with God as a she-lion's cub in her protective grip. Do you think she would abandon her cub to someone who wished to destroy it?" Another prophetic tradition tells us that when he ﷺ was on one of his military expeditions, there was a woman wandering about in search of her infant son, and as soon as she found him she leaned down and put him to her breast. As his companions looked at her in astonishment, he ﷺ declared, "Verily, God is more tender toward His believing servant than this woman is toward her son!"[56]

This mercy is manifested in the Truth's defense of them and His waging war on those who demonstrate enmity toward them, since they are the bearers of His secrets and the repositories of His light. God, may He be praised, says, "God is near those who have faith" {Al-Baqarah [The Cow] 2: 257}[57] and, "Verily, God wards off [all evil] from those who attain to faith" {Al-Ḥajj [The Pilgrimage] 22: 38}.

Even so, the encounter with the Truth for someone who has maltreated His saints may not necessarily occur in the immediate future. After all, by God's reckoning, the time we spend on this earth is quite brief; besides, God deems this earthly life an unworthy sphere in which to chastise His enemies, just as He deems it an unworthy realm in which to reward His loved ones. If one's punishment is immediate, however, it may take the form of a hardening of one's heart, a dullness in one's perceptive faculties, a reluctance to obey God, a fall into wrongdoing, a cooling of one's eager enthusiasm, or being robbed of one's delight in serving Him.

A certain man of the children of Israel had been seeking God diligently, after which he turned away from Him. He then said, "O Lord, how frequently do I disobey You, yet You punish me not!" After which God, exalted is He, inspired the prophet of that era to say to the man, "How frequently do I punish you, yet you perceive it not! Have I not robbed you of the sweetness of My remembrance and the rapturous joy of our intimate conversations?" What this account tells us is that if someone has brought harm to a friend of God, he is not safe from harm himself. Hence, if you have not seen him suffer some tribulation which affects his own person, his wealth, or his children, it may be because his tribulation is too great for human beings to be made privy thereto.

[Let us now return to] the words of the Prophet in which he ﷺ speaks for God, saying, "No one has ever drawn near to Me by any means as [perfect as] the performance of the obligations which I have required of them." The religious duties which the Truth requires of His servants are of two types: outward and inward. Outward religious duties include such things as the five daily ritual prayers, payment of zakāh, fasting the month of Ramaḍān, performing the ḥajj, enjoining the doing of what is right and forbidding the doing of what is wrong, and kindness to one's parents.

As for the inward duties, they include knowledge of God, love for God and reliance upon Him, trust in God's promises, fear of God, hope in God, etc. Our duties toward

God are also divided into two types which might be referred to as "commissions" and "omissions," in other words, things which the Truth requires you to do, and things which He requires you to refrain from doing. These two types of duties are mentioned together in a single verse of the Qur'an where God, may He be praised, says, "Behold, God enjoins justice, the doing of good, and generosity toward [one's] fellow men...," thus presenting you with something which God calls upon you to do. He then says, "...and He forbids all that is shameful and all that runs counter to reason, as well as envy" {Al-Naḥl [The Bee] 16: 90}, thereby presenting you with something which God calls upon you to refrain from doing.

You should also understand, may God be gracious to you, that God neither commands nor recommends that His servants do something unless it is in their best interest to do this or that thing. Nor does He require or recommend that they refrain from a given action unless their welfare lies in refraining from the action concerned. We are not saying, as would be said by someone who has turned away from the path of right guidance, that God must provide for His servants' best interests; rather, we say: This is the Truth's wont, if you will, His enduring manner of being and His way of relating to His servants in accordance with His gracious disposal toward them. Hence, when they say, "God must provide for His servants' best interests," would that I knew who it is that imposes upon Him this obligation!

Upon considering the matter further, we have found that every action which is either commanded or recommended requires the concentration of one's whole being[58] on God, while every action which is forbidden or deemed offensive entails separation from Him. Hence, what God seeks from His servants is the concentration of their entire beings upon

Him. Acts of obedience are the causes behind such concentration and the means by which it is achieved, which is why God has commanded them, while acts of disobedience are the causes for separation and the means by which it comes about, which is why God has forbidden them.

Outward religious obligations are inseparable from inward ones, while the inward obligations are the conditions for the outward ones and that which sustains them. In addition, there are obligations which are both outward and inward, or somewhere in between the two. It is in this context that I understand the words of the Prophet ﷺ, "The believer's intention is better than his action."[59]

Similarly, inward sins, both minor and major ones, are more serious than outward sins. Given that the Truth has required His servants to perform the various religious obligations in a binding manner which leaves them no choice but to perform them, it follows that the servant only performs them by God's having chosen for him to do so. Hence, the servant is moved by a desire to perform such acts because God, may He be praised, has appointed their numbers, their times and their causes. This being the case, the servant's fulfillment of these obligations has nothing to do with his choice for himself, and everything to do with God's choice for him. Moreover, such actions require a closeness to God which nothing else does. It is for this reason that He declared, "No one has ever drawn near to Me by any means as [perfect as] the performance of the obligations which I have required of them,"[60] and, "My servant never ceases to draw near to Me through supererogatory acts of worship until I love him."

As for the word rendered here as "supererogatory acts of worship," namely, *nawāfil* (singular, *nāfilah*), it refers to something which is additional. The word *nawāfil* likewise refers to spoils of war which the imam grants as he sees fit [to this or that fighter] over and above his appointed share. God, may He be praised, says, "And rise from thy sleep and pray during part of the night [as well], as a free offering [*nāfilah*] from thee" {Al-Isrā' [The Night Journey] 17: 79}, that is, as an addition which you offer, thanks to Our gracious bounty, over and above what your obligations require of you.

Know that the Truth, may He be praised, has, for the most part, not required any duty but that He has likewise provided some supererogatory act of the same type so that if one of His servants performs the duty in question imperfectly, the imperfection may be compensated for by the supererogatory act which belongs to the same category. Hence, we have a tradition which says, "He [God] looks upon the ritual prayer performed by His servant, and if he has performed it as God commanded Him to, he will be rewarded for it and it will be recorded to his credit, whereas if it contained some imperfection, it will be completed through a supererogatory prayer."[61] Those with knowledge have likewise said, "A supererogatory act of worship which you have performed will only be recorded to your credit if your performance of the obligatory act of worship [of the same category] was sound."[62]

Knowing that among His believing servants there would be some who are strong and others who are weak—as the tradition says, "The strong believer is more beloved to God, exalted is He, than the weak believer," (or in some versions, "better than the weak believer," though there is goodness in both)[63]—God has opened the way for the weak to content themselves with nothing but the duties required of them, while opening for the strong the door of abundant blessings. However, servants who have been moved to perform the duties required of them out of [nothing but] fear of God's punishment, in order simply to deliver themselves from perdition, will not have done so out of longing for God or in pursuit of His divinity. Hence, if they were to be brought to judgment, these acts of worship would not be accepted of them, since they only did what they did for themselves and in pursuit of their own fortunes. As such, they fulfilled their duties toward God dragged along, as it were, by the chains of obligation. Hence we read in one tradition, "Your Lord marvels at a people who are led to Paradise in chains."[64] Other servants, by contrast, so overflow with passionate longing and ardor that they are not content with the mere performance of their duties; rather, their hearts are attentive to God despite the impediments of this world. Hence, were they not forbidden to perform supererogatory prayers at certain times, their prayers would have neither beginning nor end, and they would impose upon themselves more than they could bear.

Among the evidences for the notion that people are divided into these two types is the fact that the Messenger of God ﷺ once said, "Make haste to perform good works before you are overtaken by [the following] seven [events]. Is there any of you who is certain never to acquire wealth that threatens to drown out all other concerns, suffer poverty so dire it causes one to forget [one's duties toward God and neighbor], be afflicted with illness which weakens, old age which refutes [the notion that one can go on being young] or death which ruins, or meet the antichrist? [Should you compare] the worst possible event you might anticipate with the Last Hour, [know that] the Last Hour will be more calamitous and bitter."[65]

This tradition requires that one muster the utmost zeal to relate to God, may He be praised and exalted, that one hasten to obey Him, anticipating obstacles and accidents of fate before they present themselves. This tradition is addressed to the first group mentioned above, with the Apostle ﷺ calling upon them to act without delay. Other traditions, by contrast, command God's servants to be moderate in their obedience lest they act upon zealous impulses and, as a consequence, burden themselves with more than they can tolerate, thereby rendering themselves incapable of obeying or, in their obedience, of performing those actions for which God holds them accountable. He ﷺ said, "You must perform no more labor than you can tolerate for—and God is my witness—God does not grow weary until you yourselves do."[66] He ﷺ also said, "Aim for moderation, moderation";[67] "Verily, this religion is demanding, so enter into it gently;"[68] and, "Do not make the worship of God odious to yourself."

The person who contents himself with performing his duties and nothing more, and the person who performs both his duties and additional acts of worship along with them may be likened to two servants who were sent out by a monarch to labor however they wished provided that they brought him four dirhems every day. The first servant brought his master four dirhems every day and no more, whereas the second servant sought out choice fruits and rare gems which he purchased and presented to his master. This latter servant, without a doubt, will be deemed more worthy of the master's affection than the former.

In the tradition which reads, "And if I love him, I become the hearing by which he hears, the sight by which he sees, the hand by which he strikes and the foot on which he walks...," what is being described is permanence (*baqā'*) following annihilation (*fanā'*) such that your own attributes are effaced, having vanished with the appearance of the Master's attributes within you.

I once heard our shaykh, Abū al-ᶜAbbās (may God be pleased with him) say, "God has servants who have obliterated their actions with His actions, their attributes with His attributes, and their selves with His self. He has caused them to be bearers of secrets which the more ordinary friends of God would be unable to hear. It is these who have drowned in the sea of the Divine Self and in the stream of [His] attributes. Hence, there are three annihilations: for Him to annihilate you to your actions with His actions, to your attributes with His attributes, and to yourself with Himself. It has thus been said:

> Some people wander in a desert wilderness,
> While others wander in the land of His love.
>
> They are annihilated, then annihilated,
> then annihilated,
>
> Yet they are preserved in permanence through
> the nearness of His nearness.

If He annihilates you to yourself, He will preserve you in Himself, for annihilation is the portal through which one enters the realm of permanence. He whose annihilation is genuine will find genuine permanence, and he who is annihilated to everything other than God will find his permanence in God. It is for this reason that they say: He whose ruin is through God, through God will his successor be raised up. Annihilation requires that they be excused, while permanence requires that they be granted victory. Annihilation requires their absence from everything, while permanence causes them to be present with God in everything such that by nothing are they separated from Him. Annihilation puts them to death, and permanence brings them to life. When the mountains of one's existence have been crushed, he will hear the Summoning Voice of his vision: "And they will ask thee about [what will happen to] the mountains [when this world comes to an end]. Say, then: 'My Sustainer will scatter them far and wide, and leave the earth level and bare [so that] thou wilt see no curve thereon, and no ruggedness. On that Day, all will follow the Summoning Voice from which there is no escape. All sounds will be hushed before the Most Gracious, and thou wilt hear nothing but a faint sough[69] in the air" {Ṭā Hā [O Man] 20: 105-108}.

The one who has attained permanence calls others to the truth on God's behalf; as for the one who has experienced annihilation, God calls others to the truth on his behalf.

[Let us now reconsider] God's words, "there is no act in the face of which I hesitate as I do in the face of [taking] the soul of a believer who abhors death, for I [myself] abhor causing him anguish despite the fact that it [death] is something from which there is no escape." Know that the word "hesitation" must be understood figuratively rather than literally; for hesitation can only be attributed to creatures, either due to opposing attractions, or due to uncertainty concerning outcomes. However, neither of these situations [that is, being torn between conflicting attractions or uncertainty concerning consequences] is possible where God is concerned. Rather, what is meant by "hesitation" here is that God's foreknowledge requires that the servant's death take place at the time at which God knew it would. At the same time, however, the divine attribute of mercy would require that God prevent the servant's death from occurring were it not for His foreknowledge thereof. The

Truth, may He be praised, alludes to His attribute of mercy in the words, "for I [myself] abhor causing him anguish," while in the words, "despite the fact that it [death] is something from which there is no escape," He alludes to His attribute of knowledge.

* * *

Know, may God be gracious unto you—by His devotion to you and His causing His lights to reach you—that there are two types of sainthood, or friendship with God: There is the saint who has allied himself with God, and the saint with whom God has allied Himself. Concerning the first type of sainthood, God says, "…for all who ally themselves with God and His Apostle and those who have attained to faith—behold, it is they, the partisans of God, who shall be victorious" {Al-Mā'idah [The Repast] 5: 56}. Speaking of the second type of sainthood, He says, "…for it is He who protects[70] the righteous" {Al-Aᶜrāf [The Faculty of Discernment] 7: 196}.

Shaykh Abū al-Ḥasan (may God be pleased with him) said, "For the sake of God's gifts to us, [we should] be content with whatever He decrees, endure with patience when misfortune descends, rely upon God in times of affliction, and look to Him in the midst of life's vicissitudes." If anyone brings forth these four virtues out of the treasure houses of [good] works on the path of spiritual warfare, emulation of the prophetic Sunnah and imitation of the imams,[71] his friendship toward God, His Apostle and the believers will be proved genuine: "…for all who ally themselves with God and His Apostle and those who have attained to faith—behold, it is they, the partisans of God, who shall be victorious." Similarly, if anyone brings forth [such virtues] out of the treasure houses of grace on the path of love, God's friendship toward him will be perfected: "...for it is He who protects the righteous."

The difference between these two types of sainthood, or friendship between the servant and God, is that the first is characterized by the servant's allying himself with God, while the second is characterized by God's allying himself with the servant. The first might be thought of as a lesser sainthood, as it were, and the second, as a greater sainthood. Your alliance with God emerges from spiritual warfare, your alliance with His Apostle emerges from your emulation of his Sunnah, and your alliance with those who believe emerges from your imitation of the imams. This may be understood from God's words, "...for all who ally themselves with God and His Apostle and those who have attained to faith—behold, it is they, the partisans of God, who shall be victorious."

Know, may God be gracious unto you—by the gifts which He grants and your understanding of the subtleties of His [divinely given] knowledge—that the righteousness being spoken of in the words, "...for it is He who protects the righteous" is not the righteousness which is meant by followers of the path when they identify [spiritual] ranks; they might say, for example, that so-and-so is righteous, a martyr, and a saint. Rather, the "righteous" being spoken of here are those who have become fit for His presence by attaining annihilation to His creation.[72] Have you not heard God's words, spoken through Joseph, upon him be peace, "Let me die as one who has surrendered himself unto Thee, and make me one with the righteous!" {Yūsuf [Joseph] 12: 101}. By "the righteous" here, he meant those of his forebears who had been sent by God, since God had rendered them fit to be His prophets and messengers.

If you wish, you might refer to these two types of sainthood as the sainthood of faith, and the sainthood of certainty. The former is illustrated in the words of God, may He be praised, "God is near unto those who have faith, taking them out of deep darkness into the light" {Al-Baqarah [The Cow] 2: 257}. Moreover, this verse from the holy Qur'an presents us with a number of lessons:

The first lesson has to do with the fact that the divine name "Allāh" in particular, and no other, is used in this context. He says, "God (Allāh) is near unto those who have faith..." He does not use the appellation, "al-Raḥmān" ("the Most Gracious"), nor "al-Qahhār ("the One who holds absolute sway over all that exists"), nor any of the other names which describe the divine attributes. The reason for this is that by using that name which encompasses all [of the divine] names, He wants you to realize the comprehensiveness of His protection of, and nearness to, His believing servants. For if He had used a name which points to [only] one of the divine attributes, it would appear that sainthood pertained exclusively to that particular name or attribute.

The second lesson offered by this verse has to do with the connection between sainthood and faith. Through this connection, He wants to acquaint you with the abundance of faith's power and the sublimity of its station. So great is faith's power and so elevated is its station that it has contributed to the constancy of God's nearness to and protection of His servants. However, it should not be thought that, because this verse is worded in the past tense, God's nearness and protection are thereby restricted to those who attained to faith before these words were revealed. Rather, what it means is that no matter when this or that servant attains to faith, God's nearness and protection are thereby necessitated. Hence, verbs may be placed in a particular tense without the import of the statement being restricted to the tense in which it is expressed. One might say, for example, "Whoever believes will prosper" or, "Whoever denies the truth will fail,"[73] the meaning of which is not restricted to a given time frame, but rather, applies to the past, the present and the future.

The third lesson is that in the words, "taking them out of deep darkness into the light" {Al-Baqarah [The Cow] 2: 257}, God shows us the expansiveness of His mercy and the abundance of His grace. When He says, "God is near unto those who have faith, taking them out of deep darkness into the light," He knows that those who have faith may, in fact, enter the deep darkness. However, due to His nearness to them and His protection of them, He undertakes to bring them out of it. He describes the believers elsewhere as those "...who, when they have committed a shameful deed or have [otherwise] sinned against themselves, remember God and pray that their sins be forgiven—for who but God could forgive sins?—and do not knowingly persist in doing whatever [wrong] they have done..." {Āl ᶜImrān [The House of ᶜImrān] 3: 135}. God utters these words in praise of those who believe just as, when He says that He will "tak[e] them out of deep darkness into the light," He is bringing them good tidings. He does not describe them as those "who commit no shameful deeds" since, if He did, no one would be included among the believers but those who have been granted the most supreme divine providence.

He likewise describes believers as those "who, when they are moved to anger, readily forgive..." {Al-Shūrā [Consultation] 42: 37} and as those who "hold in check their anger" {Āl ᶜImrān [The House of ᶜImrān] 3: 134}. God thus praises them for forgiving after they have been moved to anger. He does not describe them as "those who are not moved to anger," as though they never felt anger in the first place. After all, the humanity in which they share does not necessitate this.

The fourth lesson is that the Truth, may He be praised, informs believers through this verse of marvelous glad tidings concerning His nearness and protection. Indeed, God's nearness to those who believe encompasses all the blessings of this world and the world to come: light and knowledge, openings and visions [of the divine realities], forgiveness and inward certainty, support and continual increase, palaces and companions, rivers and fruits, a vision of God, joyful contentment with God and God's joyful contentment with them, being gathered together with the God-conscious, taking the record of one's deeds in one's right hand, having one's weight of good deeds be heavy in the balance, and being established firmly on the straight path which leads to paradise, not to mention all the other gifts and graces encompassed within God's nearness to His believing servants. Hence, these are glad tidings to end all glad tidings.

Know also that the friendship of God encompasses both benefit and defense, as it were. As for the benefit, it is spoken of in God's words, "For alas, there has never yet been any community that attained to faith, and thereupon benefited by its faith…" {Yūnus [Jonah] 10: 98} and, "But their attaining to faith after they had beheld Our punishment could not possibly benefit them…" {Ghāfir [Forgiving] 40: 85}. These words are a description of those who deny the truth, from which one may also understand that faith benefits those who believe even when they experience misfortune and hardship. Similarly, God says, "[But] on the Day when thy Sustainer's [final] portents do appear, believing will be of no avail to any human being who did not believe before or who, while believing, did no good works" {Al-Anᶜām [Cattle] 6: 158}, from which we may understand that those who, by contrast, had believed before the Day of Judgment *will* benefit from their faith.

As for defense, it is spoken of in God's words, "Verily, God wards off [all evil] from those who attain to faith" {Al-Ḥajj [The Pilgrimage] 22: 38}. Such defense likewise includes God's succor of the believers:"...for We had willed it upon Ourselves to succor the believers" {Al-Rūm [The Byzantines] 30: 47} as well as deliverance: "...for thus do We deliver all who have faith" {Al-Anbiyā' [The Prophets] 21: 88}.

The fifth lesson is likewise reflected in His words, "taking them out of deep darkness into the light." In other words, He takes them:

-out of the darkness of unbelief into the light of faith,

-out of the darkness of innovation into the light of conformity to the prophetic Sunnah,

-out of the darkness of heedlessness into the light of vigilance;

-out of the darkness of seeking one's personal fortunes into the light of seeking to give God and neighbor their due,

-out of the darkness of seeking this world into the light of seeking the world to come,

-out of the darkness of disobedience into the light of obedience,

-out of the darkness of densities into the light of subtleties,

-out of the darkness of false claims into the radiant light of deliverance from [reliance on one's own] power and strength,

-out of the darkness of earthly desires into the light of godly fear,

-out of the darkness of the created world into the light of the vision thereof,

-out of the darkness of disposing of one's own affairs into the light of entrusting [one's affairs to God], not to mention the innumerable other types of darkness out of which God brings His believing servants and the corresponding types of light into which He brings them.

The second type of sainthood, i.e., that which is based on certainty, includes both faith and reliance upon God. About this type of sainthood God has said, "and for everyone who places his trust in God, He [alone] is enough" {Al-Ṭalāq [Divorce] 65: 3}. It is not possible to rely fully upon God unless one has certainty, nor is it possible to have certainty and to rely fully upon God unless one has faith, since certainty is a kind of settling of the knowledge of God in one's heart. As such, the meaning of the term "certainty" (*yaqīn*) is derived from the verb *yaqina* as in the phrase, *yaqina al-mā'u fil-jabal* ("The water settled, i.e., was still, on the mountain"). All certainty entails faith, though not all faith entails certainty. The difference between them is that while faith might be attended by heedlessness, such is not the case with certainty.

If you wish, you may refer to them as the sainthood of the sincere (*al-ṣādiqīn*), and the sainthood of those fully realized in righteousness (*al-ṣiddīqīn*). The first type of sainthood comes about through sincere effort for God and loyalty to Him in pursuit of His reward. As for the second type, it comes about through annihilation to everything other than God, while remaining present in everything through God. Shaykh Abū al-Ḥasan (may God be pleased with him) once said, "In one of the scriptures which He revealed to His prophets, God declares, 'If anyone obeys Me in everything, I will obey him in everything!'"

In explanation of this saying, Shaykh Abū al-Ḥasan said, "If anyone obeys Me in everything by his abandonment of everything, I will obey him in everything by disclosing Myself to him in everything so that he will see Me as nearer to him than everything. This is a superior path, the path of the spiritual wayfarers, a majestic way: If anyone obeys Me in everything by approaching everything in light of his Master's goodwill expressed therein, I will obey him in everything by disclosing Myself to him in everything until he sees Me as the essence of everything."

Once you have realized this, you will understand that there are two types of saints: one who has been annihilated to everything in such a way that he sees nothing but God, and another who remains in everything in such a way that he sees God in everything. However, this[74] is an imperfection, because God, may He be praised, only revealed the kingdom in order that He might be seen therein. Created entities are the mirrors of the [divine] attributes; hence, if someone is absent to the created universe, he will likewise be absent to the vision of the Truth therein. Created entities were not set up in order for you to see them, but rather, in order for you to see their Master within them. Hence, what the Truth desires of you is for you to see created entities with the eye of one who sees them not; that is, for you to see them not with a view to their creatureliness but rather, with a view to His appearance in them. This message is expressed in the following lines:

> I only revealed the worlds to you
> That you might see them with the eye of one
> who sees them not,
>
> Detached therefrom with the upward vision of one
> who contents himself not
> With any condition unless [therein] he sees His
> Master.

The one who looks at created entities without seeing the Truth therein is in a state of heedlessness, while the one who has been annihilated to them is a servant dazzled by the "assaults" of the divine vision. As for the one who sees the Truth in created entities, he is a servant completed and set aside [for his appointed mission]. Attention is turned away from the created universe only with respect to its creatureliness, not with respect to the Truth's appearance therein; hence, this is due not to His failure to appear in everything but rather, to their inability to perceive Him in everything. For He does appear in everything; in fact, He appears even in those entities through which He is veiled. Hence, there is, in reality, no veil. As one poet expressed it:

> I see everything in need, while all wealth is Yours,
> It is in my nature to sin, while it is in Yours to pardon.
>
> Demonstrating loving-kindness out of Your gracious bounty,
> It is in Your nature to nurture, and in my nature to turn away.
>
> No life is sweet without Your loving communion,
> Nor is it tranquil—no, by God!—for how could it be so?

I have resolved to abandon the entire universe
And to follow love's path as do those whom God has chosen.

Both the vision of You and the veil serve to disclose,
For when realization comes, it becomes itself the unveiling.

How fine are the loved ones in every state,
For to God belongs what they reveal, and to Him
belongs what they conceal.

As for those who have had no vision of You,
Their hearts are dull to the longing to win the secret
of passionate love.

You are the One who brought to light, then came to light
In all manifestations as even the most ordinary have
born witness.

You have become visible to the entire universe, so the
universe itself is a manifestation
Both within and for itself, as the revealed scriptures came.

What heart would turn away from Your love,
And what eye, after Your nearness to me, would close
in slumber?

What soul has not been inclined toward You by the
longing You inspire?
On Your love do the souls of all humankind depend.

If you wish, you may say that there are two types of sainthood: a sainthood of evidence and proof, and a sainthood of witness and direct sight. The former is for those who rely on reflection and contemplation, while the latter is for those who rely on intuitive perception. In the following words God speaks of those in the former group, saying, "In time We shall make them fully understand Our messages in the utmost horizons [of the universe] and within themselves, so that it will become clear to them that this [revelation] is indeed the truth" {Fuṣṣilat [Clearly Spelled Out] 41: 53}. As for the second group, He addresses them thus, "Say: 'God [has revealed that divine writ]!'—and then leave them to play at their vain talk" {Al-Anᶜām [Cattle] 6: 91}.[75]

Those who are given to seeking evidence and proofs are mere laity, as it were, by comparison with those who have witnessed [the divine realities] and seen them with their own [inner] eyes. The reason for this is that the latter group so hallow the Truth in His appearance [in created entities] that He has no need [to present them with] evidence of His presence. After all, how can the One who has provided the evidence need [further] evidence? And how can He be known through it [i.e., the evidence] when He is the One who has made it known?

Shaykh Abū al-Ḥasan (may God be pleased with him) said, "How can the One through whom the gnostic sciences have been known be Himself known through the gnostic sciences? Or, how can the One whose existence preceded the existence of all things be known through any of these things?" A disciple once asked his shaykh, "O Teacher, where is God?" To which his shaykh replied, "May God crush you! After a vision [of the Divine] with your own eyes, you seek to know where He is?"

One gnostic sang:

> You became manifest so that You were hidden from no one
> But the blind man who cannot see the moon.
>
> Then You were concealed from view, O Ṣamad,[76]

For how can One shrouded in almighty power be known?

The Truth has thus been veiled from His servants by the very magnificence of His appearance, while their sight has been prevented from witnessing Him by the very brilliance of His light. Hence, the very intensity of [your] nearness [to Him] has absented you from the vision of that nearness. Shaykh Abū al-Ḥasan (may God be pleased with him) said, "The reality of nearness is for you to be so intensely near that you are absent, in the nearness, from the nearness. The experience might be likened to that of someone who, smelling the fragrance of musk, continues drawing nearer to it, and the nearer he approaches, the more powerful its fragrance becomes. However, when he enters the house where the musk is, its fragrance ceases to be perceptible to him."

One gnostic sang:

How many a soul has camouflaged himself in al-
Shiᶜbayni and ᶜAlam
When his secret was plain for all to see?

I hear you asking about Najd when you are
already there,
And about Tihāmah—what suspicious conduct!

I also found the following lines written in our shaykh Abū al-ᶜAbbās's own script:

Have you from Laylā any words uncensored
Which, when they come, raise dry bones to new life?

Ours has been a long acquaintance, yet I,
Even so, have been neglectful of her love.

Her apparition would visit me in days of yore,
But when it faded, why should it have become elusive?

Has she withheld even her apparition,
Or has it grown so delicate it no longer appears to
my mind's eye?

From Laylā's face the sunrise seeks light,
While in the sun human sight is confounded.

She was only veiled by the lifting of her veil,
What a marvel that appearance itself is a concealment!

Know that evidence is only provided for those who are seeking the truth, not for those who have witnessed it. The witness, by virtue of the clarity of his vision, has no need for evidence, while knowledge—considering the [various earthly] means which have led to it—will [at first] be something acquired, after which, in its final stage, it will become a necessity.[77]

Moreover, if there are created entities which, thanks to their clarity, need to present no evidence [on their own behalf], then how much less would the Creator be in need thereof? Shaykh Abū al-Ḥasan (may God be pleased with him) said, "We view God with the perceptive powers of faith and certainty, which has freed us from the need for evidence and proof. Indeed, we see no creature. After all, is there, in all of existence, anything but the True Sovereign? And even if we must acknowledge other entities, they differ little from the fine dust particles in the air which, when you examine them carefully, you find to be nothing at all." It is thus most astonishing for created entities to be capable of leading [someone] to God, and would that I knew how they might possess existence with Him such that they can, in fact, lead [someone] to Him, or how they might possess a clarity which He lacks such that it is they that make Him manifest!

If created entities do lead [us] to God, they do so not out of some capacity which they possess in and of themselves. Rather, God is the One who has assigned them this function and they, accordingly, perform it. For nothing can lead to Him but His own divinity. Nevertheless, the truly Wise One has established [earthly] causes which, for those who fail to see beyond them to His [divine] power, are the veil *par excellence*. A narrator once said, "The Messenger of God ﷺ awoke one morning following a night's rain, and he said, 'Do you know what your Lord says?' Those listening replied, 'God and His Messenger know best.' And he told them, 'Of My servants who awaken in the morning, some have faith in Me, and others deny Me. Those who say, "We have received rain by virtue of God's bounty and mercy" have faith in Me, but deny [the role of] the heavenly bodies. And as for those who say, "We have received rain on account of such-and-such a star or such-and-such a storm," they deny Me and have faith in the heavenly bodies."'"

This tradition was narrated by Mālik in his *Muwaṭṭa'*.[78]

Hence, [earthly] causes must needs exist, while at the same time, one must be absent to them in order to witness [the divine causality behind them]. After all, how can created entities manifest Him when He is the One who manifested them? Or, how can created entities bring about the knowledge of Him when He is the One who has brought about knowledge of them?

You might say: The prophetic tradition according to which, "Whoever knows himself knows his Lord"[79] indicates that self-knowledge leads to the knowledge of God. Moreover, since self-knowledge is a kind of created existence, this tradition demonstrates that created entities can lead to Him. In this connection, I heard our shaykh Abū al-ᶜAbbās (may God be pleased with him) say, "This tradition may be interpreted in two ways. According to the first interpretation, the tradition means that if someone knows himself in his lowliness, helplessness and poverty, he will come to know God in His glorious might, power and self-sufficiency; hence, one comes to know oneself first, and to know God thereafter. According to the second interpretation, the words, 'Whoever knows himself knows his Lord' mean that if someone knows himself, this is evidence that he had already known God before this. The first interpretation describes the condition of spiritual wayfarers (*al-sālikīn*),[80] while the second describes the condition of the divinely possessed (*al-majdhūbīn*).[81]

And know—may God grant you His grace in full measure and cause you to be among those who dwell in His presence—that if He, may He be praised, takes a saint under His care, He will preserve his heart from everything other than Himself and guard it with unceasing light. Hence, one gnostic has said: If God, may He be praised, has guarded the heavens with the stars and flaming meteors lest anyone overhear its secrets,[82] how much worthier of such protection will the believer's heart be? As God declares through His Messenger ﷺ, "Neither earth nor heaven can contain Me, but I am contained by the heart of My believing servant."[83]

Behold—may God be gracious to you—the superlative honor which was given to this heart such that it became worthy of this rank.

Shaykh Abū al-Ḥasan (may God be pleased with him) once said, "If the light possessed by the disobedient believer were made visible, the heavens and the earth would collapse into one another. How much more overpowering, then, must the light of the obedient believer be?"

I once heard our shaykh Abū al-ᶜAbbās (may God be pleased with him) say, "If the saint's true nature were disclosed, he would be worshipped, since his attributes and qualities are derived from His [Lord's]." In this connection, a certain disciple once said to me, "When I was performing a certain ritual prayer behind my shaykh, I saw something that left me dumbfounded. I saw the shaykh's body filled with light, and it radiated from his being until I could look at him no longer." Hence, if the Truth were to unveil the radiances of His saints, the light of the sun and the moon would be engulfed by the radiance of their hearts. After all, what is the light of the sun and the moon by comparison with their lights? The sun is eclipsed and sets; as for the lights of the saints' hearts, they are eclipsed not, nor do they set. It is for this reason that someone once said:

> The daytime's sun goes down by night,
> But the sun of hearts never sets.

The light of the sun is witnessed to by effects, while the light of certainty is witnessed to by the Cause of all effects. As we read in the following lines:

> This sun has met us with a light,
> But verily, the sun of certainty casts a light
> more dazzling.
>
> For we, by the former, have seen, but
> By the latter we have beheld the Giver of light.

Nevertheless, the Truth, may He be exalted, does justice to the essences of created entities, giving each its proper measure. He decrees for every created entity its specific rank and grants it in full its sphere and time of influence. It is for this reason that He has concealed the secret of the unique distinctions which mark human existence. The sun needs a cloud, and the beautiful woman a veil. After all, is it reasonable to expect a treasure not to be buried, or a secret not to be guarded? God, may He be praised, has established things in this manner in order that the secret of sainthood might remain in the realm of the unseen; as such, he who believes in this secret will be a believer in the unseen. Moreover, He has esteemed His saints too highly to manifest them in a realm devoid of permanence. Hence, He has lowered a veil of protection over them until the advent of the final realm (i.e., the life to come), which He has deemed worthy of their appearance, approach and unveiling. It is in this latter realm that God unveils the secret of sainthood, granting it the highest of stations and raising its light aloft.

Know—may God be gracious to you—that when God wills for one of His saints to call others to Him, He must of necessity disclose this saint to the rest of His servants, since it is only in this manner that the call to God may be issued. Not only so, but He must clothe this saint in two garments: the garment of majesty, and the garment of splendor.

As for majesty, it is granted in order that God's servants might hold the saint in the highest esteem and, as a consequence, comport themselves toward him with the proper courtesy. He causes His servants to hold the saint in such awe that when he commands and prohibits, his commands and prohibitions will be heard and obeyed. The Truth has placed this awe and reverence in His servants' hearts as a means of empowering the saint to achieve victory on His behalf. God describes this saint as being among "those who, if We firmly establish them on earth, remain constant in prayer, give in charity, enjoin the doing of what is right and forbid the doing of what is wrong; with God rests the final outcome of all events" {Al-Ḥajj [The Pilgrimage] 22: 41}.

This [i.e., the awe and veneration inspired by the one whom God has chosen to call others to the truth] is likewise a manifestation of the honor and strength which the Truth grants to His believing servants. He says, "…all honor belongs to God, and [thus] to His Apostle and those who believe…." {Al-Munāfiqūn [The Hypocrites] 63: 8}.

This awe and reverence which the Truth has placed in His servants' hearts toward His saints is a result of the dignified rank of the one they follow having been extended to them. Have you not heard the saying of the Prophet ﷺ, "I was granted victory by terror from a month's march away"?[84] The Truth has arrayed them in the vestments of His awesome splendor and through them has caused His majestic grandeur to appear. Whenever they descend into the land of servanthood, He lifts them into the heavenly realm of His elect. Hence, they are kings even if no flags flutter over their processions, and mighty rulers even if no soldiers march before them.

How aptly it has been said concerning Mālik Ibn Anas (may God be pleased with him):

> As he declines to reply, others retreat from
> consulting him, so awed are they by his presence,
> While his inquirers approach with heads bowed.
>
> [Enjoying] the courtesy commanded by his dignified
> bearing and the renown born of the authority
> of the God-fearing,
> He is obeyed though he possesses no [earthly] power.

He whom God has possessed commands himself and his passions, for God has given him dominion. As God, exalted be He, declares, "Say: 'O God, Lord of all dominion!

Thou grantest dominion unto whom Thou willest…" {Āl ʿImrān [The House of ʿImrān] 3: 26}.

I once heard our shaykh Abū al-ʿAbbās (may God be pleased with him) say, "A king once said to a gnostic, 'Request of me anything you wish.' The gnostic replied, 'To me you say this? I possess two servants who have taken possession of you, and whom I have vanquished but who have vanquished you, namely, lust and miserliness. Hence, you are my servant's servant. And why should I make any request of my servant's servant?'"

As for the second garment with which the Truth, may He be praised, clothes those saints whom He has set aside to call others to the truth, it is, as we have seen, the garment of splendor. God clothes His saints in this garment in order to adorn them in the hearts of His servants so that they will look upon them with affection and love which will, in turn, move them to follow them. Do you not see how God, may He be praised, said concerning Moses, upon him be peace, "…I spread Mine Own love over Thee" {Ṭā Hā [O Man] 20: 39}. He also declares, "Verily, those who attain to faith and do righteous deeds will the Most Gracious endow with love " {Maryam [Mary] 19: 96}.

God decks them out in the robes of venerability in order that His servants might love them, and in order that their love for them might draw them into the love of God. Love in God necessitates, in turn, love from God. As the Prophet ﷺ said, speaking on God's behalf, "My love must be granted to those who love one another in Me."

There are four stages involved here: Love for God, love in God, love through God and love from God. Love for God is thus the beginning, love from God is the end, while love in God and love through God are intermediary stages between them. Love for God means for you to prefer Him above all, and not to prefer anything or anything over Him. Love in God is for you to love, in Him, those whom He has befriended. Love through God is for the servant to love whomever he loves and whatever he loves without any thought for himself and his own desires, while love from God is for God to take you from everything such that you love nothing and no one but Him.

The mark of love for God is constant remembrance of Him, with one's mind and heart fully present. The mark of love in God is that you love those who are obedient and perform righteous deeds even if they have not brought you any worldly benefit. The mark of love through God is for the motivation to seek one's personal fortunes to have been vanquished by God's light, while the mark of love from God is for Him so to draw you unto Him that He causes everything other than Himself to be concealed from you.

Shaykh Abū al-Ḥasan (may God be pleased with him) once said, "If anyone has loved God and has loved for God, his sainthood has been perfected through love." The true lover is one over whose heart no one but his beloved has power or authority, and who has no will but the will of his beloved. Hence, the person whose sainthood from God has been established will not abhor death. This may be seen from the words of God, exalted be He, "Say: 'O you who follow the Jewish faith! If you claim that you are close to God to the exclusion of all other people, then you should be longing for death if what you say is true!" {Al-Jumᶜah [The Congregation] 62: 6}. Hence, the true saint will not spurn death if it is offered to him.

He who loves God is someone who has no beloved but Him; he who loves for God is someone who loves nothing and no one for the sake of his own desires, while he who loves to meet God is one who has tasted the intimacy of his Master.

Love for Him is purified in the following ten: in the Apostle ﷺ, Abū Bakr, [c]Umar, the Prophet's companions and their followers, the saints and the scholars who guide us to God, the martyrs, the righteous, and the believers, all of whom I ask you to consider in light of what follows:

If matters are divided following faith into ten categories—that is, into orthodoxy and innovation, right guidance and error, obedience and disobedience, justice and injustice, and truth and falsehood—and if you distinguish among them, loving one and hating the other—then love for Him and hate for Him without concern for which of the two you are encountering, since both phenomena might be manifest within one and the same person, in which case you must do equal justice to both of them. If you believe that you love for God's sake the ten individuals and groups mentioned above, then observe to see whether earthly desire has some role therein. Likewise consider the love you have for your sincere brethren, the righteous shaykhs, the rightly guided scholars, and any and all others, be they present or among those who are absent or deceased. If you find that your heart has no special attachment either to those who are present or to those who are absent or deceased, then your love has been purified of earthly desire and your love for God's sake has been confirmed. If, on the other hand, you discover some attachment in yourself to someone or something which you love, then return to the pursuit of knowledge and gain a thorough understanding of the five categories of actions, namely, obligatory, recommended, offensive, forbidden, and permissible.

Know, moreover, that the shaykh's saying that "the person whose sainthood from God has been established will not abhor death" is a standard which he has given disciples by which to judge themselves if the claim is made, whether by them or others, that they have attained sainthood, since people are prone to make [false] claims and to leap [prematurely] to advanced spiritual ranks without their having trodden the path which leads thereto. It is for this reason that God, may He be praised, says, "Say: 'Produce your evidence—if you truly believe in your claims!'" {Al-Naml [The Ants] 27: 64} And He says here, "Then you should be longing for death—if what you say is true!" {Al-Jum^c^ah [The Congregation] 62: 6}

The Apostle ﷺ once said to Ḥārithah, "Everything has a reality, so what is the reality of your faith?" Then when he asked Ḥārithah, "How did you awake this morning?" he replied, "I awoke a true believer." As for him in whom there are still the remains [of his attachment to this world], he will not love death, nor will he who still clings to some type of sin. God has [thus] made the desire for death a witness to the saint's sainthood, and the lack of desire for death a witness to the error of those who have gone astray. God, may He be praised, has said, "Weigh, therefore, [your deeds] with equity" {Al-Raḥmān [The Most Gracious] 55: 9}.

Death is likewise a measure of actions and states, just as it is a measure of spiritual ranks. As it pertains to spiritual ranks, we have discussed this matter above. With regard to actions and states, if there is some action which is unclear to you in the sense that you do not know whether it would please God for you to engage in it or not or, in the case of a state you are in, whether you entered this state in truth or based on your own desires, you should bring the thought of death to bear on the action or state with which you are concerned. Every state or action which is confirmed rather than defeated by the thought of death's advent may be considered to be truth, while every state or action which is defeated by the projection of death's advent is falsehood, since death is truth, and truth defeats and crushes falsehood. As God, almighty and majestic be He, declares,

> "Nay, but We hurl the truth against falsehood, and it crushes the latter, and lo! It withers away" {Al-Anbiyā' [The Prophets] 21: 18}

> "Say: 'Verily, my Sustainer hurls the truth [against all that is false]—He who fully knows all the things that are beyond the reach of a created being's perception!'" {Saba' [Sheba] 34: 48}

> "And say: 'The truth has now come, and falsehood has withered away: for behold, all falsehood is bound to wither away!'" {Al-Isrā' [The Night Journey] 17: 81}

Hence, whatever you are undertaking in truth will not be defeated by death, since it is truth; death is truth, and truth does not defeat truth.

I once had a conversation with a seeker of knowledge concerning the fact that one's intention in such an endeavor must be pure, and that one must undertake this endeavor for God alone. I said to him, "The person who seeks knowledge for God is the one who, were you to say to him, 'Tomorrow you will die,' would not put the book down."

The unaware seeker of knowledge might be misled by the statement, "We sought knowledge for the sake of some aim other than God, but He refused to allow it to be for anything but Him."[85] There is nothing in this statement which would justify the pursuit of knowledge for the sake of earthly authority and advantage over others. Rather, the person who uttered these words was speaking of a blessing which had been bestowed upon him, and of a temptation from which God had delivered him. Hence, there is no need to apply this statement to anyone else. Such a situation might be likened to someone afflicted with a chronic intestinal ailment who, enervated from treatment and despairing of a cure, takes a dagger and stabs himself in the abdomen in order to kill himself. However, in so doing, he happens to puncture the afflicted intestine, thereby causing the illness to drain out of him. Such an action would not be approved by anyone in his right mind, even if it happened to lead to success. In other words, a pleasant final outcome does not absolve from blame those who cast themselves into perdition. As someone once said: One who is deceived is not praiseworthy even if he escapes harm.

The shaykh's saying, "He who loves God is someone who has no beloved but Him" requires that we understand what love is. Know that love is one of the sublimest stations of certainty. In fact, the people of God have differed over which is closer to perfection: the station of love, or the station of contentment? We hold that the station of contentment is closer to perfection, because love's power may hold sway over the lover, thereby intensifying his earthly passions, which in turn may lead him to seek the vision of that which ill befits his station. Do you not see that the lover wants to see the beloved at all times, while the person in the station of contentment with God is content with Him whether he sees Him or is prevented from doing so? The lover desires constant communion, while the person who is content with God is content with Him whether He grants him intimate communion or cuts him off, since he is not in pursuit of what he wants for himself, but rather, what God wants for him. The lover seeks unceasing communication with the beloved, while the contented soul seeks nothing. This truth is conveyed in the following lines:

I once sought communion with Him,
But when I attained to knowledge and ignorance was lifted,

I knew for a certainty that the true servant seeks nothing.
If He draws near, He does so out of His bounty,
and if He draws away, He does so for good reasons.

If He discloses, He discloses none but His own attributes,
And if He conceals, I shall deem the concealment,
for His sake, as sweet.

Shaykh Abū al-Ḥasan (may God be pleased with him) said, "Love entails God's taking His servant's heart away from everything but Him." Hence, you find the soul desiring to obey Him, the mind fortified with the experiential knowledge of Him, the spirit captivated by His presence, and the innermost being steeped in the vision of Him. The servant seeks more and more is given, and he is made privy to that which is sweeter than the most rapturous secret conversations. Clothed in the vestments of intimate approach on the path of loving adoration, he touches virginal realities as well as the "experienced" sciences. Thus it has been said, "God's friends are brides, and brides are not seen by criminals."

Someone asked him, "I know what love is. But what is love's nectar? What is love's cup? Who is the cupbearer? What is 'tasting'? What is 'drinking'? What is it to have one's thirst quenched? What is intoxication? What is sobriety?"

He replied, "Love's nectar is the brilliant light which emanates from the beauty of the Beloved.

"The cup is the subtlety which delivers the light to hearts' mouths.

"The cupbearer is the Supreme Protector of the elect of His friends and His righteous servants, namely, God, the Knower of the destinies and best interests of His loved ones. As for one to whom this beauty has been disclosed and who has enjoyed some measure thereof—if even just a sip or two—after which the veil is lowered once again over his eyes, this is the one who has tasted and who now lives in a state of longing.

"He for whom this [tasting] lasts for as much as an hour or two is one who has truly drunk.

"When someone has successive experiences of this nature and continues to drink until his veins and joints are filled with God's store of lights, this is the quenching of one's thirst.

"Such a person may withdraw from the world of sense and rationality to the point where he is unaware of what is being said or what he is saying; this is intoxication.

"The cup may be passed among them and they may experience a variety of states, after which they are restored to conscious remembrance and to acts of obedience; even so, the [divine] attributes will not be hidden from them by the press of this life's inevitable preoccupations. This is the time of their restored sobriety, the expansion of their vision, and the increase of their [true] knowledge.

"Thus it is that by the stars of knowledge and the moon of divine unity they are guided by night, and by the suns of the gnostic sciences they are illumined by day."

"They are God's partisans: oh, verily, it is they, the partisans of God, who shall attain to a happy state!" {Al-Mujādalah [The Pleading] 58: 22}

The shaykh and pole, ᶜAbd al-Salām Ibn Mashīsh, the shaykh of Shaykh Abū al-ᶜAbbās (may God be pleased with them both) said, "Keep yourself pure of *shirk*.[86] Whenever you have an occurrence of ritual impurity,[87] cleanse your-

The Tomb of Ibn Mashīsh

"Abū al-Ḥasan al-Shādhilī (May God be pleased with him!) was born in the village of Ghamara in North Africa near Sabtah (Ceuta) in Morocco in the year 1196. He received the Shādhilī *ṭarīqa* and inherited the function of Pole of the age from his shaykh, the Imam Abū ᶜAbd Allah ᶜAbd al-Salām Ibn Mashīsh (may God sancitfy his Secret)."

From the autobiography, *Two Who Attained*, of Fatima al-Yashrutiyya, a Sufi woman descended from this lineage.

self of the contamination that results from the love of this world. Whenever you feel inclined to satisfy some lust, repair through repentance what you have damaged, or nearly so, through craving.

"Moreover, you must love God with reverence and unblemished intention. Become addicted to drinking from [love's] cup, with alternating intoxication and sobriety. Whenever you awaken or regain your sobriety, drink again until both your intoxication and your sobriety come in turn and until, so [taken are you] by His beauty, you lose consciousness of love, of the nectar, of the drinking and of the cup by virtue of the light that appears to you, that is, the light of His beauty and of the holiness of His consummate majesty.

"Of course, I may be speaking to those who know nothing of love, the nectar, the drinking, the cup, intoxication, or sobriety."

To which his conversant replied, "Indeed. How many are those who have drowned in something while knowing nothing of their drowning? Hence, grant me knowledge and awaken me to that of which I am ignorant, or to what has been graciously bestowed upon me without my being mindful thereof."

I have told you: Yes, love is for God to captivate the heart of the one He loves by the light He discloses to him, namely, the light of His beauty and of the holiness of His consummate majesty.

The nectar of love is the mixture of attributes with attributes, morals with morals, lights with lights, names with names, qualities with qualities, and deeds with deeds, in which vision is broadened for those for whom God wills this, mighty and majestic be He.

Drinking is the giving of this nectar to hearts, limbs and veins until one is intoxicated. However, this process takes place by training after one has been melted and refined; hence, each one is given to drink according to his capacity. There are those who are given to drink without mediation, and whom God, may He be praised, Himself gives to drink. There are those who are given to drink through mediaries such as the angels, scholars, and great souls who have been drawn near. There are those who are intoxicated by the mere sight of the cup, even before they have had a taste. How much more sublime will their state be, then, once they have tasted, once they have drunk, once their thirst has been quenched, and once they have been intoxicated with the nectar itself?

Just as intoxication takes places in varying degrees, so also, subsequently, does sobriety. The cup is "Truth's ladle" by which He dips out the limpid, unadulterated, purifying nectar for those whom He wills of His chosen servants. Sometimes the drinker sees the cup as an image; at other times he will see it in a spiritual form, and at others, in an intellectual form. The image is the portion of bodies and souls, the spiritual form is the portion of hearts and minds, while the intellectual form is the portion of spirits and the inmost consciousness. Oh, what a nectar it is, and how sweet! Blessed are those who imbibe therein and persevere in doing so, and who are never deprived thereof. "Such is God's bounty; He grants it to anyone who is willing [to receive it]:[88] for God is limitless in His great bounty" {Al-Jumᶜah [The Congregation] 62: 4}.

A community of lovers might gather and be given to drink either from a single cup or from numerous cups, while a single lover likewise might be given to drink from a single cup or from numerous cups. The nectars might differ from one cup to another, while conversely, more than one nectar might be contained by a single cup from which a multitude of lovers drink.

* * *

Know, moreover—may God open your spiritual eyes to the vision of His lights and bless you unceasingly with His gnostic sciences and secrets—that one of the sublimest of God's gifts to His saints is that of verbal expression [on God's behalf].

I heard our shaykh, Abū al-ᶜAbbās (may God be pleased with him) say, "The saint is so charged with knowledge, both intellectual and experiential, and with realities which he himself has witnessed, that when he expresses himself in words, it is as if he has been given God's permission to speak. Thus, you must understand that if someone has been granted permission to speak [on God's behalf], his listeners will hear his words as beautiful and refined, and his exhortations will be given a welcome reception."

I also heard him say (may God be pleased with him) say, "When someone has been granted God's permission to speak, his words emerge clothed in vestments of eloquence and grace, whereas if he has not been granted such permission, his words come out obscure and lightless. In fact, if two men speak about one and the same reality, the message of one may be received readily, while that of the other may be spurned."

Know, moreover, that the saint founds his life upon sole dependence on God, contentment with the knowledge He grants, and cultivation of the vision of Him. God, may He be praised, declares: "and for everyone who places his trust in God, He [alone] is enough" {Al-Ṭalāq [Divorce] 65: 3}. And He asks: "Does he, then, not know that God sees [all]?" {Al-ᶜAlaq [The Germ-Cell] 96: 14}; "Is not God enough for His servant?" {Al-Zumar [The Throngs] 39: 36}; and, "Is it not enough [for them to know] that thy Sustainer is witness unto everything?" {Fuṣṣilat [Clearly Spelled Out] 41: 53} In the beginning, saints flee from the created realm and seek solitude with the True Sovereign; they conceal their good works and their mystical states as a means of achieving their annihilation, confirming their denial of the world, ensuring the well-being of their hearts, and expressing their desire to perform all their deeds in perfect sincerity to their Master.

Then, once certainty has been firmly established and once they have been sustained by thorough understanding and God-given empowerment and have attained to the reality of annihilation, they arrive at the state of permanence. Once they have achieved permanence, God will reveal them if He wills, or conceal them if He wills. If He wills, He will reveal them as those who guide other servants to Him, and if He wills, He will conceal them and set them apart from everything, reserving them for Himself, as it were. Hence, the saint's appearance is not a matter of his own will but rather, a matter of God's will for him. In fact, if he had any say in the matter, the saint would always choose to remain hidden, as we have seen. However, if God, may He be praised, wills to manifest the saints and does, in fact, manifest them, He grants them His nearness and protection through His sustenance and abundant blessings. As the Prophet ﷺ declared, "O ᶜAbd al-Raḥmān Ibn Samurah, seek not rulership for yourself, for if it is granted to you without your asking, you will receive [divine] succor in bearing its burdens, but if it is granted to you because you sought it out, you will bear its burdens alone."[89]

Those who attain realization through servanthood to God seek neither to remain hidden nor to be manifested; rather, their wills are subject to what their Master chooses for them. Shaykh Abū al-ᶜAbbās (may God be pleased with him) said,

"He who wishes to appear [before others] is a slave to appearances, while he who wishes to remain hidden is a slave to hiddenness. As for the one who is a slave to God, it makes no difference to him whether God manifests him or conceals him."

Let us conclude this introduction with mention of the miracles performed by God's friends, the saints, both as possibility and as actual occurrence, and with a brief summary of their various types. This is a theme which has been dealt with exhaustively by others who, in so doing, have relieved us of the need to do so here. However, we draw attention to a number of beneficial points for those with hearts given to understanding, unveiling their beauty in order to prepare you to accept the miracles of those belonging to this community and the glorious signs which we will ascribe to them, God willing.

An Interlude on the Theme of Saints' Miracles

Our discussion of miracles will be presented within the framework of two aspects thereof: possibility and actual occurrence. It is clear that the performance of miracles by the saints is a possibility since, if it were not, it would be either a necessity or an impossibility. It would be invalid to consider them an impossibility, since an impossibility is something which, if its existence is posited, necessitates an absurdity. As for the positing of the occurrence of miracles, it necessitates no absurdity. Moreover, it would be false to say that the performance of miracles by the saints is a necessity, since this community [i.e., the Sufi community] is in unanimous agreement that someone may be a saint even if he performs no extraordinary feats.

Hence, it follows that the occurrence of miracles must be a possibility. Now, a possibility is something which is not ruled out by reason. If, moreover, miracles are not ruled out by reason and if no written statement has been handed down by tradition to the effect that they did not occur, it must therefore be possible for God to honor His saints by allowing them to perform them.

Miracles include such things as a collapsing of the distance between one place and another, walking on water, flying through the air, cognizance of entities which used to exist [but exist no longer], or of entities which have not yet come into existence through supernatural means, multiplying food or drink, producing fruit [on a tree, for example] out of season, causing water to flow from the ground without digging for it, taming wild animals, responding to someone's petition by producing rain at a time when rain would not normally fall, abstaining from nourishment for an extraordinary length of time, causing a barren tree to produce fruit other than the fruit it would naturally bear, etc. All of these belong to the realm of purely visible miracles.

However, those miracles which are considered by the people of God to be superior to and more sublime than these are miracles of the spirit, such as the experiential knowledge of God, reverent fear of Him, constant observance of Him, hastening to obey His commands and to avoid what He forbids, firm establishment in certainty, strength and empowerment, perseverance in following God and listening to Him, acquiring understanding on His authority, unceasing confidence in Him, sincere reliance upon Him, etc.

I heard our shaykh Abū al-ᶜAbbās (may God be pleased with him) say, "The phenomenon of 'collapsing' is of two types: lesser and greater. The lesser 'collapsing,' which occurs among the more ordinary members of this community, is for the earth to 'collapse' for them, as it were, from the east to the west in a single breath. As for the greater 'collapsing,' it is the 'collapsing' of the attributes of souls.[1] He spoke truly (may God be pleased with him) in so saying, since "collapsing" the earth is a feat which, if God rendered you incapable thereof, or if He deprived you of your [previously existing] ability to perform it, this would not detract from your standing with Him so long as you were loyal to Him in your servanthood, whereas if you were unable to bring about the "collapse" of the soul's attributes through Him, you would be among the blameworthy, and relegated to the ranks of the heedless.

Shaykh Abū al-Ḥasan (may God be pleased with him) said, "These two miracles are all-encompassing: the miracle of faith with the increase of certainty and being an eyewitness [to the divine realities], and the miracle of laboring to emulate and follow [the examples of the righteous] and to eschew false claims and deceit. Hence, someone who has been granted these two miracles, then begins to long for something else, is a slanderous, lying servant who has missed the mark with respect to knowledge and sound action. Such a person may be likened to someone who, having been granted the honor of appearing before the king and enjoying his favor, begins longing to go out and drive beasts of burden and foregoes the king's favor. If any miracle is not attended by contentment with God and God's contentment with the person who performed it, he is either deficient, deluded and seeking to lure others [into error], or perishing and headed for destruction.

Know that God's saints' awareness of certain unseen realities is not ruled out by reason; moreover, there are written reports of this phenomenon which have been passed down by tradition. We find, for example, that when Abū Bakr was suffering from the illness which was to lead to his death, he said to ᶜĀ'ishah (may God be pleased with them both), "[Take care of] your two brothers, your two sisters, and a woman great with child from whom I see a female emerging!"[2] In so saying, Abū Bakr announced that his wife was pregnant with a girl, and his words proved to be correct.

Another example is the incident in which ᶜUmar (may God be pleased with him) said, "Sāriyah! The mountain!" while Sāriyah was in the furthest regions of Iraq, in spite of which Sāriyah heard ᶜUmar's voice. God had given ᶜUmar awareness of the fact that Sāriyah was surrounded by the enemy; hence, he commanded him to veer in the direction of the mountain. Sāriyah and the army which was with him did as ᶜUmar had directed them to, as a result of which they were victorious in battle. When ᶜUmar was given this awareness, he was standing at the pulpit delivering a sermon; hence, he stopped preaching and said, "Sāriyah! The mountain!" after which he went back to his sermon. Some of the Prophet's companions came after this to ᶜAlī (may God be pleased with him) and said, "While ᶜUmar was delivering a sermon today, he stopped preaching and said, 'Sāriyah! The mountain!' Then he went back to preaching." ᶜAlī replied, "Woe be to you! Leave ᶜUmar alone, for never has he entered into anything but that he has known the way out." It was after this that Sāriyah came and informed them that he had heard ᶜUmar's summons at the very time when ᶜUmar had called to him.

As for ᶜAli Ibn Abī Ṭālib (may God be pleased with him), the most astonishing things have been reported of him in this regard. We find, for example, that historians have recorded that while he was in Kufa, a rumor began to circulate that Muᶜāwiyah had died. When this report reached him (may God be pleased with him), he said, "By God, he has not died, nor will he die before he takes possession of what is beneath these two feet of mine. The son of Hind[3] wished to spread this rumor in order to elicit a response from me." Following this, the people of Kufa wrote to Muᶜāwiyah and learned that governing authority had passed to him.

Indeed, such accounts concerning the saints, circulated in every time and place, demonstrate the reality of this phenomenon, having been handed down on the basis of so many independent chains of transmission that their reliability cannot be doubted.

I will now direct you—may God be gracious to you—to a point which will make it easier for you to believe in this [i.e., the saints' miracles], namely, that the chosen servant's priviness to a reality which God has concealed from others comes about not through his physical senses nor [even] through his powers of inner perception, but rather, by the Truth's light within him. This may be seen in the words of the Prophet ﷺ, "Beware of the believer's discernment, for he sees by the light of God."[4] Is it any surprise, then, that a believer should be given cognizance of some reality which God has concealed from others given the fact that the Apostle ﷺ has testified of him that he sees not by his own powers, but by the light of his Lord?

Evidence of this phenomenon is likewise provided by the prophetic tradition which was cited earlier and in which the Prophet ﷺ speaks on God's behalf, saying, "And if I love him, I become the hearing by which he hears, the sight by which he sees, the hand by which he strikes and the foot on which he walks...." In the case of someone for whom the Truth is his sight, it is not surprising that he should have cognizance of some reality which God has rendered invisible [to the general populace]. (According to some chains of transmission the wording of this tradition is, "And if I love him, I become for him hearing, sight, a tongue, a heart, a mind, a hand, and a support.")

At this juncture you might say: How do you account, then, for the words of God, "He [alone] knows that which is beyond the reach of a created being's perception, and to none does He disclose aught of the mysteries of His own unfathomable knowledge unless it be to an apostle whom He has been pleased to elect [therefore]" {Al-Jinn [The Unseen Beings] 72: 26-27}? According to this declaration, no one but the apostle is excepted. Know, however, that I once heard our shaykh, Abū al-ᶜAbbās (may God be pleased with him) say, "The word 'apostle' as used here includes the sense of someone fully realized in righteousness (*ṣiddīq*) or a saint (*walī*)."

You might also say: This is going beyond what is stated in the Qur'an. Know, however, that if it were said, "The sultan has granted permission [to enter his presence] today to no one but the vizier," it might happen that the vizier's mamluks could enter the sultan's presence with him, since the permission granted to the one to whom they are subordinate is tantamount to permission for them as well. Similarly in the case of the saint, if God grants him cognizance of some reality which He has concealed from others, this will be because of the saint's inclusion within the honor and glory of prophethood and his sincere emulation of the Prophet ﷺ. Hence, he will not have seen this reality by his own powers but rather, by the light of the one to whom he is subordinate.

[You might also object, saying:] This Qur'anic verse points likewise to the fact that no servants are made privy to unseen realities unless God makes them privy thereto. However, God, may He be praised, has made clear the reason for which He has given knowledge of unseen realities to those to whom He has given such knowledge, namely, that the servant to whom He grants such knowledge is one "whom He has been pleased to elect [therefore]." Moreover, the use of the word "apostle" singles out the apostle for mention. He does not, for example, mention the prophet (*al-nabī*), the one realized in righteousness (*al-ṣiddīq*), or the saint (*al-walī*) despite the fact that each of them would be a person with whom God is pleased, since the apostle is more worthy of this than anyone else.

In order to make it easier for you to believe in the miracles of God's friends, rather than looking upon them as beyond their ken, I shall mention the following points:

Firstly, you should know that it is the power of God, greater than which no power exists, which causes this or that miracle to be performed at the hands of this or that saint. Look not, then, at the frailty of the servant but rather, at the power of the Master. For denial that a miracle could be performed by a saint is a denial of the power of the All-Powerful One, and a blindness which has prevented you from seeing the grandeur of His attributes, may He be praised and exalted.

Secondly, one reason which leads people to deny the performance of miracles by saints may be that they think such a miracle to be beyond the capacity of the particular servant to whom it has been attributed. However, the miracle in question is only performed at his hands as a testimony to the validity of the path initiated by the one he follows. As such, the supernatural feat performed at the hands of this or that saint is to be classified as a *karāmah,*[5] whereas with respect to the person by virtue of whose blessings his follower has performed the feat in question, it is to be classified as a *muᶜjizah.*[6] It has thus been said: Every miracle (*karāmah*) performed by a saint is a miracle (*muᶜjizah*) performed by the prophet of whom the saint is a follower. Look not, then, at the follower but rather, at the exalted standing of the one being followed.

Thirdly, you should know that what God, may He be praised, has given to His friends by way of faith and certainty—and which you believe in and affirm—is greater than that which you have denied and deemed preposterous, namely, their being given knowledge of unseen realities, flying through the air, or walking on water. If you find it preposterous that such things could be performed by a believer, you are like someone who finds it astonishing that, after a certain servant has been chosen as part of the king's inner circle and given a basket filled with precious sapphires, with every sapphire worth ten thousand dinars, this servant says (or it is said concerning him) that the king has given him one hundred dinars. But would this astonishment of yours be considered fitting by someone with understanding and insight?

Of all the things with which God, may He be exalted, has honored His servants in this world and in the next, there is nothing so great as the honor of faith in Him and the experiential knowledge of His lordship. After all, every blessing of this life and the life to come is simply a product of faith in God, be it a mystical state or station, the words of divine remembrance required of a shaykh's followers morning and evening and the various God-given blessings and disclosures, light, knowledge and "openings," insight into an unseen reality, hearing divine words addressed to oneself, the performance of a miracle, or the blessings of Paradise — such as mansions, companions pure, rivers and fruits, its inhabitants' contentment with God and God's contentment with them, the vision of the Divine, etc. All of these blessings are none other than fruits of faith, its effects, and the extension of its light.

May God cause both us and you to be among those who believe in His lordship with that faith which God is pleased to grant His chosen servants, and may He grant both us and you complete submission to Him in everything He wills. Know that there are people whom God has consigned to failure, as a result of which they have denied the saints' miracles from the very start. We seek refuge in God from this path, which it would be more fitting not even to mention. However, we have chosen to mention it in order for you to know that if God wills to lead a servant astray, neither reason nor knowledge will be of any benefit to him. As God, may He be praised, has declared, "...if God wills anyone to be tempted to evil, thou canst in no wise prevail with God in his behalf" {Al-Mā'idah [The Repast] 5: 41}; "if you should stumble after all evidence of the truth has come unto you, then know that, verily, God is almighty, wise" {Al-Baqarah [The Cow] 2: 209}; and, "...who is it that protects, the while there is no protection against Him?" {Al-Mu'minūn [The Believers] 23: 88}

Thus it is that states, words, deeds and the stages through which a servant passes as he ascends toward the Truth are all dependent upon the success granted by God alone. They do not necessitate lights[7] and they merit no acceptance, nor does the servant with whom they are associated have any claim upon [God's] gracious approach until he has been aided by this divinely granted success (*tawfīq*). So highly esteemed is this grace in God's sight that He only mentions it once in the entire Qur'an, saying, "the achievement of my aim depends on God alone" {Hūd 11: 88}. What brings about such divinely granted success, and the sign of its presence, is a sincere return to God as one commences any act or refrains therefrom, by affirming one's poverty and utter need for Him, immersing oneself in the sea of humble submission and spiritual penury in His presence, and by maintaining this inward attitude until one has completed the action in question and indeed, at all times. As God, may He be praised, declares, "for indeed, God did succor you at Badr when you were utterly weak" {Al ᶜImrān [The House of ᶜImrān] 3: 123}; and, "The offerings given for the sake of God are [meant] only for the poor and needy" {Al-Tawbah [Repentance] 9: 60}.

Enter not, then, the garden of your labor and [pursuit of] knowledge with the opening and light you have been given saying, as did the one who met with disillusionment and of whom God reports, "And having [thus] sinned against himself, he entered his garden, saying, 'I do not think that this will ever perish!'" {Al-Kahf [The Cave] 18: 35} Rather, enter it as He has instructed you, saying, as it pleases God for you to, "'Whatever God wills [shall come to pass, for] there is no power save with God!'" {Al-Kahf [The Cave] 18: 39} From this you will understand the words of the Prophet ﷺ, "[The saying], 'There is no power nor strength save in God' is one of the treasures of Paradise." (Another version of the same saying reads, "...one of the treasures beneath the Throne.")[8] As for the treasure being spoken of here, it is that of true detachment of oneself from [one's own] power and strength and reliance upon the power and strength of God.

As for those who deny the miracles of God's friends, there is evidence both in the realm of reason and in that of written tradition which refutes this denial. Not only so, but it is to be feared that those who adopt this stance will meet a doleful end.

There is one group of people who believe in the miracles performed by saints who were not their contemporaries, such as Maᶜrūf,[9] Sarī,[10] al-Junayd[11] and others like them, while disbelieving in the miracles performed by saints who are their contemporaries. Shaykh Abū al-Ḥasan (may God be pleased with him) likens such people to Jews who believed in the miracles performed by Moses and Jesus, upon them be peace, but disbelieved in Muḥammad ﷺ because they were his contemporaries.

There is another group of people who believe that within God's kingdom there are saints who perform miracles, yet without acknowledging that this could apply to any of their contemporaries in particular. Hence, whenever mention is made to them of a saint or of a miracle attributed to a saint, they resist the proof of this on the basis of criteria imposed by their minds, which are shackled by the bonds of heedlessness and deceived by their submission to their own desires. Belief [in the miracles of the saints] will not be brought about by their emulation of others, nor [even] by the light of guidance, since one does not emulate some anonymous saint but rather, a saint to whom God has led you, having acquainted you with his unique qualities and his chosen status, thereby obscuring your vision of his humanity by [the vision of] his chosenness and uniqueness. Once this has taken place, you submit to his lead and he, in turn, conducts you along the path of right guidance, enabling you to see your soul's thoughtless ways and its hidden recesses, as well as its buried treasures. He [i.e., the saint whom you emulate] shows you what it means to concentrate your entire being upon God, teaches you to flee from all but God, and accompanies you along your path until you reach Him. He causes you to be aware of ways in which your soul offends and helps you to see God's goodness to you. The realization of the offenses of which your soul is guilty teaches you to flee from your self and from reliance upon it, while the knowledge of God's goodness to you teaches you to devote yourself to Him, to offer Him thanksgiving, and to linger in His presence with the passing of the hours.

You may say: Where is a person such as the one you describe? You are directing me to something rarer than the legendary phoenix! Know, however, that you are not in need of those you can guide you; rather, what you may need is sincerity in your search for them. Find sincerity,[12] and you will find a guide. You will likewise find your guide in the following verses from the Qur'an: "Nay—who is it that responds to the distressed when He calls out to Him...?" {Al-Naml [The Ants] 27: 62}; and, "it would be but for their own good to remain true to God" {Muḥammad 47: 21}.

If your longing for someone to lead you to God is as urgent as the thirsty man's longing for water or the frightened man's longing for safety, you will find him nearer to you than your pursuit itself. If your longing for God is as urgent as a mother's longing for her child when she has lost him, you will find the Truth near to you and responsive to your plea, you will find that arrival [at your desired aim] presents you with no difficulty, and the Truth will draw near to you, making all things clear. What I am saying here, I say with respect to both possibility and actual occurrence.

The varieties of miracles which the pious ancestors (may God be pleased with them) are agreed to have performed are too numerous to mention. However, Abū al-Qāsim al-Qushayrī has dealt with them exhaustively in his *Risālah*, in which he devotes a section to this theme in particular. Know that a miracle is sometimes manifested to the saint in himself, while at other times it is manifested in him for others' sake. In the former case, the purpose behind the miracle is to acquaint the saint himself with God's power, His incomparability, and His unity in order that the saint might understand that His power is not dependent on earthly causes, and that it is not the familiar chains of cause and effect which stand in judgment over Him, but He who stands in judgment over them. Rather, He has made the familiar chains of cause and effect, mediating forces and earthly causes to be like veils which conceal His power, and like the clouds which obscure the suns of His oneness. Hence, he who stops at these is bound to meet with disillusionment, while he who sees beyond them to God is a recipient of the grace of divine providence.

Shaykh Abū al-Ḥasan (may God be pleased with him) said, "The benefit of a saint's miracle is that through it, God provides us with a clear definition of knowledge, power, will and the pre-eternal divine attributes, of a union which knows no separation and a command which knows no multiplicity, as if it were a single attribute subsisting within the essence of the One. Can one to whom God has made Himself known by His light be equated with one who has come to know God through his reason?

Moreover, given that miracles are meant as a confirmation [of God's power, for example] for those to whom they are manifested, they may be taken note of by spiritual seekers who are still at the start of their journey, while they may be overlooked by those who have reached the end of their spiritual treks. The reason for this is that due to their rootedness in certainty, strength and empowerment, those who have reached the end of their spiritual journeys are not in need of such confirmation. And thus it is that by the Truth's grace, may He be praised, the pious ancestors (may God be pleased with them) had no need for tangible miracles due to what God had given them by way of knowledge of unseen realities and sciences inspired by their vision of the divine. After all, a mountain has no need of an anchor. Hence, a miracle serves to unsettle doubts concerning divine grace, to [bring about] experiential knowledge of God's bounty toward the one at whose hands it was performed, and to bear witness to his uprightness before God, may He be praised.

People may be classified into three groups based on their attitudes toward saints' miracles. The first group treat such miracles as an end in themselves; hence, if they witness a miracle, they venerate the person at whose hands it was performed, whereas if they do not witness such a miracle, they will not. The second group are those who say: What are miracles? They are nothing but ruses by which those with the desire to attain to higher and higher spiritual stations are deceived lest they exceed their boundaries, and lest they enter a mystical station which is not for them.

Abū Turāb al-Nakhshabī once said to Abū al-ᶜAbbās al-Raqqī, "What do your companions say about these [miracles] with which God honors His servants?"

Abū al-ᶜAbbās replied, "I have never found any of them who didn't believe in them."

Abū Turāb replied, "Whoever does not believe in them has renounced faith. I only asked you in order to ascertain their spiritual condition [with respect to this phenomenon]."

Abū al-ᶜAbbās said, "I have never known them to say anything [about them]."

"Nay," said Abū Turāb, "but your companions have claimed that they are ruses from the Truth. However, this is not true. Rather, [they are only] ruses in cases where people content themselves with the miracles alone.[12] As for those who do not adopt this attitude, it is they who occupy the rank of the lordly ones."

This conversation took place after Abū Turāb's followers had grown thirsty and he, in response, had struck the ground with his hand, causing water to gush forth. A boy there said, "I want to drink it out of a cup." Thereupon, he struck the ground again and handed him a white glass cup, after which he drank from it and gave us to drink as well.

Abū al-ᶜAbbās al-Raqqī said, "And the glass remained with us until we reached Mecca."

The definitive word in this regard is that as an expression of courtesy toward God, you must not seek [miracles]. Nevertheless, a person at whose hands a miracle is manifested is held in high esteem, since the miracle bears witness to his uprightness before God.

As for a miracle which is manifested through a saint for others' sake, the purpose behind it is to enable the servant who witnessed it to see the validity of the path being followed by the saint at whose hands the miracle was performed. In such a case, the servant may be a denier [of the reality of miracles] who, after witnessing the miracle, returns to an acknowledgment [of their reality], an unbeliever who then returns to faith, or someone who, after doubting the uniqueness and chosenness of the saint who performed the miracle, comes to perceive the storehouses of goodness which God has placed within him.

The discussion presented in this introduction has been lengthier than we would have preferred. Nevertheless, it has presented the reader with sciences and secrets, bestowing radiant light upon those who have been given a share of grace.

It is now time to commence what we have set out to do. God is the One who makes all things clear, and He is the Master of bounty and beneficence. To Him belongs all praise as His majesty merits, and to Him belongs all thanksgiving for His unceasing blessings and bounties. He is our Sufficiency, and a most excellent Protector.

The *maqam* of Abū al-Ḥasan al-Shādhilī at Tunis.
A mosque is built over the site of the Shaykh's devotional retreat, a small cave, cool and tranquil.

"Upon receiving the initiation, his Shaykh ordered him to travel to a town called Shadhila near Tunis and it was there that he began to be known. Later he moved to Tunis, and from there to the more eastern lands. He made the pilgrimage many times and died on the way to Mecca in the year 1258. He was buried near the shore of the Red Sea in the village of Ḥumaythirā in Egypt, and to this day people from all regions of the earth make pilgrimage to his tomb."

From the autobiography of Fatima al-Yashrutiyya

Chapter One

An introduction to his shaykh from whom he received this status, and a testimony from the eminent scholars who were his contemporaries that he was the pole of his time and the standard bearer of his era for those who have been eye witnesses [to the divine realities]

That is, the shaykh and imam, the supreme apologist for Sufism, the signpost of the rightly guided, the most wonderful of gnostics, the instructor of the greatest, he who was unique in this time for his sublime gnosis and his praiseworthy traits and qualities, the knower of God, the guide to God, the wellspring of secrets,[1] the storehouse of lights, the all-encompassing pole and source of succor: Taqī al-Dīn Abū al-Ḥasan ᶜAlī Ibn ᶜAbd Allāḥ Ibn ᶜAbd al-Jabbār Ibn Tamīm Ibn Hirmiz Ibn Ḥātim Ibn Quṣayy Ibn Yūsuf Ibn Yūshaᶜ Ibn Ward Ibn Baṭṭāl Ibn Aḥmad Ibn Muḥammad Ibn ᶜĪsā Ibn Muḥammad Ibn al-Ḥasan Ibn ᶜAlī Ibn Abī Ṭālib, may God be pleased with him.

Known as al-Shādhilī, he was born and raised in Morocco and first appeared [as a teacher] in Shādhilah, a town near Tunisia from which his appellation as al-Shādhilī (the Shadhilite) is derived.

Widely traveled, having fought majestic battles and acquired copious knowledge, he only entered the path to God after he was considered to have mastered numerous fields of knowledge for scholarly debate in the visible sciences.[2]

Shaykh Ṣafī al-Dīn Ibn Abī al-Manṣūr (may God be pleased with him) mentions him in his book, in which he praises him highly.

Shaykh Quṭb al-Dīn al-Qasṭalāni (may God be pleased with him) mentions him among the shaykhs he had encountered, and praises him highly also.

Shaykh Abū ᶜAbd Allāh Ibn al-Nuᶜmān (may God be pleased with him) mentions him and testifies to his being a pole.

Shaykh ᶜAbd al-Ghaffār Ibn Nūḥ (may God be pleased with him) mentions him in his book, *Al-Waṣīd* and praises him highly.

No one with an enlightened heart, nor any gnostic endowed with insight has ever disputed his being a pole. He performed amazing feats along this path, laid important groundwork in the science of [the divine] reality, and opened wide vistas for spiritual wayfarers. Indeed, I heard the shaykh and imam, the muftī of Islam Taqī al-Dīn Muḥammad Ibn ᶜAlī al-Qushayrī, may God have mercy upon him, say, "Never have I seen anyone more knowledgeable of God than Shaykh Abū al-Ḥasan al-Shādhilī (may God be pleased with him)."

The shaykh and gnostic Makīn al-Dīn al-Asmar (may God be pleased with him) told me, "In [the city of] al-Manṣūrah, I entered a tent where al-Qushayrī's *Risālah* was being read aloud to the shaykh, imam and muftī of the human race, ᶜIzz al-Dīn Ibn ᶜAbd al-Salām, Shaykh Majd al-Dīn Ibn Taqī al-Din ᶜAlī Ibn Wahb al-Qushayrī the teacher, Shaykh Muḥyī al-Dīn Ibn Surāqah, Shaykh Majd al-Dīn al-Akhmīmī and Shaykh Abū al-Ḥasan al-Shādhilī (may God be pleased with them), all of whom were engaging in scholarly discussion with the exception of Shaykh Abū al-Ḥasan, who remained silent.

When they were all finished speaking, they said to him, 'Master, we wish to hear from you.'

He replied, 'You are the masters and eminent figures of the time, and you have spoken.'

They said, 'No, but we must hear from you.'

The shaykh then remained silent for an hour, after which he spoke of marvelous secrets and magnificent sciences.

Shaykh ^{c}Izz al-Dīn then rose and left the tent, saying, 'Listen to these extraordinary words, which arise out of nearness to God!'"

I was told by Shaykh Abū ^{c}Abd Allāh Ibn al-Ḥājj, who was told by Shaykh Abū Zakariyā Yaḥyā al-Balansī, who said, "I became a companion [follower] of Shaykh Abū al-Ḥasan al-Shādhilī (may God be pleased with him), then set out for Andalusia. As I bid him farewell, Shaykh Abū al-Ḥasan said to me, 'When you arrive in Andalusia, meet with Shaykh Abū al-^{c}Abbās Ibn Maknūn, for he has been given such knowledge of existence that he knows his own station, whereas people have not been given knowledge of Abū al-^{c}Abbās such that they know his station.' When I arrived in Andalusia, I went to see Shaykh Abū al-^{c}Abbās Ibn Maknūn, and when he caught sight of me, he said (although he had never seen me before), 'You have come, Yaḥyā! You have come, Yaḥyā! Praise be to God for your meeting with the pole of the era. O Yaḥyā, what Shaykh Abū al-Ḥasan told you, speak of to no one.'"

Rashīd al-Dīn Ibn al-Rāyis told me, "I once had a dispute with the companions of a certain shaykh, after which I came to Shaykh Abū al-Ḥasan and told him of our disagreement. In reply, he said, 'You were saying to him, "I have been nurtured and educated by the pole," whereas whoever has been nurtured and educated by the pole has been nurtured and educated by forty substitutes.[3]'"

I was told by my father, may God have mercy upon him, "I went in to see Shaykh Abū al-Ḥasan al-Shādhilī (may God be pleased with him) and I heard him say, 'You may ask me about a given matter and I may not have an answer, but I [then] see the answer written in the inkwell, on the mat, and on the wall.'"

I was told by one of his companions, "Shaykh Abū al-Ḥasan al-Shādhilī said one day, 'Verily, He causes the sustenance to descend upon me, and I see Him flowing through the whale in the water and through the bird in the sky.' Shaykh Amīn al-Dīn Jibrīl, who was present when he made this statement, said to Shaykh Abū al-Ḥasan, 'You, then, are the pole. You, then, are the pole!' But Shaykh Abū al-Ḥasan replied, 'I am the servant of God. I am the servant of God.'"

I was told by one of our companions, "Shaykh Abū al-Ḥasan al-Shādhilī said, 'Verily, never has God granted His friendship and protection to a saint but that He first placed love for him in my heart, and never has He spurned a servant but that He first caused me to hate him.'"

I was also told by one of our companions, "When Shaykh Abū al-Ḥasan returned from the pilgrimage to Mecca, he came to see the shaykh and imam ᶜIzz al-Dīn Ibn ᶜAbd al-Salām before coming to his own home. [When he arrived at Shaykh ᶜIzz al-Dīn's home], he said to him, 'The Apostle ﷺ sends you his greetings.' However, Shaykh ᶜIzz al-Dīn considered himself too insignificant to be worthy of such a greeting. He then invited Shaykh ᶜIzz al-Dīn to the Sufis' centers of worship and instruction in Cairo; he was accompanied by Muḥyī al-Dīn Ibn Surāqah and Abū al-ᶜAlam Yāsīn, one of the companions of the shaykh and knower of God, Muḥyī al-Dīn Ibn ᶜArabī. Shaykh Muḥyī al-Dīn Ibn Surāqah said to Shaykh ᶜIzz al-Dīn, 'I congratulate you on what we just heard, sir. Indeed, it is a joyous thing for there to be, in this era, someone to whom the Messenger of God ﷺ sends his greetings.' Shaykh ^{c}Izz al-Dīn replied, 'May God conceal us.' To which Shaykh Abū al-^{c}Alam Yāsīn rejoined, "O God, expose us, in order that the bearer of truth may be distinguished from the bearer of falsehood!' They then gestured to the itinerant musician among them to sing, since he had heard the words they had exchanged, and the first words he sang were:

> The transmitter of traditions has spoken truly, and
> the tradition [relates events] as they came to pass,
> While the conversation of those who have witnessed
> the Truth can in no wise be falsified.

Thereupon, after his pleasant session [with his companions], Shaykh ^{c}Izz al-Dīn rose, and everyone rose with him."

The jurisprudent Makīn al-Dīn al-Asmar told me, "I once heard the Truth addressing me." "How did that happen, sir?" I asked him. He replied, "There was, in Alexandria, a certain righteous man who had become a companion of Shaykh Abū al-Ḥasan, after which he heard about so many imposing sciences and matters that transcend the rational and the conceivable that his mind could no longer grasp it, as a result of which he parted company with Shaykh Abū al-Ḥasan (may God be pleased with him). Then one night, I heard [God say], 'So-and-so called upon Us at such-and-such a time, making six requests. If he wants his supplications to be answered, let him be an adherent of Shaykh Abū al-Ḥasan al-Shādhilī. He asked Us for such-and-such and for such-and-such until I had counted up six requests.' Then the divine address came to an end. I looked to the mid-point [of that period of time], and I knew at what time the man had made his supplications. The following morning, I went to the man and I said to him, 'You called upon God yesterday, making six requests. You asked Him for such-and-such and for such-and-such, until you had made six requests.' 'Yes, I did,' the man replied. So I said to him, 'Do you want your requests to be granted?' 'And who might make this possible for me?' he asked. I said to him, 'I have been told, "If he wants his requests to be granted, let him be an adherent of Shaykh Abū al-Ḥasan al-Shādhilī."'"

I heard our shaykh, Abū al-ᶜAbbās say, "The shaykh said to me, 'If you want to be my companion, ask nothing of anyone.' So I lived in accordance with his instructions for one year, then he said to me, 'If you want to be my companion, accept nothing from anyone.' Thereafter, when hard times would come upon me, I would go out to the shore of the Alexandria sea and gather whatever wheat was cast ashore when it was being unloaded from the boats. One day as I was gathering wheat, who should I encounter but ᶜAbd al-Qādir al-Naqqād—one of God's saints—who was doing the same thing I was. He said to me, 'Yesterday I was granted a vision of the station of Shaykh Abū al-Ḥasan.'

'And what is the shaykh's station?' I asked him.

'At the throne,' he said.

'That is a station from which the shaykh had descended in order to allow you to see him there.'

He and I then went in to see the shaykh, and when we had all taken our seats, the shaykh (may God be pleased with him) said, 'Yesterday I saw ᶜAbd al-Qādir al-Naqqād in a dream and he said to me, "Are you of the throne, or of the seat?" I said to him, "Desist from such questions. Clay is of the earth, the soul is of heaven, the heart is of the throne, the spirit is of the seat, and the innermost being is with

God, without 'where'. The command descends in the midst of all this, and is followed by that which witnesses thereto.'"

A certain man who guides to God came to Alexandria, and Shaykh Makīn al-Dīn al-Asmar said, "This man invites people to God's door, but Shaykh Abū al-Ḥasan used to bring them into God's very presence."

Shaykh Abū al-ᶜAbbās (may God be pleased with him) said, "I was with Shaykh Abū al-Ḥasan in Qayrawān. It was a Friday night during the month of Ramaḍān and, specifically, the 27th of the month. The shaykh went to the mosque and I went with him. When he entered the mosque and had begun his ritual prayer, I saw saints descending upon him as flies descend upon honey. When we left the mosque the following morning, the shaykh said, 'Last night was a magnificent night. It was the night of power. I saw the Apostle ﷺ and he said to me, "Alī, cleanse your garments of all impurity, and you will enjoy God's sustenance during your every breath." "O Messenger of God," I said, "and what are my garments?" He said, "Know that God has clothed you in five garments: the garment of love, the garment of knowledge, the garment of affirmation of the divine unity, the garment of faith, and the garment of submission. When someone loves God, he attaches no importance to anything else. When someone knows God, everything of his own appears insignificant to him. When someone affirms God's unity, he no longer associates any partner with Him. When someone has faith in God, he becomes safe from everything. When someone submits himself to God, rarely will he disobey Him, and if he does disobey Him, he apologizes to Him, and when he apologizes to Him, his apology is accepted." It was then that I understood the meaning of the command, "Thy garments purify!"[4] '"

Shaykh Abū al-ᶜAbbās (may God be pleased with him) said, "I went wandering through the kingdom of God and I saw Abū Madīn, a fair-skinned man with blue eyes, clinging to the leg of the throne. I said to him, 'What are your fields of knowledge, and what is your station?' He replied, 'As for my fields of knowledge, they are seventy-one, and as for my station, I am the fourth of the caliphs and the first of the seven substitutes (*abdāl*).' I asked him, 'What do you say about my shaykh, Abū al-Ḥasan al-Shādhilī?' He replied, 'He has forty more fields of knowledge than I do. He is the sea which cannot be contained.'"

One of our companions told me, "The shaykh was once asked, 'Who is your shaykh, master?' He replied, 'I was once associated with Shaykh ᶜAbd al-Salām Ibn Mashīsh, but now I am associated with no one. Instead, I float in ten seas. Five of them are human, namely, the Prophet ﷺ, Abū Bakr, ᶜUmar, ᶜUthmān, and ᶜAlī, while five of them are of the spiritual realm, namely, Jibrīl, Mīkā'īl, Isrāfīl, ᶜIzrā'īl, and the Greater Spirit.'"

His son and our master, the imam and gnostic Shihāb al-Dīn Aḥmad told me, "The shaykh said upon dying, 'Verily, I have brought something along this path which no one else has.'"

It has been widely circulated that when he was buried at Ḥumaythirā and his body was washed in its water, the water thereafter became so copious and sweet that it sufficed the traveling parties that encamped there, whereas this had not been the case before.

Abū ᶜAbd Allāh Ibn al-Nuᶜmān (may God be pleased with him) composed verses of poetry for the shaykh in which he charged me to watch after Shaykh Abū al-ᶜAbbās (may God be pleased with him), saying:

> The gift of the throne's Divinity on the frontier,
> Aḥmad,[5]
> I took delight in him among the companions, and
> to God do I render praise.

He likewise composed the following about Shaykh Abū al-ᶜAbbās (may God be pleased with him):

> The heir to Shādhilī's knowledge in truth,
> He is a pole, matchless, so recognize him as such.
>
> After his death I witnessed his wonders,
> Standing as evidence against those who his illuminations deny.

By the words, "After his death I saw his wonders," Shaykh Abū ᶜAbd Allāh meant that the water became sweeter and more abundant than it had been before he was washed in it.

One of our companions told me, "The shaykh said, 'I was once told: Nowhere on the face of the earth is there a gathering [for the study] of Islamic jurisprudence more splendid than that of Shaykh ᶜIzz al-Dīn Ibn ᶜAbd al-Salām. Nor is there a gathering for the study of the science of prophetic traditions more splendid than that of Shaykh Zakī al-Dīn ᶜAbd al-ᶜAẓīm, nor is there a gathering for the study of the science of [divine] realities more splendid than yours.'"

Shaykh Abū al-ᶜAbbās (may God be pleased with him) said, "When I was staying in Tunisia after coming from Murcia—at which time I was a young man—I heard mention of Shaykh Abū al-Ḥasan al-Shādhilī (may God be pleased with him). A man said to me, 'Will you come with me to see him?' I replied, 'Once I have sought God for guidance in the matter.' As I slept that night, I saw a vision of myself ascending toward a mountain top. When I had reached the peak, I saw a man there donned in a green burnoose. He was seated, with a man to his right and a man to his left. I looked at him and he said to me, 'You have found the vicegerent of the age.' I awoke, and after the dawn prayer, the man who had invited me to visit the shaykh with him came to me, and I went with him. When we went in to see the shaykh, I was astounded to find him seated on the very bench I had seen on top of the mountain. The shaykh said to me, 'You have found the vicegerent of the age. What is your name?' So I told him my name and my line of descent. He said to me, 'You were lifted up to me ten years ago.'"

Shaykh Abū al-ᶜAbbās (may God be pleased with him) said, "When we came from Tunisia to Alexandria, we stayed on the outskirts of ᶜAmūd al-Sawārī. We arrived just as the sun was turning a yellowish hue, and we were exhausted and famished. An upright man of Alexandria sent us some food, and when the shaykh was told of it, he said, 'Let none of you eat any of it.' Hence, we spent the night just as hungry as we had been when we arrived. The following morning, the shaykh led us in the dawn prayer, then said, 'Spread out a cloth, and fetch the food.' We did as he said, then approached and ate. The shaykh (may God be pleased with him) said, 'I had a dream in which I saw a man who said, "The most permissible of the permissible is that of which you had no expectation, and which you have requested of neither man nor woman."'"

Shaykh Abū al-ᶜAbbās (may God be pleased with him) said, "One night I was sleeping in Alexandria when someone said to me, 'Mecca and Medina!' So the following morning, I determined to set out on a journey. At that time, Shaykh Abū al-Ḥasan (may God be pleased with him) was at al-Muqassam[6] in Cairo, so I went to where he was. When

I appeared before him, he said to me, 'Mecca and Medina.' I said, 'This is why I have come, master.' 'Be seated,' he said. So I sat down. Just then a man came in to see him and said, 'Master, I have determined to undertake the pilgrimage to Mecca, but I have nothing to my name.' The shaykh then said to me, 'What do you have with you?' 'Ten dinars,' I replied. 'Give them to this man,' he told me. So I did so.

The shaykh then told me, 'Go out to the shore tomorrow and buy me twenty ardabbs of wheat.'[7]

The following morning I went down to the shore and bought twenty ardabbs of wheat, took it to the warehouse, then came back to the shaykh. He said to me, 'I have been told that this wheat is wormy, so we can take none of it.'

I was in a quandary then, not knowing what to do. Three days went by, during which time the owner of the wheat did not demand its price of me.[8] On the fourth day, a man came around to see me and asked, 'Are you the owner of the wheat?' I replied that I was, and he said, 'You will take one thousand dirhams for it.' 'Very well,' I said. So he weighed out one thousand dirhams for me and God placed His blessing upon it. And if I told you that I'm living off of it till this very day, I would be speaking the truth."

Abū al-ᶜAbbās (may God be pleased with him) said, "We went on a journey with the shaykh (may God be pleased with him) in the year in which he died. When we were near Akhmīm, the shaykh said to me, 'I had a vision of myself yesterday in the midst of a tumultuous storm at sea. The winds descended upon us, the waves clashed, the boat began to leak, and we were on the verge of sinking. Approaching the side of the boat, I said, "O sea! If you have been commanded to hear and obey me, all grace belongs to God, the Hearer and Knower of all. If, on the other hand, you have been commanded otherwise, all judgment belongs to

God, the Almighty, the truly Wise." I then heard the sea say, "I shall obey! I shall obey!'"

The shaykh (may God be pleased with him) died and we buried him at Ḥumaythirā in the ᶜĪdhāb desert, after which we went on another journey. We found ourselves in the midst of a tumultuous storm, and when we were far out at sea, the winds descended upon us, the waves clashed, the boat began to leak, and we were on the verge of sinking. By this time I had forgotten the shaykh's words, but when the situation became dire, I recalled them. So, approaching the side of the boat, I said, 'O sea! If you have been commanded to hear and obey God's saints, all grace belongs to God, the Hearer and Knower of all.' (I did not say, as the shaykh had, 'to hear and obey *me*.') Then I said, 'If, on the other hand, you have been commanded otherwise, all judgment belongs to God, the Almighty, the truly Wise." I then heard the sea say, 'I shall obey! I shall obey!'

The sea then grew still and the [remainder of the] journey was pleasant."

Shaykh Abū al-ᶜAbbās (may God be pleased with him) said, "I was with the shaykh on the ᶜĪdhāb sea; we were being buffeted by violent winds, and the boat had sprung a leak. The shaykh then said, 'I saw the heavens open and there descended two angels. One of them said, "Moses is more knowledgeable than al-Khaḍir," while the other said, "Al-Khaḍir is more knowledgeable than Moses." Still another angel descended as well, saying, "Verily, al-Khaḍir knew no more of what Moses knew than the hoopoe knows of what Solomon knew when he said, 'I have comprehended what you have not comprehended.'" I then understood that God would deliver us safely to our destination, since He had given Moses command over the sea."

Shaykh Abū al-ᶜAbbās (may God be pleased with him) said, "A man once asked the shaykh, 'What do you say about al-Khaḍir? Is he alive or dead?' The shaykh (may God be pleased with him) replied, 'Go to the jurisprudent Nāṣir al-Dīn Ibn al-Abyārī, who has issued a legal decision to the effect that he is alive, and that he is a prophet. Not only so, but Shaykh ᶜAbd al-Muᶜṭī once met him, and was silent for an hour thereafter.' He also said, 'I have met him, and his index and middle fingers are the same.'"

Know that al-Khaḍir's continued existence is a matter of unanimous agreement among the members of this community, while the saints of every age recount having met him and received teaching on his authority. In fact, such accounts are so well-known and have been passed down based on so many independent chains of transmission that their veracity is undeniable. There are thus numerous stories told in this connection.

Shaykh Abū al-Ḥasan (may God be pleased with him) said, "I met al-Khaḍir in the ᶜĪdhāb desert once and he said to me, 'Abū al-Ḥasan, may God cause wonderful kindness to attend you, and may He be a companion to you in times of both rest and itineration.'"

Shaykh Muḥyī al-Dīn Ibn ᶜArabī (may God be pleased with him) mentioned that one day Abū al-Saᶜūd Ibn al-Shibl was sweeping the school of Shaykh ᶜAbd al-Qādir al-Kīlānī (may God be pleased with him). As he was bent down over his broom, al-Khaḍir stood at his head and said, 'May peace be upon you!' Raising his head, Abū al-Saᶜūd replied, 'And upon you be peace!' then went back to his work. Al-Khaḍir said to him, 'Why do you take no notice of me, as though you did not recognize me?' 'But I do recognize you,' replied Abū al-Saᶜūd. 'You are al-Khaḍir.' 'So why do you take no notice of me?' asked al-Khaḍir. Then, looking at me, Abū al-Saᶜūd said to him, 'Shaykh ᶜAbd al-Qādir al-Kīlānī has left no room in this shaykh[9] for anyone else.'"

Recounting an experience of his own, Shaykh Muḥyī al-Dīn Ibn ᶜArabī (may God be pleased with him) said, "I was once with a companion of mine in al-Maghrib[10] along the seashore, where there was a mosque to which certain 'substitutes' repaired for shelter. My companion and I saw a man who placed a mat in the air, four cubits above the ground, then prayed on it. My companion and I approached the man and, as I stood beneath him, I said,

> The lover has been distracted from his beloved
> By the love of the One who created the air
> and subjected it to His command.
>
> Gnostics' minds are bound [to Him],
> Purged of every created entity in which they
> might find satisfaction.
>
> For they, in His presence, are graced with honor,
> And with Him their secrets are preserved and
> consecrated to His service.

The man prayed briefly, then said, 'I only did this for the sake of the denier who is with you. I am Abū al-ᶜAbbās al-Khaḍir.' I hadn't known that my companion was someone who denied the miracles of the saints, so I turned to him and said, 'So-and-so, did you used to deny the miracles of the saints?' 'Yes, I did,' he said. 'What do you say now?' I asked him. He replied, 'After one has seen with one's own eyes, there is nothing more to be said.'"

Shaykh ᶜAbd al-Muᶜṭī al-Iskandarī said to his disciple as he was dying, "Take this robe. Many times have I embraced al-Khaḍir in it."

The wife of al-Qurashī (may God be pleased with him) said, "I left the shaykh's presence one day, and when I left, there was no one else with him. However, after I had left, I heard a man speaking with him. I paused until the talking had stopped, then I went in and said, 'Master! When I left your presence, there was no one else here with you, but just now I heard someone speaking to you.' The shaykh said, 'Al-Khaḍir brought me an olive from the land of Najd and said to me, "Eat this olive, for in it is your healing." But I said to him, "Depart, and take your olive with you, for I have no need of it."'" The shaykh was afflicted with leprosy.

It has been reported that when the Messenger of God ﷺ died, they heard someone speaking from inside the house, though they could not see him, and the person said, "In God there is a successor for everyone who perishes and a compensation for everything that passes away. Indeed, the one afflicted is he who is denied the reward." The narrator notes that those who heard it thought that the speaker was al-Khaḍir.

Know—may God be gracious unto you—that whoever denies al-Khaḍir's existence is in error; the same applies to anyone who says that he is other than the Khaḍir who spoke with Moses, or whoever holds that every age has a Khaḍir and that the rank of "Khaḍir-hood," if you will, is occupied by someone in every age. Moreover, he who denies al-Khaḍir's existence thereby confesses that he has not received the divine grace of meeting him. However, even if he has failed to receive this grace, would that he could have faith in the possibility of doing so.

Be not deceived by what is stated by Abū al-Faraj Ibn al-Jawzī in his book entitled, *ᶜUjālat al-Muntaẓir fī Sharḥ Ḥāl al-Khaḍir* ("The Haste of Those Awaiting an Explanation of the State of al-Khaḍir"), in which he denies al-Khaḍir's existence. He states, "Those who say that he exists say so based on their own fixed ideas and delusions." As evidence of al-Khaḍir's non-existence, al-Jawzī cites the words of God Almighty, "Never have We granted life everlasting to any mortal before you [O Prophet]" {Al-Anbiyā' [The Prophets] 21: 34}.

Curious, that this man should cite this verse when it provides no evidence for what he claims. After all, "life everlasting" refers to a permanence which is not followed by death; however, this is not being claimed with respect to al-Khaḍir. Rather, what is being claimed with respect to al-Khaḍir is an extended stay on earth, as it were, to be followed ultimately by death. Be amazed, then—may God be gracious to you—at a man who believes in such an extended existence for Iblīs, while denying it of al-Khaḍir.

As for the tradition attributed to the Prophet ﷺ, "If al-Khaḍir were alive, he would visit me," it has not been confirmed by scholars of prophetic traditions. Moreover, if they say, "If this were so, it would have been passed down in written accounts," you should realize that not everything which God revealed to the Prophet ﷺ was something which he was to pass on to others. After all, it has been reported concerning him ﷺ that he said, "My Lord has taught me three types of knowledge: one type which He has commanded me to spread, another type which He has forbid me to spread, and still another type which He has left me free either to spread or to conceal."

A certain gnostic has said that God, exalted be He, gave al-Khaḍir knowledge of the spirits of the saints [before they entered earthly life]. Hence, he asked his Lord to preserve him in the realm of the visible in order for him to be able to see them in the world of the visible just as he has seen them in the realm of the hidden.

Shaykh Abū al-ᶜAbbās (may God be pleased with him) said, "I was once on a journey with the shaykh, and as we were headed from Tunisia to Alexandria, I was overcome with such intense distress that I was too weak to bear it. I came to Shaykh Abū al-Ḥasan (may God be pleased with him), and when he became aware of my presence, he said, 'Aḥmad?' 'Yes, master,' I replied. He said, 'God created Adam with His own hands and caused His angels to bow down to him. He caused him to dwell in Paradise for half a day, [that is,] five-hundred years,[11] after which He brought him down to earth. Verily, He did not bring Adam down to earth in order to diminish him but rather, to complete him. Moreover, He brought him down to earth before creating him; God declares, 'And lo! Thy Sustainer said unto the angels, "Behold, I am about to establish on earth one who will inherit it"' {Al-Baqarah [The Cow] 2: 30}. God did not say, 'in Paradise,' nor did He say, 'in heaven'. Hence, his descent to earth was a descent of honor and dignity, not one of degradation and abasement. While in Paradise, Adam worshipped God based on the direct knowledge of Him, after which He brought him down to earth in order for him to worship Him based on legal obligation. Once he had experienced both types of servanthood, he was worthy to be a vicegerent. You, also, have a share in Adam: Your beginning was in the heaven of the spirit, in the Paradise of experiential knowledge, after which you were brought down to the land of the soul to worship Him based on legal obligation. Hence, once you had experienced both types of servanthood, you became worthy to be a vicegerent."

One of Shaykh Abū al-Ḥasan's companions said to me, "The shaykh said one night, 'I met with al-Sharīf al-Būnī and Sharaf al-Dīn Ibn al-Majallī, who informed me that they had gone in to see a woman in western Alexandria. They said, "She told us to show her our hands, whereupon she smelled our hands and said, 'Two righteous brothers.' Then she told us, 'In my experiential knowledge I reached the station of perplexity. Then I said: My God! How can gnostics find their way out of perplexity? I have been told that it is through affirmation of the divine unity (*tawḥīd*). Hence, is there among you someone who knows this *tawḥīd* by which gnostics can find their way out of perplexity?' We said to her, 'We have only come in order to receive your blessing.' Then Shaykh Abū al-Ḥasan (may God be pleased with him) said, 'Verily, guide her to the one who himself has been beleaguered. Verily, guide her to the one who himself has been beleaguered!' Then he turned in the direction in which the woman was located and said, 'The *tawḥīd* by which gnostics find their way out of perplexity is [the words], "There is no god but He" (*lā ilāha illā huwa*). Gnostics emerge from perplexity by "There is no god but He" (*lā ilāha illā huwa*).' One of the shaykh's companions rose the following morning and went to the woman. When he found her, she was saying, 'My need has been met! My need has been met!' Hence, we knew that the shaykh had provided her with spiritual sustenance at that very hour."

One of Abū al-Ḥasan's companions told me, "'ᶜAbd al-Qādir al-Naqqād went in to see Shaykh Abū al-Ḥasan (may God be pleased with him), whereupon the shaykh asked him, 'ᶜAbd al-Qādir, does a saint disobey [God]?' ᶜAbd al-Qādir replied, 'Yes, by the one and only God as He beholds the essence of reality!' To this Shaykh Abū al-Ḥasan replied, 'I bear witness that you are the saint of God.'"

Shaykh Abū al-Ḥasan said, "Once while on a journey, I sought shelter in a cave in Tunisia near a city of Muslims. I went without food for three days, after which some Byzantines whose ship had put down anchor there came in to where I was. When they saw me, they said, 'A cleric of the Muslims!', whereupon they brought me food and plentiful provisions. I was amazed, wondering how it could be that I had been provided for by unbelievers, and had been deprived by Muslims. As I was thinking thus, someone said to me, 'The [true] man is not one who has been succored by his loved ones; rather, the [true] man is one who has been succored by his enemies.'"

Shaykh Abū al-Ḥasan (may God be pleased with him) said, "Once while traveling, I spent the night atop a hill. As I slept, some lions came and walked in circles around me, then remained with me till morning. Never have I experienced intimate companionship as I did that night. When I arose the following morning, it occurred to me that I had experienced something of the station of intimacy with God. I then descended into a valley, where there were some partridges that I hadn't noticed. When they became aware of my presence, they suddenly flew away and my heart fluttered in alarm. No sooner had this occurred than someone said to me, 'O you who only yesterday were finding pleasant company among beasts of prey, who do you now tremble with fear at the fluttering of partridges? Yesterday you were in Us, while now you are in yourself.'"

Shaykh Abū al-Ḥasan (may God be pleased with him) said, "One day as I was in a cave during one of my journeys, I said, 'My God, when will I be a servant who is truly grateful to You?' Just then I heard someone saying to me, 'When you see no one but yourself as blessed.' I said, 'But God, how can I see no one but myself as blessed when You have blessed prophets, scholars, and kings?' Then I heard someone saying to me, 'Were it not for the prophets, you would not have been guided aright. Were it not for the scholars, you would have had no one to emulate. And were it not for kings, you would not have experienced safety. Hence, all are a blessing from Me to you.'"

Shaykh Abū al-Ḥasan (may God be pleased with him) said, "Once while on a journey, and while still at the beginning of my spiritual path, I was undecided: Should I remain in the wilderness and uninhabited regions in order to devote myself to obedience and divine remembrance, or should I return to the cities and inhabited areas for the company of the finest scholars? I was told of a certain saint on a mountain peak, so I went up to find him, but by the time I arrived, night had fallen. I said to myself: I shan't go in to see him at this time. Meanwhile, I heard him in the cave, saying, 'O God, there are people who have asked You to subject Your creation to them, and when You have granted their plea they have been content with You on this account. O God, as for me, I ask you to cause people to act perversely toward me lest I take refuge in any but You.' Reflecting on myself, I said, 'O my soul, behold the sea from which this shaykh dips!' The following morning, I went in to see him, and I was terrified by his awesome presence. 'How are you, master?' I asked. He replied, 'I complain to God of the coolness of contentment and surrender, just as you complain of the heat of disposing of your own affairs and choosing for yourself.' I said, 'Master, as for the heat of disposing of my own affairs and making my own choices, you have tasted the same [suffering], while I still experience it. As for your complaining of the coolness of contentment and surrender, why is that?' He replied, 'I fear that their sweetness will distract me from God!' I said, 'Master, I heard you saying yesterday, "O God, there are people who have asked You to subject Your creation to them, and when You have granted their plea they have been content with You on this account. O God, as for me, I ask you to cause people to act perversely toward me lest I take refuge in any but You."' He smiled, then said, 'My son, rather than saying, "Cause Your creation to be subject to me," say, "O Lord, be Thou mine!" If He is yours, do you think you will lack anything? So what an injustice it is [to ask for anything else].'"

Shaykh Abū al-Ḥasan (may God be pleased with him) said, "Once a companion of mine and I had repaired to a cave, seeking to reach God. We were saying, 'Tomorrow He will open up [understanding] to us,' and 'the day after tomorrow He will open up [understanding] to us.' A man with an awe-inspiring presence then came in to where we were and we said to him, 'Who are you?' He replied, 'I am the king's slave.' From this we knew that he was a saint of God. 'How are you?' we asked him. And he replied, 'How is one who says, "Tomorrow He will open up [understanding] to me," and "the day after tomorrow He will open up [understanding] to me"? For he enjoys neither friendship and protection from God, nor prosperity. O soul, why do you not worship God for Himself?' Realizing whence he had come, we repented to God and sought His forgiveness, after which He opened up our understanding to us."

Shaykh Abū al-Ḥasan (may God be pleased with him) said, "One day when I was in the presence of the teacher, I thought to myself: I wonder whether the shaykh knows the greatest name of God? The shaykh's son, who was at the back of the place where we were located, said to me, 'Abū al-Ḥasan! What matters is not who knows the greatest name but rather, who is Himself the essence of the name.' Then, from the front of the place, the shaykh said, 'My son has spoken truly, and has understood you well.'"

Shaykh Abū al-Ḥasan (may God be pleased with him) was once asked, "Why do you not listen to *samā*ᶜ?"[12] He replied, "Listening to the creation is rudeness [to the Creator]."

One of my companions once told me, "A certain student once sought Shaykh Abū al-Ḥasan's good offices with Judge Tāj al-Dīn Ibn Bint al-A^{c}azz, in hopes that he would agree to increase his allowance by ten dirhams. The shaykh went to the judge, who considered it an event of great moment for the shaykh to have come to him, and he said, 'Master, what has brought you here?'

The shaykh replied, 'I've come on behalf of so-and-so, the student, to see if we might increase his allowance by ten dirhams.'

Judge Tāj al-Dīn said to him, 'Master, this student has such-and-such in such-and-such a place, and in another place such-and-such, and elsewhere, such-and-such.'

Shaykh Abū al-Ḥasan said to him, 'Tāj al-Dīn, do not deem it excessive to increase a believer's allowance by ten dirhams. After all, God is not content with Paradise as the believer's reward until, in addition, He has allowed him to behold His noble face therein.'"

Shaykh Abū al-Ḥasan (may God be pleased with him) said, "I heard the tradition passed down on the authority of the Messenger of God ﷺ in which he says, 'A veil is lowered over my heart, so I seek forgiveness from God seventy times a day.'[13] The meaning of what he had said was unclear to me; then I saw the Messenger of God ﷺ and he said to me, 'O blessed one! What I was speaking of was the veil of lights,[14] not the veil of "others."'"[15]

Shaykh Abū al-Ḥasan (may God be pleased with him) said, "I heard the tradition narrated on the authority of the Messenger of God ﷺ, 'If the fear of poverty comes to dwell in one's heart, none of his good works will be lifted [before God].' I then went an entire year thinking that none of my good deeds was being brought before God and I said, 'Who can be free of this?' I then saw the Messenger of God ﷺ in a dream in which he said to me, 'O blessed one, you have brought yourself to ruin! Rather, learn to distinguish between fear's merely passing through your heart, and its taking up residence there.'"

He (may God be pleased with him) also said, "I once saw Abū Bakr in a dream and he asked me, 'Do you recognize the sign that one's heart has been freed from love of the world?'

'No, I don't,' I replied.

'The sign that one's heart has been freed from love of the world is that when one acquires worldly possessions, one disposes of them freely, and when one loses them, one experiences a sense of relief.'"

He (may God be pleased with him) said, "My heart was enlightened one day and I saw the kingdom of the seven heavens and the seven earths. I then committed a minor sin, after which the vision was concealed from me. I was astonished that such a trifling occurrence could conceal from me something so momentous. Just then someone said to me, '[Spiritual] insight is like [physical] sight: The tiniest thing that gets in the eye can obstruct one's vision.'"

Let us restrain ourselves from saying more lest we stray from the purpose of this book. After all, the words of the shaykh (may God be pleased with him) are too well-known for there to be any need for us to draw attention to them. Most of what we have mentioned here is not found among the sayings which have been attributed to him. We have included some of his sayings in the introduction, while still others will be included later in the book, God willing. Hence, it should suffice you to be aware of what he has said concerning the pole's miracles, the path of the chosen and lay persons, and sciences, realities and secrets. Consider the sweetness and succinctness of [his] language, its abundant meanings, and the sense of awe which you experience when you recall or hear his words, for rarely will you find the same in the sayings of [other] followers of the path.

Concerning the pole's miracles, he (may God be pleased with him) said, "The pole has fifteen miracles. Hence, anyone who makes a claim to all or any of them must be distinguished by the [divine] provision of mercy, sinlessness, viceregency, proxyhood, and the sustenance granted to those who carry the majestic throne. In addition, he must have received illumination into the reality of the divine essence and an all-encompassing comprehension of the [divine] attributes. He must likewise be honored with the miracle of judgment, the ability to distinguish between the two existences, the separation of the first from the first, that from which it was separated until its end and those who have been established therein, the judgment concerning what is before and what is after and concerning the One who has neither before nor after, and the knowledge of the beginning, that is, that knowledge which encompasses every science and everything known, from the first secret until its end, then returning to it again. This, then, is a criterion which God gave the shaykh by which to test anyone who makes a claim to this lofty rank, which guards secrets and encompasses the divine provision of lights.

This is similar to what is mentioned by the knower of God, Abū ᶜAbd Allāh al-Tirmidhī al-Ḥakīm in his book, *Khatm al-Awliyā'* ("The Seal of the Saints'), where he states that if someone makes a claim to sainthood, one should say to him, "Describe for us the stations of the saints." He also makes mention of other criteria for judging someone who claims sainthood.

Shaykh Makīn al-Dīn al-Asmar said, "For forty years I found it difficult to understand the matter of the Sufi path without finding anyone to speak [with me] about it and remove the difficulties with which it presented me, until Shaykh Abū al-Ḥasan appeared and clarified everything which I had found difficult to understand."

When Shaykh Ṣadr al-Dīn al-Qūnawī came to Egypt as a messenger, he met with Shaykh Abū al-Ḥasan and spoke in his presence of many fields of knowledge. Shaykh Abū al-Ḥasan kept his head bowed until Shaykh Ṣadr al-Dīn had finished speaking. Then he raised his head and said, "Tell me, where is the pole of the era today? Who is his friend, and what are his fields of knowledge?"

Shaykh Ṣadr al-Din remained silent and gave no reply.

His approach (may God be pleased with him) was that of the greater riches and the magnificent "causing to arrive." In fact, he used to say, "The shaykh is not one who leads you to that which will tire you; rather, he is one who leads you to what will give you rest." And [not a few] men received their education under his tutelage (may God be pleased with him).

These men include some who resided in al-Maghrib, such as Abū al-Ḥasan al-Ṣiqillī, who was among the greatest of those realized in righteousness, and ᶜAbd Allāh al-Jībī, who was among the greatest of God's saints. They also include some who came with him and emigrated to Egypt, such as our master, the supreme apologist for Sufism and the signpost of the chosen, Shihāb al-Dīn Aḥmad Ibn ᶜUmar al-Anṣārī al-Mursī (may God be pleased with him). They likewise include al-Ḥājj Muḥammad al-Qurṭubī, Abū al-Ḥasan al-Bajāwī, Abū ᶜAbd Allāh al-Bujā'ī, al-Wajhānī, and al-Kharrāz. Others of these men came to be his companions in Egypt, such as Shaykh Makīn al-Dīn al-Asmar, Shaykh ᶜAbd al-Ḥakīm, Shaykh al-Sharīf al-Būnī, Shaykh ᶜAbd Allāh al-Laqqānī, Shaykh ᶜUthmān al-Būranjī[16] and Shaykh Amīn al-Dīn Jibrīl.

Every one of these men had fields of knowledge, secrets, teachings and companions who received knowledge under their tutelage; we have nevertheless refrained from speaking of their miracles and their unique qualities and achievements lest we digress from the purpose of this book.

His [Sufi] path (may God be pleased with him) is associated with Shaykh ᶜAbd al-Salām Ibn Mashīsh, while Shaykh ᶜAbd al-Salām was associated with Shaykh ᶜAbd al-Raḥmān al-Madanī, beyond which the path is traced one by one back to al-Ḥasan Ibn ᶜAlī Ibn Abī Ṭālib (may God be pleased with him). I heard our shaykh, Abū al-ᶜAbbās (may God be pleased with him) say, "This path of ours is not associated with those of the East, nor with those of the West. Rather, [it may be traced back] one by one to al-Ḥasan Ibn ᶜAlī Ibn Abī Ṭālib (may God be pleased with him), who was the first of the poles.

It is necessary to identify the shaykhs upon whom a person's path rests. Hence, if someone follows a path which requires the donning of the cloak, it must be donned based on a line of succession. Moreover, it is necessary to identify the men who make up a given line of succession and this, in turn, is right guidance. At the same time, God may draw a servant unto Himself in such a way that he is not indebted to any teacher for the grace he has received. Hence, He may unite a servant with the Messenger of God ﷺ such that he receives [teaching] directly from him, which is in itself a sufficient grace.

Shaykh Makīn al-Dīn al-Asmar (may God be pleased with him) said to me, "I have been educated and nurtured by no one but the Messenger of God ﷺ." He also mentioned that Shaykh ᶜAbd al-Raḥīm al-Qanāwī (may God be pleased with him) used to say, "I am beholden for grace to no one but the Messenger of God ﷺ, and if God wills, He may choose out of his gracious bounty to exempt a servant of the need for a teacher in order that he not have any predecessor therein."[17]

A king once said to one of his table companions, "I wish to make you a minister." The king's companion replied, "But I have no predecessor to this position." The king replied, "I wish to make you a predecessor to the one who comes after you."

Let us limit ourselves to what we have said thus far, since this will suffice as an introduction to Shaykh Abū al-Ḥasan (may God be pleased with him). It is simply as one person stated:

> The place for words I have found to be spacious,
> So if you find a tongue with which to speak, then speak.

Despite the fact that our purpose in writing this book is to mention the virtuous traits and deeds of our shaykh Abū al-ᶜAbbās, we have nevertheless begun by speaking about Shaykh Abū al-Ḥasan (may God be pleased with him). The reason for this is twofold: One reason is that in this manner, one may become acquainted with the standing of Shaykh Abū al-ᶜAbbās (may God be pleased with him), since the eminence of the follower is derived from the eminence of the one followed. The second reason is that the shaykh (may God be pleased with him) himself adopted this very approach: He would mention his shaykh (may God be pleased with him) and draw attention to him while refraining from mentioning his own unique qualities or virtues. Someone once said to him, "Master, we hear you saying, 'The shaykh said,' but rarely do you attribute anything to yourself." The shaykh replied, "If I wished to say, 'God said,' I would say, 'God said' with every breath I breathe; if I wished to say, 'The Messenger of God said,' I would say, 'The Messenger of God ﷺ said' with every breath I breathe. And if I wished to say, 'I said,' I would say 'I said' with every breath I breathe. However, I say, 'The shaykh said,' desisting from any mention of myself out of courtesy to him."

With this the first chapter is now complete, praise be to God, the Lord of the worlds.

Maqam of Abū al-ʿAbbās al-Mursī (d. 1288), Alexandria, Egypt, near the place where the ancient Pharos lit the harbor.

He said, "And in fact, Shaykh Abū al-Ḥasan said to me, 'Abū al-ʿAbbās, I only took you as my disciple in order for you to be me, and me, you.'"

Chapter Two

On the shaykh's testimony that he was heir to the station of sainthood and the one who held the position of unquestioned preeminence, his reports concerning himself of the momentous blessings which had been bestowed upon him, and the testimony of the friends of God that through his arrival at the knowledge of God, he had attained the utmost that one could possibly desire

Let us first present the following introduction:

Know that a man's heir is the one who brings to light his knowledge and [spiritual] state. It is at his hands that the path of the one to whom he is heir becomes manifest, as he expounds its overall meaning and simplifies that which has been presented with such succinctness that it is difficult to grasp. The heir raises aloft the light of the path, causing it to spread near and far, and enables people to see what his teacher had been given by way of the knowledge of God, both intellectual and experiential, his penetration into the divine reality and his enjoyment of God's light. Thus it is that if people failed properly to love and revere this or that great man during his lifetime, they may correct this error after his death. After all, everything which is within our reach tends to be rejected, while everything that is beyond our reach is passionately sought after. I once heard Shaykh Abū al-ᶜAbbās (may God be pleased with him) say, "A man may be among the most prominent of his contemporaries, yet they pay him no mind. Then when he dies they say, 'He was so-and-so!' It is thus possible that after a man's death, more people will enter his path than those who entered it during his lifetime." If there is anyone to whom this statement applies, it applies to Abū al-ᶜAbbās (may God be pleased with him).

It was Abū al-ᶜAbbās who circulated the knowledge of Shaykh Abū al-Ḥasan, spreading the light of this knowledge and revealing its secrets. People came to him from far and wide, hastening to reach him from every part of the globe. Men were raised [to spiritual maturity] under his tutelage, he succored them and made them known in both word and deed until his companions, and his companions' companions, had spread to the furthest horizons, and the shaykh's fields of knowledge were disclosed on people's lips and through their written words.

The righteous, faithful and trustworthy shaykh Zakī al-Dīn al-Aswānī told me, "Shaykh Abū al-Ḥasan (may God be pleased with him) once said to me, 'Zakī, you must meet Abū al-ᶜAbbās, for in truth, a Bedouin will come and urinate on his legs, and before the sun has set he will have led him to God. Zakī, you must meet Abū al-ᶜAbbās, for in truth, never has there been a saint of God but that God has given him knowledge of him. Zakī, Abū al-ᶜAbbās is the complete man.'"

I heard Shaykh Abū al-ᶜAbbās say about himself, "Verily, the saints and the 'substitutes' will travel from one end of the terrestrial world to the other in order to find someone like us, and if they find him, their quest will have been fulfilled." Then he said, "By the one and only God, never has there been, nor is there, a saint of God but that God has given me knowledge of his name, his lineage and his degree of nearness to God."

I have heard reports that Abū al-Ḥasan used to say, "Abū al-ᶜAbbās is a sun and ᶜAbd al-Ḥakīm is a moon." (This ᶜAbd al-Ḥakīm was a great saint and a companion of Shaykh Abū al-Ḥasan's who has been mentioned earlier.)

I heard Shaykh Abu al-ᶜAbbās say, "Shaykh Abū al-Ḥasan (may God be pleased with him) said, 'I heard it said to me: Death will not come to a nation in which the following four are found: an imam, a saint, a man realized in righteousness, and a generous man.' Then Shaykh Abū al-Ḥasan said, 'The imam is Abū al-ᶜAbbās.'"

I heard Shaykh Abū al-ᶜAbbās say, "What matters is not who rules. What matters is who rules and has the power to cause others to rule, and I, in truth, have ruled and have had the power to cause others to rule for thirty-six years."

I heard him (may God be pleased with him) say, "The saint, if he wills to do so, causes others to become rich." I also heard him say, "Verily, all I have to do is to look at a man and I will have made him rich."

I also heard him say, "Shaykh Abū al-Ḥasan said, 'Abū al-ᶜAbbās, I only took you as my companion in order for you to be me, and me, you.'"

I heard him say, "The shaykh said to me, 'Abū al-ᶜAbbās, you have what the saints have, but the saints do not have what you have.'"

Someone from al-Bahansā once said to me, "Shaykh Abū al-ᶜAbbās once came to us and said, 'I am now twenty-five years old, and never has the vision of God been concealed from me for so much as the twinkling of an eye.' Then he was absent from us for fifteen years, after which he came to us again and said, 'I am now forty years old, and never has the vision of God been concealed from me for so much as the twinkling of an eye.'"

One day he said, "Verily, if the vision of the Messenger of God ﷺ were concealed from me for as much as the twinkling of an eye, I would not consider myself a Muslim."

One of his companions told me, "A man once came in to see him in Damanhūr, and when he wished to leave, he said, 'Master, shake my hand. For you have encountered lands and servants.' When he had gone, the shaykh asked, 'What did he mean by "lands and servants?"' Someone replied, 'He meant that you have shaken hands with servants and traveled through lands whose blessings you have acquired. Hence, if he shakes your hand, he will obtain a blessing for himself from you.' The shaykh laughed, then said, 'By God, the only person whose hand I have ever shaken with this hand is the Messenger of God ﷺ!'"

There was once a saint of God in Nashīl al-Qanāṭir known as Khalīl and who is now buried there. He said, "Shaykh Abū al-Ḥasan al-Shādhilī (may God be pleased with him) came in to where I was and performed his ritual ablutions in my presence. Then he took a bow of mine and drew it three times. I said to him, 'Master, who will be your successor?' He replied, 'The one who comes to you here and performs his ritual ablutions in the same manner in which I have done so and who draws this bow three times.' After this, all of the shaykh's companions came in to where I was, and I watched to see whether any of them did as he had done. None of them did as Abū al-Ḥasan had done until Abū al-ᶜAbbās (may God be pleased with him) came in. When he entered, he performed his ritual ablutions as the shaykh had, then looked up and saw the bow hanging and said, 'Hand me that bow.' So I handed it to him, and he drew it three times, then said, 'Khalīl, the shaykh's promise has come to you.'"

I have received reports that Shaykh Abū al-Ḥasan (may God be pleased with him) said, "Since the time Abū al-ᶜAbbās attained to the vision of God, it has never been concealed from him, and [even] if he sought a veil with which to conceal it from himself, he would not find it."

Shaykh Abū al-ᶜAbbās (may God be pleased with him) said, "One night I was sitting in Alexandria writing a letter to one of my companions when suddenly I saw Shaykh Khalīl in the air. I asked him, 'Where has your journeying led you this night?' He replied, 'I left Nashīl and went to the Zaytūn Mountains in Morocco. I would like to go to Jerusalem, then return home, and if a greater distance were unfolded before me, I would traverse that as well.'

I said to him, 'What matters is not that you go to the Zaytūn Mountains and return on the same night. If I wished right now to take your hand and place you on the peak of Qāf[1] while remaining where I am, I could do so.'"

Abū ᶜAbd Allāh Ibn Sulṭān, who was a saint of God, told me, "I wanted to send some honey to Shaykh Abū al-ᶜAbbās, so I told one of my companions. He said to me, 'I have two small jars,' and he brought them to me. Then I closed them and wrote on them: 'To be deposited with Shaykh Abū al-ᶜAbbās al-Mursī.' Then I brought them to the Tunisia Sea and lowered them into the water, after which I received news from him that they had reached him. One of my companions informed me saying, 'One day the shaykh was sitting and said to one of his companions, "Let us rise." He then came to the Silsilah Sea and lowered his hand into the water and brought out the two jars.'"

ᶜAbd al-Dā'im, son of Shaykh Māḍī (Māḍī being one of the companions of Shaykh Abū al-Ḥasan, may God be pleased with him, and the brother of Abū ᶜAbd Allāh Ibn Sulṭān) said, "One night during Ramaḍān I prayed with

Shaykh Abū al-ᶜAbbās. When he had finished praying, he said to his son, 'Take your paternal cousin and go up.' So we went up to the shaykh's house, and he served us fried cakes and honey, saying, 'This honey is from your uncle.' When I returned home to my father, he said to me, 'You were so late getting back last night, you had me worried!' I replied, 'I was at the home of Shaykh Abū al-ᶜAbbās and he fed me fried cakes and honey. And he said, "This honey is from your uncle."' 'Strange!' my father replied. 'I've been in Egypt for twenty years, and my brother has never sent me anything at all.' It was after this that he learned that the honey had reached the shaykh in the manner described above."

He used to say, "Truly, if the vision of the Garden of Paradise were concealed from me for so much as the twinkling of an eye, I wouldn't count myself a Muslim."

He also used to say, "Truly, if I missed the opportunity to stand on Mt. ᶜArafah for a single year, I wouldn't count myself a Muslim."

I once heard him say, "Whenever any of his companions would hurt me in some way, the shaykh would say to me, 'Bear it patiently, for in truth, it belongs to you alone (meaning, the inheritance will go only to you).'"

I once found the following written in Ibn Nāshi's script: "We were told by Shaykh Jalāl al-Dīn that Shaykh Abū al-Ḥasan al-Shādhilī (may God be pleased with him), had said, 'Abū al-ᶜAbbās was clothed with the garments of "substitute-hood" today when they arrived from al-Ḥijāz at the ports of al-Jadīd.'"[2] Ibn Nāshi' said, "So I wrote the following lines to my shaykh, Abū al-ᶜAbbās (may God be pleased with him)":

To that lovely face, my greetings!
O my Lord, bring me to my exemplar's door.

I kiss feet which have hastened toward a solitude
In which the shaykh is unveiled, the most glorious
unveiling.

Thus do I emerge from the anguish of wayward-
ness into right guidance
For his having set aright my pact, my covenant
and my intention.

Lights radiated from every direction
By his teaching of the *dhikrs* on every visit.

I beheld what I beheld of the One who...
So ask not, O people, about that Which[3]

I lament and part of Which I reveal not,
For if I do so, I lament with my tears.

Highest praises to the One who has blinded hearts
to the one who
Has disposed of hearts' inner beings with such ardor.

Who is it that has been nurtured and taught in the
presence of his shaykh?
What a noble presence among presences!

He was worthy in al-Jadīd of a vestment
Which has become the vestment of "substitutes"
on the first journey.

Thus did the shaykh say to the riding party while
on a journey
Without pause in a year of pause:[5]

Has He nurtured and taught me now like Aḥmad[6],
Who came to me, nurtured me and taught me
during a time when no apostles have appeared?[7]

My praise for him is praise for Aḥmad, who
Ascended to the heights, the sublimest station of love.

God's blessings will descend upon him so long as
there are those who
Make their way to his tomb following pilgrimage.

The shaykh, imam and gnostic Najm al-Dīn ᶜAbd Allāh al-Iṣbahānī, a resident of Mecca, told me, "I was told by a shaykh to whom I had become a companion while in the lands of the non-Arabs, 'You will meet the pole in the land of Egypt.' Hence, I left my country and headed for Egypt. While on my way, I was accosted by a band of Tatars who seized me and said, 'This is a spy.' They bound me and consulted with one another as to whether to kill me, with some of them saying, 'Let us kill him!' and others saying, 'Let us not kill him!' I spent the night bound, thinking about my situation and saying: I left my country in the hope of meeting the one who would bring me to the knowledge of God. Truly, I have no fear of death, but how can I die before having attained my quest? I then composed some verses of poetry in which I included words from Imru' al-Qays:

My sandals have trodden upon every land
Till absence from home has wearied my soul.

So long have I wandered over the horizons
That in return for my spoils, I would be content with a simple homecoming!

No sooner had I composed these verses than I saw a man with a thick beard and an imposing demeanor. Approaching me as a falcon swoops down upon its prey, he loosed my bonds and said, 'Rise, ᶜAbd Allāh, for I am the one whom you seek.' I then came to Egypt and was told, 'There is a man here by the name of Abū al-ᶜAbbās al-Mursī.' I went to him and what should I find but that he was the very man who had loosed my shackles. He said, 'I was pleased by your verse on the night you were taken captive and by the words you spoke,' whereupon he recited all of my verses to the end."

Shaykh Najm al-Dīn also told me, "My shaykh said to me, 'When you meet the pole, do not pray with him behind you.' When Shaykh Abū al-ᶜAbbās was in Alexandria (may God be pleased with him), I came to him at the time for the mid-afternoon prayer. When I came in to where he was, he asked me, 'Have you prayed?' 'No,' I replied. 'Rise and pray,' he told me. In the place where he was there were two recess-like sitting rooms, one of them closer to the qiblah and the other closer to the sea. The shaykh was seated in the room closer to the sea, and when I rose to pray, I remembered what my shaykh had told me: 'When you meet the pole, do not pray with him behind you.' And I realized that if I prayed from where I was, the shaykh would be behind my back. It was then that God brought my heart to a mystical state and I said, 'Wherever the shaykh is, there is the qiblah.' So I turned to face the shaykh, and just as I was about to commence my prayer by uttering the words, '*Allāhu akbar*', the shaykh said, 'No! No! It does not please Him to depart from the Sunnah!'"

He (may God be pleased with him) also said, "I have nothing to do with chemistry. Verily, I have been a companion to people, one of whom might pass by a dry tree, and no sooner had he pointed to it than it would bear pomegranates right on the spot. Once one has been a companion to men such as these, what need does he have for chemistry?"

One of my companions told me, "In the city of Qūṣ I was the companion of Shaykh Abū al-ᶜAbd Allāh al-Bujā'ī, one of the companions of Shaykh Abū al-Ḥasan al-Shādhilī (may God be pleased with him). I would sometimes encounter things I didn't understand, in which case I would ask Shaykh Abū ᶜAbd Allāh about them and he would reply, 'This is not for me to explain. However, when God has brought you together with Abū al-ᶜAbbās al-Mursī, you will find in him that which you seek.'"

And he said, "I had a dream in which I had a plate of dates just beginning to ripen and fine white meal from which to eat. So I related the dream and I was told, 'This is a great man under whose tutelage you will acquire many fields of knowledge after their time has come.' When Shaykh Abū al-ᶜAbbās came to the city of Qūṣ, I went in to see him and I asked him about the matters which had been difficult for me to understand. He answered all my questions and said, 'Remember your vision of the dates beginning to ripen and the white meal for you to eat. I am that fine white meal.'"

As I was conversing one day with Shaykh Makīn al-Dīn al-Asmar (may God be pleased with him), I told him about Shaykh Abū al-ᶜAbbās. I said, "The shaykh does such-and-such and such-and-such" until we had spoken for quite some time. The jurisprudent Makīn al-Dīn was amazed at the things I was telling him about the shaykh. At last he said, 'Truly, we have not known Abū al-ᶜAbbās."

This was a recognition on the part of Shaykh Makīn al-Dīn al-Asmar of the greatness of Abū al-ᶜAbbās and that he had not really known him, despite the fact that Shaykh Abū al-Ḥasan al-Shādhilī (may God be pleased with him) testified of Shaykh Makīn al-Dīn al-Asmar that he was one of the seven "substitutes."

One day I was with Shaykh Abū al-ᶜAbbās al-Damanhūrī, and also present was a companion of Shaykh Abū al-ᶜAbbās. Someone then said to him, "Master, this is one of the companions of Shaykh Abū al-ᶜAbbās al-Mursī." Shaykh Abū al-ᶜAbbās al-Damanhūrī replied, 'My master Abū al-ᶜAbbās al-Mursī is one of the royal personages of the life to come."

Sulaymān Ibn al-Bākhis said to me, "I went in to see Shaykh Abū al-ᶜAbbās al-Damanhūrī and I heard him say, 'O Lord, there is Abū al-ᶜAbbās, and I am Abū al-ᶜAbbās,' after which he continued to repeat these words. So I said, 'Master, who is Abū al-ᶜAbbās?' He replied, 'Al-Mursī. My son, there is no man like him between Aswān and Alexandria.'

Then he said, 'There is no man like him between Aswān and Dumyāṭ, nor between Dumyāṭ and Alexandria.'"

This same Sulaymān told me, "One day I encountered Shaykh Abū al-ᶜAbbās al-Mursī as he was leaving the public bath. I invited him to come up to my home, and he accepted the invitation. I served him some watermelon from al Ṣāliḥiyah, and as he ate, I asked him about a man who enjoyed great fame, who took great numbers of people out marching with banners and who did not attend the Friday congregational prayer. When I mentioned him to the shaykh, a change came over him and he said, 'Truly, if I'd known that you would mention him to me, I wouldn't have come to your home. You mention followers of innovation in the presence of saints and "substitutes"!'"

I heard him say, "By God, there have never been two people who possess this knowledge in a single age; rather, it has been passed down from one person to another, going back to al-Ḥasan."

A group of people from Ashmūm told me, "Shaykh Abū al-ʿAbbās al-Bujāʾī, a companion of Shaykh Abū al-Ḥasan al-Shādhilī (may God be pleased with him) came to us and was speaking to us. We were pleased by his words, and when he noted our admiration he said, 'How would it be, then, if you were to see Abū al-ʿAbbās al-Mursī? If Shaykh Abū al-ʿAbbās were to loosen my tongue, I would speak of knowledge even more extraordinary.'"

I heard him [Shaykh Abū al-ʿAbbās] say, "There used to be three shaykhs who spoke of this knowledge: Shaykh Abū al-Ḥasan, his companion Shaykh Abū al-Ḥasan al-Ṣiqillī, and I. Then the shaykh (may God be pleased with him) died, as did Abū al-Ḥasan al-Ṣiqillī, and I know no one on the face of the earth, apart from me, who speaks of this knowledge anymore."

When Shaykh Abū al-ʿAbbās died, I was in Cairo, so one day I went into the *zāwiyah*[8] of Shaykh Ṣafī al-Dīn Ibn Abī al-Manṣūr and sat down. As I sat there, a certain Sufi said to another, "Brother, a great man died today." "Who is that?" the other man replied. "Shaykh Abū al-ʿAbbās al-Mursī," said the first. The two men speaking did not know that I had been one of the shaykh's companions. The first man asked, "Do you know what happened to him with our shaykh, Ṣafī al-Dīn?" "No," he replied. "One night the shaykh heard a *dhikr* here which was unfamiliar to him and he said to me, 'Go see who that is.' So I went, and who should I find but Shaykh Abū al-ʿAbbās and his companions. I returned to Shaykh Ṣafī al-Dīn and informed him of what I had seen and he said, 'This man comes here and does not visit us? How strange!' The next morning, Shaykh Ṣafī al-Dīn said to his companions, 'Yesterday I had a vision in which I was in a waterless desert. Abū al-ᶜAbbās was on a mound and was saying to me, "Brother, only in this manner will God allow us to meet.""'

Shaykh Abū ᶜAbd Allāh Ibn al-Nuᶜmān said, "Shaykh Abū al-ᶜAbbās al-Mursī is truly the heir to Shaykh al-Shādhilī's knowledge."

A jurisprudent from al-Bahansā told me, "Shaykh Amīn al-Dīn Jibrīl once asked me, 'Would you like me to show you one of God's saints?' 'Yes,' I replied. 'Let us go,' he said, whereupon he brought me to Shaykh Abū al-ᶜAbbās and said, 'Here he is.'"

One of his companions told me, "The shaykh was invited home by a certain man, who served him food in order to test him. The shaykh, however, turned away from the food and refused to eat it. Then he turned to his host and said, 'Al-Ḥārith Ibn Asad al-Muḥāsibī had a vein in his hand which, if he reached out to take food which he should be suspicious of, would twitch to warn him. As for me, I have in my hand sixty veins which twitch to warn me in such a situation.' Thereupon his host sought God's forgiveness and offered his apologies to the shaykh."

It has been widely circulated among the companions of Shaykh Abū al-Ḥasan and others that one day, as al-Niffarī's book *al-Mawāqif* was being read to him in the home of al-Zakī al-Sirāj in Cairo, the shaykh said, "Where is Abū al-ᶜAbbās?" When Abū al-ᶜAbbās had come, he said to him, "Speak, my son. Speak! Speak—may God bless you—and you will never be silent again!" Shaykh Abū al-ᶜAbbās said, "Thus it was that at that time, I was given the shaykh's tongue."

The scholars of his time used to concede to him this status. In fact, our shaykh, the learned imam, the sword of scholarly disputants and supreme defender of the scholastics, Shams al-Dīn al-Iṣbahānī, and the learned shaykh Shams al-Dīn al-Aykī, were sitting in his presence as disciples, receiving his teaching and the knowledge which he possessed when one of them asked him about a certain shaykh who was manifest at that time. "Do you know him, Master?" he asked. The shaykh replied, "I know him here (pointing to the earth), but I do not know him there (pointing to heaven)."

One of them asked him about a person in Damascus who spent most of his time in a state of intoxication and "absence". The shaykh (may God be pleased with him) replied, "Whoever does not have a shaykh on this path is not a cause for rejoicing."

Moreover, he (may God be pleased with him) held the view that it is not necessary for the pole to be a descendent of al-Ḥasan,[9] but might have some other line of descent.

He spoke one day about the distinguishing marks of the pole. Then, pointing to himself he said, "And certain saints are not far from polehood."

One of his companions reported to me, saying, "The shaykh lay on his back one day and grasped his beard, saying, 'If the scholars of Iraq and Syria knew what lies beneath these hairs, they would come after it, even if they had to crawl to get here!'"

He used to say, "I tell you truly, we only study the words of those who follow the Sufi path in order to see God's bounty toward us." And concerning Imam Abū Ḥāmid al-Ghazālī (may God be pleased with him), "We bear witness that he was among the greatest of those realized in righteousness."

Shaykh Abū al-Ḥasan used to say, "If you sense some need before God, request it from Him through the mediation of Imam Abū Ḥāmid."

Shaykh Abū al-ᶜAbbās used to quote his shaykh, Abū al-Ḥasan (may God be pleased with him) as saying, "[Al-Ghazālī's book] *Iḥyā' ᶜUlūm al-Dīn* will give you knowledge, but *Qūt al-Qulūb* [by Abū Ṭālib al-Makkī] will give you light."

He also used to quote Shaykh Abū al-Ḥasan as saying, "Read from *al-Qūt* [*Qūt al-Qulūb*], for it will give you sustenance."

He [Shaykh Abū al-ᶜAbbās] and Shaykh Abū al-Ḥasan used to venerate the godly imam, Muḥammad Ibn ᶜAlī al-Tirmidhī, whose words held the highest place in both of their hearts. In fact, he used to say that he [Shaykh Abū al-Ḥasan] was one of the four "stakes."[10]

I entered his presence one day and found him engrossed in the recitation of a *wird*[11] which he had been assigned, and he said, "I heard someone saying to me yesterday, 'Peace be upon you, My servants!'" Then he said, "This is something I may hear once or twice a year."

The following are among the lines composed about him by Abū al-ᶜAbbās Ibn al-ᶜArīf:

There has appeared to you a secret which was long concealed,
And a dawn has broken whose darkness you once were.

For you are the veil which conceals from the heart the secret of His revelation,
And were it not for you, it would not be sealed shut.

[But] once you are absent,[12] the revelation descends upon it,
The tents of unveiling's well-guarded caravan come to abide,

And speech of which one never tires is heard,[13]
Delectable to us in its prose[14] and its verse alike.

Entrance to the shrine of Abū al-ᶜAbbās al-Mursī

"As for God's command, 'And do not allow death to overtake you ere you surrender yourselves unto Him,' it means that we should perform only those actions which, were we to die while engaging in them, we would die in a state of surrender to God."

Abū al-ᶜAbbās al-Mursī

Chapter Three

On his spiritual states and strivings, his disciples' experiences with him and his unveilings (*mukāshafāt*)

I heard Shaykh Abū al-ᶜAbbās, may God be pleased with him, say, "Once when I was a young boy, I was with my teacher at the Qur'anic school when a man came along and found me writing on a tablet. He said to me, 'The mystic does not blacken that which is white.'[1] 'It is not as you say,' I replied. 'Rather, the whiteness of the heavenly records is not blackened by the darkness of sins.'"[2]

I also heard him say, 'When I was a young boy, there was a shadow play being put on beside our house, so I went to see it. When I went the next morning to see the teacher at the Qur'anic school, who was a friend of God, he uttered the following lines of poetry when he saw me:

> You who behold shadow images in wonderment,
> You yourself are the shadow if only you could
> perceive it!

He also said, may God be pleased with him, "One night I had a vision in which I was in the celestial realm, when there appeared to me a dark-skinned man of short stature with a large beard. He said to me, 'Say: O God, forgive Muḥammad's people. O God, have mercy upon Muḥammad's people. O God, cast Your veil of protection over Muḥammad's people. O God, restore Muḥammad's people. This is the prayer of al-Khaḍir. Whoever utters it every day will be counted among the substitutes. I was told that this was Shaykh Ibn Abī Shāmah. When my vision had come to an end, I came to see Shaykh Abū al-Ḥasan, may God be pleased with him, whereupon I sat down but told him nothing about my vision. He then said, 'O God, forgive Muḥammad's people. O God, have mercy upon Muḥammad's people. O God, cast Your veil of protection over Muḥammad's people. O God, restore Muḥammad's people. This is the prayer of al-Khaḍir. Whoever utters it every day will be counted among the substitutes.'"

He also said, may God be pleased with him, "Every day I used to go out the sea gate toward the lighthouse. One day I went out to the lighthouse and went to sleep along the eastern side with the thought: I wonder why it is that Abū Bakr, may God be pleased with him, related so few ḥadīths on the authority of the Apostle ﷺ despite the close companionship between them? I then heard someone say to me, 'The most knowledgeable of all people after the Messenger of God was Abū Bakr the Veracious, may God be pleased with him; however, he related so little on the Prophet's authority because he was so fully realized in him ﷺ.'"[3]

He said, may God be pleased with him, "I had entered the spiritual station of mercy when someone said to me, 'Truly, God's mercy is so vast that on the Day of Resurrection, even Ibn Abī al-Ṭawājin will attain a portion thereof.' Ibn Abī al-Ṭawājin is the one who murdered Shaykh and Pole ᶜAbd al-Salām Ibn Mashīsh, who was shaykh to Shaykh Abū al-Ḥasan al-Shādhilī, may God be pleased with them both."

He said, may God be pleased with him, "I was once with the shaykh in the city of the Apostle ﷺ and I wanted to visit Ḥamzah, may God be pleased with him. I left the city and was followed by a certain man, so we came to the tomb together. The door was closed; however, it opened by the blessing of the Messenger of God ﷺ, and we went in. Once inside, we saw a man who was one of the substitutes. I said to the man who had followed me, 'At this time you may ask of God whatever you wish, and your prayer will be granted.' The man then prayed for God to give him a dinar. When we returned to the city, he was met by a man who gave him a dinar. When we went in to see Shaykh Abū al-Ḥasan, may God be pleased with him, he said to the man, 'You unaspiring soul! You came upon a time when your prayers would be answered, and all you asked of God was a dinar?! If only you had asked of Him what Abū al-ᶜAbbās did, namely, that He spare him worldly anxiety in this life and God's chastisement in the life to come! For indeed, God has granted his supplication.'"

He said, may God be pleased with him, "One day I was seated in the teacher's presence when a group of righteous men came in to see him. After they had departed, he said, 'These men are substitutes.' When I examined them with my inner eye, however, I did not find them to be so. Hence, I was in a quandary as to which to believe: what my shaykh had reported, or what my inner eye had discerned. Several days later the shaykh said, 'Everyone whose unrighteous deeds have been replaced by acts of righteousness is a substitute.'[4] And from this I understood that [when he described his visitors as 'substitutes'], he had been speaking of the lowest ranks of 'substitutehood.'"

Gnostic shaykh Najm al-Dīn al-Iṣbahānī once told me, "One day Shaykh Abū al-ᶜAbbās asked me, 'What's the name of such-and-such in Persian?' After that it occurred to me that the shaykh really ought to become acquainted with Persian, so I brought him a book entitled, *The Translator*.[5] 'What is this book?' the shaykh asked me. 'It's *The*

Translator,' I replied. The shaykh laughed and said, 'Ask me whatever you wish in Persian and I will answer you in Arabic. Ask me whatever you wish in Arabic and I will answer you in Persian.' So I asked him questions in Persian and he answered me in Arabic; I also asked him questions in Arabic and he answered me in Persian. Then he said, 'O servant of God, when I asked you about the name of such-and-such in Persian, I only did so as a way of conforming to the way you perceived me. After all, no one could have attained the station I have and be ignorant of languages.'"

Shaykh Najm al-Dīn al-Iṣbahāni also told me, "One day Shaykh Abū al-ᶜAbbās asked me, 'How many rivers are there between this and that village in Persia?' 'There are four,' I replied. 'And what about the river you drowned in?' he asked. I then realized that I had forgotten a river which I crossed one day, and in which I had nearly drowned."

Gnostic shaykh Yāqūt once told me, "Someone invited me to his house and served me some food. However, I sensed a kind of 'darkness' over it, as though it had come from a garbage dump. So I said to myself: This food is unclean, and I refrained from eating it. I then went in to see Shaykh Abū al-ᶜAbbās, may God be pleased with him, and the minute I sat down he said, 'It is only ignorant disciples who, when food is served to them, perceive darkness in it and proclaim it unclean. Hapless man! Your pious circumspection doesn't merit your thinking ill of your fellow Muslim. Rather, you should have said simply, 'This is food which God has not willed me to partake of.'"

I myself went in to see Shaykh Abū al-ᶜAbbās one day, with the desire to abandon reliance on all worldly causes, devote myself entirely to worship and devotion, and cease my pursuit of outward knowledge, saying: This is the only way one can reach God. Then, without my giving any indication of what was on my mind, he said, "I had a disciple in Qūṣ by the name of Ibn Nāshī who was a teacher and a deputy governor. Having experienced something of the spiritual path under our tutelage, he said, 'Master, shall I leave my profession and devote myself entirely to following you?' 'There is no need to do that,' I said. 'Rather, remain where God has placed you, and whatever you receive through us will be yours as well.'" Then he said, "This is the way of the just and veracious. They do not abandon anything until the Truth Himself, exalted be He, removes them from it." When I left his presence, God had cleansed my heart of such thoughts as though they were a garment which I had shed, and thenceforth I contented myself with God in that in which He had established me.

One of the shaykh's fellow disciples once told me, "When I was in Tunisia, I saw a circle of men. One man stood in the center, and those around the periphery were all facing him. I said to myself: That must be the pole. I recognized the man on this basis, and whenever I was told about a man [with spiritual knowledge], I would come to him thinking: Perhaps he is the one I saw in the center of the circle. At last I was told about Shaykh Abū al-ᶜAbbās al-Mursī, so I came to him, and found him indeed to be the same man whom I had seen in the center of the circle. I told him what I had been thinking, and he said, 'Yes, I am the pole. Those who stand opposite my stomach draw upon my inward reality, those who stand opposite my back draw upon my outward knowledge, while those who stand on either side of me draw upon all the types of knowledge which I carry within me.'"

One of the shaykh's fellow disciples told me, "A certain man of knowledge and virtue had a vision in which he was in the smaller Qarāfah cemetery. People were gathered there, peering skyward, and someone said, 'Shaykh Abū al-Ḥasan al-Shādhilī is coming down from the heavens, and Shaykh Abū al-ᶜAbbās is awaiting his descent.' I then saw Shaykh Abū al-Ḥasan come down from the sky wearing white garments. When Shaykh Abū al-ᶜAbbās saw him, he planted his feet firmly on the ground and made ready for Abū al-Ḥasan's descent, whereupon Abū al-Ḥasan descended upon him and disappeared into his head. Then I awoke from my vision."

Shaykh Muḥammad al-Sirāj, may God have mercy upon him, told me, "One night as I was sleeping, someone appeared to me and said, 'Leave Alexandria through the Sidrah Gate. Enter the first garden you come to on your left, and you will find a group of people. The one sitting under the tallest date palm is a man of greatness.' Then I was told, 'At the mosque there is a circle which, if anyone enters it, he will be safe.' The following morning, I went to the outskirts of Alexandria and entered the first garden on the left, and there I found a circle. As I looked up to see which date palm was the tallest, someone said to me, 'All of them are tall.' The speaker turned out to be Shaykh Abū al-ᶜAbbās al-Mursī, may God be pleased with him. I greeted him and sat down, then said, 'Master, I dreamed such-and-such last night,' and told him of my vision. He said, 'The "mosque" refers to me, and the circle is my disciples. Whoever enters this circle—that is, whoever adheres to our conditions—is safe.' Then he said, 'Tonight I will come to you.' 'Master,' I said, 'Shall I wait for you at the door, or shall I leave it open for you?' 'Neither,' he replied. 'Rather, leave it closed, and I will come to you.'

Shaykh Muḥammad continued, "When night fell, I grew uneasy, thinking: From which direction will he come? From over here? No, from other there! And I couldn't sit still. So

I went out to Ribāṭ al-Wāsiṭī and ascended the minaret. As I stood there praying, Shaykh Abū al-^{c}Abbās came to me through the air and said, 'Muḥammad, did you really think that if you came here, I wouldn't know where you were?' 'Master,' I said, 'I only came here because I couldn't bear to sit still any longer!' Hearing myself speak frightened me, though, because the language with which I addressed him was different from the one in which I had been reciting."

One of the shaykh's fellow disciples told me, "We were once with the shaykh in the city of Qūṣ. One of Abū al-^{c}Abbās's disciples was a man by the name of Abū al-Ḥasan al-Mursī, who was prone to be hot-tempered. The shaykh's son went down to play one day as young boys are wont to do, and Shaykh Abū al-Ḥasan al-Mursī said to him, 'Get back up there, and may God not help you!' Shaykh Abū al-^{c}Abbās heard him and said, 'Abū al-Ḥasan, learn to deal with people more gently. You have only a year left to live.' And in fact, he died exactly one year later."

Abū ^{c}Abdallāh al-Ḥakīm al-Mursī, may God have mercy on him, told me, "The shaykh once came to see us in Ashmūm. When night had fallen, he summoned me and said, 'Ḥakīm, come close to me.' So I came close to him. He placed his hand behind my back, and I placed mine behind his. Then he embraced me and wept. I wept to see him weep, though I didn't know what had caused him to do so. Then he said, 'Ḥakīm, I've only come to bid you all farewell. I'll go to al-Muqassam to bid farewell to my brother; then I'll return to Alexandria and spend the night there, and the next day I will enter my grave.' Hence, he departed and stayed with his brother for a short time, after which he went down to Alexandria and spent the night there. And the following day, just as he had said, he entered his grave, may God have mercy on him."

My master Jamāl al-Dīn, the shaykh's son, may God be pleased with them both, once told me, "A European envoy once came to Alexandria, so I went to see him, but I didn't inform the shaykh.

When I returned, he said, 'Where have you been?'

'Right here,' I said.

'No,' he replied, 'you went to see the envoy from Europe. Do you really think that any of your affairs are hidden from me? The envoy was wearing such-and-such and riding a such-and-such. So-and-so was to his right, and so-and-so was to his left.'

And in this way he described the situation exactly as it had been."

ᶜAbd al-ᶜAzīz al-Madyūnī told me, "The shaykh once asked me, 'ᶜAbd al-ᶜAzīz, did you water the mare?'

'Yes, I did,' I replied.

He repeated the question several times, and each time I replied that I had. After asking the question for the last time, he said, 'O Lord!' and took off into the air until he disappeared from sight.

The next day he said to me, 'ᶜAbd al-ᶜAzīz, 'What would make it necessary for you to speak anything but the truth? You were about to say that you hadn't watered the mare. And what would I have done to you if you hadn't?'"

I once heard some students saying, "Those who keep company with the shaykhs acquire nothing in the realm of the outward sciences."

It distressed me to think of missing the opportunity to acquire such knowledge; however, it also distressed me to think of losing the shaykh's companionship, may God be pleased with him. After this I came to see the shaykh and found him eating meat with vinegar, and I thought to myself: If only he would give me a bite from his hand! I'd barely finished thinking the thought before he thrust into my mouth the bite that was in his hand.

Then he said, 'If a merchant becomes our disciple, we do not tell him: Leave your business and come. Similarly, if a craftsman becomes our disciple, we do not tell him: Leave your craft and come. Nor do we tell a student: Abandon your pursuit of knowledge and come. Rather, we confirm everyone in that in which God has established him, and whatever portion he receives through us will be his as well. The Companions became disciples of the Messenger of God ﷺ, but never once did he say to a merchant, "Leave your business," nor to a craftsman, "Leave your craft." On the contrary, he confirmed them in their various means of livelihood, instructing them to be conscious of God therein.'"

I heard him say, "I once traveled to Qūṣ with five people: Ḥājj Sulayman, Aḥmad Ibn al-Zayn, Abū al-Rabīᶜ, Abū al-Ḥasan al-Mursī, and one other person.

Someone asked me, 'What do you intend to do on this journey, sir?'

I replied, "I plan to bury these people in Qūṣ, then return.'

And in fact, I buried all five of them there. However, Ḥājj Sulaymān did not die until he had drunk from the pool of Kawthar.[6]

One of his companions told me, 'A man of note once came to stay with him, and he said to himself: How I would like for someone to wake me up a bit before dawn, bring me a pitcher of warm water and a lamp, and show me where to do my ritual ablutions. And in fact, before dawn someone came and knocked on the door. He went out and who should he find but the shaykh, who said: It is now a bit before dawn. Here is a pitcher of warm water and a candle. Come, let me show you where to do your ritual ablutions.'"

I once said to one of the shaykh's disciples, "I would like the shaykh to regard me with solicitude and grant me a special place in his thoughts."

The disciple then relayed my words to the shaykh. When I later went in to see the shaykh, may God be pleased with him, he said, 'Demand not that the shaykh grant you a special place in his thoughts. Rather, require yourselves to grant the shaykh a special place in your thoughts. For to the degree that you revere the shaykh, he will revere you.' Then he said, 'What do you want to be? Verily, you will be someone of influence. Verily, you will be someone of great influence. Verily, you will have such-and-such. Verily, you will have such-and-such.' The only part which I recall is his statement, 'Verily, you will be someone of great influence.' And I came to have, by God's abundant grace, exalted be He, an authority which I cannot deny."

My master Jamāl al-Dīn, the shaykh's son, told me, "I told the shaykh, 'They want to grant Ibn ᶜAṭā' Allāh a leading position in Islamic jurisprudence.' The shaykh replied, 'They grant him a leading position in Islamic jurisprudence, and I grant him such a position on the mystical path.'"

I once went in to see the shaykh and he said, "When the jurisprudent Nāṣir al-Dīn recovers, he will grant you the position once occupied by your grandfather. The jurisprudent will sit on one side, and I on the other, and you, God willing, will speak to us on both outward and inward knowledge." And what he predicted, may God be pleased with him, came to pass.

I also heard him say, "I would like to copy the book entitled *Al-Tahdhīb* for my son, Jamāl al-Dīn." So I went and copied it without telling him about it.

When I brought him Volume I, he asked, "What is this?"

"It's the book, *Al-Tahdhīb* which I've copied for you," I replied.

He took the book, and as he rose, he said, "Mark my words: A saint never receives anything from anyone but that he repays it in full. May you find this good deed recorded to your credit on the Day of Resurrection."

As I left his house after bringing him Volume II, I was met by one of his disciples, who said, "The shaykh spoke of you, saying, 'So help me God, I will make him an object of God's special providence and favor, who will be emulated for his knowledge of both outward and inward realities.'"

When I brought him Volume III, I was met again as I left his home by one of his disciples, who said to me, "I went up to see the shaykh and I found a book with a red binding, and he told me, 'This is a book which was copied for me by Ibn ʿAṭā' Allāh. I swear by God, I will not be content for him simply to occupy the position of his grandfather; rather, I want him to enjoy an increase in mystical knowledge.'"

One of the shaykh's disciples told me, "One day the shaykh said, 'When Ibn ʿAṭā' Allāh, the jurisprudent of Alexandria, comes, let me know.' Hencc, when you came, we informed the shaykh of your arrival."

[When I came in to see him], he said, "Come forward." So I stepped forward. Then he said, "When the Messenger of God ﷺ was disbelieved by the Qurayshites, Gabriel, upon him be peace, came to him with the angel of the mountains and said, 'This is the angel of the mountains. God has commanded him to obey your instructions concerning Quraysh.' The angel of the mountains then greeted the Prophet ﷺ and said, 'O Muḥammad, if you wish, I will cause the two mountains of Mecca to close in upon them.' The Messenger of God ﷺ replied, 'No. Rather, my hope is that God will bring forth from among their descendents those who affirm the oneness of God and associate no partners with Him.' Thus it was that the Messenger of God ﷺ patiently endured the Qurayshites' unbelief, in hopeful anticipation of their [believing] descendents.[7] And we, likewise, patiently endured this jurisprudent's grandfather for the sake of his grandson."[8]

One day I left the house of the jurisprudent Makīn al-Dīn al-Asmar, may God be pleased with him, together with Abū al-Ḥasan al-Jazīrī (who was a disciple of Shaykh Abū al-Ḥasan). I greeted him and he, in return, greeted me in such a friendly, enthusiastic way that I asked him, "How do you know me?"

"How could I not know you?" he replied. "One day I was sitting in the house of Shaykh Abū al-ᶜAbbās, and you were there as well. When you left, I said to him, 'Master, I'm impressed by that young man. So-and-so and so-and-so have fallen away from their commitment to the path, but this young man remains steadfast.'"

The shaykh replied, "Believe me, Abū al-Ḥasan, this young man is destined to become one who calls others unto God."

And what the shaykh predicted has come to pass, may God be praised.

This same Abū al-Ḥasan [al-Jazīrī] told me, "One night I was at the home of Shaykh Abū al-Ḥasan, and he was reading to us from the book *Khatm al-Awliyā'* by al-Tirmidhī al-Ḥakīm. As we sat there, I saw someone sitting in the room who had not come up with us, and who had not been at the shaykh's house when we arrived. So I asked the person sitting beside me, 'Who is that man sitting beside so-

and-so?' He replied, "There is no one here but the people you already know.' So I kept quiet after that, realizing that he had not seen the man. When everyone else had left, I asked Shaykh Abū al-Ḥasan, may God be pleased with him, about the matter, saying, 'Master, I saw a man here who had not come up with us, and who was not here before we arrived.' The shaykh replied, 'That was Abū al-ᶜAbbās al-Mursī. He comes every night from al-Muqassam in order to hear what we have to say at the appointed hour, then he goes home.' Shaykh Abū al-Ḥasan was in Alexandria at that time."

I used to have frequent obsessive doubts as to whether I was in a state of ritual purity. When news of this reached Shaykh Abū al-Ḥasan, he said to me, "I've heard that you're prone to obsessive doubts as to whether you've performed your ablutions or not."

"Yes, I am," I replied.

Then he said, may God be pleased with him, "This group of ours calls the shots with Satan, not the other way around."

Several days then passed and I went in to see him again. "How are you doing with your obsessive doubts?" he asked.

"There hasn't been any change," I replied.

He said, "If you don't abandon this obsessive preoccupation, don't come back to see me again."

What the shaykh had said caused me such anguish that from that time forward, God delivered me from my inward tormentor.

Moreover, the shaykh, may God be pleased with him, used to instruct people who were prone to such devilish insinuations to recite the words, "Limitless in His glory is the Sovereign, the Creator. 'If He so wills, He can do away with you and bring forth a new mankind [in your stead]:

nor is this difficult for God' {Al-Fāṭir [The Originator] 35:16-17}."

I once composed a poem in which I praised the shaykh and which, God willing, I will mention at the end of this book. When I recited the poem to him, he said, "May God uphold you with the Holy Spirit." I then composed another poem about him in response to a poem in which someone from Akhmīm praised him as well, and which I also intend to mention, God willing, at the end of this book. When the poem was recited to him, he said, "When this jurisprudent became my disciple he suffered from two maladies from which God has now delivered him; and he is destined to speak on knowledge of both inward and outward realities."

The shaykh was referring here to the obsessive doubts from which I had once suffered. I was delivered from them through his blessing, however. In fact, the inner respite which I then experienced was so remarkable that I began to fear that I had become too lenient with myself in some matters!

As for the other malady, it was headaches that I used to suffer. However, I complained to him of the problem and after he had prayed for me, God healed me and restored my vitality.

One night when I was worried and anxious, I saw the shaykh in a dream and complained to him of the state I was in. He said, "Be still, and I swear by God, I will most surely teach you a great science." After I woke up, I came to see the shaykh, may God be pleased with him, and I told him of my vision. He said, "Thus will it be, God willing."

Before becoming the shaykh's disciple, I denied that he had anything distinctive to offer and I objected to his message, though not on account of anything I had heard him say or which he was reported to have said or done. Then one day I got into an argument with one of his followers. I said to the man, "The only people I trust are those who profess outward knowledge. These people, on the other hand,[9] make great claims which are refuted by the straightforward meaning of Islamic law."

After I, too, had become the shaykh's follower, this same man asked me, "Do you know what the shaykh said to me on the day when you and I got into an argument?"

"No," I replied.

He said, "I went in to see him and the first thing he said to me was, 'People like that are like rocks: The ones that miss you are better than the ones that hit you!'"

I knew then that the shaykh had been granted supernatural knowledge of what transpired between us that day. And believe me: I followed the shaykh for twelve years, and contrary to the things which he had been quoted as saying by those who wished to do him harm, never once did I hear him say anything which would be denied by the outward sciences.

What led me at last to meet the shaykh was that after the altercation between me and this disciple of his, I thought to myself: Let me go see this man [the shaykh]. After all, those who speak the truth are marked by clearly recognizable signs. Hence, I went to his gathering place, where I found him speaking of the spiritual 'draughts' of which the Lawgiver has commanded us to partake.

"The first," he said, "is submission (*islam*), the second is faith (*īmān*), and the third is virtue (*iḥsān*)."

"If you will," he continued, "you may say that the first is worship (*ᶜibādah*), the second is servanthood (*ᶜubūdiyah*), and the third is servitude (*ᶜubūdah*)."

"If you will, you may say that the first is law (*sharīᶜah*), the second is reality (*ḥaqīqah*), and the third is realization (*taḥaqquq*), or the like."

He kept on saying, "If you will, you may say...," and "if you will, you may say..." until he dazzled my mind, and I knew that this man was drawing upon the abundance of a divine ocean, a celestial storehouse. Thus it was that God caused all my doubts and resistance to flee. I went home that night, but felt none of my usual desire to meet with family. Instead, I experienced a peculiar sensation the meaning of which I was uncertain. Hence, I went somewhere to be alone. As I gazed at the sky and the celestial bodies and what God had placed therein of the wonders of His power, I felt moved to go back to him again. When I arrived, permission was requested of him for me to enter. When I came in to see him, he rose and received me with such warmth and enthusiasm, I was both astonished and abashed, feeling myself too insignificant to be worthy of such a reception. The first thing I said was, "Sir, God knows, I love you!"

"May God love you as you have loved me," he replied, whereupon I complained to him of my cares and sorrows.

Then he said, may God be pleased with him, "There are only four states in which the servant of God will find himself: blessing, affliction, obedience and disobedience. If you are in a state of blessing, what the Truth requires of you is that you be thankful. If you are in a state of affliction, what the Truth requires of you is that you bear it patiently. If you are in a state of obedience, what the Truth requires of you is that you bear witness to His grace towards you; and if you are in a state of disobedience, what the Truth requires of you is that you seek forgiveness."

As I got up to leave, the cares and sorrows which had burdened me seemed like nothing but a garment which I had now cast off. Some time later he asked me, "How are you?"

"I look for something to worry about," I replied, "and I find none!"

Then he said, may God be pleased with him:

> "By your face my night is moonlit
> As its darkness among others spreads.
> Others find themselves in the approaching gloom,
> While we bask in the light of day.

Remain steadfast on your path, for if you do, you will most surely be one who issues legal rulings in both schools."

By this he meant: both the school of those who stress adherence to Islamic law and outward knowledge, and the school of those who stress experience of Reality and inward knowledge.

Al-Mursī Mosque complex and entrance to his tomb

"Indeed, Shaykh Abū al-Ḥasan (may God be pleased with him) once said to me, 'Abū al-ʿAbbās, you possess the qualities that mark the saints, while even the saints lack the qualities that you possess.'"

Chapter Four

On his knowledge, his renunciation, his abstinence, his detachment from the world, his forbearance, his long-suffering and the rightness of his path

If anyone spoke with Abū al-ᶜAbbās, may God be pleased with him, about this or that field of knowledge, and particularly, the fields of Qur'anic interpretation and prophetic traditions, he would engage the person in such learned conversation on the topic that his listener would say: He must not be well-versed in any field but this! And he would say, "We have shared with the jurisprudents in what they know, but they have not shared with us in what we know."

The book on which he relied in teaching the principles of religion was *Al-Irshād*, in teaching the science of prophetic traditions, *Al-Maṣābīḥ*, in teaching jurisprudence, *Al-Tahdhīb wal-Risālah*, and in teaching Qur'anic interpretation, Ibn ᶜAṭiyah's book.[1]

He used to be recited to by individuals fully versed in the Arabic language, yet even among them he would detect errors which required correction.

As for the gnostic sciences (*al-maᶜārif*) and the sciences of the mysteries (*ᶜulūm al-asrār*), he was their fulcrum and guiding light. If you heard him speak on such things, you would say: These are the words of someone whose homeland is none other than the divine realm of the unseen, and who is more familiar with the denizens of Heaven than he is with those of Earth.

I once heard Shaykh Abū al-Ḥasan say of him, "Abū al-ᶜAbbās is more conversant with the ways of Heaven than he is with the ways of Earth."

You would hear him speak of nothing but the Supreme Intelligence, the Most Excellent Name and its four branches, the names, the letters, the saints' varied spheres of influence, the spiritual stations of those with inward certainty, the angels with near access to the Throne, the sciences of the mysteries, the spiritual resources released through phrases of divine remembrance, the day on which human beings' destinies were determined, divine providence, the science of the beginning, the science of the [divine] will, the divine "grasp" in which the cosmos exists and the men with an understanding thereof, the sciences of the Solitaries (*ᶜulūm al-afrād*), and what will take place on the Day of Resurrection by way of God's dealings with His servants: His forbearance, His grace, and His vengeance. In fact, I once heard him say, "I tell you truly, if it weren't for people's limited understanding, I would speak to them of the future manifestations of God's mercy."

When he did descend to the level of worldly affairs and matters pertaining to day-to-day transactions among people, he would do so only briefly in view of people's need for such. Consequently, he had few followers in the aforementioned [esoteric] realms of knowledge. After all, there may be many who will purchase small pearls, but only rarely will sapphires find a buyer. Consequently, he used to say, may God be pleased with him, "The followers of truth are few." As the Truth has declared: "...how few they are!" {Ṣād 38:24); "few are the truly grateful among My servants" {Saba' [Sheba] 34:13}; "but most people know it not" {Al-Rūm [The Byzantines] 30:6}; and concerning the Companions of the Cave He states, "none but a few have any real knowledge of them" {Al-Kahf [The Cave] 18:22}. Hence, the friends of God are those who dwell in the cave of refuge, as it were, and are recognized by few.

I heard him say, may God be pleased with him, "It is more difficult to recognize the friend of God than it is to recognize God Himself. After all, God is recognized by virtue of His perfection and beauty. By contrast, how long will it take you to come to know another creature like yourself, who eats as you eat and drinks as you drink?"

As for his renunciation of the world (*zuhd*), evidence for this may be found in his renunciation of worldly power, while evidence of his renunciation of worldly power may be found in his refusal to meet with those who possessed it. May God be pleased with him, he lived in Alexandria for 36 years, during which time he neither saw nor sent for its mayor, and although the mayor of Alexandria requested to meet with him, the shaykh did not agree to it.

Al-Zakī al-Aswānī said to him, "Master, the mayor of Alexandria has said that he would like to meet with you. He would like to take your hand and for you to be his shaykh."

The shaykh replied, "Zakī, I am not someone to be toyed with. I tell you truly, I will meet God without being seen by the mayor, and without seeing him." And what he said came to pass.

If, while staying in this or that town, the shaykh was told, "The town's mayor will be coming to see you tomorrow," he would depart that very night.

He was sometimes called upon by the mayor and the administrator of the border town, as well as its bookkeeper. However, on the nights when they came, he would invariably be gripped by a kind of spiritual oppression and wouldn't speak freely as he did when they weren't present. Hence, we used to say, "If only, on the nights when they come, he would say the things he says in their absence!"

The shaykh was once paid a visit by al-Shujāʿī in all of his pomp, splendor and power, yet he wasn't in the least impressed, nor was he distracted by this worldly display from his high-aspiring spiritual ambition. In fact, I was told that when al-Shujāʿī made a show of his wealth, al-Zakī al-Aswānī said to the shaykh, "Master, ask him for our land, that your disciples might till it." But the shaykh replied, "Zakī, this is something which will never be."

His renunciation of the world, may God be pleased with him, is likewise evidenced by the fact that he died without having built a dwelling for himself, planted an orchard, or adopted a profession. Nor did he leave behind any writings. For even though renunciation is a quality of the heart which God creates in those who love Him, there are, nevertheless, outward signs which point to its presence.

Shaykh Abū al-Ḥasan, may God be pleased with him, said, "I once saw [Abū Bakr] the Righteous in a dream, and he asked me, 'Do you recognize the sign that one's heart has been freed from love of the world?'

'No, I don't,' I replied.

'The sign that one's heart has been freed from love of the world is that when one acquires worldly possessions, one disposes of them freely, and when one loses them, one experiences a sense of relief.'"

Shaykh Abū al-ʿAbbās, may God be pleased with him, once said, "I saw ʿUmar Ibn al-Khaṭṭāb, may God be pleased with him, in a dream and I said to him, 'O Commander of the Faithful, what is the sign of love for the world?'

He replied, 'The fear of censure and the love of praise.'

Hence, if the sign of love for the world is the fear of censure and the love of praise, then the sign of renunciation of and antipathy for the world is that one neither fears censure nor loves praise."

As for his abstinence (*wara*[c]), one of his disciples told me that one day, he entered the home of a member of the community in the tower in which he was, and found him driving a peg into the wall. Greatly distressed at what he saw, the shaykh asked him, "How dare you do something for which you haven't received permission on property which has been set aside as a religious endowment?"

Shaykh Abū al-[c]Abbās used to say, "Never once has anything forbidden entered my stomach," and, "The abstemious person is one whom God Himself causes to abstain."

He said, may God be pleased with him, "A certain upstanding man of Alexandria once invited us to an orchard of his in al-Raml. Hence, I went out with a number of the upstanding men of the border town; however, the owner of the orchard did not go out with us at that time. Instead, he simply described the location to us. As we were on our way there, we got into a conversation about 'abstinence,' and everyone had something to say on the topic. As for me, I told them, 'The abstemious person is one whom God Himself causes to abstain.' When we got to the orchard, it being the mulberry season, everyone made a beeline for the trees and began eating. However, every time I approached a tree to eat, I would get a stomachache. I would then withdraw, and the pain would go away. This happened again and again until finally, I sat down without having eaten anything. Then, as my companions were eating, somebody shouted, 'How dare you eat from the fruit of my orchard without my permission!' And sure enough, they had come to the wrong orchard. So I said to them, 'Didn't I tell you that the abstemious person is one whom God Himself, glory be to Him, causes to abstain?'"

Know—may God have mercy on you—that the abstinence of the elect is understood by few. It includes, for example, their wariness of relying on any being but God, inclining in love toward anything or anyone other than Him, or aspiring to anything but His grace and goodness. The abstinence of the elect likewise includes their wariness of reliance on intermediaries and earthly causes, and their repudiation of [the competition which arises among] peers and [attempts to please] earthly authorities.

The abstinence of the elect also includes their wariness of relying upon habits, acts of obedience, and the lights of divine self-disclosures.

Lastly, the abstinence of the elect includes their vigilance against being enticed by this world or diverted by the life to come [from seeking God Himself]. They are wary of this life out of loyalty [to God], and of the life to come out of the desire to be devoted purely to God alone.

Shaykh ᶜUthmān ᶜĀshūrā' said, "I once left Baghdad for Mosul, and as I traveled, this earthly life was displayed before me in all of its glory, its [promise of] fame, it prestige, its carriages, its raiment, its adornments, and its luxuries; yet I turned away from it. Then Paradise was displayed before me in the same way: with its companions pure, its palaces, its rivers and its fruits; yet I turned away from it as well. I was then told, 'ᶜUthmān, if you had contented yourself with the former, We would have concealed the latter from you, and if you had been content with the latter, We would have concealed Ourselves from you. As it is, however, We belong to you, and your portion of both this life and the life to come will be yours as well.'"

Shaykh ᶜAbd al-Raḥmān al-Maghribī, who resided in east Alexandria, said, "One year I performed the pilgrimage to Mecca, and after completing it I decided to return to Alexandria. Then I heard someone say to me: Next year you will be with Us. So I thought to myself: If I'll be here next year, then I won't return to Alexandria. I had the thought of going to Yemen, so I went to Aden, and as I was walking along one of its beaches one day, I was accosted by merchants who had brought out their merchandise and set up their stalls. Then I looked up, and what should I see but a man who had spread a carpet on the sea and was walking on the water. I said to myself: I'm fit neither for this world nor for the world to come! Yet as I thought thus to myself, I heard someone say to me, 'Whoever is not fit for this world or the world to come, is fit for Us.'"

Shaykh Abū al-Ḥasan said, "Abstinence is the blessed path of those for whom—[given their renunciation of this world]—it is as if they had already died and bequeathed their worldly possessions to others, yet they are in no haste to receive their reward. Hence, their abstinence has led them to a state in which they receive [knowledge] from God and on His authority, speak by God's grace, and labor on God's behalf and by His grace; and all of this on the basis of clear evidence and rare insight."

Such individuals—throughout the hours of their day and in whatever conditions they find themselves—knowingly plan, choose, will, ponder, observe, speak, strike, walk, and move solely by God's grace and for His sake. Their knowledge has brought them to an awareness of the true nature of things; hence, their entire beings are centered [upon God], undistracted by other concerns, be they sublime or earthly. As for the most earthly of the earthly, God Himself causes them to eschew it as a reward for their piety, while maintaining the Islamic law's demands upon them.

As for those whose action and knowledge are not rooted in a [tried and true] inherited tradition, their spiritual perception will be clouded by some worldly concern, or they will be alienated from God by some delusive claim. Hence, all that such individuals have inherited is the habit of self-aggrandizement, arrogance toward others like them, and the illusion that they have guided others to God through their knowledge. This, however, is manifest loss. Almighty God forbid that any one of us should follow such a path.

People of discernment will be wary of this type of abstinence and seek God's refuge from it. Those whose knowledge and action do not lead them to a greater sense of their utter dependence upon God and humility before other human beings are doomed to perdition. Glory be to the One who has caused many of the righteous, by virtue of this very righteousness, to lose sight of that which is in their true interest, just as He has separated those who spread corruption on earth, by virtue of their corruption, from the One who brought them into existence. Hence, seek refuge in God, for He is All-hearing, All-knowing.

Behold, then—may God grant you understanding of the path of His friends and the grace to follow in the footsteps of those whom He loves—the type of abstinence about which the shaykh spoke, may God be pleased with him, when he said, "Their abstinence has led them to a state in which they receive [knowledge] from God and on His authority, speak by God's grace, and labor on God's behalf and by His grace; and all of this on the basis of clear evidence and rare insight."

This is the abstinence of the substitutes and the just and veracious, not of those who speak in such a way as to impress others with their knowledge, and which gives rise to distrust and delusion.

As for the shaykh's detachment from the world, it led him to conduct himself in the most astonishing ways. We have already made mention of such detachment as it was reflected, for example, in his dealings with those in positions of authority when they would display their worldly wealth before him and seek to engage him in conversation.

Once he told his disciples, may God be pleased with him, "I was paid a visit today by the eunuch Bahā' al-Dīn (the government bookkeeper at that time) and the jurisprudent Shams al-Dīn al-Khaṭīb (who was the overseer of religious endowments), and they said to me, 'This fortress [in which you live] is in need of mats, oil and lamps, while the poor who live here are in need of food. Moreover, we, being the current rulers, could contribute something to it every month.'"

So I said to them, 'Let me first consult my companions.'

You are my companions; so what would you advise me?"

However, no one made any reply. He repeated his question several times, but received no response.

Then he prayed, "O God, enrich us so that we have no need of them, and enrich us not through them. You are capable of all things."

Hence, he did not agree to their proposal, and when he died, may God be pleased with him, the place still had no fixed allotment [from the government].

I heard him say, may God be pleased with him, "Truly, I have never seen genuine glory and honor come through anything but detachment from God's creatures."

I also heard him say, "One day I saw a dog along the road. I had some bread with me, so I placed it between his paws, but he paid no attention to it. I brought it close to his mouth, yet he still paid no attention to it. Then I heard someone say to me, 'How insufferable are those who are less willing to renounce the world than a dog!'"

I also heard him say, "I once went to buy something from someone I knew for half a dirhem. As I was on my way, I thought to myself: Perhaps he won't be willing to take the money from me. But just then I heard someone say to me, 'Well-being in one's religion consists in abandoning greed toward other creatures.'

Then I returned home, came into the house and closed the door. After I had sat down, someone opened the door all of a sudden and said to me, 'What makes for well-being in one's religion?'

'Abandoning greed toward other creatures,' I replied. And he latched onto my statement as if it were exactly what he had been seeking. It then became apparent that Shaykh Abū al-Ḥasan had instructed this man to go to the granary and measure out three whibas for himself.[2] However, he went and measured out for himself an ardeb.[3] When news of what he had done reached the shaykh, he said, 'Leave what he measured out where it is, and give him the three whibas which we promised him.'"

He said, may God be pleased with him, "[The word] 'greed' consists of three letters, each of which is hollow.[4] Hence, it's a bottomless pit,[5] and the greedy person is never satisfied."

He used to say, may God have mercy on him, "All people are motivated by something. As for us, we are motivated by faith and consciousness of God. As God, glory be to Him, has declared, 'Yet if the people of those communities had but attained to faith and been conscious of Us, We would indeed have opened up for them blessings out of heaven and earth' {Al-Aᶜrāf [The Faculty of Discernment] 6:96}."

Know, then, that detachment from the creation is the mark of those who follow the [Sufi] path and who strive for spiritual realization.

Junayd was once asked, "Might the gnostic commit sexual sin?"

He replied, "He might, if God had foreordained him to do so."

However, I am certain that if he had been asked, "Might the gnostic desire anything but God?" he would have said, "No. Rather, what the Truth, glory be to Him, wills is for His servants to worship Him in everything out of love and trust and in a spirit of reliance, fear and hope. For this is what His uniqueness merits."

One gnostic expressed this truth in verse, saying:

How unthinkable that someone who affirms His
    Lord's oneness and worships
Him alone should seek a gift from anyone [but Him].

My companion, help me to stand in the Truth's presence,
That I might die [to myself] in holy rapture,
Then live having found true Existence.

Say to the kings of earth: Strive as you may, [your
    dominion is bound to pass away].
As for that dominion [to which I have attained],[6] it
    can be neither bought nor bestowed.

Detachment from the world arises solely from genuine trust in God, while genuine trust in God arises solely from faith in God based on a personal vision of and encounter with Him. Hence, such people's faith requires that they exult in God. As God has declared, glory be to Him, "All honor belongs to God, and [thus] to His Apostle and those who believe..." {Al-Munāfiqūn [The Hypocrites] 63:8}.

Likewise does all succor come from God: "We had willed it upon Ourselves to succor the believers" {Al-Rūm [The Byzantines] 30:47}.

Similarly, it is God who delivers us from those impediments which threaten to keep us from Him: "Thus have We willed it upon Ourselves: We save all who believe [in Us]" {Yūnus [Jonah] 10:103}.

Hence, the glory and honor of one who believes in God derive from his trust in his Master, the victory which He grants him over himself and his worldly passions, and His deliverance from those impediments which threaten to cut him off from the path of divine guidance.

The byword and source of protection for those with the will [to obey their Lord] is: contentment with God alone, detachment from everything other than Him, and keeping the garments of faith from being defiled by the desire for that which is merely temporal or aspiring after anything other than the Ever-gracious Sovereign.

This truth is conveyed by the following verses:

[My soul] awakened early, reproaching an age
which had dealt unjustly,
Yet I disregarded her in hopes that she would desist.

Cast not undue blame on your fate, as though one
could expect it to be loyal and pure of heart.

No harm will come to me should I be unknown in
my time:
The full moon remains a full moon be it visible or
concealed.

God knows that mine is a resolution which,
In its purity and extremity, shuns all that is base.

Why should I not protect myself from [abasement
by] others,
Revealing to them instead the might of kings and an
honor even greater [than theirs]?

Shall I present myself as one who stands in need of
them,
When all alike are impotent?

How shall I seek sustenance from His creation?
Were I to do so, that would most surely be an estrange
ment [from God Himself].

For the weak to complain to another no less weak
than he
Is an infirmity which will set him on the brink [of
perdition].

Hence, seek your sustenance from God, whose
goodness
Embraces all creation in grace and compassion.

Seek refuge in Him, turn not back from His door,
And you will find your heart's desire.

What necessitates your detachment from any and all other than God is your knowledge that He could only have brought you into His kingdom by virtue of having protected you and granted you [so many blessings and gifts] that you no longer need anything from anyone but Him. Hence, if the understanding which they [God's friends] have been granted on His authority leads them to refrain from asking Him for what they need—content in the realization that He knows their needs before they ask—how could this same understanding and realization not lead them to refrain from seeking what they need from other creatures?

Those to whom the Truth, glory be to Him, has disclosed some of what He has made known to His loved ones are thereby called upon to detach themselves from all else but Him—just as this is required of others, yet to a greater extent. Have you not heard God's words, "Indeed, We have bestowed upon thee seven of the oft-repeated [verses] and [have, thus, laid open before thee] this sublime Qur'ān: [so] turn not thine eyes [longingly] toward the worldly benefits which We have granted unto some of those [that deny the truth]" {Al-Ḥijr 15:87}.

After all, how could His grace toward you, His gifts, the openings[7] He grants through His providential care and the unique signs of His friendship fail to prevent you from becoming attached to anything or anyone else?

One gnostic expressed it thus:

> After penetrating the depths of the divine realities,
> After taking delight in my Creator's gifts
> And commanding a view of His kingdom,
> Shall I be found with my palm outstretched to someone
> other than my Provider?

Would a human being of high rank be willing for you to attribute to him a position which grants someone else the authority to give or to withhold, to embrace or to banish? Beware lest you be counted among those about whom God, glory be to Him, has said, "And most of them do not even believe in God without [also] ascribing divine powers to other beings beside him" {Yūsuf [Joseph] 12:106}. For it is an odious thing to be a recipient of His hospitality and, at the same time, to be casting covetous glances in someone else's direction.

The following verses make the same point:

> Is it fitting for me, a guest in Your house,
> To place my hope in Your servants?

Rather, it is to You that I turn,
Leaving all else behind.

Hence, seek nothing from those who are distant from you while neglecting to make requests of the Sovereign who is nearer to you than your jugular vein. Have you not heard what God, exalted be He, has declared? He says:

- "And if My servants ask thee about Me—behold, I am near: I respond to the call of him who calls, whenever he calls upon me. Let them, then, respond unto Me, and believe in Me, so that they might follow the right way" {Al-Baqarah [The Cow] 2:196}.
- "Now, verily, it is We who have created man, and We know what his innermost self whispers within him: for We are closer to him than his jugular vein" {Qāf 50:16}.
- "Call unto Me, and I shall respond to you!" {Ghāfir [Forgiving] 40:60}.
- "Ask, therefore, God [to give you] out of His bounty" {Al-Nisā' [Women] 4:32}.
- "For no single thing exists that does not have its source with Us" {Al-Ḥijr 15:21}.

God has made all such declarations in order to encourage His servants to set their aspirations entirely upon Him, and to bring their needs to Him alone.

As for his long-suffering, may God be pleased with him, it was manifest in the fact that he refused to avenge or defend himself.

I went in to see him one day and he asked me, "What do you think of so-and-so (referring to a man who had done great harm to the shaykh)?

"I was approached by the companions of so-and-so (a certain man of influence in those days who used to visit the shaykh regularly), and they said,

'Master, concerning this man who did you such harm, we want to strike him and expose him in both Cairo and Alexandria.'[8] So, what do you say?"

"[It would be in your best] interest," I said.

"What?" he asked in disbelief.

I said, "For us to take revenge on him."

"I take revenge on no one," he replied.

"Rather," I explained, "I meant [that] your followers [would take revenge on your behalf]."

He said, "I would never instruct my followers to take revenge."

Upon hearing his response, I hung my head in shame. And from then on, if anyone did harm to any of us and if, following this, some misfortune befell him and we were tempted to gloat over his suffering, we would remember the shaykh's words, "I take revenge on no one," as if he had uttered them at that very moment, and our desire for revenge would be extinguished. It also happened that about fifteen years later, the same man who had sought to harm the shaykh sought to do us harm as well, after which he was struck by some misfortune. However, God preserved and protected me from taking satisfaction in his suffering.

The shaykh used to say, "The man concerning whom I consulted you—the same thing that I went through with him, you will go through with him as well. When that happens, respond to him in the same way that I did."

Such are the words of the greatest of God's saints, which are recorded on the pages of their disciples' hearts in such a way that when the [appropriate] time comes, the Truth, glory be to Him, brings them to mind so vividly that it seems as though they were hearing them for the first time.

God might cause your shaykh who thus addressed you to be present to your mind in his appearance and dress; or, it might take place in the "discontiguous imagination."[9] He might also appear physically at a time of misfortune or affliction as a means of strengthening and teaching his disciple.

I heard him say, may God be pleased with him, "What you have heard from me and understood, place it in God's safekeeping, and He will bring it back to you when you need it. And whatever you have not understood, entrust likewise to God, and He Himself will make it clear to you."

Thus, the words of such extraordinary souls yield their fruits to their disciples at the time when they need them. The disciple will think that he has learned nothing, when in fact, he has. Wisdom consists of both the seed and the plant, but the time for sowing the seed is distinct from the time for the plant's emergence and growth. The seeds of wisdom may have been sown within you, but the plant's emergence and growth depend on the arrival of a rain cloud; once the cloud appears, it reveals what lay dormant in the earth. Thus, that which has been deposited in servants' minds and hearts remains hidden until its time has come.

I once heard that Shaykh Abū al-Ḥasan had said, "There is no veil but time."

One day I heard him [Shaykh Abū al-ᶜAbbās] say, "It used to be that whenever anyone did me harm, he would perish immediately. Now, however, I am not like that. For he [Shaykh Abū al-Ḥasan] saw me, may God be pleased with him, aspiring to a change in this state of affairs, and he said to me, 'Knowledge has increased.'"

I also heard him say, "The flesh of the friends of God is poisoned."[10]

Know—may God instruct you in the knowledge to which He Himself leads, and cause you to dwell constantly in His presence—that the Truth comes to His friends' defense not because they asked Him to do so, but rather, because of their sincere dependence upon Him and their surrender of the matter to Him. Have you not heard the Truth's words, "We had willed it upon Ourselves to succor the believers," and, "and for everyone who places his trust in God, He [alone] is enough."

Do not say, "These are people who defend themselves against others. Rather, count them among those whom God defends. After all, He is the Victorious One who cannot be defeated, the All-Powerful One who knows no infirmity, and the Irresistible One in the face of whose scourge nothing and no one in heaven or on earth could stand. Indeed, were He to place even an atom's worth of His destructive power upon the mountains, they would melt.

What the shaykh meant when he said, "Knowledge has increased," is that when the disciple first sets out upon the path, he relies upon his high-aiming aspiration, whereas, once he nears the path's end, he comes to rely upon his knowledge. Hence, if, in the beginning, he turns to God in sincere resolution, appealing to Him for vengeance against those who have done him harm, the Truth will come to his defense because of his having turned to Him for succor with sincere determination, and because of his inability to endure patiently any delay in requital. In the case of the gnostic, however, the sea of knowledge has so expanded within him that his personal aspiration, willing and planning have given way to God's willing on his behalf and His divine providence. For once one has had a vision of the divine will and come under the sway of this vision, what [personal] ambition could possibly remain to him?

It can thus be seen that if the punishment of someone who has caused [the gnostic] harm is delayed, he will perceive the wisdom in his Lord's choice. Consequently, he will not seek to hasten God's defense of him because, in contrast to the inexperienced disciple, there is no danger that he will be unable to endure patiently if vengeance on his behalf is delayed.

In addition, we find that when the gnostic comes to God seeking vengeance against someone who has wronged him, the mercy and compassion which lie within him are awakened by virtue of the fact that his character has been conformed to that of the One whom he knows, thereby preventing him from seeking to avenge himself even if he would have been capable of doing so. After all, how can one seek vengeance on God's creatures when he sees God at work through them?

It may also be said that when God's friends are wronged, their responses divide them into different classes. One class is represented by the person who calls down evil upon the person who wronged him. In such a person's case, the harm he has suffered has provoked such a sense of injury that he feels himself compelled to utter such a prayer. Such a plea, moreover, will not go unanswered, and it is about this type of person that the Prophet ﷺ was speaking when he said, "Beware of the prayer [for vengeance] uttered by one who has been wronged, for it is heard directly by God."[11]

As for the second class, it consists of those who, if they are wronged, appeal to God, glory be to Him, for succor and seek a swift response. However, such individuals have come to realize that God knows all mysteries and has concealed them; consequently, they quietly surrender the matter to Him. These individuals are the most worthy of God's defense of them due to their reliance upon and trust in Him, and their complete surrender of their affairs into His hands. God, glory be to Him, has declared, "and for everyone who places his trust in God, He [alone] is enough" {Al-Ṭalāq [Divorce] 65:3}.

It is related that a certain woman had a single chicken whose eggs she lived on. One day, a thief came and stole the chicken, but the woman did not call down evil upon him. Rather, she surrendered the matter to God, glory be to Him. The thief then slaughtered the chicken and plucked out its feathers, whereupon the feathers sprouted on his face. He tried to get rid of them, but to no avail. He then sought help from other people as well, but no one was able to relieve him of what had befallen him until, at last, he came to a Jewish rabbi, who said to him, "I know of no cure for you except for the woman whose chicken you stole to call down evil upon you. If she does so you will be healed."

Hence, the man sent some people to speak to the woman.

"Where is the chicken you used to have?" they asked her.

"It was stolen," she replied.

"The person who stole it did you an injustice," they said.

"He certainly did," she replied.

"Not only that, but he deprived you of its eggs!"

"Yes, he did," she agreed.

And they kept after her this way until they had worked her into a fury, whereupon she called down evil upon him, and the feathers fell out of his face.

The rabbi was asked, "How did you know that this would happen?"

He replied, "When her chicken was stolen, she did not call down evil upon the thief; rather, she appealed to God with her concern, and God Himself came to her defense. However, when she called down evil upon him, she came to her own defense, so the feathers fell out of the thief's face."

The third class is represented by people who, when they are wronged, neither call down evil upon those who wronged them nor appeal to God to avenge them. Rather, they recognize God as the ultimate arbiter in the matter, thereby committing the choice to Him.

As for the fourth class, it consists of those who, when they are wronged, have compassion on the one who wronged them. Shaykh Abū al-Ḥasan, may God be pleased with him, said, "If some malefactor does you harm, you must patiently endure. Beware of wronging yourself, thereby causing yourself to suffer doubly: first, from the wrong done to you by another, and secondly, from the wrong you have done to yourself."

If you fulfill your commitment to exercise patient endurance, God will reward you with long-suffering (*ḥilm*) so that you will be able to forgive and pardon. He may even reward you—out of the light of His goodly acceptance—with the wherewithal to have such compassion on the one who wronged you that you call down blessing upon him and see your prayer answered.

And what a joyous state will be yours if, through you, the one who wronged you receives mercy. This is the rank of the merciful and righteous: "...place your trust in God, for verily, God loves those who place their trust in Him" {Āl ᶜUmrān [The House of ᶜUmrān] 3:159}.

Of relevance in this regard is the story told by Shaykh Abū al-Ḥasan about what happened to Ibrāhim Ibn Adham, may God be pleased with him. A soldier once asked him, "Where is the populated area?"

In reply, he pointed to the cemetery.

The soldier, thinking that Ibrāhīm Ibn Adham was mocking him, beat him until he had fractured his skull.

Hanging his head, he said, "Yes! Beat the head which has disobeyed God Almighty for so long!"

The soldier was then told, "The man you just beat is Ibrāhīm Ibn Adham, the holy man of Khurāsān."

Upon hearing this, the soldier fell on his feet with kisses and apologized profusely.

Ibrāhīm Ibn Adham then said to him, "Believe me, no sooner had you finished beating me than I asked God to forgive you. After all, I knew that God would reward me for what you had done to me and hold what you had done against you. Hence, I felt ashamed that I should receive good from you while you received evil from me."

Shaykh Abū al-Ḥasan said, "This is not perfection, however. Rather, perfection may be seen in what was done by Saᶜd, one of the ten.[12] A certain woman claimed falsely that he had taken something from her orchard. In response, he prayed, 'O God, if what she claims is false, blind her and strike her dead where she is.' Thereafter, the woman went blind. Then one day as she was walking through her orchard, she fell into a well and died. If what Ibrāhīm did was perfection, then what this Companion did is even more worthy to be described thus. Saᶜd was among those to whom God had entrusted the knowledge of the unseen, and who therefore viewed himself and others as one and the same. Hence, he did not call down a curse upon the woman because she had done harm to him personally, but rather, because she had harmed the Companion of the Messenger of God ﷺ. Ibrāhīm, by contrast, had not yet reached this level; he refrained from calling down curses upon the soldier lest this be a way of avenging himself, whereas in Saᶜd's case, may God be pleased with him, God had delivered him from himself and given him a unique standing among people. God likewise delivers whomever He wills of His servants. In short, the Sufi claims no right for his own sake; rather, whatever right he claims, he claims for the sake of his Lord.

Moral:

Know that when God's friends first embark on the Sufi path, God empowers other people over them in order to purge them of what remains of their spiritual vices and weaknesses, and in order for their virtues to be brought to perfection. He also deals with them in this manner lest they rely on other human beings. Someone who does you harm frees you from slavery to his kindness, whereas someone who shows you kindness enslaves you by putting you in his debt. The Messenger of God ﷺ declared, "Hearts are naturally disposed to love those who treat them with kindness."

He also said, "If someone does you a favor, reward him, and if you are unable to do that, then call down blessings upon him."

The purpose behind all of this is thus to free the servant's heart from other people's benevolence, thereby enabling him to attach himself [solely] to the true Sovereign.

Shaykh Abū al-Ḥasan, may God be pleased with him, said, "Flee from people's kindness more than you flee from the evil they commit against you. For their kindness affects you in your spirit, whereas their evil affects you only in your body. To be affected in your body is better for you than to be affected in your heart, and an enemy through whom you draw near to God is better for you than a friend who alienates you from Him. Consider their friendly approach toward you by night and their shunning of you by day: Do you not see that when they thus approach you, they beguile?

God's manner of dealing with His sincere friends and loved ones as they first embark on the Sufi path is to give other human beings power over them. Thus, Shaykh Abū al-Ḥasan, may God be pleased with him, said, "O Lord, You sentence Your people to abasement in order that they might receive glory and honor, and You sentence them to loss in order that they might find. All glory and honor which alienates from You, we ask You to replace with abasement which brings with it the subtleties of Your mercy, and every gain which veils You, we ask You to replace with loss which brings with it the lights of Your love."

That this is, in fact, God's manner of dealing with His true friends and loved ones is evidenced by His saying, glory be to Him:

- "Misfortune and hardship befell them, and so shaken were they that the Apostle, and the believers with him, would exclaim, 'When will God's succor come?' Oh, verily, God's succor is near!" {Al-Baqarah [The Cow] 2:214}.
- "...but at last—when those apostles had lost all hope and saw themselves branded as liars—Our succor attained to them" {Yūsuf [Joseph] 12:110}.
- "But it was Our will to bestow Our favor upon those [very people] who were deemed [so] utterly low in the land, and to make them forerunners in faith, and to make them heirs [to Pharaoh's glory], and to establish them securely on earth..." {Al-Qaṣaṣ [The Story] 28:5-6}.
- "Permission to fight is given to those against whom war is being wrongfully waged—and verily, God has indeed the power to succor them—those who have been driven from their homelands against all right for no other reason than their saying, 'Our Sustainer is God!'" {Al-Ḥajj [The Pilgrimage] 22:39-40}.

Numerous other verses from the Holy Qur'ān communicate this same truth as well.

The state in which God's friends find themselves at the beginning of their spiritual journey is evidenced by Ibrāhīm Ibn Adham's having lowered his head when he was beaten by the soldier, saying, "Yes! Beat the head which has disobeyed God Almighty for so long!" It may likewise be seen in his saying, "There are two times when I've really rejoiced. The first time was when, while in a mosque, I suddenly got diarrhea. I kept getting up, then sitting down again until the proprietor of the mosque came and instructed me to leave. However, I was so weak, I couldn't do as he asked. So he grabbed me by the leg and dragged me out.

The other time was when a number of us boarded a ship where there was a wag who was saying, 'This is the way we used to take hold of the louts in Byzantium.' And as he said it, he reached out and yanked on my beard, which pleased me because this way, I knew he considered me the most contemptible person on board!"

This is the way in which they experience things in the beginning of their journey along the path given their awareness of their remaining spiritual flaws and weaknesses. As a consequence, they are wary of defending themselves lest they do so for selfish motives and fall out of favor with God, exalted be He. Instead, they exercise clemency and refrain from defending or avenging themselves, since they realize the baneful effects of doing so. Hence, the Truth's accustomed manner of dealing with His true friends and loved ones is to surround them with enemies, then to grant succor in their dealings with them.

Shaykh Abū al-Ḥasan, may God be pleased with him, said, "Someone once persecuted me so terribly that I was at my wits' end. Then I had a vision of someone in a dream who said to me, 'A sign of true righteousness is that one has a plethora of enemies, yet takes no notice of them."

You should know that people tend to enjoy remaining in situations or places of honor, glory, power and status. However, if the Truth, glory be to Him, allowed them what they desire, they would perish. Hence, He rouses them out of such states by means of the harm they suffer due to persecution and the opposition of the envious. As one gnostic has declared, "The enemy's derisive laugh is the whip with which God lashes people's hearts if they find repose in anything or anyone but Him." Otherwise, the heart would go on resting in the cool shade of glory and fame, which are a thick veil between the soul and God. Truly did he speak, may God be pleased with him.

This is a manifestation of the favor with which God looks upon His friends and loved ones and His loving guardianship over them; as God, mighty and majestic is He, has declared, "God is near unto those who have faith" {Al-Baqarah [The Cow] 2:257}.

If their lights reach perfection and their inner beings are purified of what remains of their spiritual weaknesses and flaws, God gives them power over other human beings and humbles others before them; when this takes place, the chosen servant becomes a sword in God's hand, exalted be He, with which He avenges Himself. It was in this capacity that Sa^c^d called down a curse upon the woman who had made a false claim about him, saying, "O God, blind her sight and cause her to die where she is," and his plea was answered. Similarly, when ^c^Uthmān Ibn ^c^Affān's assassins entered his home, one of the men slapped his wife in the face, and ^c^Uthmān, may God be pleased with him, said to him, "May God cut off your hands and your feet and cause you to enter the Fire." When, some time later, the man was seen in Damascus with both his hands and his feet cut off, he said, "The first two parts of ᶜUthmān's prayer have been answered, and now only the third remains."

Such men's spiritual conditions may not be clearly understood by the general populace. Hence, do not favor a friend of God who, after being wronged, pardons, over one who, when he is wronged, avenges himself or calls down a curse on the one who wronged him. After all, the former's having pardoned may be due to his awareness of remaining impurities in his own heart, while the latter's prayer for vengeance may be due to his awareness that he has been purged of such impurities, as a result of which he seeks vengeance [not for his own sake, but rather] for the sake of his Lord.

As for his patient endurance, he was among those in whom this trait has been firmly ingrained. He was afflicted with a number of illnesses which, if even some of them were placed on the mountains, would cause them to melt away. He had kidney stones, suffered from pain in his kidney when the weather was cold, and had twelve hemorrhoids which caused him particular discomfort when he was sitting with others. However, he would not interrupt a session or moan as he sat. Hence, those who were with him would not even be aware that there was anything wrong with him. Nor did his illnesses cause jaundice in his face or any other visible change in his bodily appearance. Hence, he used to say, "Look not at the ruddiness of my face, for the ruddiness of my face comes from my heart."

A particular man went in to see him one day and found him in pain. The man said, "May God grant you well-being, Master."

However, the shaykh remained silent and made no reply. The man stayed an hour longer, then said, "May God grant you well-being, Master."

The shaykh then replied, "I have asked God for well-being, and the condition I am in is, itself, perfect well-being."

The Messenger of God ﷺ asked God for well-being. However, he also said, "The food I ate in Khaybar still causes me suffering, and now it has affected my aorta."[13]

ᶜUmar, may God be pleased with him, asked God, exalted be He, for well-being, after which he was stabbed to death.

ᶜUthmān, may God be pleased with him, asked God for well-being, after which he had his throat slit.

ᶜAlī, may God be pleased with him, asked God for well-being, after which he was killed.

Hence, if you ask God for well-being, ask Him with the realization that He knows best that in which your true well-being lies.

He used to say, may God be pleased with him, "The phrase, 'patient endurance' (*ṣabr*) is derived from the word, *aṣbār*, which refers to the target used by archers. Hence, the person with patient endurance is one who sets himself up as a target for the arrows of divine decree."

Moreover, it was his custom to ask God to deal graciously with him, and rarely would he flag in his mention of it.

I went in to see him one day and found him in pain. "Master," I said, "I think you are weak."

"The weak person," he replied, "is the one with neither faith nor consciousness of God."

Know that patient endurance may be divided into three categories: (1) perseverance in the performance of duties, (2) self-control in the face of that which is forbidden, and (3) steadfastness and equanimity in affliction.

As for the patient endurance exhibited by the greatest of God's saints, it is reflected in:

- Their patient endurance of the need to conceal the divine mysteries and to refrain from reliance on earthly effects or the lights [they have received].
- Their willingness to endure persecution and their steadfastness under the blows of divine decree.
- Their willingness to bear others' burdens and to submit gladly to whatever God wills.
- Their resoluteness in performing what is required of them as God's servants, and their steadfast surrender to His lordship.
- Their constancy in exhibiting noble traits of character, and their submission and conformity to what God requires.
- Their determination to center all their aspirations on God and to commit all their affairs to Him.
- Their steadfastness in making themselves available to others and pointing them to the true Sovereign.

Indeed, Shaykh Abū al-ᶜAbbās, may God be pleased with him, used to say, "I tell you truly, I only began making myself available to people when I had been threatened with dispossession. I was told, 'If you do not sit with people,[14] We will take away what We have given you!'"

As for the rightness of his path, may God be pleased with him, it may be seen in the extreme care he would take not to violate others' rights, so much so that he would rush to repay what he owed before it was due. Similarly, he would urge his disciples to free themselves of any debts they owed to others.

If he owed a debt, he would repay it in full, and if someone owed him a debt, he would claim his right in the most fitting manner. He kept himself aloof from people of wealth and influence, neither lifting a foot to approach them, nor sending for them or writing to them [even] if he was requested to do so. Once when someone asked him to write such a missive, he replied, "I will present your need before God." If the person who had made the request was content with this, it meant that his effort had met with success. His Lord thus dealt graciously with him as he endured the trials involved in making himself available to others; indeed, whether you came to him by night or by day, you would always find him.

I went to see him one day and asked permission to go in, but I was told, "You'll have to wait for a bit." This left me feeling unsettled, and I thought: The shaykh must have heard something about me which he will insist that I change.

An hour later I was given permission to go in, and he said, "Please forgive me. Shaykh Abū al-Ḥasan's daughter was here, and I hated to cut her off. Believe me, I count myself nothing but a servant."

He would not allow a disciple to be put off if he came to him. He would say, "The disciple comes to me filled with burning aspiration, but if someone says to him, 'Wait for an hour,' the flame with which he came will be extinguished."

In expression of this same spirit, he would not guide a disciple into things which would cause him hardships and troubles, nor would he require such things of him. He used to quote his shaykh, Abū al-Ḥasan, as having said, "The true man is not one who leads you into difficulty, but rather, the one who leads you into what will bring you respite."

The foundation of his path, may God be pleased with him, was total centeredness upon God without allowing oneself to be distracted by any other object or concern, and regular spiritual retreats and remembrance of God.

He would assign to each of his disciples the particular discipline which was most suited to him, but he did not like disciples who had no means of livelihood.

He would encourage his disciples to be united in their love for him; however, he would never forbid any of them to see some other shaykh. Rather, he would quote his own shaykh, may God be pleased with him, as saying, "Be my companions, and I will not forbid you to be another's companions as well. If you find a spring sweeter than this one, drink from it."

If any of his disciples adopted a *wird*[15] on his own initiative and based on his own desires, he would insist that he discontinue it.

If he was eulogized in a poem or verses, he would receive the one who had eulogized him, and perhaps even with a gift.

He would honor jurisprudents, scholars and students when they came to him, and if a leader or person of rank came, he would say to his companions, "Introduce me to him."

He was, of all people, the least willing to seek favors from those in positions of worldly power and influence; even so, he would treat them hospitably if they came to him, and might even take a few steps forward to receive them upon their arrival.

He had the utmost reverence for his shaykh, Abū al-Ḥasan, may God be pleased with him, so much so that others used to observe that he considered himself nothing in comparison with him.

If mention was made of the shaykh, may God be pleased with him, he would recite these lines:

I have masters who, so great is their honor and glory,
One would gladly be the ground on which they tread.

And though I may not be counted among them,
By loving them, I, too, receive glory and honor.

If food had been stored up for him, he would refuse to eat it, and he disliked knowing of food or a gift before it had reached him.[16]

If someone did him a kindness, he would not call down blessings on the person in his presence, but only after he had departed.

If he was given a simple gift, he would receive it gladly and enthusiastically, while if he was given a large or sumptuous gift, he would receive it with a reserve that bespoke an inner detachment.

He would never praise a disciple or draw attention to his progress in the presence of his peers lest he be envied, and his canonical prayers were always brief, albeit complete, in explanation of which he would say, "The substitutes' prayers are light."

When he recited the Qur'ān, you would feel as though the entire universe was listening to him, and one year he prayed the special Ramaḍān evening prayers for the entire year. Then he said, "I recited the Qur'ān this year as though I were reciting it to the Messenger of God ﷺ." The following Ramaḍān rolled around and he said, "I recited it this year as though I were reciting it to Gabriel, upon him be peace." When the third Ramaḍān arrived, he said, "I recited this year as though I were reciting to God, mighty and majestic be He."

When the Night of Power had arrived, he would inform his companions. On that night, he would utter three times the same supplications which he uttered every night. And he would say, "Thanks be to God, all of our times are a 'night of power!'"

On this same theme, one of our peers recited the following verses to some followers of the path, saying:

Had I not witnessed Your beauty within me,
I would not be content with so much as an hour of my life.

What is the magnificent Night of Power
If my [other] hours are not filled with You?

Once the lover has mastered love and its passion,
What need has he of special meeting times?

One year the jurisprudent Makīn al-Dīn al-Asmar, may God be pleased with him, came and said to him, "Master, I witnessed the Night of Power, but not as I have in years past. This year, it was lightless."

"Makīn al-Din," he replied, "its light was outshone by yours!"

I was once with Shaykh Makīn al-Dīn al-Asmar at Alexandria's western mosque during the last ten days of Ramaḍān. On the 26th of the month, he said, "I see angels ascending and descending as if they were making ready for something. Have you not seen the way families make preparations on the night before a wedding? That's what I see the angels doing." The following night, that is, the 27th of the month and a Friday, he said, "Now I see angels with saucers of light; one of them is parallel to the minaret, and there are others above it and below it. This is the Night of

Power." On the third night, that is, the night of the 28th, he said, "I saw tonight as though it were angry and saying, 'Suppose the Night of Power does have the right to be recognized. Well, don't I have the right to be recognized, too?'"

Shaykh Makīn al-Dīn al-Asmar, may God be pleased with him, was a man of discernment and keen insight who had drawn near to God, mighty and majestic be He. Shaykh Abū al-Ḥasan al-Shādhilī, may God be pleased with him, used to say of him, "Among you there is a man known as ᶜAbdullāh Ibn Manṣūr, with black skin and a white heart. I tell you truly, he discloses things to me when I am with my family or on my bed."

Shaykh Abū al-Ḥasan also said of him, "Never have I traversed one of God's unseen realms but that his turban was beneath my feet."

Shaykh Makīn al-Dīn al-Asmar told me, "I once entered the mosque of the Prophet Daniel in Alexandria (in al-Dīmās), and as I came in, I found the prophet who was buried there, clothed in a striped outer garment and praying. He said to me, 'Come pray in front of me.'

'No, you pray in front of me,' I replied.

'You pray in front of me,' he said, 'for you belong to the nation of a prophet whom we should not attempt to precede.'

I said to him, 'By the honor of this prophet, you *must* pray in front of me!'

But just as I was saying, 'By the honor of this prophet,' he placed his mouth over mine out of reverence for the word 'prophet,' to keep it from emerging into the air.

So I came and prayed in front of him."

Shaykh Makīn al-Dīn al-Asmar also told me, "One Friday night I spent the night at the Qarāfah Cemetery. When the [other] visitors rose, I rose with them. They were reciting the Qur'ān, and they continued reciting until they reached Sūrat Yūsuf, upon him be peace, and specifically, the verse in which God states, 'Joseph's brothers came.' They concluded their visit with the tombs of Joseph's brothers. When we got there, I saw a tomb split open, and out of it emerged a tall man with a sparse beard, a small head and a dark complexion who said, 'Who told you our story? That is exactly what happened to us!'"

One day as I was lying down, feeling calm and tranquil, a disturbance suddenly came over me, and I felt impelled to go meet with Shaykh Makīn al-Dīn al-Asmar, may God be pleased with him. I got up quickly and knocked on his door, whereupon he came out. When he saw me, he smiled and said, "Don't come until people come marching behind you!"

"[But] I have come, sir," I said.

He then went inside and brought a vessel out to me, saying, "Take this to Shaykh Abū al-ᶜAbbās and say to him, 'I've written verses from the Qur'ān in it and washed them off with zamzam water and a bit of honey.'"

So I took the vessel to Shaykh Abū al-ᶜAbbās, may God be pleased with him.

"What's this?" he asked.

"It was sent to you by the jurisprudent Makīn al-Dīn al-Asmar," I told him.

He dipped a single finger into it and said, "This is for the blessing."

He then emptied the vessel and filled it with honey, saying, "Take it back to the jurisprudent."

So I took it back to him. When I returned to see him later, he said, "Yesterday I saw angels who had brought me glass containers filled with drink, and they said to me, 'Take this in place of what you gave to Shaykh Abū al-ᶜAbbās, may God be pleased with you both.'"

Shaykh Abū al-ᶜAbbās, may God be pleased with him, was full of hope for God's servants, with a special proclivity for seeing the wideness of God's mercy.

Moreover, may God be pleased with him, he used to relate to people in accordance with their standing before God. He might, for example, be visited by someone living a life of obedience to God, yet pay him little attention, while someone who had been disobedient might come to see him and be treated with deference and hospitality, the reason being that the obedient person had come with an attitude of arrogant pride in his good works, while the disobedient person had come broken-hearted over his disobedience and in a spirit of meekness and submissiveness born of his transgression.[17]

He had a profound dislike for obsessive doubts concerning one's ritual purity and the validity of one's canonical prayers, and he found it burdensome to be with people who were prone to such preoccupations. One day when I was with him, someone said to him, "Master, so-and-so is a man of knowledge and integrity, but he's prone to obsessive doubts."

"Where is his knowledge and integrity, then?" the shaykh asked. "[True] knowledge is imprinted on the heart as whiteness [inheres] in that which is white and as blackness [inheres] in that which is black."

Chapter Five

On Verses from the Book of God, Exalted Be He, Whose Meaning He Clarified and Whose Import He Expounded

God, glory be to Him, says, "Praise be to God, the Cherisher and Sustainer of all the worlds."[1] Commenting on these words, the shaykh, may God be pleased with him, stated, "God, aware of His creatures' inability to praise Him [as truly befits Him], praised Himself in His pre-eternal existence. When He then brought creatures into being, He called upon them to praise Him in the words with which He had praised Himself, by saying, 'Praise be to God, the Cherisher and Sustainer of all the worlds.' In other words, it was as if He were saying to them, 'Say: Praise be to God, the Cherisher and Sustainer of all the worlds.' Moreover, the praise with which He praised Himself is for Him alone, and must not be for anyone or anything else. Hence, the definite article which precedes the word 'Praise' [in the Arabic] reflects the fact that these words are part of a covenantal relationship between creatures and God alone."

Concerning the subsequent phrase, "Thee alone do we worship, and unto Thee alone do we turn for aid," I heard him say, "'Thee alone do we worship' is law (*sharīᶜah*), and 'unto Thee alone do we turn for aid' is reality (*ḥaqīqah*). 'Thee alone do we worship' is surrender (*islām*), and 'unto Thee alone do we turn for aid' is virtue (*iḥsān*). 'Thee alone do we worship' is adoration (*ᶜibādah*), and 'unto Thee alone do we turn for aid' is servanthood (*ᶜubūdiyah*). 'Thee alone do we worship' is separation (*farq*), and 'unto Thee alone do we turn for aid' is union (*jamᶜ*)."

Know—may God have mercy upon you by drawing near to you in His love and cause you to be among those who are faithful to His covenant—that God, glory be to Him, has called upon His servants to worship Him, and to indicate this in words just as they have already done so in action.

He requires His servants to affirm His singularity.

He calls upon them to allow their worship to bring order to both their outward faculties and their inward reality and experience.

He likewise calls upon them to turn toward Him and away from claims of self-sufficiency in worship through a sincere renunciation of the claim to their own power and strength.

Hence, when the servant worships God through concrete action, the Truth requires that he acknowledge his worship through spoken words as well, in order that this might be a covenantal agreement between him and the Truth, mighty and majestic be He. If, then, the servant falls away from worship [at one time or another] and finds it burdensome to persevere in obedience to God's prescriptions, God's claim upon him will be vindicated due to the verbal acknowledgment which he has given to God, glory be to Him, that he worships none but Him ("Thee alone do we worship").

Moreover, by using the words, "we worship," God requires that His servants' worship of Him encompass both their outward faculties and their inner beings as well. Commenting on God's use of the plural pronoun "we" rather than the singular "I," [the shaykh notes that] the use of the pronoun "we" generally indicates that the speaker is either someone who regards himself as very important or someone who enjoys power and lofty status. However, neither of these situations applies here, since the servant does not come before God in the capacity of someone powerful or important; hence, we have no choice but to conclude that the "we" here refers to a single entity accompanied by others, the "others" being the totality of one's outward faculties and inward being.

As for God's requirement that His servants turn toward Him and away from claims of self-sufficiency in worship, this may be seen in the fact that when He says, "Thee alone do we worship," He attributes the act of worship to His servants, requiring that they acknowledge this within the realm of separation (*farq*) which results in the religious prescriptions which God lays down for His servants (*taklīf*). Then He adds, "and unto Thee alone do we turn for aid" lest the servants claim that they worship on their own initiative and by their own strength. Wanting us to do justice to both reality (*ḥaqīqah*) and law (*sharīᶜah*), He has joined the two: performance of worship in recognition of His lordship, and renunciation of claims to our own power and strength in recognition of His divinity.

He then says, glory be to Him, "Show us the straight way." Concerning this verse the shaykh, may God be pleased with him, said, "[This supplication] is a plea for God to establish the one praying in what he has already attained, and to guide him toward that which he has not yet attained." This interpretation is mentioned by Ibn ᶜAṭiyah in his commentary, and simplified by the shaykh as follows: "When ordinary believers pray saying, 'Show us the straight way' in a plea for God to establish them in what they have already attained and to guide them toward that which they have not yet attained, they do so having attained to belief in the divine unity, but without having yet attained to the ranks of the righteous.

When the righteous say, "Show us the straight way" in a plea for God to establish them in what they have already attained and to guide them toward that which they have not yet attained, they do so having attained to righteousness, yet without having attained to the ranks of the martyrs.

When martyrs say, "Show us the straight way" in a plea for God to establish them in what they have already attained and to guide them toward that which they have not yet attained, they do so having attained to the ranks of martyrs, yet without having attained to the ranks of the just and veracious (*al-ṣiddīqīn*).

When the just and veracious say, "Show us the straight way" in a plea for God to establish them in what they have already attained and to guide them toward that which they have not yet attained, they do so having attained to the ranks of the just and veracious, yet without having attained to the ranks of the poles.

And when the pole says, "Show us the straight way" in a plea for God to establish him in what he has already attained and to guide him toward that which he has not yet attained, he does so having attained to the rank of polehood, yet without having attained to knowledge which, had God wished to do so, He would have revealed to him.

***

Commenting on the verses which speak of those "who believe in [the existence of] that which is beyond the reach of human perception, and are constant in prayer..." {Al-Baqarah [The Cow] 2:3}, the shaykh stated that, "Every passage in which those who pray are mentioned by way of praise speaks of those who are constant in prayer, either by use of the specific phrase "being constant in prayer" (*al-*

iqāmah), or by the use of some phrase with a closely related meaning. God, glory be to Him, says:

- "O my Sustainer, cause me and [some] of my offspring to remain constant in prayer!" {Ibrāhīm [Abraham] 14:40}.
- "Be constant in prayer..." {Al-Isrā' [The Night Journey] 17:78}.
- "Only he should visit or tend God's houses of worship who believes in God and is constant in prayer..." (Al-Tawbah [Repentance] 9:18}.
- "[It is] they who [truly] follow God's revelation, and are constant in prayer..." {Al-Fāṭir [The Originator] 35:29}.
- "And give thou the glad tiding [of God's acceptance] unto all who are humble...and all who are constant in prayer" {Al-Ḥajj [The Pilgrimage] 22:34-35}.

When mentioning those who pray as being negligent or inattentive, He declares, "Woe, then, unto those praying ones whose hearts from their prayer are remote" {Al-Mā'ūn [Assistance] 107:4-5}. He does not say, "Woe unto those who are constant in prayer." Constancy in prayer is a situation in which, when a believer performs a prayer and it is accepted by God, God creates, out of this prayer, an image in His kingdom, bowing and prostrating until the Day of Resurrection, the reward for which goes to the person who performed the prayer.

***

Commenting on God's words, glory be to Him, "Behold, God bids you to sacrifice a cow" {Al-Baqarah [The Cow] 2:67), the shaykh said, "each person's 'cow' is himself, and God bids him to sacrifice it."

***

God declares, "Whatever good happens to thee is from God; and whatever evil befalls thee is from thyself" (Al-Nisā' [Women] 4:79). Commenting on this verse, the shaykh said, "It has been said that the manner in which this verse is worded is a kind of chastisement from God in that He attributes good things to Himself and evils to us, despite the fact that all of the servant's actions, be they good or bad, are God's creation. As He has stated, "Thy Sustainer willed it that when they came of age they should bring forth their treasure..." {Al-Kahf [The Cave] 18:82},[2] thereby attributing the action to God. Concerning the ship,[3] he [al-Khaḍir] says, "As for that boat, it belonged to some needy people who toiled upon the sea—and I desired to damage it because [I knew that] behind them was a king who is wont to seize every boat by brute force" {Al-Kahf [The Cave] 18:79}. In order to express himself in the most seemly manner, he [al-Khaḍir] refrained from saying, "Your Sustainer desired to damage it." Similarly, Abraham, upon him be peace, declared, "...and when I fall ill, [God] is the One who restores me to health" {Al-Shuᶜarā' [The Poets] 26:80}, thus attributing illness to himself and healing to God, exalted be He.

There are those who say that this [that all things are from God] is implied in what is being said [in these verses], and that these statements are simply quotes by God of things His servants have said. "But what hath come to these people, that they fail to understand a single fact?" {Al-Nisā' [Women] 4:78}.[4] "Whatever good happens to thee is from God; and whatever evil befalls thee is from thyself" {4:79}; however, God likewise tells the Prophet, "Say: 'All is from God'" {4:78}.

***

"God merges Night into Day, and He merges Day into Night" {Al-Ḥajj [The Pilgrimage] 22:61}.[5] Commenting on this verse the shaykh said, may God be pleased with him, "He merges disobedience into obedience, and He merges obedience into disobedience. When the servant obeys, he is impressed with his own obedience, whereupon he comes to rely upon it, feeling contempt for those who do not do likewise and expecting God to reward him for it. This, then, is a good deed encompassed by evil ones. When, on the other hand, the servant commits sin, he takes refuge in God, seeks His forgiveness, and feels contempt for himself while holding in high regard those who do not do as he has; this is an evil deed encompassed by good ones. Which of them, then, is obedience, and which is disobedience?"

***

God, exalted be He, stated, "Said some of them, 'We heard a youth speak of these [gods with scorn]: he is called Abraham'" {Al-Anbiyā' [The Prophets] 21:60}.

Commenting on this verse, he said, may God be pleased with him, "The heroic youth is the one who shatters the idols."[6]

***

"Who is it that responds to the distressed when he calls out to Him?" {Al-Naml [The Ants] 27:62}. Concerning these words of God, mighty and majestic be He, he said, "The saint is constantly in distress." What the shaykh meant by this statement is that ordinary people only sense their great need for God in the face of certain distressing life events. Once these events are past, however, their sense of need for God likewise passes. The reason for this is that their vision is dominated by the realm of sensory experience. For if they could see God's complete, all-encompassing grip [upon all that exists], they would know that their need for God is never-ending. After all, the creature's need for God is a function of the servant's essential nature, since he is a contingent being, and every contingent being is in need of an external source of supply, as it were. Moreover, just as the Truth, glory be to Him, is ever and always the Self-Sufficient One, so also is the servant ever and always in need of Him. Nor does this need ever cease for the servant, whether in this life or in the life to come. For even if he enters Paradise he will need God there, although his sense of neediness will be submerged in the grace in whose raiment he will be clothed. These are realities the outcome of which is unchanging, whether in the world of the seen or the world of the unseen, whether in this world or in the world to come.

For knowledge is characterized by disclosure, regardless of what kind of knowledge it is or at what time it is revealed, while will is characterized by specificity, whatever will it happens to be and at whatever time it comes about; yet even those whose lights have expanded never cease to need God.

God reproaches people who seek refuge in Him when faced with distressing circumstances which force them to do so but who, once the circumstances are past, no longer sense their need for Him. He declares:

- "Whenever danger befalls you at sea, all those [powers] that you are wont to invoke forsake you, [and nothing remains for you] save Him; but as soon as He has brought you safe ashore, you turn aside [and forget Him]—for, indeed, bereft of all gratitude is man!" {Al-Isrā' [The Night Journey] 17:67}

- "For [thus it is]: when affliction befalls man, he cries out unto Us, whether he be lying on his side or sitting or standing. But as soon as We have freed him of his affliction, he goes on as though he had never invoked us to save him from the affliction that befell him! Thus do their own doings seem goodly unto those who waste their own selves" {Yūnus [Jonah] 10:12}.
- "Say: 'Who is it that saves you from the dark dangers of land and sea [when] you call unto Him humbly, and in the secrecy of your own heart: If He will but save us from this distress, we shall most certainly be among the grateful?' Say: 'God alone can save you from this and every distress—and still you ascribe divinity to other powers beside Him!'" {Al-Ancām [Cattle] 6:63-64}

There are, in addition, numerous other verses which convey the same meaning.

Given that the minds of ordinary people are unable to grasp the truths reflected in their inward beings, the Truth afflicts them with [outward] conditions which alert them to their need for Him, thereby enabling them to experience the overwhelming power of His lordship and the greatness of His divinity and majesty. The supreme importance of a sense of one's need for God is evidenced by the fact that the Truth, glory be to Him, has made His answer to prayer conditional upon it, saying, "Who is it that responds to the distressed when he calls out to Him?" {Al-Naml [The Ants] 27:62}

If God, glory be to Him, wishes to give a servant something, He gives him a sense of his need to seek it from Him; consequently, he asks God for it with a sense of need and He gives it to him. If, on the other hand, God wishes to deny a servant something, He denies him a sense of his need to ask Him for it and, as a consequence, denies him the thing itself such that God may rightly say to the servant, "If you had sensed your need and asked for it, We would have given it to you." Hence, there is no danger that you might, sensing your need, ask God for something and not be given it; rather, the danger is that you might be denied the sense of need, as a consequence of which you are denied the act of making the request, or that you might make the request without a sense of need, and hence not be given it.

***

God tells us, mighty and majestic be He, that "Whenever Zachariah visited her in the sanctuary, he found her provided with food. He would ask, 'O Mary, whence came this unto thee?' She would answer, 'It is from God; behold, God grants sustenance unto whom He wills, beyond all reckoning" {Āl ᶜImrān [The House of ᶜImrān] 3:37}. Moreover, God said to Mary, "Shake the trunk of the palm tree towards thee; it will drop fresh, ripe dates upon thee" {Maryam [Mary] 19:25}. Concerning these verses, he said, "Some people have offered an interpretation of these passages which is not acceptable and which should be given no consideration, namely, that in the beginning, Mary loved God alone, but that when she gave birth, her love was divided. Those who put forward this interpretation are mistaken, because Mary was a woman of truth (*ṣiddīqah*). As God declared of her, "His [Christ's] mother was a woman of truth" {Al-Mā'idah [The Repast] 5:75}. Now, the man or woman of truth will never shift from a given state to one that is inferior, but only to one which is superior. From the beginning, Mary was recognized as someone whose life was marked by the miraculous and the suspension of the usual laws of cause and effect; then when her certainty [in faith] reached perfection, she was brought back to a dependence on [ordinary] causality. Hence, the latter state was superior to the former one.

***

The shaykh, may God be pleased with him, said, "True youthful valor consists in faith and right guidance. As God has declared, 'They were youths who believed in their Lord, and We advanced them in guidance' {Al-Kahf [The Cave] 18:13}."

***

Reporting the words of Satan, God says, "Then will I assault them from before them and behind them, from their right and their left; nor wilt Thou find, in most of them, gratitude" {Al-Aᶜrāf [The Faculty of Discernment] 7:17}.[7] Commenting on this passage, the shaykh, may God be pleased with him, said, "He [Satan] did not say that he would assault believers from above or below; after all, above them is belief in the divine unity, and below them is surrender to God (*islām*), and Satan can approach neither the believer's faith in the divine unity nor his surrender to God."

***

Concerning God's words, "For God did take Abraham for a friend" {Al-Nisā' [Women] 4:125}, the shaykh, may God be pleased with him, stated, "He was called a 'friend' (*khalīl*) because his inmost being had been permeated (*khālala*) with God's love. As one poet expressed it:

> You have permeated (*takhallalta*) my spirit and its path.
> Thus is the friend called a friend (*khalīl*).

If I speak, You are my words,
And if I am silent, you are a burning thirst.[8]

***

Speaking of God's reference to "Abraham, who to his trust was true..." {Al-Najm [The Unfolding] 53:37}, he said, "He was true to his trust by virtue of his saying, 'God is my sufficiency.'"

***

God, glory be to Him, speaks of those who "in the hours of early dawn [are found] praying for forgiveness" {Al-Dhāriyāt [The Dust-Scattering Winds] 51:18}. Commenting on this verse, the shaykh, may God be pleased with him, said, "[They are seeking forgiveness for] the acts of obedience and the things which they have done for God during the night [for fear that they might] view them as having originated with themselves." Evidence for what the shaykh said, may God be pleased with him, may be found in the fact that God, mighty and majestic be He, describes such individuals immediately before this as sleeping only "a small part of the night." Hence, they have committed no sin during the night for which they would need to ask forgiveness.

We know from authentic Prophetic hadiths that after completing any of the canonical prayers, the Prophet ﷺ would pray three times for God's forgiveness. And al-Wāsiṭī states, "When it comes to acts of worship, it is [almost] more fitting to seek forgiveness for them than it is to seek reward."

God, exalted be He, declares, "Say, 'In [this] bounty of God and in His grace—in this, then, let them rejoice: it is better than all that they may amass!" {Yūnus [Jonah] 10:58} In other words, it is better than all the acts of worship and good deeds they might amass. This same truth is likewise conveyed in God's saying, mighty and majestic is He, "and this thy Sustainer's grace is better than all that they may amass" {Zukhruf [Gold] 43:32}.

***

God, mighty and majestic is He, declares, "Limitless in His glory is He who transported His servant by night..." {Al-Isrā' [The Night Journey] 17:1}. Concerning these words, the shaykh said, "God does not say here that He transported His Prophet or His Messenger, although he [Muḥammad] was both God's Prophet and His Messenger. Rather, He refers to him here as His *servant* because He desires to open the door to such [supernatural] transport to his followers as well, thereby communicating to us that such a night journey is possible simply by virtue of one's servanthood. The Prophet ﷺ was possessed of perfect servanthood and was granted, accordingly, the perfect night journey in that God transported both his spirit and his body, both his outward frame and his inward being. God's friends enjoy a measure of servanthood; hence, they are granted a measure of [the Prophet's] night journey in that God transports their spirits, but not their bodies.

***

God declares, "Behold, the God-conscious will find themselves in a [paradise of] gardens and running water, in a seat of truth in the presence of a Sovereign who determines all things" {Al-Qamar [The Moon] 54:54-55}. Concerning these words I heard him say, may God be pleased with him, "'Behold, the God-conscious are in [a paradise of] gardens and running water' both in this world and the world to come. In this world, they are in the gardens of knowledge and the rivers of the gnostic sciences, while in the world to come, they will be in the Garden which they have been promised. They are in a 'seat of truth' both in this life and in the life to come; likewise, they are, both in this world and the next, 'in the presence of a Sovereign who determines all things.'"

The essence of what the shaykh said, may God be pleased with him, is that the subtleties of the bliss of paradise are made available to the God-conscious in the here and now such that what they will enjoy in Paradise on a sensory level, they enjoy now on a spiritual level. This same truth is reflected in the verse which states, "Behold, the truly virtuous will be in bliss" {Al-Infiṭār [The Cleaving Asunder] 82:13}.[9] In other words, they are in bliss in this world, just as they will be in bliss in the life to come. In this world, they enjoy the bliss of witnessing (*shuhūd*) [of the lights and divine realities which God discloses to them], while in the world to come they will enjoy the bliss of the vision [of God Himself] (*ru'yah*).

As for the wicked, God declares that they "will be[10] in a blazing fire" {82:14}. In other words, they are in such a fire both in this life and in the life to come. In this life, they are in the blazing fire of alienation, and in the life to come, they will be in the blazing fire of punishment.

[The God-conscious] are "in a seat of truth" both in this life and in the life to come. In this life, they are in the seat of truth in which they are placed by virtue of their servanthood, and in the life to come, they will be in the seat of truth by virtue of being God's elect. Likewise, they are "in the presence of a Sovereign who determines all things" both in this life and in the life to come. In this life, they experience His presence through the spiritual riches (*amdād*) to which He gives them access, and in the life to come, through direct vision (*ashhād*).

***

"Nowise has God created this but in truth..." {Yūnus [Jonah] 10:5}.[11] Concerning this verse the shaykh said, may God be pleased with him, "The truth with which God created everything was the word, 'Be'. God, glory be to Him, declared, 'Whenever He says, "Be," His word comes true' {Al-Anᶜām [Cattle] 6:73}."

***

Concerning God's words, "Be grateful towards Me and towards thy parents" (Luqmān 31:14}, he said, "The reason He links gratitude towards them [your parents] with gratitude towards Him is that your parents have a share in bringing you into existence."

***

"'Now, what is this in thy right hand, O Moses?' He answered, 'It is my staff; I lean on it, and with it I beat down leaves for my sheep. And [many] other uses have I for it.' Said He, 'Throw it down, O Moses!' So he threw it—and lo! It was a snake moving rapidly. Said He, 'Take hold of it, and fear not: We shall restore it to its former state'" {Ṭā Hā [O Man] 20:17-21}.

Concerning these verses, the shaykh, may God be pleased with him, said, "The saint is asked, 'What is that in your hand?' 'It is my earthly existence,' he replies. 'I lean on it, and with it I beat down leaves for my sheep (his sheep being his bodily members). And I have numerous other uses for it as well.' He is then told, 'Throw it down by absenting yourself from it.'[12] So he throws it down, whereupon its true nature is revealed to him and he sees that it is, in fact, 'a snake moving rapidly.' He is then told, 'Now, take hold of it and fear not.' He takes hold of it again, and is not harmed by it because he has taken hold of it by God's permission just as he cast it down by God's permission. Hence, he takes it up again in the same way that he initially cast it down: in obedience to God."

***

"And on the day when the skies, together with the clouds, shall burst asunder, and the angels are made to descend in a mighty descent—on that day [it will become obvious to all that] true sovereignty belongs to the Most Gracious [alone]..." {Al-Furqān [The Standard of True and False] 25:25-26}.

Concerning these words of God, glory be to Him, he said, "God states here that true sovereignty will be seen to belong solely to the Most Gracious, and not to the Irresistible, Almighty One, since the bursting asunder of the skies and the clouds and the angels' mighty descent are manifestations of God's overwhelming power and authority. Hence, had He used the terms Irresistible and Almighty to speak of Himself here, His creatures would be unable to bear it and their hearts would be broken. Consequently, He says that on that Day true sovereignty will be seen to belong to 'the Most Gracious'. The same consideration applies, moreover, when God speaks of 'the Day when We shall gather the God-conscious unto [Us], the Most Gracious, as honored guests...' {Maryam [Mary] 19:85}. He does not say 'unto the Irresistible, Almighty One,' since God's gathering of His creatures evokes images of a frightful, dismaying event; hence, He demonstrates His kindness and mercy toward us in the manifestations of His authority and mighty power."

***

"O you who have attained to faith! Be conscious of God with all the consciousness that is due to Him, and do not allow death to overtake you ere you have surrendered yourselves unto Him" {Āl ᶜImrān [The House of ᶜImrān] 3:102}.

In connection with these words of God, the shaykh was once asked, "How can the servant possibly be conscious of God with all the consciousness that is due to Him? And how can he possibly die having surrendered himself unto Him?"

The shaykh, may God be pleased with him, replied, "It has been said that this verse was abrogated by God's exhortation, 'Remain, then, conscious of God as best you can...' {Al-Taghābun [Loss and Gain] 64:16}. People were first addressed with the words, 'Be conscious of God with all the consciousness that is due to Him'; in other words, they were commanded to obey God and never to disobey Him, to remember Him and never to forget Him, to thank Him and never to deny His bounty. Later, however, God mitigated this demand, saying, 'Remain, then, conscious of God as best you can.'"

Then he continued, "These two verses may also be brought together as follows: The words, 'Remain, then, conscious of God as best you can' apply to the level of concrete action, while the words, 'Be conscious of God with all the consciousness that is due to Him' apply to the level of belief in the divine unity. As for God's command, 'And do not allow death to overtake you ere you surrender yourselves unto Him,' it means that we should perform only those actions which, were we to die while engaging in them, we would die in a state of surrender to God."

***

He said, may God be pleased with him, "One day as I prayed the dawn prayer behind the shaykh [Abū al-Ḥasan], he recited the surah which begins with the letters *ḥā, mim, ᶜayn, sīn, qāf.* When he came to the words, 'He bestows the gift of female offspring on whomever He wills' {Al-Shūrā [Consultation] 42:49}, it occurred to me that through the phrase 'female offspring' God was speaking of good works. He then recited the words, '...and the gift of male offspring on whomever He wills' (42:49), and I thought to myself that the phrase 'male offspring' must refer to various types of knowledge. He continued reciting with the words, '...or He gives both male and female [to whomever He wills].' 'Both knowledge and good works,' I thought to myself. And as he recited the words, 'and causes to be barren whomever He wills,' I thought, 'neither knowledge nor good works.'

When the shaykh had completed his prayer, he summoned me and said, 'I realize that during the prayer, you understood the words, "He bestows the gift of female offspring on whomever He wills" as referring to good works, the words, "male offspring" to refer to the various branches of knowledge, the words, "or...both male and female" as referring to both knowledge and good works, and the word, "barren..." as referring to those who are given neither knowledge nor good works.'

I was amazed that the shaykh would be aware of how I had understood these verses.

He asked me, 'Are you amazed that I should be aware of what you were thinking during the prayer? So-and-so understood the verses in question to mean such-and-such, while so-and-so understood them to mean such-and-such,' whereupon he proceeded to enumerate the interpretations of everyone who had prayed behind him that morning."

***

"Behold, Satan is a foe to you, so treat him as a foe" {Fāṭir [The Originator] 35:6}. May God be pleased with him, he commented on this verse saying, "There are those who have understood these words to mean that they are commanded to demonstrate enmity toward Satan. However, they have so preoccupied themselves with this enmity that they have been distracted from loving the Beloved. There are, in addition, those who have understood this verse to mean, 'Satan is an enemy to you, and I, therefore, am your Beloved.' Given this understanding, they have devoted themselves to loving Him, as a result of which He has preserved them from all who are other than Him."

Someone was once asked, "How could [God] have created you with Satan?"

"And what of Satan?" he replied. "We are a people who have so centered our aspirations on God that He has preserved us from all who are other than Him."

***

May God be pleased with him, he said, "I was once reciting the surah which begins, 'Consider the fig and the olive...,' and I came to the verse which reads, 'Verily, We create man in the best conformation, and thereafter We reduce him to the lowest of low' {Al-Tīn [The Fig] 95:4-5}. As I thought about the meaning of these verses, the 'Imperishable Tablet' was disclosed to me, and upon it were written the words, 'We create man in the best conformation in spirit and mind, and thereafter We reduce him to the lowest of low in self-indulgence and craving.'"

***

"And, indeed, she desired him, and he desired her; [and he would have succumbed] had he not seen [in this temptation] an evidence of his Sustainer's truth" {Yūsuf [Joseph] 12:24}.

Commenting on this verse, he said, "She[13] desired him with the will to act on her desire, whereas he [Joseph] desired her not with the will to act on his desire, but rather, with a [mere] sense of longing."

***

"God turned with favor to the Prophet, the Muhājirs, and the Anṣār—who followed him in a time of distress, after that the hearts of a part of them had nearly swerved [from duty]; but He turned to them also" {Al-Tawbah [Repentance] 9:117}.[14]

In speaking on this verse, he quoted his own shaykh, Abū al-Ḥasan, may God be pleased with him, who said, "God mentions the repentance of those who had committed no transgression[15] lest those who *had* been guilty of transgression lose hope. He first mentions the Prophet, the Emigrants and the Helpers, none of whom were guilty of wrongdoing; then in the following verse He mentions 'the three who were left behind.'[16] He first made mention of those who had not committed wrongdoing in order to bring solace to those who had done so, for if He had first said that God had turned in mercy to the three who had been left behind, their hearts would have been broken."

***

May God be pleased with him, he said, "God-consciousness as set forth in the Book of God falls into several categories: consciousness of the Fire, as in God's saying, 'And beware of the fire [which awaits those who deny the truth]!'

{Āl ᶜImrān [The House of ᶜImrān] 3:131}; consciousness of the Day of Judgement: 'And be conscious of the day on which you shall be brought back unto God' {Al-Baqarah [The Cow] 2:281}; consciousness of God's lordship: 'O mankind! Be conscious of your Sustainer'[17] {Al-Nisā' [Women] 4:1}; consciousness of God's divinity: 'And remain conscious of God' {Al-Nisā' [Women] 4:1}; and consciousness of God's selfhood: 'Remain, then, conscious of Me' {Al-Baqarah [The Cow] 2:197}."

***

Commenting on God's reference to "those who eagerly listen to any falsehood, greedily swallowing all that is evil" {Al-Mā'idah [The Repast] 5:42}, he said, "These words were revealed of the Jews, and of all the [spiritually] poverty-stricken of this age who have a predilection for hearing whatever suits their fancy and who consume that which has been forbidden by their Master." This, he says, "is a Jewish tendency, because the prattler speaks of romantic love without being in love himself, of charity without being charitable, and of ecstasy without having tasted ecstasy for himself. Such a person utters lies, and his listeners hear him eagerly. Moreover, those of the poor who, when invited to listen, partake of the food of oppressors, are rightly described by God as "those who eagerly listen to any falsehood, greedily swallowing all that is evil."

***

Once he related, may God be pleased with him, that "some of the Prophet's Companions happened upon some Jews as they were reciting the Torah, and were moved [to humble reverence]. When, after this, they came in to see the Messenger of God ﷺ, Gabriel, upon him be peace, descended upon him saying, 'Recite!'

'What shall I recite?' he asked.

Gabriel replied, 'Recite: "Why—is it not enough for them that We have bestowed this divine writ on thee from on high, to be conveyed [by thee] to them?" {Al-ᶜAnkabūt [The Spider] 29:51}.'

Thus, they were reproached for allowing themselves to be moved by some other book. And if the Companions were reproached for being moved by the Torah, which is God's word, how much more worthy of reproach, then, are those who turn away from the Book of God and are moved by worldly diversions and singing?"

***

Once someone asked him, may God be pleased with him, "Master, when Jesus, peace be upon him, said, 'If Thou cause them to suffer—verily, they are Thy servants; and if Thou forgive them—verily, Thou alone art almighty, truly wise!' {Al-Mā'idah [The Repast] 5:118}, why did he refer to God as "almighty, truly wise" and not as 'oft-forgiving, most merciful'?"

"The reason for this," he replied, "is that if he had said, 'and if Thou forgive them—verily, Thou alone are the oft-forgiving, most merciful,' this would have constituted intercession for them on Jesus's part in a plea for them to be forgiven. However, there can be no intercession for those who are bent on denying the truth. Moreover, given the fact that Jesus had been worshipped beside God, he was reticent to intercede with Him."

***

"Had We bestowed this Qur'ān from on high upon a mountain, thou wouldst indeed see it humbling itself, breaking asunder for awe of God" {Al-Ḥashr [The Gathering] 59:21}.

Commenting on this verse, the shaykh said, may God be pleased with him, "This verse contains praise for the chief of God's messengers ﷺ, as though through it God were saying, 'If this Qur'ān had been bestowed from on high upon the mountains, they would not have withstood it; but you, Muḥammad, withstood its descent by the divine strength which We had placed within you!' At the same time, it contains a rebuke for those bent on denying the truth, as though through it God were saying to them, 'Had this Qur'ān been sent down upon a mountain, it would have humbled itself and broken asunder in awe of Me; you, however, have neither humbled yourselves nor broken asunder.'"

***

Observation:

Know that this group's [the Sufis'] interpretation of God's word and the words of His Messenger ﷺ in such a way as to yield certain unexpected meanings—as reflected in the shaykh's statements to the effect that the words, "He bestows the gift of female offspring on whomever He wills" refer to good works, that the words, "He bestows the gift of male offspring on whomever He wills" refer to various types of knowledge, that the words, "...or He gives both male and female [to whomever He wills]" refer to God's granting knowledge and good works, and that the words, "and causes to be barren whomever He wills" refer to God's granting neither knowledge nor good works, as well as his interpretation of God's command "to sacrifice a cow" with the statement that "each person's 'cow' is himself, and God bids him to sacrifice it," and, as will be seen below, God willing, in his interpretation of Prophetic hadiths—know that this is not a denial of the outward or apparent meaning of such texts. Rather, the apparent meaning of each verse is a product of the situation in response to which it was revealed, and the message it yields based on people's customary use of the language. However, there are, in addition, hidden meanings of this or that verse or hadith which are disclosed to those whose hearts God has opened. Accordingly, the Prophet ﷺ declared, "Every verse has both an outward meaning and an inward meaning, a beginning and an end."

Hence, do not allow yourself to be dissuaded from accepting such interpretations by those who, by way of debate or objection, tell you that these are distortions of the words of God and His Messenger ﷺ. For this is not the case. It would, indeed, be a distortion if they were to say, "The verse [in question] has no other meaning." However, they have not said this. On the contrary, they acknowledge the outward meanings of texts as they relate to the topics with which they deal, while at the same time, they arrive at [inward] understandings which God has disclosed to them. In fact, they may understand a given statement to mean the opposite of what was intended by the person who wrote it. As we are told by the great shaykh, imam and mufti Taqī al-Dīn ᶜAlī Ibn Muḥammad al-Qushayrī, may God have mercy on him, "There was a jurisprudent in Baghdad known as al-Jawzī who was well-versed in no fewer than twelve branches of learning. One day as he was setting out for his school, he heard someone reciting:

> When the 20th of Shaᶜbān has passed,
> Carry on with your night's drinking by day,

And drink not from small glasses,
For this is not a time for meager portions.[18]

Having heard these lines, he went out wandering aimlessly until he reached Mecca, where he remained until he died."

Similarly, the following lines of poetry were recited to Shaykh Makīn al-Dīn al-Asmar, may God be pleased with him:

If wine had some happiness to offer me,
I would not wait till a time of fast-breaking to
imbibe.

An extraordinary thing is this wine you drink,
So indulge, though it lay upon you a burden of
guilt.

O ye who censure [others] for partaking of this
reddish limpidity,
Take the gardens [for yourselves] and leave me to
dwell in the Fire!

Someone who heard the recitation said, "It is not permissible to recite such lines."

Addressing the reciter, Shaykh Makīn al-Dīn said, "Go ahead, for this is a man [from whom such truths have been] veiled."

Evidence for what we are saying may be seen in the following example: Three men once a heard a voice saying to them, *yā saᶜtar birrī*, which each of them heard according to the inward understanding he had been given by God. One of them heard the statement, *isᶜa tara birrī*, which means, "Strive, and you will see My faithfulness." The second man heard the statement, *al-sāᶜata tarā birrī*, which means, "Now you will see My faithfulness," while the third man heard the words, *mā awsa^ca birrī*, or, "How all-encompassing is My faithfulness."

A single statement was heard, yet each of those who heard it understood it in a different way. As God, glory be to Him, declared, "[all these tracts of land are] watered with the same water; and yet, some of them have We favored above others by way of the food [which they provide for man and beast]" {Al-Ra^cd [Thunder] 13:4}; "and [remember] when Moses prayed for water for his people and We replied, 'Strike the rock with thy staff!'—whereupon twelve springs gushed forth from it, so that all the people knew whence to drink" {Al-Baqarah [The Cow] 2:60}.

Thus, the person who heard the statement as, "Strive, and you will see My faithfulness" was a disciple who was being exhorted to draw near to God through good deeds so as to take on the challenges of the path in all earnestness. He was thus being told, "Strive toward Me through your sincere manner of dealing with others, and you will see My faithfulness through loving communion [with Me]."

As for the second hearer, he was a traveler along the path to God who had been striving for so long that he had begun to lose patience, fearing that he had missed the mark of reunion [with the Beloved]. Hence, as a way of bringing relief to a heart consumed with longing, he was told, "Now you will see My faithfulness!"

As for the third hearer, he was a gnostic to whom God had disclosed the vastness of His bounty; hence, he was addressed in accordance with his inward vision and he heard, "How all-embracing is My faithfulness."

Shaykh Muḥyī al-Dīn Ibn ^cArabī, may God be pleased with him, said, "We were once invited by some of the poor[19] to a meal in Ziqāq al-Qanādīl in Cairo, where a number of shaykhs gathered. There was so much food that the vessels in which it was served could hardly hold it all. Among these was a new glass pot which had been acquired for use as a urinal but which had not yet been put to use. The host was dipping the food out of it, and as the group ate, it said, "Now that God has honored me by allowing such noble souls to eat from me, never will I allow myself to be a place of offense," whereupon it broke in two.

"Did you hear what the pot said?" I asked them.

"Yes, we did," they replied.

"What did you hear?" I asked.

In reply, they repeated the words above.

"It [also] said something else," I told them.

"What is that?" they queried.

I replied, "It said, 'So it is with your hearts: Now that God has honored them with faith, never again allow them to be the site of the impurity of disobedience and love of the world. God has given you and us understanding from Him and the ability to receive His disclosures thanks to His grace and bounty.'"

The mosque built at Ḥumaythirā, Upper Egypt,
next to the tomb of Abū al-Ḥasan al-Shādhilī

Indeed, I heard the shaykh and imam, the muftī of Islam Taqī al-Dīn Muḥammad Ibn ᶜAlī al-Qushayrī, may God have mercy upon him, say, "Never have I seen anyone more knowledgeable of God than Shaykh Abū al-Ḥasan al-Shādhilī (may God be pleased with him)."

Chapter Six

On Prophetic Hadiths Which He Interpreted And Whose Inner Meanings He Brought to Light Based on Sufi Teachings

The Prophet ﷺ stated, "There are seven types of people to whom God will provide shelter on that Day when there will be no shelter but in Him: the just imam, the young man who grew up worshipping God, the man who, when he left the mosque, remained attached to it inwardly until he returns, two men who came to love one another in God and who both came together and parted in this love, the man who, when allured by a woman of beauty and charm, said, 'I fear God,' the man who, when he remembered God in secret, wept out of fear and reverence for Him, and the man who, when he gave charity, concealed it lest his left hand know what his right hand was doing."

Commenting on this hadith the shaykh said, may God be pleased with him, "The just imam is the heart. The man whose heart remained attached to the mosque until he returned to it is one whose heart is attached to the Throne, since the Throne is the 'mosque' of believers' hearts. As for the man who, when he remembered God in secret, his eyes welled up with tears, he is one who remembers Him without egotism or selfish desire. And as for the man who concealed his almsgiving, he is one who concealed it from himself and his desires [for recognition and praise]."

In this connection the shaykh quoted God's words speaking of [Zachariah, who] "called out to his Sustainer in the secrecy of his heart" {Maryam [Mary] 19:3}, which he understood to mean that he called out to God free of egotism or selfish desire.

[He continued, saying], "Know, then, that these seven will be rewarded by the Truth, glory be to Him, based on their manner of relating to Him in this life. The just imam is the imam who, in dealing with God's servants, provided refuge for the oppressed by virtue of his fairness, as a result of which God will provide refuge for him on that Day when there will be no refuge but in Him.

"The young man who grew up worshipping God took refuge in God from his cravings and passions, seeking shelter beneath His Master's wing. Hence, the Truth will provide him shelter in the world to come as a reward, just as he sought shelter with God in this world as a way of life.

"The man whose heart remained attached to the mosque until he returned to it preferred obedience to God [over all else], having been conquered by God's love to the point where he became so attached to the mosque that he never wanted to part with it, since it was there that he found a sense of nearness and the sweetness of service. He betook himself to God, preferring [the acknowledgment of] His lordship; and God, in turn, will shelter and protect him on that Day when there will be no shelter or protection in anyone but Him, in reward for his former manner of life.

"The two men who came to love one another in God, and who both came together and parted in this love, found communion in the Spirit of God and intimate harmony in His love. Through this love and communion of theirs, they were fleeing to God, as it were. Hence, God will shelter them on that Day when there will be no shelter but in Him.

"The man who, when allured by a woman of beauty and charm, said, 'I fear God,' was exposed to the blaze generated by doing battle with his passions out of fear of his

Master and resisting the natural impulses which militate against the consciousness of God. Because he feared God, he fled to Him, and because he fled to Him in this situation as a way of coping with this life's temptations, God will embrace him in the afterlife in loving communion, sheltering him on that Day when there will be no shelter but in Him.

"As for the man who, when he remembered God in secret, wept out of fear and reverence for Him, his eyes welled up with tears from the wounds which had so pained his heart, whether out of shame before God, longing for Him, fear of His lordly might, or awareness of his negligence toward Him. Hence, when he experienced this in a place where he could be seen by no one but the One and Only Sovereign, this represented a manner of relating to God and fleeing to Him for refuge by seeking His forgiveness and expressing longing for Him. In all of this, he was seeking refuge in God, in response to which God will provide him with shelter on that Day when there will be no shelter but in Him.

"And as for the man who, when he gave charity, concealed it lest his left hand know what his right hand was doing, he preferred God to himself by disposing of his worldly possessions, thereby placing love for God above what he might desire himself. After all, the self's natural inclination is to love worldly possessions and not to dispense with them; hence, the only people who do dispense with them in this way are those who place God above them. It is for this reason that the Messenger of God ﷺ said, "Almsgiving is a proof," that is, a proof that the servant has preferred his Master to himself and his own desires. Hence, because this servant showed his love for God in the way he lived his life, God will bestow His grace upon him by providing him with shelter on that Day when there will be no shelter but in Him.

"These seven types of people have a single quality in common, and it is for this reason that they will receive a single reward. What they have in common is that all of them were exposed to the blazing heat generated by doing battle with their desires and passions in this world, as a result of which God will not allow them to suffer the blazing heat of the afterlife. Speaking on behalf of God, exalted be He, the Prophet ﷺ said, 'I allow my servant neither to suffer a double dread, nor to enjoy a double security: If I grant him comfort in this world, I frighten him in the next, and if I frighten him in this world, I comfort him in the next.'"

The Prophet ﷺ said, "Facilitate, do not make difficult." Commenting on this hadith, the shaykh (may God be pleased with him) said, "In other words, lead people to God, and to nothing else. He who leads you to this world has deceived you, and he who leads you to [good] deeds will wear you down; but he who leads you to God has counseled you aright."

The Prophet ﷺ declared, "When I beheld Paradise, I grasped a cluster [of grapes] which, had I taken it, you could have eaten from till the end of time." Commenting on this hadith, he said, "The Prophets see the realities of things, while the saints see their likenesses. This is why the Apostle ﷺ said, 'I beheld Paradise' rather than saying, 'It was as if I beheld Paradise.'

"When the Messenger of God ﷺ asked Ḥārithah, 'How are you this morning, Ḥārithah?' he replied, 'I woke up a true believer.' The Prophet ﷺ said, 'Every reality has a true nature, so what is the true nature of your faith?

Ḥārithah replied, 'My soul has so shunned this world that its gold and its clay are now the same to me. It is as if I were looking upon the inhabitants of Paradise as they live in bliss, upon those dwelling in the Fire as they are tormented, and upon my Lord's throne, high and lifted up. That is why I spend my nights awake [and in worship], and my daylight hours in thirst.'[1]

The Apostle ﷺ said to him, 'You know [the truth] now, so hold fast to it.'

The Prophet ﷺ then said, 'When one is a servant of God's light, [God] transforms him with the light of faith.'

Ḥārithah said, 'It is as if I were looking upon' rather than, 'I looked upon,' since such direct vision is reserved for the prophets alone. The same truth may be seen in the statement made by Ḥanẓalah al-Asadī to the Messenger of God ﷺ, 'You remind us so vividly of Paradise and the Fire that it is as if we were seeing them with our own eyes.'"

There are ten lessons to be drawn from the hadith concerning Ḥārithah:

First: When the Prophet ﷺ asked Ḥārithah, "How are you this morning, Ḥārithah?", Ḥārithah did not reply, "Rich," "Healthy" or with a description of any sort of bodily condition or worldly state. After all, Ḥārithah knew that the Messenger of God ﷺ was too spiritually minded to ask him a question with such a worldly intent. Rather, he understood that he was asking him about his condition in relation to God. Hence, the Companion replied, saying, "I woke up a true believer."

If, by contrast, those who are steeped in this world are asked such a question, they will only answer in worldly terms. If you ask them, they may tell you about their discontent with their Sovereign's laws and edicts. However, the person who poses such a question to people of this persuasion shares responsibility for the answer he has provoked through his question.

Shaykh Abū al-ʿAbbās, may God be pleased with him, once asked a man who had returned from the pilgrimage to Mecca, "How was your pilgrimage?" The man replied, "Very comfortable, with plentiful water supplies. The price of such-and-such was thus and so, and the price of such-and-such was thus and so." Turning away from the man, the shaykh said, 'You ask them about their pilgrimage, and if they haven't experienced, through it, any of God's light or self-disclosure, they reply with something about the good prices and the plentiful water supplies, as though that were all they had been asked about."

Second: Shaykhs should check up on their disciples' spiritual states, and it is permissible for disciples to inform their spiritual guides concerning such things even if this requires that they disclose [personal] matters. After all, the spiritual guide might be likened to a physician, while the disciple's condition might be likened to someone's private parts, which it is permissible to reveal to a physician when treatment is needed.

Third: Note the radiance of the light exhibited by Ḥārithah in his saying, "I woke up a true believer." If he had not been endowed with the light of perception of the sort that necessitates complete inward certainty and realization through adherence to the Sunnah, he would not have reported on his inward state as he did, describing himself as having genuine faith in the presence of the one who had the knowledge and authority to either confirm or controvert. At the same time, Ḥārithah revealed these things because he knew that since the Messenger of God ﷺ had inquired about his condition, he was duty bound to obey him rather than keeping such things to himself. Hence, he disclosed what he knew God to have graciously bestowed upon him through the blessing of following His Messenger ﷺ.

In this way, he made it possible for the Messenger of God ﷺ to rejoice for him in God's benevolence, to thank God on his behalf, and to ask God to establish him in what he had been given.

Of relevance here is the following account related by a certain gnostic scholar, who said, "An earthquake struck Medina during the caliphate of ᶜUmar [Ibn al-Khaṭṭāb], may God be pleased with him. In response, ᶜUmar said, 'What is this? How quickly you have brought about misfortune! I tell you truly, if this should happen again, I will depart from amongst you!'"

Behold, then—may God have mercy upon you—it was this flawless discernment, which enabled him to see that the earthquake was a result of some event which they themselves had caused, but of which he was innocent. Is this, then, anything other than the light of the perfect spiritual vision which ᶜUmar had been given (may God be pleased with him)?

The same reality may be seen in his [ᶜUmar's] striking of Abū Hurayrah (may God be pleased with him) on his chest when he found Abū Hurayrah holding the Messenger of God's sandals in his hand after the latter had told him that if he encountered someone beyond the wall who bore witness that "there is no god but God," he should announce to the person the glad tidings that he would attain Paradise. After this, the two of them went back to the Messenger of God ﷺ, whereupon ᶜUmar (may God be pleased with him) said, "O Messenger of God, did you tell Abū Hurayrah to take your sandals and to announce the good news of Paradise to whoever he encountered beyond the wall who bore witness that 'there is no god but God'?"

"Yes, I did," he replied.

"Don't do that, O Messenger of God!" ᶜUmar objected. "Rather, let them strive!"[2]

The Messenger of God replied, "Let them strive, then."

These two incidents should help you see the influential position which ᶜUmar enjoyed and the degree to which he received [understanding] from the Messenger of God ﷺ and drew upon his light. This hadith is narrated in Muslim's *Ṣaḥīḥ*, though I have related it here in abbreviated form.

Four: It may be understood from this hadith that faith is of two types: true faith, and formal faith. It was based on this distinction that the Companion spoke of himself saying, "I woke up a true believer," while the hadith itself also attests to this.

Al-Bukhārī related that the Messenger of God ﷺ said, "Faith is known experientially[3] by those who are content with God as their Sovereign, with Islam as their religion, and with Muḥammad as their Messenger."

He also said ﷺ, "There are three conditions in which you will taste the sweetness of faith. The first is the state in which God and His Messenger are more beloved to you than anything or anyone else; the second is the state in which, whatever you love, you love it for God alone; and the third is that state in which, if a great fire were lit, it would be preferable to you to fall into its flames than to associate partners with God."

In another hadith, the Messenger of God ﷺ said, "The strong believer is better and more beloved to God than the weak believer; however, there is goodness in both."

God, exalted be He, said, "It is they, they, who are truly believers" {Al-Anfāl [The Spoils of War] 8:4}. Believers belong to one of two categories: those who have come to have faith in God based on intellectual assent (*taṣdīq*) and submission (*idhᶜān*), and those who have come to faith in

God based on witnessing (*shuhūd*) and direct experience (*ᶜayān*). This second type of faith is sometimes referred to as faith (*īmān*), and sometimes as certainty (*yaqīn*), since it is a faith whose light has spread abroad, whose effects have become visible, which has taken firm root in one's heart, and which is continually witnessed by one's inner being. From this faith there emerges the friendship with God enjoyed by the elect, just as the other type of faith serves as the basis for the friendship with God common to all ordinary believers.

A distinction must be recognized between the faith of a believer who vanquishes his passions, and the faith of one who is vanquished by his passions. Similarly, the faith of the believer who is exposed to temptations yet who wards them off with his faith, must be distinguished from that of the believer who has purified his heart of thoughts which would lead him into temptation in the first place, as a result of which he is simply not exposed to them thanks to his witnessing and direct experience [of the divine realities]. Hence, followers of the [Sufi] path have disputed amongst themselves as to which of the following two servants should be considered more perfect: the servant who thinks of committing transgression but who does battle with himself until the thought has passed, and the servant who doesn't think of committing transgression to begin with.

There can be no doubt that this second type of faith is superior, since it reflects most closely the spiritual states of those endowed with experiential knowledge (*ahl al-maᶜrifah*); as for the first type of faith, it reflects the state of those engaged in spiritual battle (*ahl al-mujāhadah*). One's heart will only take on the quality [of this superior form of faith] when light has filled its inmost recesses; and this is why the thought of doing wrong finds no place there in which to gain a foothold.

Five: The Messenger of God's insistence that Ḥārithah provide proof of what he had affirmed about himself is evidence that when someone makes a claim, it is not necessarily granted to him. God, glory be to Him, said, "If an afterlife with God is to be for you alone to the exclusion of all other people, then you should long for death—if what you say is true!" {Al-Naml [The Ants] 27:64} Hence, the facts weighed in the balance bear witness against people, or in their favor. As God commands, "Weigh, therefore, [your words and deeds] with equity, and cut not the measure short!" {Al-Raḥmān [The Most Gracious] 55:9} If someone claims to have attained a certain state with God, the criteria for determining the truth of his claim are brought to bear. If they bear witness in his favor, we grant him his claim; otherwise, we do not. And if this earthly existence, ignoble as its status is before God, will only grant you [your claims] based on clear evidence which you put forward, then it is only fitting that the ranks of those who have attained inner certainty will not be granted to you unless they are demonstrated by some proof or reality.

Six: Shaykh Abū al-ᶜAbbās, may God be pleased with him, used to say, "If the person to whom the Apostle ﷺ addressed this question had been Abū Bakr, may God be pleased with him, he ﷺ would not have required him to provide proof of what he had claimed, since the unique status which Abū Bakr enjoyed bore witness in his favor without such proof. Hence, the Apostle ﷺ wanted to make us aware of the difference among the ranks of his Companions, some of whom were like Ḥārithah who, when he claimed to have genuine faith, was required to provide proof in support of his claim, and others of whom were like Abū

Bakr and ᶜUmar, may God be pleased with them, whose standing would have been affirmed by the Apostle ﷺ even if they had not affirmed it of themselves. Are you not aware of the hadith in which the Messenger of God ﷺ said, "An Israelite man once mounted a heifer and wore it out by riding it, whereupon the heifer said, 'My Goodness! I wasn't made for this! Rather, I was made for tilling.'"

When they heard this, [some of] the Companions said, "My Goodness! Can a heifer speak?"

In response, the Apostle ﷺ said, "I believed this account, as did Abū Bakr and ᶜUmar," though Abū Bakr and ᶜUmar were not present.

Note, then, what a sublime standing and honored position [these two men occupied]!

Concerning the Apostle's statement, 'I believed this account, as did Abū Bakr and ᶜUmar,' I heard our shaykh, Abū al-ᶜAbbās, may God be pleased with him, say, "That is to say, '[We believed the account] without a sense of incredulity. As for you, you believed it, but with a sense of incredulity.' This is why the Companions said, 'My Goodness! Can a heifer speak?'"

Abū al-ᶜAbbās used to say, "When the angels announced to Abraham's wife the good news that she would bear a son, she said, 'Shall I bear a child, now that I am an old woman and this husband of mine is an old man? Verily, that would be a strange thing, indeed!' {Hūd 11:72} In response, the angels asked, 'Dost thou deem it strange that God should decree what He wills?' After all, the decree of God is not something which should inspire incredulity. Consequently, God did not call her a woman of truth (*ṣiddīqah*). As for Mary, by contrast, she expressed no such incredulity when she received the glad tidings that she would bear a child which would have no earthly father; as a consequence, God called her a woman of truth, saying, 'His [Christ's] mother was a woman of truth' {Al-Mā'idah [The Repast] 5:75}."

Seven: Ḥārithah cited his renunciation of the world as evidence for the genuineness of his faith. When one is realized in faith, it causes one to renounce this earthly existence. After all, faith in God necessitates that you believe that you will meet Him [on the Day of Resurrection]; similarly, your awareness that your encounter with your Lord is fast approaching necessitates that you witness its nearness, which likewise engenders within you such an attitude of renunciation. Since the light of faith reveals to you the Truth's love and solicitous care for you, your enthusiasm for this earthly life wanes and you cease setting your hopes on it.

At the same time, of course, reality dictates that when we renounce this earthly realm, we are thereby affirming its existence, since we testify to its existence by renouncing it. And since we testify to its existence, we thereby glorify it in a certain sense. This is what was meant by Shaykh Abū al-Ḥasan al-Shādhilī, may God be pleased with him, when he said, "Truly, when you renounce it [this worldly life], you glorify it." Moreover, as is the ascetic in relation to what he has renounced, so is the person who experiences annihilation in relation to that from which he has passed away through annihilation. For the affirmation that you have passed away from something through annihilation is likewise an affirmation of the thing from which you have thus been annihilated. After all, it would be meaningless to speak of annihilation, renunciation or avoidance in relation to something which had no existence.

This same truth is conveyed in the following lines of poetry, which I composed for a certain companion by the name of Ḥasan:

It is right and good that you should abandon this
entire [earthly] existence,
Ḥasan, so let nothing distract you from this intent.

Yet if you have true understanding, you will know that
There can be no abandonment of that which has no
existence.

If you witness anything else, know that it is a
product of your own illusion
And the state of your forgetful heart.

It is sufficient that the Divine should bear witness to
His existence,
While God knows the truth of what the speaker is
saying.

I have pointed to the unambiguous guidance which,
Should you perceive it, is evidenced by abundant
proofs.

The hadith, "He was, and nothing else"[4]
Is attested to now by the discerning heart.

There is nothing other [than the Divine] but an attested
relationship,[5]
That those who neglect[6] might be censured, and that
those who act might be lauded.

Eight: Ḥārithah said, "My soul has so shunned this world that its gold and its clay are now the same to me." The word which he used for "shunning" here (*ᶜuzūb*) means the abandonment of something in the sense of turning away from it in contempt. If he had said, "I have abandoned the world," his abandonment of it would not have necessitated that he no longer desire it; after all, many a person has abandoned something, yet continued to long for it. Hence, the word *ᶜuzūb* is the shunning of something with a feeling of aversion and disdain for the thing shunned, and anyone to whom God has revealed the true nature of this earthly existence will inevitably take this attitude toward it. The Apostle ﷺ said, "This earthly existence is a putrid corpse."

He ﷺ once asked al-Ḍaḥḥāk, "What do you have to eat?"

"Meat and yogurt," he replied.

"To what do they revert in the end?" he ﷺ asked.

"To you-know-what, O Messenger of God," replied al-Ḍaḥḥāk.

"Thus," he ﷺ said, "God has caused what comes out of the human body to be a metaphor for this earthly existence."

Hence, whoever has come to perceive the true nature of this earthly existence will see it as a putrid corpse, and will find it only natural to withdraw from it.

At this point you might ask: Did the Apostle ﷺ not say, "This earthly existence is sweet and lush"?

In this connection, you should know that this earthly existence is a putrid corpse in the eyes of those endowed with spiritual insight, whereas it is lush and green in the eyes of those who look upon its outward appearance.

You might then ask: Of what use is it, then, to describe it as sweet and lush?

Know that when the Prophet ﷺ said, "This earthly existence is a putrid corpse," he said this in order to deter us from becoming attached to this world, whereas when he said, "This earthly existence is sweet and lush," he said this as a cautionary. In other words, it was as if he were to say: Beware lest it beguile you with its sweetness and lushness, since its sweetness, upon closer examination, is bitterness, and its green lushness, arid bleakness. This is why, when the Apostle ﷺ was asked about the friends of God, he said, "They are those who look upon the inward reality of this earthly existence, while ordinary people look upon its outward form."

Nine: In speaking of the evidence on the basis of which he merited his spiritual rank, Ḥārithah said, "It is as if I were looking upon (rather than "I look upon...") the inhabitants of Paradise as they live in bliss." For as we noted earlier, the Prophets see the realities of things, while the saints see their likenesses.

Ten: Ḥārithah's statement, "That is why I spend my nights awake [and in worship], and my daylight hours in thirst" tells us that Ḥārithah was a servant who, by virtue of God's favor, had arrived at a state of obedience to God. Note the fact that he first said, "My soul has so shunned this world," after which he said, "That is why I spend my nights awake [and in worship], and my daylight hours in thirst." In other words, his shunning of this earthly life [thanks to God's favor] preceded his manner of relating to God [in obedience].

Shaykh Abū al-ᶜAbbās (may God be pleased with him) used to say, "People belong to one of two categories: Those who, by virtue of God's favor, have arrived at a state of obedience to God, and those who, by virtue of their obedience to God, have experienced God's favor. As God has declared, glory be to Him, "God draws unto Himself everyone who is willing, and guides unto Himself everyone who turns unto Him" {Al-Shūra [Consultation] 42:13}.

When God's light enters one's heart, it leads necessarily to renunciation of the world, whereupon it radiates outward to one's physical being. The light that reaches one's eye leads to careful observation; that which reaches the ear leads one to become a good listener; that which reaches the tongue leads to *dhikr*, or the invocation of God's name; while that which reaches one's limbs leads to service.

Evidence for the fact that light leads one necessarily to detach and distance oneself from this earthly existence may be found in the words of the Messenger of God ﷺ: "When light enters one's breast, one experiences happiness and freedom."[7]

He ﷺ was then asked, "O Messenger of God, is there some sign that this has happened?"

He replied, "Withdrawal from the abode of illusion and return to the abode of permanence."

In the hadith concerning Ḥanẓalah al-Asadī, which is narrated by Muslim in his *Ṣaḥīḥ*, we read that "Once when Ḥanẓalah saw Abū Bakr, may God be pleased with him, he said, 'Ḥanẓalah is a hypocrite.'

'What's wrong with Ḥanẓalah?' Abū Bakr asked him.

'Well,' Ḥanẓalah replied, "When we're with the Messenger of God ﷺ, he makes us so aware of Paradise and Hellfire, it's as if we could see them with our own eyes. But when we leave him, we occupy ourselves with our livelihoods and our wives, and forget much of what we know.'

Abū Bakr (may God be pleased with him) replied, 'We experience the same sort of thing, Ḥanẓalah.'

The two of them then went to see the Messenger of God ﷺ, and Ḥanẓalah said, 'O Messenger of God, Ḥanẓalah is a hypocrite!'

'What's wrong with Ḥanẓalah?' he ﷺ asked.

Ḥanẓalah replied, "When we're with the Messenger of God ﷺ, he makes us so aware of Paradise and Hellfire, it's as if we could see them with our own eyes. But when we leave you, we occupy ourselves with our livelihoods and our wives, and forget much of what we know.'

The Messenger of God ﷺ replied, 'Ḥanẓalah, I assure you by the One Who holds my soul in His hand, if you remained in the state in which you find yourselves when you're with me and when engaging in the remembrance of God, the angels would greet you as you walked down the road and as you lay in your beds.[8] But as it is, let there be a time for this, and a time for that.'"

This hadith offers eight lessons:

The first lesson has to do with Ḥanẓalah's statement, "Ḥanẓalah is a hypocrite." The word rendered here as "hypocrisy" (*nifāq*) is derived from the term used for the way in which a jerboa builds its tunnel (*nāfiqā'*): it creates two exits with the result that if it is pursued at one of them, it can escape through the other. Similarly, the hypocrite appears to be a believer despite the fact that he has a hidden strain of unbelief. If unbelievers reproach him for the faith which he exhibits, he opens up an "exit" from within his concealed unbelief in order to dodge their criticism. If, on the other hand, he exhibits signs of being a hypocrite and faces criticism for this [among believers], he protects himself from such criticism through the veneer of belief which he puts on. This is why God speaks of them, saying, "And when they meet those who have attained to faith, they assert, 'We believe [as you believe],' but when they find themselves alone with their evil impulses, they say, 'Verily, we are with you; we were only mocking!'" {Al-Baqarah [The Cow] 2:14}

When Ḥanẓalah observed that when he was with the Messenger of God ﷺ, he would be in a particular spiritual state, but that when he went out and came in contact with the world and its various demands, his spiritual state would change, he feared that this was hypocrisy on his part due to the inconsistency between these two conditions. Consequently, he complained of this to the Messenger of God ﷺ, having been moved by his faith to reveal his difficulty in order to seek relief from it. In so doing, he complained of his distress to the one with whom he knew he would find relief. When he complained of his problem to Abū Bakr, may God be pleased with him, Abū Bakr said to him, "We experience the same sort of thing, Ḥanẓalah." Since the Messenger of God ﷺ was still in their midst, Abū Bakr did not think it necessary to answer Ḥanẓalah himself. However, if Ḥanẓalah had come to Abū Bakr with his complaint after the Prophet's death, he would have answered him himself.

The second lesson to be derived from this hadith concerning Ḥanẓalah is that if someone is led by honesty to disclose a personal struggle, he or she will experience relief, either by being told that what he or she thought was a disorder is not, in fact, a disorder, or by being guided to the remedy which will cure it. As for Ḥanẓalah, he was told that what he thought was a disorder was not, in fact, a disorder.

The third lesson of relevance here concerns Ḥanẓalah's saying to the Messenger of God ﷺ, "You remind us so vividly of Paradise and the Fire that it is as if we were seeing them with our own eyes." He did not say, "You remind us so vividly of Paradise and the Fire that we see them with our own eyes," based on the fact that, as we pointed out earlier, the prophets see the realities of things, while the friends of God see their likenesses. Consequently, as in the case of Ḥārithah who, instead of saying, "I looked upon the inhabitants of Paradise," said, "It is as if I were looking upon the inhabitants of Paradise," Ḥanẓalah likewise did not say, "we see them with our own eyes," but rather, "it is as if we were seeing them with our own eyes."

The fourth lesson to be derived from this hadith is that as far as possible, we should minimize our involvement with the affairs of this earthly existence. As Ḥanẓalah said, "When we leave you, we occupy ourselves with our livelihoods and our wives, and forget much of what we know." As the Messenger of God ﷺ said, "Just a bit of this world distracts one from a great deal of the world to come." Similarly, he ﷺ, "With every rising sun there are two angels who call out, 'O people! Come to your Lord! For that which is scant, yet sufficient is better than that which is plentiful, yet diverts one's attention [from the hereafter]!'"

The fifth lesson has to do with the Prophet's statement, "If you remained in the state in which you find yourselves when you're with me and when engaging in the remembrance of God, the angels would greet you as you walked down the road and as you lay in your beds." What this statement tells us is that to remain in such a spiritual state is a precious, yet rare phenomenon, and that for the servant not to remain in such a state is, therefore, no cause for reproach. After all, human beings are predisposed by nature to a lack of mindfulness, as a result of which it is a very difficult thing to remain in such a spiritual state.

The sixth lesson has to do with a statement made by Shaykh Abū al-ᶜAbbās, may God be pleased with him, who used to say, "The Messenger of God ﷺ did not say that it would be utterly impossible for someone to remain in such a state of spiritual awareness that 'the angels would greet you as you walked down the road and as you lay in your beds'; rather, what he was saying was that it should only be expected to occur in special cases. After all, there may be those of God's friends to whom He does grant this experience.

As for the seventh lesson, it has to do with the reason for which the Messenger of God ﷺ singled out two places—bed, and the road—for attention in this statement of his. The bed is the site of carnal appetites, while the road is the site of distractions; hence, if the angels greet them along the road and on their beds, then how much more fitting it is for them to greet them in those places where they perform acts of obedience and engage in the sacred invocation of God's name!

As for the eighth lesson, it is that the wisdom of God, glory be to Him, dictated that the time which they spent in the Prophet's presence and in invoking God's name should not be considered equal to other times, since this would ensure a proper appreciation of the supreme importance of his teaching, the inestimable value of divine remembrance, and the sublimity of both.

He said (may God be pleased with him), "The Messenger of God ﷺ once heard Abū Bakr reciting in a very low voice, while he heard ᶜUmar reciting in a loud voice. He asked Abū Bakr, 'Why do you lower your voice?' To which he replied, 'Because the only person who needs to hear me is the One with whom I'm communing.' He then asked ᶜUmar, 'Why do you raise your voice?' To which ᶜUmar replied, 'In order to rouse the somnolent and to drive away Satan.' The Prophet ﷺ then said to Abū Bakr, 'Raise your voice a bit,' and to ᶜUmar, 'Lower your voice a bit.'

Commenting on this incident, the shaykh (may God be pleased with him) said, "He ﷺ wanted to draw each of them away from what he wanted for himself and into what he ﷺ wanted for them."

The Messenger of God ﷺ said, "I am the master of all those descended from Adam; and this is no boast." Commenting on this declaration of the Prophet's, the shaykh said, "In other words, 'I do not glory in this distinguished position of mine; rather, what I glory in is my servanthood to God, glory be to Him."

And he would often recite the following lines:

> O ᶜAmr, summon Zahrā's slave,
> Who is recognized by all who hear and see.
>
> Address me only as her servant,
> For this is the most glorious of all my names.

And he said, "Shaykh Abū al-Ḥasan al-Shādhilī (may God be pleased with him) used to say, 'In this earthly existence, the believer is a captive, and a captive can only be released in one of three ways: through trickery, ransom, or providential care.'"

This statement by the shaykh is taken from the words of the Messenger of God ﷺ: "This earthly existence is the believer's prison."

In explanation of this hadith, Shaykh Abū al-ᶜAbbās (may God be pleased with him) said, "The prisoner's concern is to observe carefully with his eyes, to listen attentively with his ears and, when he is called, to respond."

He said (may God be pleased with him), "The prophets are a gift (*ᶜaṭiyah*) to their peoples, while our Prophet ﷺ is likewise a gift (*hadiyah*). However, the difference between *ᶜaṭiyah* and *hadiyah* is that "gift" in the sense of *ᶜaṭiyah* is for the needy, while "gift" in the sense of *hadiyah* is bestowed on those who are beloved. As the Messenger of God ﷺ said, "I am a mercy bestowed."

He ﷺ said, "The sultan is a God-given protector on earth." Commenting on these words of the Prophet ﷺ, the shaykh said, "This applies if the sultan is a just ruler; if he is an unjust ruler, however, he simply serves as the protector of self-indulgence and craving."

He said (may God be pleased with him), "A certain member of the group known as *ahl al-ṣuffah*[9] died and two dinars were found in his cloak. When the Messenger of God ﷺ learned of it, he said, 'Two brands from the Hellfire.'"

Commenting on these words of the Prophet ﷺ, the shaykh said, "Many Companions died during the Messenger of God's lifetime and left wealth behind; however, he ﷺ did not say of them what he said of this man. And the reason for this is that unlike this man, the others did not make a show of being something other than what they were inwardly. This man, being one of the *ahl al-ṣuffah*, had claimed to be destitute, after which it turned out that he owned these two dinars. Hence, because he had cultivated an appearance which conflicted with what he actually was, the Apostle ﷺ described those two dinars as 'two brands from the Hellfire.'"

In this same vein he said, "The Messenger of God ﷺ said, 'The honest merchant will be resurrected together with the prophets, the men and women of truth, the martyrs and the righteous.'"

Commenting on this hadith, he said (may God be pleased with him), "On what basis will he be resurrected together with the prophets? And on what basis will he resurrected together with the men and women of truth, the martyrs, and the righteous? He will be resurrected together with the prophets because the prophets are those who deliver the trust which has been placed in their safekeeping and who give wise counsel. The honest merchant will be resurrected together with the prophets in his capacity as one who, like them, delivered the trust which had been placed in his safe-keeping, and who gave wise counsel.

"He will be resurrected together with men and women of truth, since the person of truth is someone who is characterized by purity and serenity both outwardly and inwardly, and whose outward appearance and inward reality are in full accord with one another. This description applies likewise to the honest merchant, and on this basis he will be resurrected together with the men and women of truth.

"He will be resurrected together with the martyrs because, like the martyr who engages in struggle [for God's sake], the honest merchant struggles against selfish inclinations, temptations and cravings.

"Lastly, given the fact that, like the righteous, the honest merchant takes that which is lawfully his and abstains from that which is not, he will be resurrected together with them."

The screened enclosure and cenotaph above the place where Ibn ᶜAṭaᵓ Allāh (d. 1309) is buried at the foot of the Muqattam Hills in Cairo.

"After all, never does one look with the eye of faith but that it falls upon a blessing, be it past or present. This will be confirmed to you if you examine your dealings with God, and His with you. For if you look at what has proceeded from Him to you, you will find nothing but bounty and goodness, whereas if you look at what has proceeded from you to Him, you will find nothing but heedlessness and disobedience."

"Rather, the veil which renders the world of the unseen inaccessible is the presence of faults …"

"Clay is of the earth, the soul is of heaven, the heart is of the throne, the spirit is of the seat, and the innermost being is with God, without 'where'. The command descends in the midst of all this, and is followed by that which witnesses thereto."

Ibn ᶜAṭaᵓ Allāh

Chapter Seven

On His Explanations of Difficult-to-Understand Statements by Knowers of the Truth Which Led Him to the Most Beautiful of Paths

The Shaykh (may God be pleased with him) said, "Sahl Ibn ᶜAbdallāh said, 'Be not among the time-conscious, nor among those intent on counting and calculation. Rather, be among those whose concern is with eternity, and whether [they are among those destined to be] miserable or happy.'"

Then he continued, saying, "One of them might say, 'I prayed such-and-such a number of *rakᶜahs*, I fasted such-and-such a number of months, I recited the entire Qur'ān such-and-such a number of times, I performed such-and-such a number of pilgrimages.' People who say such things are intent on counting and calculation. However, they are in greater need of counting their bad deeds than they are of counting their good ones.

"As for the time-conscious, one of them might say, 'I've been on the spiritual path for seventy years,' or, 'I've been on the spiritual path for sixty years.'

"As for you, be among those whose concern is with eternity, and whether [they are among those destined to be] miserable or happy. In other words, focus your awareness on God's pre-knowledge; rely not on your own knowledge and works, but rather, on that which has existed from all eternity."[1]

He also said (may God be pleased with him), "Bishr al-Ḥāfī (may God be pleased with him) said, 'For forty years I've craved grilled meat, but haven't been able to afford it.'"

In explanation of this statement, he said, "Anyone who thinks that this shaykh went forty years without having enough money to buy some grilled meat is mistaken. After all, how did he obtain what he needed by way of food and clothing throughout those forty years? Rather, what this statement means is that the spiritual rank occupied by people of his type is such that they neither eat nor drink, nor enter into nor abandon anything without God's permission and a sign. Hence, if God had given him permission to eat grilled meat, he would have been able to afford it."

He said (may God be pleased with him), "People's means of sustenance may be divided into four categories: indifferent (*mubāḥ*), permissible (*ḥalāl*), agreeable (*ṭayyib*) and unadulterated (*ṣāfin*). That which is indifferent is something for which one merits no punishment by partaking of it, and no reward for abstaining from it. That which is permissible is something which it has never occurred to you [to wonder about], and about which you have never asked anyone, man or woman. The agreeable is that which the servant partakes of as though it had no qualities, since he himself[2] has no qualities of his own in the presence of his Lord. As for the unadulterated, it is that which the servant sees with his own eyes from the source, that is, from the wellspring of God's power, may He be exalted and glorified."

He said (may God be pleased with him), "Junayd said, 'I came upon seventy gnostics, all of whom worshipped God based on uncertainty and error. Even my brother Abū Yazīd, if he came upon one of our least experienced disciples, would become a Muslim under his influence.'"

In explanation of this statement, the shaykh said, "What he means by saying that they 'worshipped God based on uncertainty and error' is not that they were subject to uncertainty or error in their knowledge. After all, how can gnosis, or experiential knowledge, be present together with uncertainty and error? Rather, what he meant is that they had reached spiritual stations in which they imagined that there remained no further or higher station for those with inner certainty. Hence, Junayd said, 'If he came across one of our least experienced disciples, he would become a Muslim under his influence.' In other words, it would become clear to him that beyond the station to which he had attained there was a further, higher station, and beyond this higher station, still another, and another, and so on to infinity. As for the phrase, 'he would have become a Muslim under his influence,' it means that he would have submitted himself to him, since this is what *islām* means."

Abū Yazīd once said, "I have dived into a sea on whose shore the prophets are standing." In explanation of this statement, the shaykh (may God be pleased with him) said, "In so saying, Abū Yazīd is complaining of his weakness and his inability to join the prophets, upon them be peace. Specifically, what he means is: The prophets have dived into the sea of affirmation of the divine oneness, and now stand on the shore of separation, inviting people to dive in. Hence, if I were complete, I would be standing where they stand."

The shaykh's explanation of Abū Yazīd's words is well suited to Abū Yazīd's spiritual station. As we have had occasion to mention before, Abū Yazīd once said, "All that the friends of God have of what belongs to the prophets may be likened to a skin filled with honey through whose pores some of the honey has seeped out; the honey which remains inside the skin belongs to the prophets, while that which has seeped out belongs to the friends of God."

Abū Yazīd was known for the uncompromising regard in which he held the customs associated with Islamic law and his conscientious adherence to proper etiquette. It is said that a certain man was once described to him as being a friend of God; hence, he went to pay him a visit, and sat down in the mosque to wait for him. When the man came out, he spit on the mosque wall, whereupon Abū Yazīd left without meeting with the man, saying, "This man can't be trusted to conduct himself in keeping with Islamic etiquette; so how could he be entrusted with God's secrets?" As for the actions and words of the greatest of God's saints—whose integrity before God, may He be glorified and exalted, is beyond doubt—we interpret them on the basis of our knowledge of their uprightness and the goodness of their spiritual teachings when and if, taken at face value, such actions or words are problematic. As the Prophet ﷺ said, "Do not think ill of any word spoken by a Muslim if you can find some positive manner in which to interpret it."

He said (may God be pleased with him), "If al-Ḥārith Ibn Asad al-Muḥāsibī began to partake of some food of which there was reason to be suspicious, his finger would move over it."

Someone then asked the shaykh, "Master, it has been said that once when Abū Bakr the Veracious was served some yogurt, he ate some of it, at which point he sensed its impurity in his heart."

"Where did you get this yogurt?" he asked.

In reply, a servant boy said, "I used to serve as a fortuneteller for people during the days before Islam, so they paid me wages in return for the service."[3]

When he heard the servant boy's reply, Abū Bakr vomited up the yogurt, then said, "Believe me, if it had only come out through my intestines, I would still have expelled it!"

Abū Bakr had no vein which would quiver in warning when he was served food which was suspect; however, he, of all members of the Muslim nation, merits having the utmost virtue attributed to him, for if he were placed in the balance with the entire nation, he [his faith and good deeds] would outweigh them all.

The shaykh (may God be pleased with him) said, "Abū Bakr (may God be pleased with him) was like an authorized representative in the sense that as someone who had been purified of any remaining traces of his ego, he was not in need of any type of sign. Al-Ḥārith Ibn Asad, by contrast, still retained traces of ego and, as a result, was in need of a sign lest he enter into something based on self-indulgence and craving. Abū Bakr, unlike al-Ḥārith, had been purged of self-indulgence and craving, and was therefore not in need of a sign.

Know that it was God's wise choice of Abū Bakr (may God be pleased with him) that he should partake of that yogurt and then be required to vomit it up again so that God could reward him for this. In addition, it was allowed to take place so that Abū Bakr could be an example to others who, not having known before that it would be best to vomit up such a thing, will follow his example if they eat anything which is suspect.

There is no basis for anyone to say here, "He vouched for its harmlessness by eating it, and he incurred no guilt by partaking of it since he had no knowledge of its origin. After all, Abū Bakr only asked about the yogurt after he sensed its impurity in his heart." However, what this tells us is that food which is forbidden or suspect may affect someone's heart through a sense of impurity or distress even if the person concerned is unaware at the time when he eats the food that it is contaminated in some way.

And thus it is that people such as these are dealt with by God according to His special purposes. In other words, if such a thing happens to them, it is based on God's wise choice for them, in order that through them He might make His grace available to His other servants. In accordance with this same principle, it was God's wise choice for Adam to eat of the tree after he was forbidden to do so in order that he might repent of what he had done and, in this way, become a model for all those who repent. God chose this for Adam in order that he might recognize God for His magnanimity and know that He is the Most Munificent of the munificent. Similarly, God chose this for him in order to make Adam aware of His gracious protection and kindness, thereby teaching him that He is the One who is most kind to his believing servants. In addition, Adam's eating from the tree was intended to be the occasion of his descent [from Paradise to Earth], just as this descent was intended to be the occasion of Adam's becoming God's vicegerent on Earth. This is why Shaykh Abū al-Ḥasan (may God be pleased with him) said, "What an auspicious act of disobedience it was which led to [Adam's] vicegerency."

He said, "Truly, God caused Adam to descend to Earth before He created him, saying, 'Behold...I will create a vicegerent on earth' {Al-Baqarah [The Cow] 2:30}."[4] We have explained this statement in *Kitāb al-Tanwīr*[5]; hence, we will not repeat our discussion of it here.

In his *Risālah*, al-Qushayrī begins with a discussion of al-Faḍīl Ibn ᶜIyāḍ and Ibrāhīm Ibn Adham, because these two men had both been through a period of estrangement from God, after which they approached Him again, whereupon God Himself approached them in His grace. He begins by mentioning these two men in order to spread hope among those disciples who have suffered moral lapses and committed transgressions, after which they have come knocking once again at the doors of divine grace. For if he had begun by speaking of figures such as Junayd, Sahl Bin ᶜAbdullāh al-Tusturī, ᶜUtbah al-Ghulām and others who, like them, grew up adhering to the spiritual path, there are those who would say, "And who could possibly come up to their standard? They've never had moral lapses or committed transgressions!"

There is a well-known story about Samnūn al-Muḥibb, who said,

> My fortune lies in none but Thee,
> So however Thou desirest, put me to the test!

After this he was afflicted with a condition in which he was unable to pass urine. He endured for one day, but the pain increased. He endured the second day, and the pain still increased. He endured a third day, and a fourth, and the pain went on getting worse. On the morning of the fourth day, a companion of his came to him and said, "Master, I heard your voice yesterday along the Tigris River; you were crying out to God to remove the affliction that had been visited upon you." He was then visited by a second, a third and a fourth, even though he had not, in fact, asked God to remove his suffering. He knew then that this was a sign from God telling him to ask. So he began making the rounds among the young boys in the Qur'an schools and saying, "Pray for your lying uncle!"

Commenting on this story, he said (may God be pleased with him), "May God have mercy on Samnūn! Thereafter, instead of saying, 'However Thou desirest, put me to the test!' he began to say, 'However Thou desirest, pardon me!' For to ask for pardon is more fitting than to ask to be put to the test."

There is another well-known story told by Abū al-Qāsim al-Qushayrī in his *Risālah* in which Junayd says, "I once went in to see al-Sarī,[6] and I noticed that a change had come over him.

"What's wrong, Teacher?" I asked. "Why do you appear changed?"

He replied, "A young man came in to see me earlier and asked me, 'What is repentance?' So I said, 'Repentance is not to forget your sin.'"

"No," he said, "'Repentance is to forget your sin.' So what do you say, Abū al-Qāsim?"

"I personally agree with the young man," I replied, "because if I am in a state of alienation, after which God brings me into a state of harmony, then remembering the alienation at a time of harmony is alienation."

The shaykh (may God be pleased with him) said, "Al-Sarī's reply was more fitting than those of Junayd and the young man, since what al-Sarī said is indicative of the principles which govern the spiritual stations. Someone who serves as an example for others is required to speak about the spiritual stations of people [in general], including both their beginnings and their ends, and recognizing that ends are determined by beginnings."

Now, neither Junayd at that time, nor the young man mentioned here, had reached a spiritual station which would have qualified him to be an example to others. They spoke in their replies about those who have reached advanced stations and who are approaching the end of their spiritual paths. As such, they spoke only about their own particular states, whereas al-Sarī's reply might be likened to a broad, even thoroughfare which can serve as a source of guidance to all those traveling the spiritual path. This, then, is what was meant by the shaykh, may God be pleased with him.

He said (may God be pleased with him), "The Sufi is not a Sufi until he has gone twenty years without the angel on his left recording a single transgression."

What this means is not that the person commits no transgressions for twenty years; rather, what it means is that if he commits some transgression, he seeks God's forgiveness for it. The angel who is assigned to recording the person's bad deeds does not record anything until he has first waited to see whether the person concerned will change his mind before committing the act or, having committed it, whether he will repent. And whenever he wants to record some evil deed, the angel on the person's right says to him, "Wait, don't write anything down yet! Maybe he or she will repent!" until the number of sins [for which the person has not repented] comes to either seven or ten—I'm not certain which—and only then does he record the evil deed. This is why it has been said, "The angel on one's right holds sway over the angel on one's left."

Overview of mosque, tomb, and resthouse complex at Ḥumaythirā

Building above the tomb of Abū al-Ḥasan al-Shādhilī,
who was buried here in 1258 C.E.

Chapter Eight

On What He Had to Say Concerning Spiritual Realities and Stations And His Clarification of Difficult Matters Relating Thereto

He said (may God be pleased with him), "Longing (*shawq*) is of two types. The first type is the longing born of absence, which only ceases when one meets the Beloved; this is the longing of souls. The second type is the longing of spirits, which is experienced even while one is in the presence of the Beloved and one sees Him with one's own [inner] eyes."

If God lifts you up to the place where you witness the divine presence in a manner which is free of all defects, this is the station of God-given knowledge (*ta*ᶜ*rīf*) through true faith; this is the realm of the descent of the mysteries of pre-eternity (*asrār al-azal*). If, on the other hand, God brings you down to the place of perseverance and struggle, this is the station of legal prescriptions (*taklīf*) which is bound by defects; this is true Islam, or surrender to God, and this is the realm in which the realities of post-eternity (*ḥaqā'iq al-abadiyah*) are manifested.

The realized person is one to whom it makes no difference which of these stations he or she occupies. After all, it is not you, but your basic attributes which tend in this or that direction.[1] Moreover, an attribute is "from essence to essence"—that is, your existence. The name is for the tongue, that is, verbal expression; moreover, the name discloses the reality of the attribute, the attribute discloses the reality of existence, and the mysteries descend from the divine existence to the [station of] *ṣiddīqiyah*.[2] [The divine] realities are manifested through the [divine] attributes via friendship with God (sainthood) to those who concern themselves with the outward sciences,[3] [and] on the basis of the name via evidence to those who strive in the pursuit of knowledge.

Reference to this is made in the Prophet's words to Abū Juḥayfah, "O Abū Juḥayfah, you who inquire of scholars, associate with sages, and sit with the greatest of saints: the scholar guides you through knowledge based on the names, which leads to Paradise. The sage brought near to God carries you forward through certainty and the realities revealed through the attributes, which leads to the various levels of nearness [to the Divine]. These things are spoken of by God, exalted be He, when He says, "Remain conscious of God, and seek to come closer to Him" {Al-Mā'idah [The Repast] 5:35}. As for the greatest of the saints, he will lead you, via the mysteries revealed through [the divine] existence, along the path of purity, tranquillity and integrity, which leads to God."

These three ranks come together in the greatest of saints, since he carries one group forward by means of knowledge, another group by means of the realities, and another by means of the mysteries. Such people are the successors to the prophets, the substitutes for God's messengers, and those endowed with insight. "Say [O Prophet]: 'This is my way: Resting upon conscious insight accessible to reason, I am calling you all unto God—I and they who follow me' {Yūsuf [Joseph] 12: 208}." That is to say, he calls people based on direct vision: For each group of people, he has direct insight into their path and he bears them along it, which is a kind of substitutional representation (*niyābah*). As for him, however, he is so near to God that his state is unique to him alone and cannot be known by others.

He used to recite the following lines:

> My heart sang, for me and from me,
> So I sang along.
>
> Wherever they were, so were we,
> And wherever we were, so were they.[4]

He said (may God be pleased with him), "There are four times in which the servant will find himself, of which there is no fifth: blessing, affliction, obedience, and disobedience. In each of these times, there is an aspect of servanthood which the Truth requires of you by virtue of His lordship. If it is a time of obedience, your path is to bear witness to God's grace, since it is He who has guided you into this obedience and has made it possible for you. If it is a time of disobedience, your path is to seek God's forgiveness and repent. If it is a time of blessing, your path is to give thanks, which means for your heart to rejoice in God. If it is a time of affliction, your path is to be content with God's decree and to endure patiently. Contentment (*riḍā*) is to break (*raḍḍ*) oneself of one's passions, while the word for patient endurance (*ṣabr*) is derived from the word *aṣbār*, which refers to the target used in archery practice. The person who exhibits patient endurance is one who sets himself up as a "target" for the arrows of divine decree; if, then, one is unmoved by them, he or she is said to have patient endurance.

Patient endurance is the heart's steadfastness in the hands of the Lord. The Messenger of God ﷺ said, "Those who, when they receive, give thanks; who, when they are afflicted, endure patiently; who, when they are wronged, forgive; and who, when they are guilty of wrongdoing, seek forgiveness…."

He then fell silent and his listeners asked, "What about them, O Messenger of God?"

He replied, "…it is they who shall be secure, since it is they who have found the right path!" {Al-Anᶜām [Cattle] 6:82}

That is to say, they will find security in the afterlife, and in this earthly life, they are rightly guided.

He said (may God be pleased with him), "People belong to one of two groups: Those who, by virtue of God's favor, have arrived at a state of obedience to God, and those who, by virtue of their obedience to God, have experienced God's favor. As God has declared, glory be to Him, 'God draws unto Himself everyone who is willing, and guides unto Himself everyone who turns unto Him' {Al-Shūra [Consultation] 42:13}."

What the shaykh meant by this was that there are people in whom God stirs up the determination to reach Him, as a result of which they set out to traverse the wild, desert-like expanses of their egos and their natural dispositions until they arrive in their Lord's presence. Of such people God spoke truly when He declared, "But as for those who strive hard in Our cause—We shall most certainly guide them onto paths that lead to Us" {Al-ᶜAnkabūt [The Spider] 29:69}.

There are, in addition, people who are taken unawares by God's providence, without their having sought it out or prepared themselves for it. Of such people God speaks, glory be to Him, when He says, "God singles out for His grace whom He wills" {Al-Baqarah [The Cow] 2:105}.

The former condition is that of wayfarers along the spiritual path (*al-sālikīn*, singular, *sālik*), while the latter is that of the "God-possessed" (*al-majdhūbīn*, singular, *majdhūb*).

Those who begin by striving through concrete action (*al-muᶜāmalah*) end with communion (*al-muwāṣalah*), while those who begin with communion are then brought back to striving through concrete action.

Do not think that the *majdhūb* has no path to follow, for in fact, he does; however, God has shortened the distance for him, as it were, so that he has been able to traverse it quickly. You often hear it said by those who are associated with the spiritual path that the *sālik* is more perfect than the *majdhūb*, since the *sālik* has become acquainted with the path and knows the point he has reached along the way, whereas this cannot be said of the *majdhūb*. Such statements are based on these people's notion that the *majdhūb* has no path to follow. However, this claim of theirs is incorrect. For although the distance has been shortened for the *majdhūb*, he has not thereby been exempted from traversing it. For when the distance is thus shortened for someone, he does not miss the path as a result, nor is it absented from him. Rather, what he misses are its hardships and the long period of time which the path generally requires. The *majdhūb* may be likened to someone for whom the distance to Mecca has been shortened, while the *sālik* may be likened to someone who is traveling there on the back of a camel.

He said (may God be pleased with him), "The gnostic is one who has no earthly existence, since his earthly existence is subsumed within his existence in the world to come, and his existence in the world to come is subsumed within his Lord."

He also said, "The person who has renounced this earthly existence (*al-zāhid*) has come from this life to the afterlife, while the gnostic (*al-ᶜārif*) has come from the afterlife to this life. The *zāhid* is a stranger in this world, since the world to come is his homeland, while the gnostic is a stranger in the world to come, since he is in God's presence."

You may ask: What does the shaykh mean by "stranger" in these statements, and what does this word mean in the Prophetic hadith, "[The Islamic] religion began as a stranger, and will become a stranger again as it was in the beginning; hence, blessed are the strangers"?[5]

Know that in speaking of "strangerhood," this hadith is referring to the scarcity of those who are willing to offer assistance toward acting upon the truth. As a result, those who seek to live in accordance with the truth will be strangers given the absence of those who will help or support them. Rather, the only thing which gives such people strength is the power of their own faith and the steadfastness of their own certainty. This is why the Prophet ﷺ said, "[The Islamic] religion began as a stranger, and will become a stranger again as it was in the beginning; hence, blessed are the strangers."

What the Prophet ﷺ was saying through this hadith is that [when Islam first began], its followers sought to obey God's commands in his land and among his people at a time when most people had no zeal to do so.

As for the meaning of "strangerhood" in the shaykh's words (may God be pleased with him), what it means is that the person who has renounced this earthly existence is given a vision of the supremity of the world to come such that it remains his heart's true home and his spirit's resting place. As a consequence, he is a stranger, or exile in this temporal realm, since it is not his heart's true home. He has seen the eternal abode with his own eyes, as it were; hence, his heart is so taken by what it has seen of the afterlife's reward and favor, and it so recoils from what it has witnessed by way of its chastisement and torment, that he has become a stranger to this world.

As for the gnostic, he is a stranger in the afterlife, since he has received a vision of known attributes, and his heart has been so taken by what is there [in this vision] that he has become like a stranger in the world of the hereafter, since his inner being is with God "without where." For servants such as these, the divine presence itself has become their hearts' abode; to this presence they repair and in it they find repose. If they descend to the realm of legal prescriptions, moral responsibility and the demands of their earthly natures, they do so only by permission, [in the station of] stability and assurance (*tamkīn*) and deep-rooted certainty. They do not descend to the realm of their own personal needs and desires out of craving and the appetite for pleasure; and when they find themselves in the realm of legal prescription and moral responsibility, they do not fall into ill-mannered conduct and heedlessness. Rather, in all of this they adhere to the rules of etiquette prescribed by God and His messengers and prophets, acting always in accordance with what their Lord requires of them.

He said (may God be pleased with him), "Fear is of two types: the fear experienced by ordinary believers, and the fear experienced by the elect. The fear experienced by ordinary believers is the fear that their physical beings will be exposed to the Fire, while the fear experienced by the elect is the fear that the garments in which their Lord has clothed them will be defiled by disobedience."

What the shaykh meant by this is that ordinary believers' powers of spiritual perception have not yet enabled them to perceive the garments with which the Truth has clothed them, that is, the garments of faith, Islam, experiential knowledge, belief in the divine oneness, and love. All that they know is that God, exalted be He, has warned those who disobey Him of His chastisement, as a result of which they fear falling into disobedience lest this be a cause for them to suffer punishment; hence, their fear is, in essence, the fear for themselves lest they be punished by God.

As for the elect, the Truth has given them light by which He enables them to see the garments of grace in which He has clothed them; as a consequence, they strive to preserve themselves in order that when they approach Him, their garments will be unstained and unaltered, spotless and pure, bright and resplendent. They have thus understood the meaning of God's command: "And thy garments keep free from stain" {Al-Muddaththir [The Enfolded One] 74:4}.[6]

They have cleansed their garments of faith and certainty of the defilement caused by their heedlessness and disobedience. Hence, they have understood the meaning of God's declaration: "O children of Adam! Indeed, We have bestowed upon you from on high garments to cover your nakedness, and as a thing of beauty: but the garment of God-consciousness is the best of all" {Al-Aʿrāf [The Faculty of Discernment] 7:26}.

As they pass through this earthly existence, they keep their skirts raised, as it were, lest they become defiled by its impurities, in order to come into God's presence clothed in the raiment of grace which He has bestowed upon them. They are loyal to Him in what He requires of them, and faithful stewards of what He has entrusted to them.

One gnostic used to recite these lines:

> They said, "Tomorrow is the holiday, so what
> will you wear?"
> "A robe [given me by] a Cupbearer from whose
> love I've drunk deeply," I replied.

Poverty and patient endurance are my robes,
beneath which there is a heart
That finds its most intimate companion in holidays and days of gathering.

The holiday for me is but a funeral ceremony if
You, my Hope, are absent,
But as long as You fill my eyes and ears, the celebration goes on.

Is it not most fitting, on the day of visitation, to
come decked out
In the robe which your Beloved has given you to
wear?

He said (may God be pleased with him), "When ordinary believers are given reason to fear, they feel afraid, and if they are given reason to hope, they feel hopeful. When the elect are given reason to fear, they feel hopeful, and when they are given reason to hope, they feel afraid." What the shaykh meant by this is that ordinary believers deal with things based on their outward appearances; hence, if they are given an apparent reason to fear, they feel afraid, since they, unlike the people nearest to God, do not have the light of understanding which would enable them to see beneath the surface of things.

When the people of God feel afraid, they also feel hopeful, knowing that beyond both their fear and that which has caused their fear are the attributes of the One in Whom they have placed their hope, and of Whose mercy and graces they must never despair. Hence, they rely upon His magnanimity, realizing as they do that He has only frightened them in order to cause them to focus upon Him alone, and thereby to bring them back to Himself.

Conversely, when they feel hopeful, they also feel afraid. What they fear is the unseen dimension of His will—His will being the basis for their hope. They fear that the visible reasons he has given them for hope are a test of their minds, that is, a test of whether they rely solely on hope which is visible and perceptible, or whether they see beyond this to the need to fear that which is, as yet, unrevealed of His will. Hence, hope has aroused their fear. [This dichotomy bears a similarity to] their judgment on the spiritual states of "contraction," or dejection (*qabḍ*) and "expansion," or gaiety (*basṭ*). *Basṭ* can be a snare, as a result of which it calls for great caution and frequent resort [to God for His help].

One Sufi stated, "A door to *basṭ* was opened to me, so I entered it, and my spiritual station was inaccessible to me for thirty years thereafter."

The shaykh (may God be pleased with him) used to recite these lines:

> Complete the journey to Him, the journey to Him in all haste,
> But when you reach Him,
> Knock on the door ever so gently.

And:

> Beware of *basṭ* and call upon the Beloved from afar,
> And you will be called upon from nearby.

His saying, "Beware of *basṭ*," or gaiety, is consistent with what we have stated above. For when such gaiety is among the lights with which one has been endowed, there is the danger that its presence will lead one into wrongdoing. As God has declared, glory be to Him, "For if God were to grant abundant assistance[7] to [all of] His servants, they would behave on earth with reckless insolence" {Shūrā [Consultation] 42:27}.

As for *qabḍ*, or dejection, it is more in keeping with a person's true well-being, since it is, in effect, the servant's "home." After all, we are all in God's grip (*qabḍah*), and the Truth encompasses us from all sides. How, then, are servants to have a sense of gaiety when this is their condition? Gaiety is inconsistent with the nature of the time through which we are passing, whereas dejection is the most fitting state for one living in this earthly realm, since it is the realm of legal prescriptions and responsibility; it is the realm in which final outcomes are as yet unknown; it is the realm in which we lack knowledge of what has gone before us; and it is the realm in which we are called upon to act in accordance with God's rights over us.

A certain Sufi once told me, "Our shaykh once saw his shaykh in a dream after the latter's death, and he was in a state of dejection (*qabḍ*). 'Teacher, why are you dejected?' he asked. The shaykh replied, 'My son, gaiety (*basṭ*) and dejection (*qabḍ)* are two stations which, if you have not experienced both of them fully in this life, you will be required to complete them in the life to come.' This shaykh was someone who, during his lifetime, had most often been in a state of gaiety."

As for his saying, "Call upon the Beloved from afar," it means that we are to call upon the Beloved without claiming to be worthy to receive an answer, with a sense of His lordship over us, and with an awareness of the ways in which we have offended against Him. As Shaykh Abū al-Ḥasan once said, "Never have I asked God to meet a need but that I have kept my own offenses before me."

You may object to this point by citing the hadith about three men who entered a cave, after which a boulder fell down and blocked the cave entrance. They then said, "Let each of us mention the most praiseworthy thing he has ever done for God." The first mentioned his goodness to his parents; the second mentioned his chaste behavior toward his paternal cousin despite his love for her and the opportunity he had had to possess her; and the third mentioned his having invested the wages due to a worker he had hired and how, when he had recovered the money with increase, he had paid it to the worker in full. God then delivered them from their predicament, as the boulder was removed from the mouth of the cave and they came out. This is the gist of the hadith, which was narrated by Muslim in his *Ṣaḥīḥ*.

Know, however, that these three men only made mention of their various acts of obedience in recognition of them as signs of God's favor toward them. Hence, they sought one blessing from God by bearing witness to another. As God reports of Zachariah, "Never yet, O my Lord, has my prayer unto Thee remained unanswered {Maryam [Mary] 19:4}." In so saying, Zachariah was making supplication to God by citing God's previous gracious dealings with him.

A woman once approached a certain king with a request for help. She said to him, "You extended your favor to us last year, and we are in need of your assistance this year as well." The king replied, "Welcome to those who seek our beneficence by citing our beneficence!" Whereupon he gave to her most generously.

For those to whom this door has been opened, it is permissible to inform others of their acts of obedience and the virtuous manner in which they have dealt with others, since in so doing, they are speaking of God's blessings, glory be to Him.

A certain pious ancestor used to wake up in the morning and say, "Yesterday I prayed such-and-such a number of rak^c ahs, I recited such-and-such a number of suras from the Qur'ān," and so forth. He was then asked, "Are you not afraid that you might just be doing eye service?" And he replied, "What a question to ask! Have you ever heard of someone seeking to impress others with things that someone else has done??"

When another person did the same thing, he was asked, "Why don't you keep such things to yourself?" He replied, "Did God not say, 'And of thy Sustainer's blessings shalt thou [ever] speak' {Al-Ḍuḥā [The Bright Morning Hours] 93:11}? Yet here you are, telling me not to speak!"

He said (may God be pleased with him), "Human beings came to exist after having not existed, and they will cease to exist after having existed. From both ends, therefore, they are nothingness. It follows, then, that they are, in essence, nothingness."

What the shaykh meant by this is that created entities cannot be said to be characterized by absolute existence, since absolute existence can be attributed only to God, Who is solitary in this respect. As for the created worlds, they only have existence insofar as this has been granted to them.

Know that someone whose existence is derived from another is, in and of himself, nothingness. Shaykh Abū al-Ḥasan (may God be pleased with him) said, "The Sufi is someone who, in his inward being, sees human beings as so much fine dust in the air—neither existent nor non-existent—just as they are in the knowledge of the Lord of the worlds."

He also said (may God be pleased with him)—in a quote which appeared earlier[8]—"Indeed, we see no creature. After all, is there, in all of existence, anything but the True Sovereign? And even if we must acknowledge other entities, they differ little from the fine dust particles in the air which, when you examine them carefully, you find to be nothing at all."

Or, as we have stated the same truth in our book *Al-Ḥikam*, "the [created] worlds are established by His establishment of them, yet they are rendered as nothing by the singularity of His being."

Shaykh Abū al-Ḥasan (may God be pleased with him) said, "I had a companion who would often come to me speaking of the unity of existence, and I said to him, 'If you want that in which there is no cause for censure, then let distinction (*farq*) be what you speak of to others, and let unity (*jamᶜ*) be what you witness in your heart.'"

The phenomenon with which you could most usefully compare the existence of created entities when viewed with the eye of inward perception is that of shadows. A shadow is neither existent in the full sense, nor non-existent in the full sense. If you affirm the shadow-like nature of effects (creatures), you do not thereby negate the singularity of that which produces them (the Creator). For a thing is only doubled by adding an identical entity to it. Hence, those who testify to the shadow-like nature of effects are not thereby prevented from [affirming] God's unique existence. Similarly, the shadows cast by trees on the surface of a river do not prevent boats from moving through its waters.

From these observations it should be clear to you that the veil which you perceive between yourself and God is not something which actually exists. For if there were an actual veil between you and God, the veil would of necessity be closer to you than God is, whereas there is nothing closer to you than God. Hence, the presumed reality of the veil is the product of an illusion. You are not veiled from God by some entity which exists with Him, since nothing exists with Him. Rather, what has veiled Him from you is the illusion that something else exists with Him. The situation might be likened to that of a man who spent the night in a shelter of some sort and who wanted to come out; however, he heard the sound of wind blowing through a hole in the building and thought it was the roaring of a lion, which prevented him from venturing out. When he woke up the next morning, he found that there had been no lion, but rather, simply the wind whistling through the hole. Hence, what prevented him from coming out was not the existence of a lion, but rather, the illusion of there being a lion.

I once heard him say, "If God were to chastise all creatures, none of their torment would reach you, and if He were to usher them all into bliss, none of their bliss would be yours, as though you were alone in all of existence." Then he recited these lines:

> You are the one being addressed, O human being,
> So lend me your ear and the proof will appear to you.

I also heard him say, "I once went in to see Shaykh Abū al-Ḥasan, thinking that I would like to begin eating only the plainest fare and wearing coarse clothing. But he said to me, 'Abū al-ᶜAbbās, know God and be however you like!'"

Shaykh Abū al-Ḥasan was visited once by a dervish who was wearing a hair shirt. When the shaykh had finished speaking, the man came up to him, took hold of his garment and said, "Master, it's impossible to worship God in clothes like the ones you're wearing."

The shaykh then took hold of the man's clothing and, finding them to be coarse, said, "Nor is it possible to worship God in clothes like the ones you're wearing! My clothes tell people, 'I have no need of you. Don't give me anything,' whereas your clothes tell people, 'I need you. Give to me!'"

This was the approach taken by Shaykh Abū al-ᶜAbbās and his shaykh, Abū al-Ḥasan (may God be pleased with them both), as well as that of their followers. That is to say, they shunned the notion of dressing in a manner which calls attention to the wearer's inward convictions and way of life, since it was their contention that whoever dresses in this way is behaving pretentiously.

Do not, however—may God be gracious to you—understand us to be saying that we condemn those who wear dervishes' attire. Rather, what we mean by this is that it is not necessary for everyone who has a share in the Sufi life to dress in this manner. The person who wishes to wear such attire is free to do so; and those who choose not to wear it are free not to do so, so long as they are doers of good. As God has declared, "There is no cause to reproach the doers of good" {Al-Tawbah [Repentance] 9:91}.

Similarly, the wearing of soft clothing, the eating of tasty food and the drinking of cold water are not to be considered actions which merit God's displeasure if those who do so give thanks to Him for these things. Shaykh Abū al-Ḥasan said, "My son, cool the water, for if you drink lukewarm water and say, 'Thanks be to God!', you will say it with a sense of aversion, whereas if you drink cold water and say, 'Thanks be to God!', every member in your body will respond with gratitude to Him."

The basis for this is God's words concerning Moses, upon him be peace, "So he watered [their flocks] for them; and then he withdrew into the shade and prayed, 'O my Sustainer! Verily, in dire need am I of any good which Thou mayest bestow upon me!'" {Al-Qaṣaṣ [The Story] 28:24} Do you not see how he withdrew into the shade with the intention of giving thanks to God for the grace he had received?

I heard him say, "People are of differing opinions concerning the derivation of the word 'Sufi.' There are those who say that it is based on Sufis' association with wool (*ṣūf*), since wool is often worn by the pious and righteous. It has also been said that it is derived from the *ṣuffah* of the Prophet's mosque, with which are associated *ahl al-ṣuffah*[9]; however, this derivation is not based on the usual pattern for Arabic adjectives of this type."[10]

Then he continued, saying, "The most convincing explanation which has been offered of this term is that it is based on an association with God's action toward the Sufi; that is, God has related to him or her in sincerity and good will (*ṣāfāhu Allāh*, passive, *ṣūfiyā*); hence, the term 'Sufi.'"

Then he recited the following verses:

People have disputed concerning the meaning of "Sufi,"
With all of them saying things which fail to persuade.

I grant this appellation to none but the courageous,
sincere soul
Who has, in turn, been dealt with in sincerity (*ṣūfiyā*),
and who is thus known as "Sufi."

I heard him say, "The word *ṣūfī* is composed of four letters: *ṣād*, *wāw*, *fā'* and *yā'*. The letter *ṣad* stands for the Sufi's patient endurance (*ṣabr*), his honesty (*ṣidq*) and his purity and tranquillity (*ṣafā'*); the letter *wāw* stands for his ecstasy in God (*wajd*), his love and affection for others (*wadd*), and his loyalty (*wafā'*); the letter *fā'* stands for his loss [of things worldly] (*faqd*), his poverty (*faqr*), and his annihilation (*fanā'*); as for the letter *yā'*, it is the *yā'* of attribution or association [which is added to a noun]; hence, if the Sufi is perfected in all of these other aspects, he or she will be "added" to the presence of his or her Master.

He (may God be pleased with him) was once asked about the statement made by Jesus, upon him be peace, "O children of Israel, truly I say unto you, no one will enter the kingdom of heaven unless he is twice born."[11]

He replied, saying, "I most certainly am among those who have been twice born. The first birth was my natural birth, while the second was my birth through the spirit in the heaven of the gnostic sciences, or experiential knowledge."

I heard him say, "The saint will not reach God until he is free of the desire to reach God."

Shaykh Abū al-Ḥasan (may God be pleased with him) said, "The saint will not reach God so long as he still has any of his worldly desires, so long as he still attempts to dispose of his own affairs, or so long as he continues to rely on his own choices."

When the shaykh said, "The saint will not reach God until he is free of the desire to reach God," he did not mean that one must be free from the desire to reach God in the sense that one has actually ceased to desire this; rather, he meant that one must give up this desire as a demand, or as something to which one clings. The person who has become "free of the desire to reach God" in the sense intended here is one whose life is marked by his or her willingness to entrust all things to God and who witnesses to the wisdom of God's choices for him or her; as a result, such a person relinquishes control to Him and places himself, unresisting, in His hands. He or she no longer seeks to make his or her own choices, but rather, leaves them to his or her Lord, knowing the misery and affliction which inevitably follow upon seeking to make one's own choices rather than leaving them to God.

This truth is conveyed in the following poem, which we have included in our book, *Al-Tanwīr*:

Be His servant, surrender to His judgment,
And beware of disposing of your own affairs, which
availeth naught.

Would you feign be the disposer when another is
Sovereign,
And would you dispute the judgments of the Divine?

The supreme goal is to obliterate volition
And every desire, so have you ears to hear?

Thus did our forebears advance and reach their goal.
Hence, let all who follow them walk in their footsteps.

He said (may God be pleased with him), "Know that God has created human beings and has divided them into three parts: tongue, bodily members, and heart. In addition, He has placed a guardian angel over each part. As God, may He be glorified and exalted, has declared:

- "Not even a word can he utter but there is a watcher with him, ever-present" {Qāf 50:18}.
- "And whatever work you may do—[remember that] We are your witness from the moment when you enter upon it" {Yūnus [Jonah] 10:61}.

As for the heart, God has undertaken to guard it Himself, saying, "And know that God knows what is in your minds, and therefore remain conscious of Him" {Al-Baqarah [The Cow] 2:235}. As for our bodily members, God has permitted Satan to assail them. Even so, God requires each part to be faithful in caring out its obligations. For the heart, faithfulness means for it not to occupy itself with worldly concerns, scheming or envy. For the tongue, faithfulness means for it not to backbite, lie or speak of things which are none of its concern. And as for one's bodily members, faithfulness means for them not to hasten to commit acts of disobedience or to hurt any Muslim.

- Those who fall with respect to the heart are hypocrites.
- Those who fall with respect to the tongue are deniers of the truth.
- Those who fall with respect to the bodily members are disobedient.

He said (may God be pleased with him), "A servant's righteousness consists in three things: knowledge of God, knowledge of self, and knowledge of this earthly existence. Those who know God fear Him. Those who know themselves are humble before others. And those who know this earthly existence renounce it."

He said (may God be pleased with him), "My shaykh told me, 'Only take as your companion those who have these four qualities: generosity even when they have little, willingness to pardon an offense committed against them, patient endurance in times of affliction, and contentment with God's decree for them.'"

He said (may God be pleased with him), "Suppose someone buys oil from a vendor and, when it runs out, he says, 'Give me more,' and the vendor pours out some more for him; such a person's religion is more tenuous than the fine stream of oil poured out for him; similarly, if someone buys some coal and, after it has run out, says, 'Give me another piece' and the vendor grants his request, then his heart is blacker than that piece of coal."

He said (may God be pleased with him), "People belong to three categories: those whose good deeds outweigh their bad ones, and who will most certainly be in Paradise; those whose good deeds and bad deeds are equal, and who will most certainly not enter the Fire; and those whose bad deeds outweigh their good deeds, and who will most certainly not remain eternally in the Fire."

He also said (may God be pleased with him), "Entrance into Paradise occurs based on faith, abiding eternally therein is based on intention, and the degrees to which one attains there are based on one's actions. Entrance into the Fire is based on *shirk*, or association of partners with God, remaining there eternally is based on intention, and the depths to which one descends there are based on one's actions."

He said (may God be pleased with him), "One may enter God's presence through two doors only: through the door of the supreme annihilation, that is, natural death, or through the door of the [spiritual] annihilation which is the concern of this [Sufi] community."

He said (may God be pleased with him), "Created entities are of four types: dense bodies, subtle bodies, transparent spirits and the undisclosed mystery. The dense body is, in itself, an inanimate object; the subtle body is, in itself, a jinn; the transparent spirit is, in itself, an angel; while the undisclosed mystery is the meaning to which obeisance was made.[12] Human beings are, in their outward appearance, inanimate objects. Given the presence of the soul, its imagination and its ability to form things, they are jinn. Given the presence of spirit, they are angels. And in addition, they have been given the undisclosed mystery, on account of which they have been counted worthy to be God's vicegerents."

He said (may God be pleased with him), "The astonishing thing is not that someone might get lost for forty years over a distance of just half a mile; rather, what is astonishing is that someone could get lost for sixty or seventy years in a space no larger than the span of one's hand, namely, the stomach!"

He said (may God be pleased with him), "That which is lower commands a view of that which is higher, yet without encompassing it; that which is higher, however, encompasses that which is lower. The saints command a view of the spiritual stations of the prophets, but they do not encompass them, whereas the prophets encompass the spiritual stations of the saints."

One of the pious ancestors once said, "If the unknown were revealed, I would have no more certainty [than I do now]." In explanation of this statement, he said (may God be pleased with him), "In other words, if the unknown were revealed to my soul, I would have no more certainty than I already do concerning what my heart has seen."

He said (may God be pleased with him), "If you were to remove a letter from any of the names of God other than *Allāh*, it would lose its meaning. This applies, for example, to the names *al-ᶜAlīm*, 'the All-Knowing,' *al-Qādir*, 'the All-Powerful,' *al-Raḥīm*, 'the Most Merciful,' and any of the other most beautiful names. However, if you drop the initial *alif* from the name *Allāh*, you still have *lillāh* (meaning "God's," "to God," or "for God"); if you then drop the first *lām*, you still have *lahu* (meaning "to Him," or "His"); and if you drop the second *lām*, you still have *hu* ("He"), which is the last and most basic element which can be used to refer to an entity. Ibn Manṣūr al-Ḥallāj recited these lines:

Four letters in which my heart has found rapture,
And in which my sorrows and thoughts have vanished.

Alif relates to the creation through pardon and forgiveness,
Followed by *lām*, for the reproach which creatures merit.[15]

Then an additional *lām* which further deepens its meanings,
And a *hā'* in which I find both ecstasy and knowledge.[14]

He said (may God be pleased with him), "The spirits of the men and women of truth (*al-ṣiddīqīn*) were revealed to me as they ascended to the Higher Realm, and a voice said to me, '[c]Alī, my horses weren't cowardly; rather, they recalled their resting places in Barba[c]īṣa and Maysara.'" In other words, they did not flee from the creation out of cowardice; rather, they remembered the homelands in which they had come to know the Divine.

He said (may God be pleased with him), "Revelation is the casting of a meaning into a hidden place."

He said (may God be pleased with him), "All of the names of God are for appropriation except the name *Allāh*, which is for attachment."

What the shaykh meant by this was that if you call upon God saying, *Yā Ḥalīm* ("O Most Forbearing One!"), God will in turn address you in His capacity as *al-Ḥalīm*, saying, "I am the Most Forbearing. You, then, be a forbearing servant." If you call upon Him saying, *Yā Karīm* ("O Most Munificent One"), God will address you in His capacity as *al-Karīm*, saying, "I am the Most Munificent. You, then, be a munificent servant." And so on in relation to all of His names with the exception of the name *Allāh*. This name is solely to help us attach ourselves to Him, since the meaning it bears is that of divinity, and divinity is a quality which none of us could appropriate.

He said (may God be pleased with him), "The sky for us is like the ceiling, while the earth is like a house, and the true man in our view is not one who can be confined to this house."

He said (may God be pleased with him), "In this earthly life we are bodily entities together with our spirits, whereas in the life to come, we will be spiritual entities together with our bodies."

I heard him say, "The difference between an act of disobedience committed by a believer and an act of disobedience committed by a libertine may be seen in three respects: The believer does not make up his mind beforehand to commit the act, he does not rejoice in the act at the moment of its commission, nor does he insist upon its rightness after committing it. None of this is true, however, of the libertine."

He once said to one of his followers, "Let your *dhikr* be the name *Allāh*, for it is the sultan of all names. This *dhikr* has both a foundation and a fruit; its foundation is knowledge, and its fruit is light."

However, the light is not sought for itself but, rather, for the sake of disclosure and direct vision.

Once a man came to the shaykh and said to him, "Master, this is a valiant youth."

"Are you a valiant youth?" the shaykh asked.

"Yes, I am," he replied.

The shaykh said, "You know what true youthful valor is. It isn't merely water and salt.[15] Rather, it is faith and right guidance. As God, glory be to Him, has declared, 'They were youths who believed in their Lord, and We advanced them in guidance' {Al-Kahf [The Cave] 18:13}."

The valiant youth is described by God, glory be to Him, when He speaks of Abraham saying, "Said some of them,

'We heard a youth speak of these [gods with scorn]: he is called Abraham'" {Al-Anbiyā' [The Prophets] 21:60}. Abraham was spoken of as a [valiant] youth because he had shattered idols; hence, he who shatters idols is a valiant youth.

Abraham, upon him be peace, came upon physical idols and shattered them. You have spiritual idols, and if you shatter them, you too will be a "valiant youth." Specifically, you have five idols: the ego, craving, Satan, carnal appetite, and this earthly existence. If you shatter them, however, you will be the valiant youth.

Understand here: There is no sword but Dhū al-Faqār, nor is there any valiant youth but ᶜAlī.

He was once asked, "Master, why did al-Qushayrī begin his *Risālah* by speaking of Ibrāhīm Ibn Adham in particular, though other historical figures may have been superior to him?"

The shaykh replied, "The reason for this is that Ibrāhīm Ibn Adham had been an earthly king; he woke up one morning still a king, and by noon he had become one of the greatest of saints. Hence, the author of the *Risālah* began with him in order to make it known that God's grace is not based on human action."

He said (may God be pleased with him), "There are some people who are servants of their spiritual states, whereas others are servants of the One who brought them into these states. The sign that you belong to the first group is that when you come out of a given spiritual state, you grieve its loss, and when you enter it again, you rejoice, whereas the sign that you belong to the second group is that you neither rejoice when you enter a given spiritual state, nor do you grieve when you come out of it."

What the shaykh meant by this statement is that those who have been realized in God possess things without being possessed by them. Hence, spiritual states come to be subject to their control. This takes place by virtue of the person's firm establishment in knowledge, since knowledge passes judgment on spiritual states, and since it is by means of knowledge that such states are weighed. After all, spiritual states are merely a branch of knowledge; knowledge is permanent and enduring, whereas spiritual states have no permanence. That is why it has been said:

> If you did not change, you would not be called a 'state,'[16]
> And whenever you change, you cease to be.
>
> Behold the shadow as it passes away:
> After it lengthens, it begins to diminish.

In the case of the greatest of saints, God has given them mastery over their spiritual states, enabling them to pass judgement on them. Junayd was once asked, "Why is it that we see the [other] shaykhs moving about during the *samā*ᶜ ceremony,[17] while you remain still?"

He replied (may God be pleased with him) by quoting the Qur'anic words, "Thou seest the mountains and thinkest them firmly fixed: But they shall pass away as the clouds pass away" {Al-Naml [The Ants] 27:88}.[18]

Another Sufi was asked, "Why do you not move about during the *samā*ᶜ ceremony?" He replied, saying, "If there is a great saint present at the gathering, I feel bashful in his presence; hence, I keep my ecstasy to myself. However, once I get alone, I give it free rein."

Notice how he retained control over his spiritual state such that he was able to keep it in check if he so desired, and give it free rein if he so desired. If one's heart has expanded thanks to the experiential knowledge of God, incoming influences are absorbed by it. Hence, spiritual states are only expressed outwardly by those whose hearts have not yet expanded sufficiently to contain them. The gnostic has the capacity to contain spiritual states by virtue of the knowledge he possesses. Hence, if some influence comes his way, it is absorbed by the vastness of his knowledge. After all, have you ever seen a sea overflow because of the rain that falls into it from a cloud?

This is why others are unaware of the spiritual states of great saints who have attained to advanced spiritual stations. Those who exhibit their spiritual states outwardly become well-known due to the fact that the effects of the gifts they have received are visible through their actions and words; however, this is because they are too weak to keep such states hidden, and because their hearts have not yet developed the capacity to contain them. Those who exhibit spiritual states outwardly may thus have a greater following than those who have attained to advanced spiritual stations; however, the difference between the former and the latter is like the difference between heaven and earth.

The more you master the divine sciences, the more of a stranger you become in this world, with the result that there are fewer and fewer people who know and understand you and are, therefore, able to give an accurate description of who you are.

He said, "Every discourtesy which yields courtesy on your part is, itself, a courtesy."

He said, "The believer is not satisfied with himself if there is goodness within him, since beyond whatever goodness is within him there are more, and greater, manifestations of goodness; after all, would you expect him to be satisfied with evil?"

He said, "Junayd was a pole with respect to knowledge, Sahl Ibn ᶜAbdullāh al-Tusturī was a pole with respect to spiritual stations, and Abū Yazid al-Bisṭāmī was a pole with respect to spiritual states."

He said, "Kindness is a veil which conceals the One who is Most Kind."

The meaning of what the shaykh said is that if kindness is shown to someone in the realm of the self and its desires (*al-dā'irat al-nafsāniyah*), the self receives it gladly and enthusiastically; if it occurs in the realm of the spirit (*al-dā'irat al-maᶜnawiyah*), the spirit receives it with love and devotion. The person concerned thus feels an affinity for the kindness itself. This engenders a sense of repose, which is accompanied by a sense of intimate warmth toward the person with whom one has found this repose. However, God does not want you to find repose or a sense of intimacy with anyone or anything but Him. It is for this reason that the shaykh (may God be pleased with him) said, "Kindness is a veil which conceals the One who is Most Kind." That is to say, kindness is a veil when one finds repose in it and is tempted to be content with the kindness itself [rather than seeking the One who is its source].

Of relevance in this connection is the account related earlier of when Shaykh Abū al-Ḥasan al-Shādhilī (may God be pleased with him) went in to see a certain shaykh and asked him, "How are you?" The shaykh replied, "I complain to God of the coolness of contentment and surrender, just as you complain of the heat of disposing of your own affairs and choosing for yourself." Abū al-Ḥasan said, "As for my complaint of the heat of disposing of my own affairs and making my own choices, you have tasted the same [suffering], while I still experience it. As for your complaining of the coolness of contentment and surrender, why is that?"

He replied, "I fear that their sweetness will distract me from God!"

God, exalted be He, once spoke by revelation to Moses, upon him be peace, saying, "Moses, Noah would have been the best of servants had it not been for the fact that he found such rest in his pre-dawn prayers; for those who know Me find rest in nothing but Me."

In Alexandria there was a woman among us who had experiential knowledge of God. She told me that once she had heard someone saying to her, "I seek refuge in You from the light and its power to entice, and from the unseen and its power to distract."

She also said to me, "As I walked through Alexandria one day, people around me were happy and enjoying themselves. I thought to myself: Here are these people celebrating, taking pleasure in life, and all the while enjoying God's clemency and patience; as for us, we meet with afflictions and the force of the divine decrees. Then someone said to me, 'Those blessed with the divine presence and an awareness of the rules of courtesy which must be observed before God are not like those immersed in amusement and gaiety.'"

She also said, "When I'm experiencing the divine presence and my husband wants to fulfill his desire for me, I do nothing to prevent him; however, he is unable to do so. Whenever he wants something from me under these circumstances, he's unable to obtain it. Finally he reaches his wits' end and says, 'This beautiful young woman of mine just gives me grief! She doesn't withhold herself from me, yet I still can't get to her!' Then I say to him, 'So which of us is the man, and which of us is the woman?' However, at the times when God's presence is veiled, he can have his way with me."

Al-Wāsiṭī spoke truly when he said, "The enjoyment of obedience is a deadly poison." An example of this phenomenon is that if the door is opened for you to the sweetness of obedience, you begin to engage in it as a means of seeking its sweetness, as a result of which you miss the opportunity to demonstrate sincere devotion in your performance of such actions, and you want to continue in them not out of loyalty to your Lord, but rather, because of the sweetness and enjoyment that you find in them. Hence, you appear to be performing such acts for God when, in reality, you are only doing so in fulfillment of your own desires. In such a situation, the danger is that the pleasure you experience in obedience will become a reward which you seek in this life, the result being that when you come to the Day of Resurrection, there will be no reward left for you.

When I read to him out of *Kitāb al-Ḥaqā'iq* by al-Sulamī where he states, "The reasoning of the rational has ended in confusion," the shaykh quoted Shaykh Abū al-Ḥasan al-Shādhilī (may God be pleased with them both), saying, "Those who are spiritually realized suffer no confusion concerning those things which cause confusion to ordinary believers."

He also said (may God be pleased with him), "People are of three types: those who bear witness to what proceeds from them to God, those who bear witness to what proceeds from God to them, and those who bear witness to what proceeds from God to God."

What the shaykh meant by this statement is that there is one group of people who have the tendency to see their own failures and the offenses they have committed; hence, they frequently seek God's forgiveness and are burdened constantly by feelings of sorrow and anxiety. Such people are overcome with distress whenever they conduct themselves badly or receive insight into negative qualities in themselves. Those in the second group have the tendency to focus on God's bounty, goodness and generosity toward them; as a result, they are in a constant state of happiness in God and joy in His grace. As God, glory be to Him, has declared, "Say, 'In [this] bounty of God and in His grace—in this, then, let them rejoice: it is better than all that they may amass!'" {Yūnus [Jonah] 10:58}

The first group are those whose primary focus is on worship and the renunciation of this earthly life, while the second group are those whose primary focus is on the divine providence and love. Those in the first group dwell in the realm of legal prescription and responsibility, while those in the second dwell in the realm of God-given knowledge. The first group are those who live in a state of vigilance, while the second group are those who live in a state of experiential knowledge.

This is why Shaykh Abū al-Ḥasan (may God be pleased with him) said, "The gnostic is someone who recognizes the adversities of this temporal existence in the kindnesses which he or she receives from God, and who recognizes his or her own offenses in God's goodness to him or her.[19] Thus, remember God's signs in order that you might prosper.

He also said, "The performance of fewer good works while witnessing to God's grace is better than the performance of more good works while witnessing to one's own negligence or failure." As one gnostic said, "Bearing witness to one's own negligence or failure involves a degree of "association" (*shirk*) with the divine decree, or pre-determination."[20]

Shaykh Abū al-Ḥasan (may God be pleased with him) said, "One night I recited the Qur'anic verses, 'I seek refuge with the Lord and Cherisher of Mankind, the Ruler of

Mankind, the God of Mankind, from the mischief of the Whisperer [of evil], who withdraws [after his whisper], who whispers into the hearts of Mankind, among Jinns and among Men' {Al-Nās [Mankind] 114}.[21] And I was told, 'the mischief of the Whisperer' is an insinuation which comes between you and the Beloved, causing you to forget His wonderful kindnesses and reminding you of your own bad deeds. In so doing, it reduces the things recorded by the angel to your right and increases those recorded by the angel to your left, thereby drawing you away from a positive perception of God and His Messenger and toward a negative one."

Beware of entering through this door, which has led astray many of those who have renounced this earthly existence and devoted themselves to worship, as well as those committed to diligent striving [along the spiritual path].

It is for this reason, moreover, that you rarely find a person who has renounced this earthly existence or who has devoted himself or herself to the worship of God but that he or she is in a constant state of distress and sorrow, since they know that God has called them to servanthood, causing them to bear its burdens and laying upon them the responsibility which the heavens, the earth and the mountains feared to take upon themselves. As God, glory be to Him, has declared, "Verily, We did offer the trust [of reason and volition] to the heavens, and the earth, and the mountains; but they refused to bear it because they were afraid of it. Yet man took it up—for, verily, he has always been prone to be most wicked, most foolish" {Al-Aḥzāb [The Confederates] 33:72}.

Those who have renounced this earthly existence have a direct vision of the weight of what they bear, yet they have not penetrated to a vision of the kindness of God which bears these burdens for those of His servants who rely fully upon Him. Consequently, distress and melancholy are their constant companions.

As for those endowed with experiential knowledge of God, they know the weight of the responsibilities which they have been given to bear; however, they also know that they are too weak to bear them or fulfill them as long as they rely upon themselves. God, glory be to Him, declares, "For man has been created weak" {Al-Nisā' [Women] 4:28}. These people know that if they seek God's assistance, He will bear for them that which He has given them to bear. As He has declared, glory be to Him, "And for everyone who places his trust in God, He [alone] is enough" {Al-Ṭalāq [Divorce] 65:3}. They seek His assistance in all sincerity and He bears their burdens in their stead. Thus it is that they advance toward God, borne along on litters of grace and fanned with the fragrant breezes of divine compassion.

Others have advanced toward God bearing the burdens of legal prescription and its attendant responsibilities, suffering constant hardships and feeling the vastness of the distances before them. If God wills, however, He overtakes them with his compassion, taking them by the hand and leading them [away] from a focus on their own actions to a realization of the fact that it is God Himself who has enabled them to act obediently, thereby sweetening their days and causing the signs of His providential care to shine brightly within them.

As for the third group, namely, those who witness to what God has bestowed upon Himself, they have been granted a vision of the oneness of existence (*tawḥīd*) and the all-encompassing singularity of the Divine (*tafrīd*).

Those who belong to the first group, namely, those who focus on that which proceeds from them to God, have yet to emerge from inward *shirk*, or association of other entities with God, though they may have abandoned its outward manifestations. Such people upbraid themselves, bearing witness to their failures and offenses. Now, if they did not see these failures and offenses as originating with and belonging to themselves, they would not reproach themselves when they fail. It was to this that the gnostic quoted earlier was referring when he stated, "Bearing witness to one's own negligence or failure is not without a degree of association (*shirk*) with the divine decree, or pre-determination."

You may object here, saying, "If reproaching and criticizing oneself involves a kind of subtle *shirk*, then what are we to do given that God Himself has found fault with the self [which is guilty of negligence]? Indeed, God has commanded us to reproach ourselves if we fail or are negligent and reproaches us Himself if we are neglectful."

In answer to this objection, we say: Self-reproach is indeed a duty, since God has commanded you to reproach yourself. However, He has commanded you to do so without testifying of yourself that it has power [to act on its own], and without attributing to your self acts for which you view yourself as being the doer.

As for the second group, namely, those who bear witness to that which proceeds from God to them, it may be said that although this attitude is preferable to that of the first group, it is, nevertheless, still not free of a kind of affirmation of self, since one sees oneself as having been given gifts by the Truth. After all, if it weren't for such people's affirmation of themselves, they would not bear witness to this. For these two reasons, then, the people of God prefer the third group, namely, those who bear witness to that which proceeds from God to God.

He said (may God be pleased with him), "If the gnostic is given reason to fear, he feels afraid." As God stated as if on the lips of Moses, upon him be peace, "I fled from you because I feared you" {Al-Shu^{c}arā' [The Poets] 26:21}.

What the shaykh (may God be pleased with him) meant by this is that God's grace granted to the gnostic does not prevent him from seeing His justice, nor does his witnessing of God's kindness prevent him from fearing those dimensions of His will which have yet to be revealed.

You should know that the states experienced by those who have been granted experiential knowledge as they near the end of their spiritual journeys may be difficult to understand for those who are still at the beginning of the path.

As he first sets out on the spiritual path, the disciple is influenced by fears due to the fact that the power of the truth has not yet taken full possession of him; once his annihilation has been realized, he is no longer affected by external stimuli, nor is he governed any longer by habit. However, when he is brought back to the state of permanence (*baqā'*), things affect him once again just as they did when he first started out on the path. As God has declared, "Out of this [earth] have We created you, and into it shall We return you" {Ṭaha [O Man] 20:55}. Hence, you will find that the novice disciple, when given reason to fear, feels afraid, and that likewise the gnostic, when given reason to fear, feels afraid. However, although they may be similar in appearance, they are not the same; for the novice feels afraid due to what is veiled from his sight, while the gnostic feels afraid due to the perfection of his knowledge. Therefore, we should not show preference for a servant who is confident of God's kindness and grace over someone who is fearful of what he does not yet know of God's will. Similarly, we should not show preference for a servant who relies upon the manifest content of the divine promise over a servant who has been brought back to a focus on pre-eternity,[22] as a result of which he no longer stops at the gracious promise and bliss but, rather, goes beyond this to what has been known to God from all eternity, whatever it may be.

It is recorded that at the Battle of Badr, the Messenger of God ﷺ stood praying to God with his hands raised heavenward, saying, "O God, if you cause this community[23] to perish, there will thenceforth be no one left to worship You!" He went on beseeching his Lord until his cloak fell off his shoulders, whereupon Abū Bakr (may God be pleased with him) said, "O Messenger of God, these entreaties of yours are sufficient, since He has already accomplished for you what He has promised!"

In this situation the Apostle ﷺ, given his perfect knowledge of God, was bearing witness to the [unknown dimension of the] divine will, whereas Abū Bakr (may God be pleased with him) was bearing witness to God's gracious promise.[24] The Messenger of God ﷺ was aware, of course, of the gracious promise of which Abū Bakr spoke. After all, it was through him ﷺ that Abū Bakr had learned of this promise to begin with. However, God was leading the Prophet ﷺ along the more perfect path by causing him to demonstrate his sole reliance on God's will, which depends upon nothing, and upon which everything depends.

He said (may God be pleased with him), "What matters is not whether geographical distances are collapsed for someone, since he or she is merely in Mecca or some other earthly location; rather, what matters is whether one's personal qualities are 'collapsed' since, when this takes place, one is with God."

Quoting his own shaykh, he said (may God be pleased with him), "Those who have devoted themselves to worship and who have renounced earthly life leave this temporal realm with their hearts still closed to God."[25]

Quoting his own shaykh, he said (may God be pleased with him), "Whoever does not penetrate deeply into these sciences will die as one who, without realizing it, has been stubbornly persisting in the gravest of sins."

I once heard him say, quoting his shaykh Abū al-Ḥasan, may God be pleased with him, "Everything which God has forbidden to you is [like] the tree from which Adam ate; however, when Adam ate from the tree, he descended to earth to become God's vicegerent there, whereas when you eat from the forbidden tree, where do you descend? You descend to the land of estrangement."

He said (may God be pleased with him), "There was, in al-Maghrib, a certain friend of God who used to deliver public addresses. Now, this saint happened to be obese, and as he spoke to a group of people one day, a man with a large, bare head said, 'This man's looks are enough to make anybody want to renounce this world! He's huge as a bear!' The shaykh, who was given knowledge of the man's comment, said from the pulpit, 'You with the little head! The only thing that's made me so fat is love for Him!' Then he recited these lines:

Someone said to me, "You're no lover.
If you were, you would have wasted away long ago!

My heart aflame, I replied,
"You've never tasted love yourself. So how can you
know me?

My heart came to love without my body's knowledge,
For had it known, it wouldn't have stayed plump."

He said (may God be pleased with him), “Someone invited Shaykh Abū al-Ḥasan to his home one day, so he came to the man’s home along with his followers. When we prepared to leave without having drunk anything, the shaykh said to us, ‘How stingy you are! It’s stinginess on the part of a Sufi to eat [at someone’s home] without drinking as well. The Messenger of God ﷺ said, “Whoever gives a believer a drink of water when it is available is equal to someone who has freed seventy of Ishmael’s descendents.”’ Then he continued, ‘If you partake of someone’s food, then drink at his home as well in order that he might receive this great reward.’”

He said (may God be pleased with him), “I went in one day to see Shaykh Abū al-Ḥasan (may God be pleased with him) and he said to me, ‘If you want to be my follower, then ask no one for anything, and if you receive anything without asking for it, do not accept it.’

I thought to myself: The Prophet himself ﷺ used to accept gifts, and he said, ‘Whatever comes to you without your asking for it, take it.’

The shaykh then said, ‘You’re thinking to yourself: The Prophet ﷺ used to accept gifts, and he used to say, “Whatever comes to you without your asking for it, take it.” However, God said concerning the Prophet ﷺ, “Say: ‘I but warn you on the strength of divine revelation’ {Al-Anbiyā’ [The Prophets] 21:45}.” Now, when has God given you revelation? If you are going to follow his example in taking people’s gifts, then you must take them in the same way in which he did. In the case of the Prophet ﷺ, he only accepted things from people in order to reward and compensate them for what they were giving him. If your soul has been purified and sanctified to this decree, then accept what people give you; otherwise, do not.’”

He asked one of his followers, "Why have you stopped seeking me out?"

He replied, "Master, I've become self-sufficient through you."

The shaykh (may God be pleased with him) said, "No one has ever become self-sufficient through anyone. Even Abū Bakr did not become self-sufficient through the Messenger of God ﷺ, nor did he ever cease to seek him out."

He said (may God be pleased with him), "When God created the earth, it was in tumult, so he fixed it in place with the mountains. Hence He declared that He had 'made the mountains firm' {Al-Nāziᶜāt [Those That Rise] 79:32}. So also when God created the soul, it was in tumult, so he secured it with the 'mountains' of reason. Hence, when your reason is sound and your light is sufficient, a tranquillity born of His immanence will descend upon you from your Lord, and your soul's agitation will cease. You will have confidence in the One in whose hands all causes rest; hence, you will be at peace: calmly accepting your divinely decreed fates, fully endowed with His support and His lights, and gladly relinquishing all attempts to dispose of your own affairs or to dispute that which has been ordained for you. In short, your soul will rest serenely in your Lord, knowing that He sees you."

Indeed, is it not sufficient that your Lord is Witness to all things?

Such a soul is worthy to be addressed with the words, "O thou soul in [complete] rest and satisfaction! Come back thou to thy Lord, well pleased and well-pleasing unto Him! Enter, then, among My devotees! Yea, enter thou My heaven!" {Al-Fajr [The Dawn] 89:27-30}[26]

Quoting his shaykh, he said (may God be pleased with him), "It is night-time now, and night is a time of dormancy and silence until it is illuminated by the rising of the sun of gnosis, the moon of belief in the divine unity, or the stars of knowledge."

He said (may God be pleased with him), "God, mighty and majestic is He, says: Adam, I have created all things for your sake, and I have created you for My sake. Hence, do not allow yourself to become distracted by what belongs to you from the One to Whom you belong."

He said (may God be pleased with him), "All of the universes are slaves placed in subjection [to you], and you are a slave to the divine presence."

I heard him say, "The essence of intention is the negation of that which is not intended."

I also heard him say, "Jesus, upon him be peace, said, 'O children of Israel, say not, "Knowledge is in the heavens, so who will bring it down?" nor, "It is beneath the earth, so who will bring it up?" Rather, follow the moral example of those endowed with Spirit and emulate the virtues of the prophets, and I will cause such knowledge to well up from within your hearts that it will engulf you.'"

He also said (may God be pleased with him), "If, when a disciple comes to us, he still has some attachment to the world, we do not say to him, 'Abandon your worldly attachments and come.' Rather, we leave him in peace concerning the matter until we have established him so firmly in the lights of experiential knowledge that he abandons them of his own accord. Such a person's situation might be likened to that of a group of people aboard a ship at sea, and whose captain says to them, 'Tomorrow a gale so powerful will blow up that the only thing that will save you is to throw some of your possessions overboard, so you'd best throw them overboard now,' yet no one listens to what he says. When the storms blow, however, the prudent among them throw their possessions overboard of their own accord; so also when the storms of certainty blow up, it is the disciple himself who abandons his worldly attachments without anyone else prompting him to do so."

Speaking about the great saint Shaykh ᶜAbd al-Razzāq (may God be pleased with him), he said that once when a man from al-Mahdiyah came to see the shaykh, the shaykh said to him, "I see in you the evidence of grace. Where are you from, and what is your story?"

The man replied, "Master, I was once among the notables and leading personalities of al-Mahdiyah; in fact, I was the wealthiest, most influential man in the city. We were then visited by a man who claimed that he could guide others to God. Having a burning desire to reach God myself, I went to him and he said to me, 'You will only fulfill this aim of yours if you give up all of your wealth, divorce all of your wives irrevocably, and change your attire.' I did everything he had instructed me, yet my heart only grew harder. Greatly distressed and confused, I couldn't bear to remain in al-Mahdiyah after having lost all the wealth and prestige I'd once known there. And, having gained nothing inwardly in compensation for all that I'd given up, I decided to come here with the intention of performing the pilgrimage to Mecca."

Shaykh ᶜAbd al-Razzāq said, "[Such people's teachings are] claims devoid of all spiritual insight, may God chastise them!" Then he said to the man, "Stay here with us." When the time for the pilgrimage had arrived, he sent him off with some residents of Alexandria. Later the man returned to the shaykh in Alexandria, and when it had come time for him to set out for al-Maghrib, the shaykh said to him, "Go to your town, and when you get there, people will hear of your arrival and come out in haste to receive you, presenting you with clothing and carriages. Take the best of what they have to offer and enter al-Mahdiyah. What has been given to you of this world's blessings, accept them, and God will restore to you what you had before, and more. You will find that your wives have been divorced by their husbands, so take them back, and you will attain even greater power, prestige and wealth than you had previously. And once this has all come to pass for you, God will open the eyes of your heart."

[Shaykh Abū al-ᶜAbbas continued, saying,], "So, he set out on his journey, and when he reached the coast of al-Mahdiyah, people heard that so-and-so had come from the East. Now it happened that there was no one in the entire town but that this man had helped him in some way or performed some service on his behalf; hence, they rushed out to meet him with resplendent attire and the most elegant of carriages. He put on the most beautiful garments, mounted the best carriages and entered al-Mahdiyah, where he was showered with gifts, treasures and wealth. In addition, he found that his wives had been divorced by their husbands and had fulfilled their prescribed waiting periods, so he took them back. In short, everything that the shaykh had promised him came to pass on that day. Then God opened the eyes of his heart."

One day he spoke of the virtues that distinguished Abū Bakr (may God be pleased with him), saying, "The Messenger of God ﷺ said, 'Abū Bakr is not superior to you in fasting or prayer, but rather, in something which to him is an established fact.' Then he asked, 'And what is this thing which to him is an established fact?' One of those present replied, '[Self-]examination (*murāqabah*).'"

The shaykh then continued, "Such a reply merely touches on the surface. If someone who occupies a lower rank than the Veracious One (Abū Bakr) finds himself engaging in self-examination, he should seek God's forgiveness for it just as a disobedient person seeks God's forgiveness for his disobedience. The reason for this is that if one attributes the act of examination to oneself, it is as if he were saying, 'You [God] are *al-Raqīb*, or the Ever Watchful One, and so am I.' As God has declared, 'Could there be any divine power besides God? Sublimely exalted is God above anything to which men may ascribe a share in His divinity' {Al-Naml [The Ants] 27:63}."

Once when one of his followers had decided to perform the pilgrimage to Mecca, he instructed him saying, "When you reach the house,[27] let your concern be not with the house, but with the Lord of the house. Be not among those who worship idols and graven images."

He said, "Those who know God do not rest tranquilly in God, for to rest tranquilly in God is a sign that one considers oneself safe; however, no one considers himself safe from God's scheming (*makr*) but those who are spiritually lost."

This statement by Shaykh Abū al-ᶜAbbās is similar to one made by Shaykh Abū al-Ḥasan (may God be pleased with them both), who said, "I was once told, 'Never consider yourself safe from My scheming.' Hence, if I consider you to be safe, my knowledge is not comprehensive." And thus were the shaykhs in their teaching.

He also used to say, "The saint, even in his annihilation, must retain a subtle degree of discernment which results in a sense of accountability before God's law. The situation might be likened to that of a person in a darkened house, who knows that he is present there, though he cannot see himself directly."

He also used to say, "I tell you truly, never once have I sat [with my followers] but that I have placed flight through the air, walking on water and the collapsing of geographical distances beneath my carpet."[28]

Once, after I had read to him al-Muḥāsibī's book, *Al-Riᶜāyah*, he said (may God be pleased with him), "This entire book could be summed up in two statements: 'Worship God provided that you have knowledge,' and, 'Never be satisfied with yourself.'" Having said this, he would not allow it to be read anymore.

After being asked once about a certain shaykh who was his contemporary, he said, "God has constricted his freedom through abstinence born of piety (*waraᶜ*), whereas He has broadened our freedom through experiential knowledge (*maᶜrifah*)."

Now, you should not think that by his saying that the gnostic has been given broader freedom by virtue of his spiritual knowledge, he means that the gnostic would eat that which is forbidden or suspect. However, the gnostic (*al-ᶜārif*) has been endowed with enlightened spiritual vision which enables him to perceive what would be hidden to the abstinent believer (*al-wariᶜ*), as a result of which he may accept food which he knows to be lawful and sound based on what he has been allowed to see by his inward spiritual vision, whereas the abstinent believer does not have access to such knowledge. For this reason, the gnostic may partake of food which the abstinent believer would refrain from eating.

He (may God be pleased with him) used to say, "Whoever longs to meet an oppressor is himself an oppressor."

He used to express preference for those who are rich, yet grateful, over those who are poor, but patiently enduring. This is the teaching of Ibn ᶜAṭā' and Abū ᶜAbdullāh Muḥammad al-Tirmidhī al-Ḥakīm. He said, "Gratitude is a quality of those who inhabit Paradise even after they enter

Paradise, whereas this may not be said of patient endurance."

I also heard him say, "'Dejection' (*qabḍ*) is of two types: dejection which has a cause, and dejection which has no cause. The type of dejection which has a cause is experienced by both ordinary believers and the elect, while the type which has no cause is experienced only by the elect."

He used to say (may God be pleased with him), "Thanksgiving is the heart's openness to witnessing the Sustainer's grace."

The Arabic word for "thanksgiving" is *shukr*; if the letters of the verb *shakara* are rearranged, we have the verb *kashara*, which is used of an animal when it bears its teeth. A certain gnostic once said, "If Satan knew of a path which leads to God more perfectly than that of thanksgiving, he would be certain to block it. Did he not say: 'Then will I assault them from before them and behind them, from their right and their left, nor wilt Thou find in most of them gratitude [for Thy mercies]' {Al-Aᶜrāf [The Faculty of Discernment] 7:17}?[29] Note that he did not say, 'Nor wilt Thou find, in most of them, patient endurance, fear of God, or hopefulness.'"

When I met in Alexandria with the Sultan King al-Manṣūr Lājīn, may God have mercy on him, I said to him, "You should give thanks to God, since He has blessed your reign with prosperity, as a result of which your subjects are content with you. After all, prosperity is something which kings are not able to achieve or secure in the way that they are able to institute justice and openhandedness."

"What is thanksgiving?" he asked.

"Thanksgiving is of three types," I replied. "Thanksgiving of the tongue (*shukr al-lisān*), thanksgiving of the bodily members (*shukr al-arkān*), and thanksgiving of the heart (*shukr al-janān*). Thanksgiving of the tongue involves speaking of God's blessings. As God, glory be to Him, has said, 'And of thy Sustainer's blessings shalt thou ever speak' {Al-Ḍuḥā [The Bright Morning Hours] 93:11}. Thanksgiving of the bodily members involves acting in obedience to God; as God has declared, 'Labor, O people of David, in gratitude [towards Me]' {Saba' [Sheba] 34:13}. And as for thanksgiving of the heart, it is the recognition that every blessing with which you or any other human being is endowed is from God; as God has said, 'For whatever good thing comes to you, comes from God' {Al-Naḥl [The Bees] 16:53}."

Concerning the first type of thanksgiving, the Messenger of God ﷺ said, "Speaking of God's blessings is thanksgiving." In illustration of the second type, the Messenger of God ﷺ stood [praying] for so long that his feet began to swell. Someone then asked him, "Why do you impose this on yourself when God has forgiven you all your sins, past as well as future?" He ﷺ replied, "Shouldn't I be a grateful servant?" And as for the third type of thanksgiving, every morning the Messenger of God ﷺ used to pray, saying, "O God, whatever blessing I, or any of Your other creatures, enjoy this morning is from You alone."

(These hadiths, however, did not occur to me at the time I was speaking with him.)

Then the king asked, "And how should the thankful person comport himself?"

I replied, "If the person possesses knowledge, then through teaching and guiding others. If the person possesses wealth, then by spending on others and preferring them to himself or herself. And if the person possesses influence and prestige, then by treating others justly and protecting them from injury and hardship."

He said (may God be pleased with him), "God has one angel that fills one-third of the universe, another angel that fills two-thirds of the universe, another that fills the entire universe, and still another who, if he were to put one foot down on the Earth, would find no room to put down the other."

Then he continued, saying, "Someone might ask, 'If there is an angel that fills the entire universe, then where is the one that fills one-third of the universe, and where is the one that fills two-thirds of the universe?'" In reply to this question, he said, "Subtle bodies don't compete for space. One might liken the situation to a lamp which you have brought into a house so that it fills the house with its light. However, if you brought one thousand additional lamps into the house, there would be room for the light given off by every one of them."

I heard him say, "The Messenger of God ﷺ once said to Abū Bakr, "Abū Bakr, do you want me to invite you to something?"

"To what, O Messenger of God?" Abū Bakr asked.

"To that," he ﷺ replied.

I also heard him say, "The Messenger of God ﷺ said, "Abū Bakr, do you know about 'day...day'?"

"Yes, O Messenger of God," he replied. "You asked me about the day on which destinies were decreed, and at that time I heard you say, 'I bear witness that there is no god but God and that Muḥammad is the Messenger of God.'"

He said (may God be pleased with him), "Abū Bakr and ^{c}Umar were the caliphs of messengerhood, while ^{c}Uthmān and ^{c}Alī were the caliphs of prophethood."

He said (may God be pleased with him), "If ordinary believers see someone associated with the path of God who's come from the bleak desert expanses, they receive him with veneration and acclaim, while untold numbers of saints and substitutes are in their midst without their paying them the least attention, despite the fact that they are the ones who bear their burdens and direct them away from dependence on beings other than God. The situation might be likened to one in which a zebra is brought into town, whereupon everyone makes the rounds with it, marveling at its stripes and its lovely appearance, while the donkeys in their midst that bear all their burdens are hardly given a passing glance."

Shaykh Abū al-Ḥasan (may God be pleased with him) said, "Abū al-ᶜAbbās, if someone says something about you which is not true, then say, 'God knows about me what He knows, and with God rests final outcomes.'"

Shaykh Abū al-Ḥasan also said, "God, knowing what [untruths] would be uttered about His saints and the men and women of truth, began with Himself by turning away from and destroying a people who attributed to Him a wife and a son."

If it is said concerning the person of truth that he or she is an unbeliever, or if it is said of a saint that he or she is heedless of God and straying from the right path, and if the person of truth or the saint is disturbed by what has been said, then he or she is told, 'What was said about you is a description of the way you would be were it not for My favor toward you. However, things have likewise been said of Me which are unworthy of My majesty.'"

He said (may God be pleased with him), "Those who perish on account of this community outnumber those who are saved."

Know that God has afflicted those who belong to this community through other people in order that, by virtue of their patient endurance of people's persecution, He might elevate their status, bring their lights to perfection and realize their spiritual heritage through them, and in order that when they are persecuted as their forebears were, they might exhibit patience endurance just as they did. If people's unanimous acceptance of those who bring guidance were evidence of these messengers' perfection, then the one who would have been most worthy of such acceptance was the Messenger of God ﷺ. He ﷺ was accepted by some people whom God guided by His grace; however, this was not granted to others from whom the Truth concealed his messengerhood.

Thus it is that in relation to this community, people have been divided into those who recognize them and those who censure them, believers and deniers. The only people who believe in their sciences and mysteries are those whom the Truth, glory be to Him, desires to admit into their ranks. Hence, there are few who acknowledge God's election of them and providential care for them, the reasons for this being widespread ignorance, the heedlessness which has so many in its grip, and people's aversion to there being anyone who enjoys a special grace or a rank which is superior to theirs. Have you not heard God's declaration that, "most people know it not" {Al-Rūm [The Byzantines] 30:6}? And whence are people to obtain knowledge of the Truth's mysteries [manifested] in His friends and the dawning of His light in the hearts of those whom He loves?

The reason that some people perish on account of this community is that those of its members whom God makes visible must be revealed to others through the most dazzling of graces and miraculous powers; however, ordinary believers find it difficult to comprehend that such things would be granted to anyone but the prophets or that miracles might be performed by anyone but those who are sinless. Such people do not realize that every miracle performed by a saint is, in fact, a miracle performed by the prophet of whom this saint is a follower. Rather, they suppose that the performance of a miracle by a saint means that the saint has a share in the station of prophethood. Yet God forbid that the prophet and the saint should share in the same station! This could not be the case given Abū Yazīd's statement that, "All that the friends of God have received from the prophets may be likened to a skin filled with honey through whose pores some of the honey has seeped out; the honey which remains inside the skin represents the knowledge of the prophets, while that which has seeped out is the saints' share thereof."

Know—may God have mercy on you—that when you take pride in a powerful person, this does not mean that you share in this person's power or high rank. The friends of God take pride in the prophets whose guidance they have followed and whose path they have embraced; however, they do not for this reason share in their power or standing. Have you not heard the words of the Sovereign, exalted be He, "All honor belongs to God and [thus] to His Apostle and those who believe" {Al-Munāfiqūn [The Hypocrites] 63:8}? From this declaration it may be seen that affirmation of the honor (*ᶜizzah*) of the Messenger of God ﷺ and of the believers does not necessitate that they should share with God in His power and glory (*ᶜizz*).

Moreover, it is the wisdom of God which has decreed that people should not be in agreement over God's friends; on the contrary, they are divided over them, as we have explained above.

It should also be borne in mind that if everyone believed in God's friends, they would miss the opportunity to endure patiently the disbelief of those who do not believe in them; similarly, if everyone disbelieved in them, they would miss the opportunity to give thanks for the affirmation of those who do believe in them. Hence, by means of His wise choice on behalf of His friends, God wills for people to be divided concerning them, with some believing and others disbelieving, in order that His friends might worship Him through thanksgiving for those who believe them, and through patient endurance in response to those who disbelieve them. After all, half of faith is patient endurance, and the other half is thanksgiving.

You should know that given the cherished place which the saints occupy with God, He has cast a veil between them and other human beings even if they are visible among them. For the friends of God are manifested among other people by virtue of their outward knowledge and the evidence which this provides [of their advanced learning], while the secret of their sainthood remains concealed.

Shaykh Abū al-Ḥasan (may God be pleased with him) said, "Every saint has a veil, and my veil is earthly causes."

There are those whose veil is that of appearing as someone with a domineering, forceful presence. People in general tend not to tolerate the company of those who fall in this category. Hence, the reason for a saint's appearing in this guise is the Truth's self-manifestation through one of these qualities in him. If such a quality predominates in the saint's inner experience or witness (*shuhūd*), it will likewise predominate in his outward bearing (*ẓuhūr*). Consequently, the only individuals who are willing to become his followers and persevere are those whose egos and selfish inclinations God has crushed.

Our Shaykh Abū al-ᶜAbbās (may God be pleased with him) was of this type; indeed, you couldn't sit in his presence without terror gripping your heart. However, those whom God has delivered from their egos and selfish inclinations will not find it strange that he should appear in this powerful, awe-inspiring guise; after all, what dominion could be greater than this? This is the kind of dominion which even kings lack. Have you not observed that in all times and places there are saints before whom the kings of their era are reduced to humility, obedience, and submissiveness?

There are, in addition, saints whose veil is that of frequenting kings and rulers concerning people's needs. Some short-sighted person might say: If this were truly a saint, he would not frequent those endowed with worldly wealth and power. However, it is unfair to say such a thing; rather, you should take a good look at the manner in which this saint frequents such people: If he does so on others' behalf and with the aim of alleviating their suffering and enabling them to obtain what they would be unable to obtain by themselves; and if he does this with an attitude of self-denial and a lack of desire for what his hosts possess, drawing on the power of faith while seated in their presence, exhorting them to do good and discouraging them from doing evil, then there is no reason for him not to comport himself in this manner, since he is doing good. As God, glory be to Him, has said, "There is no cause to reproach the doers of good" {Al-Tawbah [Repentance] 9:91}.

This was the path adopted by our shaykh's shaykh, the great pole Abū al-Ḥasan al-Shādhilī (may God be pleased with him). In fact, I once heard the shaykh, imam and mufti of all mankind, Taqī al-Dīn Muḥammad Ibn ᶜAlī al-Qushayrī (may God be pleased with him) say of him, "Both the public in general and those in authority were ignorant of Shaykh Abū al-Ḥasan al-Shādhilī's true rank due to the frequency of his visits to them on others' behalf."

You should know that this sort of intercession would only be possible for someone who has taken on the qualities of the Divine, having spent himself on others' behalf and humbled himself in the pursuit of God's good pleasure. Such a person has come to know the vastness of God's mercy and, as a result, treats God's servants with mercy, heeding the Messenger of God's exhortation, "The merciful will receive mercy from the Most Merciful and Compassionate. Therefore, be merciful to those on earth, that He who is in Heaven may have mercy on you."

I was told that Shaykh Abū al-Ḥasan (may God be pleased with him) once summoned a Jewish eye doctor to treat someone who was at his home. The doctor replied, however, "I can only treat him by special permission. A decree has been issued out of Cairo stating that no physician can treat anyone unless he receives permission from the Chief Physician in Cairo." When the Jewish doctor had left, the shaykh told his servants to get his carriage ready, whereupon he set off immediately for Cairo, where he obtained written permission for the Jewish doctor to treat a patient. He then returned to Alexandria without staying in Cairo even for a single night. Once he had arrived in Alexandria, he sent again for the Jewish doctor, who declined a second time, giving the same reason as the first. When the shaykh then brought out a letter stating that he had obtained permission for him to administer treatment, the doctor was greatly astonished at the shaykh's generosity and nobility of character.

A saint might, on the other hand, be veiled by great wealth and worldly comfort. A certain shaykh once related the account of a man who lived in al-Maghrib. This man was among those who have renounced this worldly existence, and who are devoted to serious endeavor and striving.

Making his living as a fisherman, he gave away some of his catch as alms, and lived on the rest. One of this shaykh's followers had decided to travel to al-Maghrib, so the shaykh said to him, "If you go to such-and-such a town, visit my brother, so-and-so, and deliver him my greetings. Please also ask him to make supplication for me, since he is one of God's saints."

The shaykh's disciple said, "So I set off on my journey. When I reached the town in question, I asked about this man, and I was directed to a house which would only have been fit for a king. Bewildered, I asked for the man and I was told, 'He is with the Sultan now,' which bewildered me even more. An hour later, along he came in the most sumptuous clothing and carriage, like a king with his royal entourage. More bewildered than ever, I nearly left without meeting with him. But then I said to myself: I can't go against my shaykh's request. So I sought permission to see him and he agreed. When I came in to see him, I was appalled by the sight of slaves, servants and the most elegant finery.

"I said to him, 'Your brother, so-and-so, sends you his greetings.'

"'Have you come from him?' he asked,

"'Yes, I have,' I replied.

"Then he said, 'When you return, say to him: How long will you go on being preoccupied with this earthly existence? How long will you go on pursuing the world? And when will you stop craving it?'

"I thought to myself: Indeed, this is more astonishing than everything else thus far!

"When I went back to see the shaykh, he asked me, 'Did you meet with my brother?'

"'Yes, I did,' I replied.

"'What did he say to you?' he asked.

"'Nothing,' I replied.

"'You must tell me,' he said.

"So I recounted what his brother had said. When he heard it, he wept for a long time, then said, 'My brother has spoken the truth. God has purified his heart of the world, yet has placed it in his hand and given him the appearance of a worldly man. As for me, He has taken it out of my hand, yet I still long for it.'"

Another of the veils which conceal God's friends is their acceptance [of things] from people. If a man accepts what is given to him, his stature is diminished in others' eyes, since people only revere those who do not accept their worldly offerings and who, when they give to them, return the gifts and refuse to receive anything from them.

Now, those who behave in this manner may do so only for the sake of appearances and in an attitude of unbelief, that is to say, as a means of courting people's favor, in the hope that others will venerate and extol them.

Shaykh Abū al-Ḥasan (may God be pleased with him) once said, "Whoever seeks praise from people by refusing to receive from them simply worships himself and his own desires, and has no share in God."

Something [else] which might cause people to close their minds to God's friends is a lapse on the part of someone who dresses in the same way they do or who is associated with the same path they follow. However, basing our judgment on such a person's behavior alone will deprive us of the company of those who stand with him. As God, glory be to Him, has declared, "No bearer of burdens shall be made to bear another's burdens" {Al-Anᶜām [Cattle] 6:164}. After all, why is it necessary to conclude, just because one member of a group commits an offense or is seen to be insincere, that all others who follow the same path are like him?

Shaykh ᶜAlam al-Dīn al-Ṣūfī, may God have mercy on him, recited the following lines concerning himself, saying:

> To be concealed in every land
> Behind a veil of suspicion is a sublime calling.
>
> No harm is done to the crescent moon's beauty when, in
> the darkness of the night,
> The clouds' blackness conceals it from view.

However, no veil prevents people from recognizing God's friends more effectively than that of similarity. This is the same veil with which God concealed recognition from the Prophet's contemporaries. Quoting their words, He says, "This man is nothing but a mortal like yourselves, eating of what you eat, and drinking of what you drink" {Al-Mu'minūn [The Believers] 23:33}; "Are we to follow one single mortal, one from among ourselves?" {Al-Qamar [The Moon] 54:24}; and, "What sort of an apostle is this, who eats food [like all other mortals] and goes about in the market-places?" {Al-Furqān [The Standard of True and False] 25:7}

Hence, if God desires to enable you to recognize one of His friends, He will prevent you from looking at the person's mere humanity and cause you to see, instead, that which makes him or her one of God's elect.

ADMONITION AND GUIDANCE:

Beware, brother or sister, of listening to those who deride and detract from the members of this [Sufi] community lest you fall from God's favor and merit His wrath. For these people have sat with God in genuineness, sincerity and utter loyalty and have examined their souls in His presence. They have relinquished control to Him, casting themselves confidently into His arms. They have abandoned all desire to avenge themselves, fearing His lordship and contenting themselves with His self-subsisting, eternal nature. For He has established their rights more fully than they could ever have done for themselves, He has waged war on their behalf against those who have waged war on them, and it is He who has won victory over those who have sought victory over them. At the same time, God has tried those who belong to this community by means of other people, and most particularly, those endowed with outward knowledge. Rarely will you find among such scholars anyone whose heart God has opened to believe in this or that of His saints. On the contrary, one of them might say to you, "Yes, we know that saints exist. But where are they?" And no sooner has a particular person been mentioned to him than he begins casting doubt on God's election of him, outspoken in his objections and utterly lacking in credulity. Beware of such types; indeed, flee from them as you would from a rapacious lion. And may God in His grace cause both you and us to be among those who believe in His saints.

Shaykh Abū al-Ḥasan (may God be pleased with him) said, "Once while traveling, I spent the night atop a hill. As I slept, some lions came and walked in circles around me, then remained with me till morning. Never have I experienced intimate companionship as I did that night. When I arose the following morning, it occurred to me that I had experienced something of the station of intimacy with God. I then descended into a valley, where there were some partridges that I hadn't noticed. When they became aware of my presence, they suddenly flew away and my heart fluttered in alarm. No sooner had this occurred than someone said to me, 'O you who only yesterday were finding pleasant company among beasts of prey, why do you now tremble with fear at the fluttering of partridges? Yesterday you were in Us, while now you are in yourself.'"

Chapter Nine

On the Poetry Which He Recited, Which Was Recited in His Presence, Or Which Was Recited About Him, And Which Contains Mention of His Unique Attributes

He said (may God be pleased with him), "God granted me a vision of the angels as they prostrated themselves before Adam, upon him be peace, whereupon I joined them in their prostration and began to recite, saying:

My self dissolved, my annihilation was complete,
And the Sun of illumination was manifested to me.

I descended by degrees through the worlds, making visible
That which had been concealed of the [divine] attributes by virtue of my newfound serenity.

For my serenity, like the sun, reveals its splendor
While my existence, like the night, conceals all that is not-I.

I am the meaning of existence from A to Z,
Whoever beholds me will fall prostrate before my beauty.

Any light will be plainly visible to its kith and kin,
So behold me with your own eyes, for I have laid myself bare.

When he was asked (may God be pleased with him) about the soul and the spirit, he said,

> If you should ask me about the purest of blessings
> And about the soul's attachment to the body:
>
> About its clinging to its earthly ambitions, its habituation to
> Its imperfections and the onset of decay,
>
> About its descent into the bodily state
> Where it acquires knowledge by which to distinguish between the base and the noble,
>
> About its inclinations [toward the good] from which, by its nature, it tends to stray,
> Falling, thanks to its passions and desires, into the darkness of distress,
>
> About its true nature and constitution,
> Which turns not aside toward idols—
>
> Then lend me your ear, for I have been guided into realms of knowledge of which one would rarely find a practitioner,
> And be not deceived by those who make unfounded claims.
>
> With Truth as their aim, attestations to their validity are plain for all to see,
> While their realities emerge from both the Trunk and Its branches.
>
> You who inquire of me concerning knowledge which is grasped
> Not through understanding or intelligence

But rather, through the light bestowed on those who have
arrived at the station of *jam*^{c},[1]
Whose minds have been extinguished while the entire
creation is heavy with sleep:

Embrace such knowledge with [the help of] a truth of
which you are by no means ignorant,
For the matter has made itself clear, and the truth has
bound me.

On the authority of truth take your knowledge of affairs,
and
Let not their appearance in this world we call "home"
veil your understanding.

The condition of the soul is a mystery that eludes
Minds shackled by illusions and vice.

Even so, it emerged in the realm of discernment, carry-
ing out its charge
Until [Earth's] inhabitants came to find repose in it,

That it might be said that there are servants faithful to
the command
Issued before creation and its tribulations.[2]

The soul, as it descends through its [various] worlds, is
Like Adam in his union with Eve,[3]

While the spirit as it progresses along its routes of ascent
Readies itself to receive God-given knowledge and
blessing.

Its likeness in the upper realms is the mirror of its true
nature,

Whose subtle meanings are hidden as a secret is concealed from public view.

An olive tree whose oil is light to those who partake of it,
It holds forth its guidance to all the universe.

"All is You" in a sense that is evident for all to perceive,
Yet the light is obscured as water is concealed in milk.

The servant is eclipsed by the brilliance of his Master's glory,
While the knowledge of Him remains elusive in both time and eternity.

He used to chant the following lines:

If you were to behold the day when the earth is shaken
and the mountains are leveled,

You would see the light of Truth's sun shining forth,
And you would perceive which men are men in truth.

Concerning these lines he used to say (may God be pleased with him), "The earth spoken of here is the soul, the mountains are human reason, and the sun is experiential knowledge of God."

He also used to chant:

I stood upon Mt. Tūbādh when I saw it, and when it saw me
It shouted, "God is greatest!" to the Most Merciful.

I asked it, "Where are those I'd been accustomed to seeing
Gathered about you in safety and well-being?"

"They've departed," it replied, and "entrusted their
home lands to me.
For who can defy the vicissitudes of Time?"

He also used to chant:

Never will I be a true lover unless I make my heart
His home and sacred space:

My circumambulation is unceasing meditation upon
Him,
And He is my 'corner' when I come to place my hand
upon the Black Stone.[4]

He also used to chant, saying:

Vacillating and perplexed, we sought union with the
Beloved
In all the ways we knew:

Occasions for love encompassed us round about,
While all that would stand opposed to love weighed
heavily upon us.

He used to recite the following lines by al-Suhrawardī (may God be pleased with him):

Ever and always do [our] spirits pine for You,
For union with You is their sweet basil and wine.

The hearts of those who have known Your
lovingkindness
Find repose in the perfection of Your beauty.

Have mercy upon the lovers who have endured love's
burdens,
And whose passionate ardor they wear on their sleeves!

If they divulge the mystery they're declared outlaws,
Branded as criminals for giving the secret away!

He used to chant, saying:

[Thanks to] the times we spent at Munā and al-Khayf,
The good life we lived and the pleasures we knew,

I will most surely tread that path even it should lead me to
Caravans of lions and spears as dense as thickets.

He used to chant the following lines by Imru' al-Qays, saying:

My comrade wept when he saw the path before him
And was certain that we were approaching Caesar.

I said to him, "Let your eyes weep no longer, for we
seek dominion, and
Should we die, pardon will be ours."[5]

The shaykh (may God be pleased with him) used to explain the latter part of this line, saying, "We seek dominion through subsistence, yet should we die, we will have attained pardon, by virtue of annihilation."[6]

He used to chant the following lines from a poem by Ibn al-ᶜAṭṭār:

The stations of divine communion have so lifted my veil
that
Through You, I have been veiled from the veil itself.

I remained in my prayer niche with the steadfastness of
one who knows nothing but union
Until there I beheld the Truth's countenance.

I punctured my ship's wall to damage it
And was thus delivered from a king who would have
taken it by force.

I slew a young boy (who was part of myself),
Whose slaying would be the cause of deliverance and, as
such, the greatest of causes.

From my heart I removed the wall of its veil
To reveal its imperishable treasure.[7]

I ascended through the seven heavens on high
Until I drew nigh as nigh could be.

The following lines were chanted to him (may God be pleased with him), while I was present and listening:

From my words take fruits which yield pleasure and
delight,
Whose fragrance wafts forth with the redolence of
musk.

Having been guided to the remembrance of God, pursue
it steadfastly,
For in it both hearts and mouths find sweetness and
relief.

Let your adornment be devotion to Him, for the wise
soul,
My friend, is the one whose devotion to Him is his
adornment.

Let your thoughts labor in His kingdom,
Absorbed in unearthing its meaning.

Remove your sandals as one realized [in the divine realities],
As one who forswears both universes[8] in his upward spiritual trek.

Be annihilated even to your annihilation,
For herein lies true subsistence, and then will you behold Him.

And when He appears to you, know that you are not He,
Nor, indeed, are you anything but He.

Two entities which have not been united, but herein lies
A mystery which we are hard pressed to explain.

You who hear what we have said:
Should one's heart not ponder what one's ears have perceived?

Remove the veil, the veil of your senses,
And the mystery whose grandeur you've failed to perceive will appear.

The Divine is the most sublime entity that could ever be known,
Hence, the blindness of those who fail to see Him.

It is through Him that those endowed with discernment see Him,
And indeed, He hasn't been out of their sight for a moment.

After all, how could He be absent when nothing but He exists?
Yet the very intensity of His presence conceals Him from view!

The shaykh (may God be pleased with him) concluded his recitation with the following lines:

And when He appears to you, know that you are not He,
Nor, indeed, are you anything but He.

Two entities which have not been united, but herein lies
A mystery which we are hard pressed to explain.

Then he added, "We will never be able to make it fully clear."

I once recited to him the following poem attributed to Ibn al-Faras:

God is my Master, none but Him do I desire.
In the presence of Truth can there be anything but the Divine?

In the essence of the Divine do our essences subsist?
Were it not for Him, would anything else have come to be?

No wonder that only through Him have we seen Him,
For only as the Light manifests itself are you able to perceive it.

Travelers along the spiritual path witness His doings firsthand,
Engrossed in thoughts of Him.

As for knowers of God, they behold His essence
As though their hearts were His abode.

You who are absent when the Truth within you is
present:
How can you be absent from Him when He is all you
have ever seen?

Those who fail to see His essence with the eye of
discernment
Are shrouded in the veil of their own blindness.

But for those who never see anything but Him,
It would be unthinkable to forget Him.

For those whose thoughts travel deep into the Kingdom,
Their reward is the attainment of a blessed end.

Glory be to the One who rends the veil for His servant
And guides him in his quest until he beholds Him.

Glory be to the One who has filled existence with signs,
That what He has concealed might become visible
through what He has revealed.

Glory be to the One who, had His lights not shone on
the horizon,
We would recognize neither differences nor likenesses.

Master, You are the One, the Uncaused Cause of All
That Is, whom
We have beheld with our inner eyes in the Kingdom.

Master, Your intimate companionship allows for no
loneliness or desolation
But that it dispells their darkness with its glow.

Master, Your servant has no fear of thirst.
How could he, when the Truth has given him to drink?

Master, I seek refuge in none but You,
Since to those for whom You are not their refuge, no
guidance will come.

You are the One who hast bestowed our existence upon us
And taught us what it means.

I haven't divulged what You've entrusted to me,
For those who divulge the Truth's mystery have never
truly tasted it.

For those who know that You are the Inimitable One
Who boggles the human mind, You are their Sufficiency and Protection.

The shaykh then said, "All of this is still just so much beating around the bush, and doesn't really penetrate to the essence."

I found something in Ibn Nāshī's handwriting which reads as follows: Having received greetings from my master and shaykh, Abū al-ᶜAbbās al-Mursī, I wrote to him saying:

Greetings were brought from the Imam,
And it gladdened me to know that I was in his thoughts,
that he hadn't forgotten me.

O messenger, if you find that he is still as he was of yore,
Then congratulate me on my good fortune.

My shaykh Abū al-ᶜAbbās is unique in his time,
The Khaḍir of his age, the seat of sainthood.

I pine for a time I spent in your presence,
When you educated me in the realm of divinely given
knowledge.

I was nothing but a soul gone astray when you brought
me back
And led me onto the straight way.

You gave me to drink of the water of life and were, to me,
Like Khaḍir, for once your thirst had been quenched,
you gave me to drink as well.

Would that I could spend my entire life with him
So that after death I might live in well-being and tranquillity.

You who have let down your anchor in a sea of gnosis,
Journey to al-Mursī on a gentle breeze.[9]

For he is the path to the Prophet Muḥammad
If you should ever entertain the desire to draw near to
the Divine.

May God rain down blessing upon him whenever his
name is mentioned
In this world by a scholar with the knowledge of God.

He was praised in a poem by the eminent man of letters Sharaf al-Dīn al-Buṣīrī, a part of which follows:

Love is souls' self-denial,
So find blessedness, O my soul, in wretchedness.

The lover sheds his tears for the one he loves,
A live coal smoldering within him.

He then passed on to the following lines:

Believe and say with me: Unless someone is as he was,
No one will benefit from his teaching.

May God accept my attempt to draw near through these words of praise,
And my coming to his God-protected side.

I desired to travel to where he was but was unable,
Yet in his countenance he revealed not a trace of anguish.

Wednesday—what a lovely day for a visit,
As though it were, for me, better than a thousand Thursdays.[10]

Every contact with a blessed man is blessed,
As though one had come to him three and six times in succession.

He then passed on to the following verses:

Eminence has been granted to Shādhilah and Murcia[11]
In honor of the leaders in their midst.

No sooner do you attribute their two shaykhs to them
Than you adorn them as one adorns a bride for her groom.

When I was just entering manhood, I composed a poem about Shaykh Abū al-ᶜAbbās and it was recited in his presence. When the recitation was over he said, "May God uphold you with the Holy Spirit." As for the poem, it is as follows:

Salmā emerged from among the tents
And showed us the full moon from beneath her locks.

The camel drivers sang when they saw her face in the night
As though the morning had dawned.

But we excused them, for what wonder is it that
Salmā's face should be seen in the darkness

As though it were the radiance of dawn or the full moon in the dark of night,
Yet more perfect and complete?

If the full moon had seen her it would have beat a quick retreat,
Too bashful to look upon her face.

And if the sun had seen her, it would have refused to rise that day,
Then taken anguish and regret as its companions.

She tormented my heart with an aloofness of the sort
That has tormented lovers before me since time immemorial.

She clothed me in a garment of such distress,
I became a beacon of sorrow and weariness among my people.

She would do nothing but turn her back upon me,
While my tears would do nothing but betray my pain.

I spent the night observing the stars
And calling to mind the intimate communion that was no longer.

Every time I longed to shut my eyes
My heart would say, "Not yet! Slumber not."

She claims to be in love yet she demonstrates the
contrary.
Love for me is nothing but sleeplessness and infirmity.

Keep watch at the door in servility and sorrow,
For such are love's requirements.

Let there be no more laxness in His service,
Roll up your sleeves and have no fear of pain.

Strive diligently, that perchance you may be
Delivered tomorrow from the chastisement of the
Divine, Creator of the nations.

Do not tell me that this is an arduous age when
It is difficult to find those who are free of failings
and vices.

The friends of God have not died out!
His confederates have not been defeated.

We have seen them all in a single man,
A man of dignity, loyalty and high-minded determination.

In Abū al-ᶜAbbās one finds the sum total
Of all their knowledge and wisdom.

In Abū al-ᶜAbbās, grief has been cast out
Of people's hearts and darkness dispelled.

In him the sun of guidance has risen,
And the pearls of the sciences have been strung in
perfection.

Any light will be visible to its own people,
Any knowledge will be clear to those with understanding.

The Lord of exaltation has granted him distinction
And garbed him in robes of grace.

Tell those who desire to match him in excellence:
Spare yourselves the effort, for God has reserved it
for him!

Realizing such a goal is no easy matter.
One attains it through diligence and steadfastness.

It is none other than a portion foreordained by God,
Given to Aḥmad before the creation came into being.

They disputed the judgment of God Almighty
When they desired to conceal the most consummate
light.

For if they deny the sun that grants the morning its
brightness
As its light becomes visible and reaches completion,

They make themselves companions of ignorance and
caprice,
Filled with disquiet and remorse.

His shaykh—the pole of the whole Earth and possessor of the most all-embracing knowledge—said of him long ago:

"You are I"—whereby you should know that
This is not a matter to be concealed.

The shaykh's words concerning him have spread far and
wide
Among Arabs and non-Arabs alike.

Were we to set them forth in full, time would not suffice us,
And our explanations would grow prolix.

Yet then they could no longer disavow them,
Mixing honeycomb with poison.

Let them persist in their fury and malice,
Let them die one and all in affliction and sorrow.

As for you, may your honor outlive their enmity
For as long as the turtledove alights on the acacia branch.

When the recitation reached the following lines of my poem:

We have seen them all in a single man,
A man of dignity, loyalty and high-minded determination.

In Abū al-ᶜAbbās one finds the sum total
Of all their knowledge and wisdom,

the shaykh (may God be pleased with him) said, "Indeed, Shaykh Abū al-Ḥasan (may God be pleased with him) once said to me, 'Abū al-ᶜAbbās, you possess the qualities that mark the saints, while even the saints lack the qualities that you possess.'"

Moreover, when the recitation reached the lines that declare:

His shaykh—the pole of all the Earth and
Possessor of all-embracing knowledge—said of him
long ago:

"You are I"—whereby you should know that
This is not a matter to be concealed,

He said, "And in fact, Shaykh Abū al-Ḥasan said to me, 'Abū al-ᶜAbbās, I only took you as my disciple in order for you to be me, and me, you.'"

A number of years then passed, after which the shaykh (may God be pleased with him) returned from a trip to Upper Egypt. When I met with him he showed me a poem which someone from Akhmīm had composed about him, and he said to me, "Respond to him." So I went away [and began attempting to compose], but the words wouldn't come. I said, "Strange, that the shaykh should instruct me to compose a poem, and then for the words not to come. It must be on account of some insincerity on my part!" However, no sooner had I said this than God so opened the floodgates for me that the words poured forth like a raging torrent until I had composed an entire poem. When it was recited to him, it met so fully with his approval that from time to time he would request that it be repeated. When it was recited to him again he said, "When this scholar of jurisprudence first became my follower, he was afflicted with two maladies (referring to my headaches and my obsessive preoccupation with ritual purity), but God has cured him of both. And he is destined to instruct others in both sciences [that is, both the exoteric, or legal, and the esoteric, or mystical]."

As for the poem I composed, it is as follows:

Pause to look out over your homesteads, for their
dwellings have come within view.
After all, toward whom are you journeying, and what
else could be your desired destination?

Rest your she-camel, for she's reached the slope
After a long, arduous journey.

For such a long time now she's traversed desert expanses,
Her pastern joints stained with blood.

Morning and evening, she never wearied of the journey
Until at last she began to suffer from exhaustion and
lesions in her hoofs.

Go easy on her, O camel driver,
Goad her not, for she's goaded sufficiently by her own
longing.

Sufficient for her is the journey's discomfort,
And her ardent yearning to reach home.

Or have you not observed how she sheds her tears
Until she's wet the ground before her?

She's driven onward toward the homestead by her
fervent desire,
Led onward by her ardor toward the beloved.

She's won the prize of reunion with her loved ones,
Staggering under the weight of her longing.

She moans with yearning as she glimpses the Naqā
Valley,
Rejoicing in this sign of hope fulfilled.

Her delight is like the happiness of the days when
Abū al-ᶜAbbās became her[12] bright morning sun.

Lost in Aḥmad when he came to her as a mercy,
She began boasting of him to all she met.

She was filled with honor by his coming,
Decked out in all her finery.

He set about to guide aright the religion of Muḥammad,
Dispelling her sorrow and presenting her with gifts as a
bridegroom to his bride.

When you meet him, you find a firmly established
imam,
An upright, learned, tender-hearted man intent on
turning to God again and again.

In him all virtues have reached perfection,
Gathered together in completeness.

How many divinely given traditions had died, after
which he restored them to new life?
How many misguided innovations had taken hold, after
which he freed us from their grip?

How many have come to him with their hearts set on
disobedience,
Their souls bound by caprice and illusion,

Only for him to deliver them from their bondage,
Causing the clouds of darkness to disperse?

How many hearts had been put to death by earthly
craving,
After which he restored them to life, then through them
brought life to others?

You revived the people's knowledge at a time when
Help was scarce, causing the darkness to vanish.

You came as succor to humanity
Before which taboos had been violated and the sacred
treated as profane.

You came trailing the robes of God-given knowledge,
Clothed in the finest raiment of righteousness.

You persevered till our souls yielded to you,
Then delivered them from their ignorance and blindness.

After our selfish inclinations had won dominion over us
And our souls had strayed from the path of guidance,

After they'd been headstrong, defiant and almost beyond
hope,
You humbled them till they came in willing submission.

This is why their love for you has grown so steadfast,
A source of glad tidings for them and its own happy
reward.

For you have become their highest aspiration,
Both before others and in their inmost hearts.

You continue to guide Aḥmad's community of faith,
For through you have their righteousness and devotion
reached perfection.

Creation was deep in confusion
Till the pole of humankind came and guided it aright.

Through al-Shādhilī its darkness was dispelled
And its horizons filled with light.

A treasure trove of devotion, a signpost of true guidance,
an ocean
Of dew, the pole of creation, its life-giving rain and
refuge,

He is the one who, if the community suffers affliction,
Protects them and draws them out of misfortune and adversity.

A shelter in which all humankind can find refuge,
Their hope in times of both hardship and ease.

Until God takes him in death—
and what a desire fulfilled and cherished attainment!

I have succeeded him in his spiritual states and stations
By ascending their heights and receiving his legacy.

For others' sake God brought Aḥmad to the station of subsistence,
Causing him to dwell in their midst in order to nurture and guard them.

Those who have sought to undermine his standing
Have only brought suffering among themselves.

Though they deny God's manifest signs,
They are still visible and their splendor plain to see.

They know that he is the pole of all humanity,
Yet their souls' worldly cravings have vanquished them.

Or do you not see how the Prophet Muḥammad's people
Persisted without shame in their unbelief and ingratitude,

Despite their awareness that the Prophet Muḥammad
Was the Messenger who had brought them true guidance?

Hence, the Sovereign One allowed their wrath to persist,
While [the community of faith] remained in a state pleasing to its Lord.

You are worthy of all honor,
And of all heavenly ranks, you shall attain the most
exalted.

The line which most pleased him was:

How many hearts had been put to death by earthly
craving.
After which he restored them to life, then through them
brought life to others?

Consequently, he used to request that the poem be recited again up to this line. Then, once it had been repeated up to this point, he would ask that the line be recited still again.

May God, by His grace and bounty, cause this eulogy of ours to add to the weight of our good deeds and render us more worthy of His favor.

Pilgrims entering and performing supplications
at the tomb of Abū al-Ḥasan al-Shādhilī

In explanation of this saying, Shaykh Abū al-Ḥasan said, "If anyone obeys Me in everything by his abandonment of everything, I will obey him in everything by disclosing Myself to him in everything so that he will see Me as nearer to him than everything. This is a superior path, the path of the spiritual wayfarers, a majestic way: If anyone obeys Me in everything by approaching everything in light of his Master's goodwill expressed therein, I will obey him in everything by disclosing Myself to him in everything until he sees Me as the essence of everything."

Chapter Ten

On His *Dhikr* and the Supplication With Which He Concluded His Lectures, The *Ḥizb*[1] Which He Arranged for Those Who Were Recipients of His Knowledge and Interpretations, And Part of the Supplication of Shaykh Abū al-Ḥasan (may God be pleased with him) And His Two *Ḥizbs*, With Which This Chapter Concludes

Shaykh Abū al-ᶜAbbās's *dhikr* included the following:

- There is no god but God, the First, the Manifest and the Hidden. Muḥammad is the Messenger of God, the perfect master who opens others' understanding and seals the line of God's prophets.
- O God, O Light, O Truth, the One Who Makes All Things Clear: Revive my heart with Thy light, establish me as Thy witness, and teach me the path which leads to Thee.
- My Lord, forgive me; cause me to be a servant of Thine whose ego has been dissolved in Thy lights, whose perception has been effaced by Thy majesty; forgive me and all believers, both male and female.

One of the supplications he used to utter was this: "O God, forgive me, shield me, and expose not my offenses either in this world or the world to come; teach me, remind me, grant me understanding; have mercy upon me, grant me joy, and do good to me; empty me of everything but the remembrance of Thee, obedience to Thee and Thy Messenger, and love for Thee and Thy Messenger ﷺ."

One of the supplications he used to utter following his public addresses was: "O God, be merciful and tender toward us. Take us by the hand and lead us to Thee as those whom Thou has honored. O God, straighten our paths when we make them crooked; assist us when we act with integrity; take us by the hand if we stumble, and be ours wherever we are."

The supplications uttered by Shaykh Abū al-Ḥasan (may God be pleased with him) included the following: "O God, this earthly existence is ignoble along with everything therein, while the life to come is noble together with everything therein, while Thou art the One who has rendered the former ignoble, and the latter noble. Hence, how can one be noble while seeking anyone or anything other than Thee? And how can one renounce this earthly existence if he or she chooses this world along with Thee? Bring me to an understanding of the realities of renunciation, that I might dispense with seeking anything or anyone but Thee; and of such an experiential knowledge of Thee that I no longer need to seek Thee.

My God, how can one who seeks Thee, reach Thee? And how can one who flees from Thee, escape Thee? So seek me in Thy mercy, not in Thy vengeance, O Exalted in Might, O Avenger. Thou, indeed, art capable of all things."

Another of Shaykh Abū al-Ḥasan's supplications is as follows: "Strip me of reasoning that veils Thee from me, or which prevents me from comprehending Thy signs and the words of Thy Messenger. Grant me the understanding which Thou hast bestowed specially upon Thy prophets, Thy messengers, and those servants of Thine who are men and women of truth. Guide me by Thy light as Thou hast guided those singled out [for sainthood] by Thy will. By Thy mercy, grant me light in perfect abundance. For all true guidance is

Thy guidance, and all bounty is in Thy hands; Thou bestowest it upon whomsoever Thou willest, and Thou art the Lord of Grace Abounding."

Shaykh Abū al-Ḥasan (may God be pleased with him) also used to utter this supplication: "O God, seat us on the carpet of nearness to Thee through annihilation to everything and everyone but Thee and subsistence in Thy light. Bring us near by drawing us away from that which is ours and toward that which is Thine: in knowledge and understanding, in action and spiritual states. Grant us dominion in the *barzakh*[2] of creation: looking at Thee, through Thee, and looking from Thee at that which is not Thee. Thou art capable of all things."

Another of Shaykh Abū al-Ḥasan's supplications reads, "O Exalted in Might, Most Merciful One, All-Wise, Self-Sufficient, Most Munificent, All-Pervading, Knower of All, Lord of Grace Abounding: Cause me to be in Thy presence always, engaged in Thy service and worship, free of all that is not Thee, spellbound by Thy love, and mindful of Thy majesty and grandeur. Dissolve the breach between us, lest there be anything closer to me than Thee. Do not, by means of Thyself, conceal Thyself from me. Indeed, Thou art capable of all things."

He also used to pray saying, "O God, grant me a share of the light by means of which Thy Messenger ﷺ saw what had been and what was yet to be, that this servant might take on the likeness of his master: so rich through Thee that he has no need to reexamine any knowledge [that comes his way], and able to achieve the possibilities to which he aspires. By the essence of the [divine] mystery, he comprehends all manner of essences, living in a manner which preserves the harmony between body and soul, heart and reason, the [human] spirit and the [divine] mystery, command

and discernment, and comprehending, likewise, the Primary Intelligence derived from the Greatest Spirit which is separate from the Supreme Mystery.

"O God, sustain me out of the treasure of, 'There is no power or strength but in God,' since it is one of the treasures of Paradise; and with it, level such a blow at me that Thou crushest all strength in my heart [but that which is Thine]. Grant that through this sustenance, I might be so enriched that I cease to observe myself or the rest of creation; and by means of it, deliver me from the degradation of poverty, managing my own affairs and reliance upon my own choices, and from heedlessness, lust, self-will, distress and neediness. Indeed, Thou art capable of all things."

He also used to pray, saying, "In the name of the Guardian, the Exalted in Might, the All-Powerful, the One who marks the end of all things, the One who grants me succor *qāf, jīm, nūn, ṣād*[3]: Grant me succor, for Thou art the best of those who provide succor; open the truth to me, for Thou art the best of those who lay open the truth; provide me with sustenance, for Thou art the Best of all sustainers; guide me, and deliver me from evildoers."

Similarly he used to pray, "O Thou who wilt summon all humankind on a day concerning which there can be no doubt: summon me to obedience founded on the witnessing of Thy presence. Cast a divide between me and concern for both this earthly life and the life to come, and stand in my stead in both realms. Cause my sole concern to be Thee; fill my heart with Thy love and with joy in Thy light. Bring my heart into a state of reverence by the force of Thy grandeur, and entrust me not to myself for so much as the twinkling of an eye!"

We herewith present the *ḥizb* of our master and lord, the shaykh and imam, pole of gnostics and signpost of the rightly guided, Shihāb al-Dīn Abū al-ᶜAbbās Aḥmad Ibn ᶜUmar al-Mursī, some of which is taken from the words of his shaykh, Abū al-Ḥasan al-Shādhilī (may God be pleased with them both). We then present the *ḥizb* of Shaykh Abū al-Ḥasan (may God be pleased with him), known as the "*ḥizb* of light," followed by still another *ḥizb* of his.

The reason we have included the *ḥizb* of Shaykh Abū al-ᶜAbbās which he passed down on the authority of his shaykh, as well as the two *ḥizbs* of Shaykh Abū al-Ḥasan, namely, *ḥizb al-nūr* ("the *hizb* of light") and the one subsequent to it, is that these three *ḥizbs* have not become as well known as Shaykh Abū al-Ḥasan's two *ḥizbs* entitled *ḥizb al-baḥr*, or "the *ḥizb* of the sea" and *ḥizb wa idhā jā'aka*, or "the *ḥizb* of 'and when he comes to thee'". We have singled out these three *hizbs* for special mention and have not included the other two referred to here, since their renown has spread abroad, and their praises are celebrated among town dwellers and nomads alike.

As for the *ḥizb* of Shaykh Abū al-ᶜAbbās (may God be pleased with him), which is presented below, it served as his shaykh's *wird*[4] after the final evening (*ᶜishā'*) prayer; *ḥizb wa idhā jā'aka* was to be recited following the dawn (*ṣubḥ*) prayer, and *ḥizb al-baḥr* was to be recited following the mid-afternoon (*ᶜaṣr*) prayer. This is the way in which Shaykh Abū al-ᶜAbbās (may God be pleased with him) arranged them.

The *ḥizb* is as follows:

"All praise is due to God alone, the Sustainer of all the worlds, the Most Gracious, the Dispenser of Grace, Lord of the Day of Judgment! Thee alone do we worship, and unto Thee alone do we turn for aid. Guide us the straight way—the way of those upon whom Thou hast bestowed Thy blessings, not of those who have been condemned [by Thee], nor of those who go astray!" {Al-Fātiḥah [The Opening] 1:1-7}

"God—there is no deity save Him, the Ever-Living, the Self-Subsistent Fount of All Being. Neither slumber overtakes Him, nor sleep. His is all that is in the heavens and all that is on earth. Who is there that could intercede with Him, unless it be by His leave? He knows all that lies open before people and all that is hidden from them, whereas they cannot attain to aught of His knowledge save that which He wills [them to attain]. His eternal power overspreads the heavens and the earth. Their upholding wearies Him not, and He alone is truly exalted, tremendous " {Al-Baqarah [The Cow] 2:255}.

"The Apostle, and the believers with him, believe in what has been bestowed upon him from on high by his Sustainer: they all believe in God, in His angels and His revelations, and His apostles, making no distinction between any of His apostles; and they say: 'We have heard, and we pay heed. Grant us Thy forgiveness, O our Sustainer, for with Thee is all journeys' end! God does not burden any human being with more than he is well able to bear; in his favor shall be whatever good he does, and against him whatever evil he does. O our Sustainer! Take us not to task if we forget or unwittingly do wrong! O our Sustainer! Lay not upon us a burden such as Thou didst lay upon those who lived before us! O our Sustainer! Make us not bear burdens which we have no strength to bear! And efface Thou our sins, and grant us forgiveness, and bestow Thy mercy upon us! Thou art our Lord Supreme; succor us, then, against people who deny the truth!'" {Al-Baqarah [The Cow] 2:285-286}

"God—there is no deity save Him, the Ever-Living, the Self-Subsistent Fount of All Being. Step by step has He bestowed upon thee from on high this divine writ, setting forth the truth which confirms whatever there still remains [of earlier revelations]: for it is He who has bestowed from on high the Torah and the Gospel aforetime, as a guidance unto mankind, and it is He who has bestowed the standard by which to discern the true from the false" {Āl ᶜImrān [The House of Imran] 3:1-4}.

"O thou [in thy solitude] enfolded! Arise and warn! And thy Sustainer's greatness glorify! And thine inner self purify! And all defilement shun! And do not through giving seek thyself to gain, but unto thy Sustainer turn in patience" {Al-Muddaththir [The Enfolded One] 74:1-7}.

"Read in the name of thy Sustainer, who has created—created man out of a germ-cell! Read—for thy Sustainer is the Most Bountiful One who has taught [human beings] the use of the pen—taught them what they did not know!" {Al-ᶜAlaq [The Germ-Cell] 96:1-5}

"The Most Gracious has imparted this Qur'ān [unto man]. He has created man. He has imparted unto him articulate thought and speech. [At His behest] the sun and the moon run their appointed courses; [before Him] prostrate themselves the stars and the trees. And the skies has He raised high, and has devised [for all things] a measure, so that you [too] might never transgress the measure [of what is right]....Hallowed be thy Sustainer's name, full of majesty and glory!" {Al-Raḥmān [The Most Gracious] 55:1-8,78}

"Glory be to my mighty Lord, glory be to my mighty Lord, glory be to my mighty Lord.

"All that is in the heavens and on earth extols God's limitless glory: for He alone is almighty, truly wise! His is the dominion over the heavens and the earth; He grants life and deals death; and He has the power to will anything. He is the First and the Last, the Outward as well as the Inward, and He has full knowledge of everything. He it is who has created the heavens and the earth in six aeons, and is established on the throne of His almightiness. He knows all that enters the earth, and all that comes out of it, as well as all that descends from the skies, and all that ascends to them. And He is with you wherever you may be; and God sees all that you do. His is the dominion over the heavens and earth; and all things go back unto God [as their source]. He makes the night grow longer by shortening the day, and makes the day grow longer by shortening the night; and He has full knowledge of what is in the hearts [of men]" {Al-Ḥadīd [Iron] 57:1-6}.

"God is He save whom there is no deity; the One who knows all that is beyond the reach of a created being's perception, as well as all that can be witnessed by a creature's senses or mind: He, the Most Gracious, the Dispenser of Grace. God is He save whom there is no deity: the Sovereign Supreme, the Holy, the One with whom all salvation rests, the Giver of Faith, the One who determines what is true and false, the Almighty, the One who subdues wrong and restores right, the one to Whom all greatness belongs. Utterly remote is God, in His limitless glory, from anything to which men may ascribe a share in His divinity! He is God, the Creator, the Maker who shapes all forms and appearances! His [alone] are the attributes of perfection. All that is in the heavens and on earth extols His limitless glory; for He alone is almighty, truly wise!" {Al-Ḥashr [The Gathering] 59:22-24}

"Say, 'He is the one God: God the Eternal, the Uncaused Cause of All That Exists. He begets not, and neither is He begotten; and there is nothing that could be compared with Him.'" {Al-Ikhlāṣ [The Declaration of God's Perfection] 112:1-4}

"Say, 'I seek refuge with the Sustainer of the rising dawn, from the evil of aught that He has created, and from the evil of the black darkness whenever it descends, and from the evil of all human beings bent on occult endeavors, and from the evil of the envious when he envies.'" {Al-Falaq [The Rising Dawn] 113:1-5}

"Say, 'I seek refuge with the Sustainer of men, the Sovereign of men, the God of men, from the evil of the whispering, elusive tempter who whispers in the hearts of men, from all [temptation to evil by] invisible forces as well as men.'" {Al-Nās [Men] 114:1-6}

"O God, the One Who is thus [described in the holy revelation], and by Thy devoted servants from among the prophets, the men and women of truth, the martyrs, the righteous, the scholars endowed with inner certainty, and the saints drawn near to Thee in Thy heavens, on earth and throughout creation: By these heavens, this earth and those who dwell therein, by all of Thy signs, Thy [divine] names, and by the greatest thereof, by the Fātiḥah, by the Throne Verse, by the verses which conclude Surat al-Baqarah, and by the beginnings and the closings, I ask Thee by the "Amen!" of agreement, the *ḥā'* of *raḥmah*, or mercy, the *mīm* of *mulk*, or dominion, and the *dāl* of *dawām*, or permanence.

"Muhammad is God's Apostle, and those who are with him are firm and unyielding towards all deniers of the truth [yet] full of mercy towards one another. Thou canst see them bowing down, prostrating themselves [in prayer], seeking favor with God and [His] goodly acceptance: their marks are on their faces, traced by prostration. This is their parable in the Torah as well as their parable in the Gospel: [they are] like a seed that brings forth its shoot, and then He strengthens it, so that it grows stout and stands firm upon its stem, delighting the sowers....[Thus will God cause the believers to grow in strength] so that through them He might confound the deniers of the truth. [But] unto such of them as may [yet] attain to faith and do righteous deeds, God has promised forgiveness and a reward supreme" {Al-Fatḥ [Victory] 48:29}.

Aḥūn, qāf, Adam, ḥā' mīm, hā', amīn. Kāf, hā', yā', ᶜayn, ṣād.

Forgive me, have mercy upon me with the mercy which Thou hast bestowed upon Thy prophets and Thy messengers, and let not my prayer go unanswered, O my Lord.

Indeed, I have feared, and I now fear lest I should not be guided unto Thee, so guide me to Thee and through Thyself, grant me safety from all fear—and all those who would cause me to fear—in religion, in this earthly life, and in the life to come. Indeed, Thou art capable of all things.

O God, O Creator of the heavens and the earth, O Thou who dost remain Self-Subsistent in both this realm and the next, O Thou who dost subsist immutably in all things, O Living One, O Self-Subsistent One, O our God, we have no god but Thee. Be for us a protector, helper, and faithful preserver. Secure us, through Thyself, from everything, lest we fear anything or anyone but Thee. Place us under Thy protection and shield us by that with which Thou shielded Thy friends, for Thou seest, but none of Thy creation sees Thee. Pour out blessing upon us, the most perfect and beautiful thereof, and avert from us all evil, from the least to the greatest.

"He has given freedom to the two great bodies of water, so that they might meet: [yet] between them is a barrier which they may not transgress" {Al-Raḥmān [The Most Gracious] 55:19}.

O God, cause us to fear Thee, to place our hope in Thee, to love Thee, to long for Thee, to find intimate companionship through Thee, to content ourselves with Thee, to obey Thy commands based on a witnessing of who Thou art: looking from Thee to Thee and speaking through Thee of Thee. There is no god but Thee. Glory be to Thee, our Lord. We have wronged ourselves and have now turned to Thee in repentance in word and deed; so turn to us in Thy munificence and compassion, put us to use through action which merits Thy favor, and grant us righteous offspring. Indeed, we have turned to Thee in repentance, and we are among those who have surrendered ourselves to Thy ways.

O Most Forgiving One, O Most Loving One, O Most Righteous, O Most Beneficent One: Forgive us our sins, and draw us near by Thy lovingkindness. Bring us into communion with Thee through our belief in Thy oneness, and have mercy upon us through our obedience to Thee. Chastise us not by allowing us to fall into indifference or reliance upon anything or anyone other than Thee; bear us along on the path of right intent, and protect us from the unjust along the way. Indeed, Thou art capable of all things.

O God, Who will gather all people on a Day concerning which there can be no doubt: Gather us together with truthfulness, pure intention, sincerity, reverence, awe, contrition, self-observation, light, inward certainty, knowledge both scholarly and experiential, preservation, virtue, activity, power, covering [of faults], forgiveness, clear and eloquent expression, and understanding of the Qur'ān. Bestow upon us, from Thyself, love, chosenness and friendship with Thee. Be, for us, hearing, sight, tongue, heart, hand and succor. Grant us that knowledge which comes directly from Thee, righteous action, and a wholesome livelihood which neither veils Thee from us in this earthly realm nor engenders guilt for which we must give account, whether in this life or the life to come. Grant that our lives might be founded upon Thy law and belief in Thy unity, free of the tyranny of craving, lust and our natural inclinations. "O my Sustainer! Cause me to enter [upon whatever I may do] in a manner true and sincere, and cause me to leave it in a manner true and sincere; and grant me, out of Thy grace, sustaining strength" {Al-Isrā' [The Night Journey] 17:80}.

O God, O Most High, O Most Magnificent, O Knower, Hearer and Seer of all, Thou Whose Will is Incontrovertible, O Infinite in Power, O Ever-Living One, O Self-Subsistent Fount of all Being, O Most Merciful, O Most Beneficent, O Thou who art *huwa*, *huwa*, *huwa*, O *huwa*: I ask Thee by the greatness which permeates the foundations of

Thy throne, by the mighty power by which Thou wast able to perform Thy act of creation, by Thy mercy which embraces all things, by Thy knowledge which encompasses all, by Thy will which none can contest, by Thy hearing and Thy sight to which everything is near at hand, O Thou who art nearer to me than anything: Great has been my shamelessness, my proneness to falsehood, my distance from Thee and my wretchedness. Thou art the One who sees my distress, my confusion, my craving, my shame. Thou knowest my error, my blindness, my poverty, and my basest inclinations. I have placed my faith in Thee, in Thy names, in Thy attributes, and in Muḥammad, Thy Messenger. For who but Thee can have mercy upon me? Who but Thee can bring me happiness? Have mercy upon me, then, show me right guidance and lead me along its path; show me, likewise, the path of error and deception, and enable me to avoid it. Cause my companions to be truth, light, wisdom, clarity and the ability to distinguish truth from falsehood, and guard me by Thy light.

O God, O Light, O Truth, O Thou Who Makest All Things Manifest, open my heart by Thy light, instruct me out of Thy knowledge, grant me understanding on Thy authority, enable me to hear Thy words and to see by Thy light and grace. Indeed, Thou art capable of all things.

O God, I have awakened with the desire for goodness and a hatred for evil. Glory be to God, praise be to God; there is no god but God, and God is greatest. There is no strength or power save in God, the Most High, the Magnificent. Lead me by Thy light to Thy light through what I receive from Thee, in what proceeds from me to Thee, and in that which transpires between me and others. Envelop me with Thy nearness, veil me with the veils of Thy honor, and veil me from Thy veils.[5] Be Thou my veil in order that

I might see nothing but Thee, and do nothing but for Thy sake. As for my livelihood, place it at my service, and preserve me from avarice and from exhausting myself in its pursuit; protect my heart from preoccupation with and care-worn attachment to it, from subservience to other creatures on its account, and from planning and thinking about how to obtain it. And once I have obtained it, preserve me from niggardliness and the dangers to which the soul is exposed thereby. [I ask Thee] to create it [my livelihood] by Thy power in accordance with Thy will and knowledge, and in such a way that it responds to the needs of Your creatures. Hence, render it a cause for servanthood and a witness to the decrees of Thy lordship. Bestow upon me a *dhikr* from Thyself, and grant me a share in Thy secrets, Thy lights, Thy mysteries, and the acts of obedience performed by Thy prophets. Grant me the companionship of Thy angels, and be Thyself my Guardian, not leaving me to my own devices even for so much as the twinkling of an eye! Cause me to be one of Thy good works, a mercy to Thy servants through whom Thou guidest others to a straight path, the path of God to whom belongs all that is in the heavens and on earth. Indeed, to God belong all final outcomes.

O God, guide me to Thy light, grant me Thy grace, and protect me from every enemy who is an enemy of Thine, and from everything which would distract me from Thee. Impart to me a tongue which never wearies of invoking Thy name, a heart which truly hears Thy words, a spirit which is honored by looking to Thee, an inward being with access to the realities of nearness to Thee, and a mind which occupies itself with the majesty of Thy greatness. O Hearer and Knower of all, O Perfectly Wise One, adorn both my outward and my inward being with all manner of obedience to Thee.

O God, as Thou hast created me, so guide me; as Thou hast caused me to die, so bring me to life, and as Thou hast fed them, so feed me and give me to drink. My infirmity is not concealed from Thee, so heal me; my sins have encompassed me round about, so forgive me and grant me knowledge which conforms to Thy knowledge, and judgment which conforms to Thy judgment. Bestow upon me a tongue which utters truth among Thy servants, and allow me to be among those who inherit Thy paradise. Deliver me from the Fire by Thy pardon, and grant me entry into Paradise both now and in the future by Thy mercy. Show me the face of Muḥammad Thy Prophet, and lift the veil now drawn between me and Thee. Cause my station to be ever and always in Thy presence, and disclose to me so fully the true nature of things that Thy servant will thereafter seek nothing more apart from the increase which Thou hast so graciously promised.[6] Indeed Thou art capable of all things.

O God, O Exalted in Might, O Perfectly Wise One, Thou hast supported whomever Thou choosest, by whatever means Thou choosest, howsoever Thou choosest, toward whatever end Thou choosest. So uphold us with Thy succor by the holiness of Thy saints, expand our beings to contain the knowledge of Thee when we encounter Thy enemies, and bring to us him with whom Thou art pleased, as Thou didst for Muḥammad Thy Messenger, that we might surrender and humble ourselves before him.[7] Avert from us the wicked scheming of those upon whom Thy anger rests as Thou didst for Abraham Thy beloved friend. In this earthly existence, reward us with deliverance from that which would cause us to enter the Fire and from the oppression of every unjust tyrant, and by rendering our hearts free of attachment to anything and everyone but Thee. Cause us to scorn this earthly life just as Thou causest us to long for the life to come, and grant that in both, we might be among the righteous. Indeed, Thou art capable of all things.

O God, O Magnificent One, O Hearer and Knower of all, O Truly Righteous One, O Most Beneficent, Thy servant is encompassed round about by his sins, but Thou art the Magnificent. Though my supplication may seem not to have been heard, Thou art the Hearer of all. I am helpless to govern my own soul, but Thou art the Knower of all. How am I to have mercy upon myself when Thou art the Truly Righteous, the Most Merciful?[8] How can my transgression be great before Thy greatness? How couldst Thou answer those who ask not and abandon those who ask? How am I to guide my soul in righteousness when my weakness is so well-known to Thee? And how am I to show myself compassion when the storehouses of compassion are in Thy hands?

My God, Thy greatness has so filled the hearts of Thy saints that everything else has become of little account to them. So fill my heart with Thy greatness in order that, henceforth, nothing else will be either of little account or of great moment in my eyes. Hear my supplication by virtue of Thy kindness, for Thou, indeed, art capable of all things.

My God, because my position before Thee was concealed from me, I disobeyed Thee even while in Thy grip. After committing the transgressions I committed, how can I seek Thy pardon?

My God, Thy lure has filled me with longing for Thee, while Thy veil has caused me to despair of all else. So pierce my veil that I might reach Thee, and lure me so inexorably that never again will I seek anything or anyone but Thee.

My God, how many a good deed by those whom Thou hatest merits no reward, and how many an evil deed by those whom Thou lovest merits no punishment? Hence, cause my evil deeds to be the evil deeds of those whom Thou lovest, and let not my good deeds be the good deeds of those whom Thou hatest. For the munificence of the Munificent is revealed more perfectly in the face of evil deeds than it is in the face of good ones. Hence, cause me to witness Thy munificence and Thy mercy and cause me to be content with what Thou hast foreordained for me. Grant me the patient endurance to persevere in observing Thy commands and prohibitions, inspire me to give thanks for Thy grace, cover me with the robe of Thy pardon lest I associate anyone or anything with Thee, and lead me to that understanding which is given on Thy authority. Indeed, Thou art capable of all things.

My God, my disobedience to Thee has summoned me to obedience, and my obedience has summoned me to disobedience. Hence, in which of them am I to fear Thee, and in which of them am I to hope in Thee? If I say [that I am to fear Thee] in disobedience, Thou encounterest me with Thy favor and thus leavest me no cause to fear, and if I say [that I am to hope in Thee] in obedience, Thou encounterest me with Thy justice, and thus leavest me no cause for hope. So would that I knew: How am I to measure my virtue in the face of Thy [infinitely greater] virtue? And how can I fail to recognize Thy favor despite my disobedience?

Qāf jīm—two mysteries with Thy mystery, both of which point to that which is other than Thee. For by the all-encompassing mystery which points to Thee, abandon me not to that which is other than Thee. Indeed, Thou art capable of all things.

O God, O Opener of the Truth, Most Forgiving One, Bestower of Blessings, the One Who Guides Aright, O Helper, O Exalted in Might: Grant me, out of the light of Thy names, that through which I can behold the realities of

Thy Essence; lay open the truth for me, forgive me, bestow Thy bounty upon me, guide me, succor me, honor and strengthen me. O Exalter, debase me not by allowing me to dispose of Thy wealth, nor allow me to be distracted from Thee by that which is Thine. For all belongs to Thee: all command is Thy command, and all mystery is Thy mystery, whereas my non-existence is my existence, and my existence is my non-existence. All truth is Thy truth, and all action is Thy action. There is no god but Thee, and Thou art the true, manifest Divinity.

O Thou who knowest that which is secret as well as that which is yet more hidden, O Possessor of honor and fidelity, Thy knowledge has encompassed Thy servant, who has made himself wretched through his pursuit of Thee. How can those who seek anything or anyone other than Thee be anything but wretched? Yet, through Thy gentle kindness toward me, I came to know that my pursuit of Thee was ignorance, and that my pursuit of anything or anyone else was unbelief; hence, deliver me from ignorance and preserve me from unbelief! O Near One, Thou art the One Who has been close at hand, and I am the one who has been distant. Thy nearness has caused me to lose hope in anything or anything other than Thee, while my distance has brought me back to the pursuit of Thee. So be mine, by Thy grace, and thereby obliterate my pursuit of Thee through Thy pursuit of me. O Possessor of All Strength, O Exalted in Might, Thou indeed art capable of all things.

O God, torment us not—by virtue of our own will and our love for our own passions—such that we are preoccupied, veiled [from Thee] or caused to rejoice by the presence of that which we desire, or such that we are grieved, angered, or driven to hypocritical resignation when it is lost. Thou, of all, knowest best our hearts; so have mercy upon us by granting us the supreme bliss, the most excellent increase, and the most perfect victory. Cause us to be absent from everything [but Thee], and cause everything [but Thee] to be absent from us. Enable us to witness Thee truly, and come to our aid both in this earthly life and on the Day when the witnesses arise.

O God, O Infinite in Power, O Thou Whose Will is Incontrovertible, O Exalted in Might, O Most Wise, O Most Worthy of Praise, we ask Thee by the ultimate power, by the supreme will, by all of Thy signs and names, and by this greatest name of all, to subject to us this sea, and every sea of Thine on earth and in the heavens. Subject to us all dominion and sovereignty, just as Thou didst subject the sea to Moses, the fire to Abraham, the mountains and iron to David, and the wind, the demons and the jinn to Solomon. Subject to us all things, O Thou in whose hand resteth dominion over all things, Who granteth protection and from Whom no protection can be granted, O Most High, O Most Magnificent, O Most Forbearing One, O Knower of all. Amen. *Alif. Hā.*

And may God's blessings and peace rest upon our master Muḥammad, his household and his companions.[9]

HEREWITH IS THE "*Ḥizb* OF LIGHT," WHICH ORIGINATED WITH THE SHAYKH AND RIGHTEOUS SAINT, OUR MASTER ABŪ AL-ḤASAN AL-SHĀDHILĪ, MAY GOD BE PLEASED WITH HIM

I seek refuge in God from the accursed Satan. In the name of God, the Most Gracious, the Dispenser of Grace:

O God, O Light, O Truth, O Thou who dost make all things clear: Open my heart with Thy light, teach me out of Thy knowledge, grant me understanding on Thy authority, cause me to hear Thy words, cause me to see by Thy grace and light, establish me as Thy witness, show me the path which leads to Thee and ease its difficulties for me by Thy grace, and clothe me with the garments of righteousness which Thou Thyself dost provide. Indeed, Thou art capable of all things.

O God, remember me, remind me, accept my repentance, and grant me such forgiveness that I forget all that is other than Thee. Impart to me Thy righteousness, cause me to love and fear Thee, and provide for me—in every worry, sorrow, distress, passion, craving, thought, idea, choice, as well as every decree of fate and every affair—relief and a way of escape.

Thy knowledge encompasses all actualities, Thy power surpasses all potencies and potentials, and Thy will is far exalted above being either conceded or opposed by any of Thy creatures.

God is my sufficiency, and I disavow all that is other than Him [with the exception of His Apostle].

God, there is no god but He: In Him have I placed my trust, and He is the Lord of the Throne Supreme.

There is no god but God: The light of God's throne.

There is no god but God: The light of God's tablet.

There is no god but God: The light of God's pen.

There is no god but God: The light of God's Messenger.

There is no god but God: The light of the mystery of the essence of God's Messenger.

There is no god but God: Adam is God's viceregent.

There is no god but God: Noah is God's confidant.

There is no god but God: Abraham is God's beloved friend.

There is no god but God: Moses is God's mouthpiece.

There is no god but God: Jesus is God's spirit.

There is no god but God: Muḥammad is God's beloved.

There is no god but God: The prophets are God's elect.

There is no god but God: The saints are God's helpers.

There is no god but God: The Lord and Deity, the manifest, true Sovereign, Creator of all, the One, the Supreme and Irresistible, Lord of the heavens and the earth and all that is between them, the Exalted in Might, the Most Forgiving.

There is no god but God, the Most Exalted, the Magnificent.

There is no god but God, the Most Forbearing, the Most Munificent.

Glory be to the Lord of the seven heavens and the Lord of the Throne Supreme. Praise be to God, Lord of the worlds.

In the name of God, through God, from God, to God, and upon God let the believers rely.

God is my sufficiency, I have believed in God, I have found my contentment in God, I have placed my trust in God, and there is no power or strength save through God. I repent unto Thee, through Thee and from Thee. Hadst Thou not willed it to be so, I would not have turned to Thee in repentance. Cleanse my heart of all love for that which is other than Thee, and preserve my members from transgressing Thy commands.

By Thee I swear: If Thou dost not watch over me with Thine eye and preserve me with Thy power, I will bring about my own demise, and with me, that of a nation of Thy creation, which will bring harm, in the end, to Thy servant alone.

I seek refuge in Thy pardon from Thy chastisement; I seek refuge in Thy favor from Thy wrath; I seek refuge in Thee from Thee. I praise Thee without measure, for Thine are all the praiseworthy attributes which Thou hast attributed to Thyself; indeed, Thou art far more sublime than any praise which I might bestow upon Thee. Rather, [what I see are] mere outward manifestations of Thy bounty. Thou didst reveal these to us through the words of Thy Messenger so that, through them, we might worship Thee in a manner commensurate with our own capacities but which, even so, falls far short of Thy true majesty. After all, can the [fitting] reward for the initial, consummate act of goodness[10] be anything other than a [further] act of goodness which comes from Thee Thyself?

O Thou through whom, from whom, and to whom all things return, I ask Thee by the sanctity of the Teacher,[11] by the sanctity of the Prophet who guides aright, by the sanctity of the seventy and the eight,[12] by the sanctity of the mysteries of that which proceeded from Thee to Muḥammad, the unlettered prophet, by the sanctity of the Throne Verse, by the sanctity of the seven oft-repeated verses and the Magnificent Qur'ān, by the sanctity of [all] Thy revealed scriptures, by the sanctity of the Supreme Name in the presence of which nothing on earth or in the heavens can cause harm, and by the Hearer and Knower of all; by the sanctity of, "Say, 'He is the one God: God the Eternal, the Uncaused Cause of All That Exists. He begets not, and neither is He begotten; and there is nothing that could be compared with Him'": Preserve me from every heedless moment, every lustful desire and every disobedience, be it past or yet to come; grant me refuge from all those who would make claims upon me, by right or otherwise, whether in this life or the life to come. With Thee alone rests the final evidence of all truth, and Thou art capable of all things. Preserve me from anxiety over my daily sustenance and the fear of others, and lead me along the path of integrity. Uphold me with the truth and preserve me from every concern and sorrow except the concern to enter Thy Paradise. Protect us from all suffering, whether above us or beneath our feet, which might cause us to divide into factions and seek to lord it over one another; and protect us from all harm which lies within Thy knowledge of what has been or will be. Indeed, Thou art capable of all things.

Glory be to the Sovereign Creator. Glory be to the Creator and Sustainer. Glory be to God, who is far exalted above all that they may attribute to Him. Knower of the seen and the unseen, He is far exalted above all beings to which they attribute divinity besides Him. Glory be to the Possessor of Honor and Omnipotence. Glory be to the Possessor of Power and Dominion. Glory be to the One who gives life and deals death. Glory be to the Ever-Living One who never dies. Glory be to the Ever-Existent, All-Powerful One. Glory be to the All-Powerful, the Irresistible. Glory be to the One Who holds sway over His servants, the All-Wise, the All-Aware. Glory be to the Ever-Existent, Eternal One.

Say: God is my sufficiency; all who have placed their trust in God rely on Him alone.

I seek refuge in God from affliction and its attendant strain, from ill fate, from the depths of misery, and from the gloating of enemies. And I seek refuge in God—my Lord and your Lord—from every disdainful oppressor who believes not in the Day of Reckoning.

O Thou in whose hand resteth dominion over all things, Who granteth protection and from Whom no protection can be granted, uphold me through the fear of Thee and reliance upon Thee alone, lest I fear any but Thee, lest I hope in any but Thee, and lest I worship any but Thee.

I bear witness that Thou art capable of all things and that Thou has encompassed all things with Thy knowledge.

By this command which is the origin of all that exists, which marks the beginning and the end, the goal of all goals, we ask Thee to make this sea subservient to us—the sea of this earthly existence, including everything and everyone therein—as Thou didst make the sea subservient to Moses, the fire to Abraham, the mountains and iron to David, and the wind, the demons and the jinn to Solomon.

Make subservient to me every sea, every mountain, all iron, every wind, every demon from among jinn and human beings. Make subservient to me my own soul and all things, O Thou in whose hand resteth dominion over all things. Uphold me with inward certainty, and support me with the Spirit of Faith and Truth.

"O Man! We did not bestow the Qur'ān on thee from on high to make thee unhappy, but only as an exhortation to all who stand in awe [of God]: a revelation from Him who has created the earth and the high heavens—the Most Gracious, established on the throne of His almightiness. Unto Him belongs all that is in the heavens and all that is on earth, as well as all that is between them and all that is beneath the sod. And if thou say anything aloud, [He hears it—] since, behold, He knows [even] the secret [thoughts of man], as well as all that is yet more hidden [within him]" {Ṭā Hā [O Man] 20:1-7}.

God, there is no god but He. To Him belong the most beautiful names: We seek Thee by this great name by which Thou didst preserve Thy noble prophets. Thou art the All-Knowing Sovereign. Make me worthy of the example embodied in Abraham, upon him be peace, and those with him when they said to their people, "We declare ourselves innocent of you and that which ye worship other than God. We renounce that which you declare to be true, and henceforth there shall be enmity and hatred between us until ye place your faith in God alone."

My Lord is exalted far above being either present in things, or absent therefrom.[13] In His presence nothing on earth or in the heavens can cause harm, and He is the Hearer and Knower of all. *Alif. Hā.*

The *Ḥizb* of Shaykh Abū al-Ḥasan al-Shādhilī, May God Be Pleased With Him

I seek refuge in God from the accursed Satan. In the name of God, the Most Gracious, the Dispenser of Grace:

"All praise is due to God alone, the Sustainer of all the worlds, the Most Gracious, the Dispenser of Grace, Lord of the Day of Judgment! Thee alone do we worship, and unto Thee alone do we turn for aid. Guide us the straight way—the way of those upon whom Thou hast bestowed Thy blessings, not of those who have been condemned [by Thee], nor of those who go astray!" {Al-Fātiḥah [The Opening] 1:1-7}

"God—there is no deity save Him, the Ever-Living, the Self-Subsistent Fount of All Being. Neither slumber overtakes Him, nor sleep. His is all that is in the heavens and all that is on earth. Who is there that could intercede with Him, unless it be by His leave? He knows all that lies open before people and all that is hidden from them, whereas they cannot attain to aught of His knowledge save that which He wills [them to attain]. His eternal power overspreads the heavens and the earth. Their upholding wearies Him not, and He alone is truly exalted, tremendous" {Al-Baqarah [The Cow] 2:255}.

"The Apostle, and the believers with him, believe in what has been bestowed upon him from on high by his

Sustainer: they all believe in God, in His angels and His revelations, and His apostles, making no distinction between any of His apostles; and they say: 'We have heard, and we pay heed. Grant us Thy forgiveness, O our Sustainer, for with Thee is all journeys' end! God does not burden any human being with more than he is well able to bear; in his favor shall be whatever good he does, and against him whatever evil he does. O our Sustainer! Take us not to task if we forget or unwittingly do wrong! O our Sustainer! Lay not upon us a burden such as Thou didst lay upon those who lived before us! O our Sustainer! Make us not bear burdens which we have no strength to bear! And efface Thou our sins, and grant us forgiveness, and bestow Thy mercy upon us! Thou art our Lord Supreme; succor us, then, against people who deny the truth!'" {Al-Baqarah [The Cow] 2:285-286}

"God—there is no deity save Him, the Ever-Living, the Self-Subsistent Fount of All Being. Step by step has He bestowed upon thee from on high this divine writ, setting forth the truth which confirms whatever there still remains [of earlier revelations]: for it is He who has bestowed from on high the Torah and the Gospel aforetime, as a guidance unto mankind, and it is He who has bestowed the standard by which to discern the true from the false. Behold, as for those who are bent on denying God's messages—grievous suffering awaits them: for God is almighty, an avenger of evil. Verily, nothing on earth or in the heavens is hidden from God. He it is who shapes you in the wombs as He wills. There is no deity save Him, the Almighty, the Truly Wise" {Āl ᶜImrān [The House of Imran] 3:1-6}.

"Say, 'O God, Lord of all dominion! Thou grantest dominion unto whom Thou willest, and takest away dominion from whom Thou willest; and Thou exaltest whom Thou willest, and abasest whom Thou willest. In Thy hand is all good. Verily, Thou hast the power to will anything. Thou makest the night grow longer by shortening the day, and Thou makest the day grow longer by shortening the night. And Thou bringest forth the living out of that which is dead, and Thou bringest forth the dead out of that which is alive. And Thou grantest sustenance unto whom Thou willest, beyond all reckoning" {Āl ᶜImrān [The House of Imran] 3:26-27}.

"[He] is the One who has created me and is the One who guides me, and is the One who gives me to eat and to drink, and when I fall ill, is the One who restores me to health, and who will cause me to die and then will bring me back to life—and who, I hope, will forgive me my faults on Judgment Day! O My Sustainer! Endow me with the ability to judge [between right and wrong], and make me one with the righteous, and grant me the power to convey the truth unto those who will come after me, and place me among those who shall inherit the garden of bliss! And forgive my father—for, verily, he is among those who have gone astray—and do not put me to shame on the Day when all shall be raised from the dead: the Day on which neither wealth will be of any use, nor children, [and when] only he [will be happy] who comes before God with a heart free of evil! For, [on that Day], paradise will be brought within sight of the God-conscious, whereas the blazing fire will be laid open before those who had been lost in grievous error" {Al-Shuᶜarā' [The Poets] 26:78-91}.

"All that is in the heavens and on earth extols God's limitless glory: for He alone is almighty, truly wise! His is the dominion over the heavens and the earth; He grants life and deals death; and He has the power to will anything. He is the First and the Last, the Outward as well as the Inward, and He has full knowledge of everything. He it is who has created the heavens and the earth in six aeons, and is established on the throne of His almightiness. He knows all that enters the earth, and all that comes out of it, as well as all that descends from the skies, and all that ascends to them. And He is with you wherever you may be; and God sees all that you do. His is the dominion over the heavens and earth; and all things go back unto God [as their source]. He makes the night grow longer by shortening the day, and makes the day grow longer by shortening the night; and He has full knowledge of what is in the hearts [of men]" {Al-Ḥadīd [Iron] 57:1-6}.

"God is He save whom there is no deity; the One who knows all that is beyond the reach of a created being's perception, as well as all that can be witnessed by a creature's senses or mind: He, the Most Gracious, the Dispenser of Grace. God is He save whom there is no deity: the Sovereign Supreme, the Holy, the One with whom all salvation rests, the Giver of Faith, the One who determines what is true and false, the Almighty, the One who subdues wrong and restores right, the one to Whom all greatness belongs. Utterly remote is God, in His limitless glory, from anything to which men may ascribe a share in His divinity! He is God, the Creator, the Maker who shapes all forms and appearances! His [alone] are the attributes of perfection. All that is in the heavens and on earth extols His limitless glory; for He alone is almighty, truly wise!" {Al-Ḥashr [The Gathering] 59:22-24}

"Consider the bright morning hours, and the night when it grows still and dark. Thy Sustainer has not forsaken thee, nor does He scorn thee: for, indeed, the life to come will be better for thee than this earlier part [of thy life]. And, indeed, in time will thy Sustainer grant thee [what thy heart desires], and thou shalt be well-pleased. Has He not found thee an orphan, and given thee shelter? And found thee lost on thy way, and guided thee? And found thee in want, and given thee sufficiency? Therefore, the orphan shalt thou never wrong, and him that seeks [thy] help shalt thou never chide, and of thy Sustainer's blessings shalt thou ever speak" {Al-Ḍuḥā [The Bright Morning Hours] 93:1-11}.

"Have We not opened up thy heart, and lifted from thee the burden that had weighed so heavily on thy back? And [have We not] raised thee high in dignity? And, behold, with every hardship comes ease: verily, with every hardship comes ease! Hence, when thou art freed [from distress], remain steadfast, and unto thy Sustainer turn with love" {Al-Sharḥ [The Opening-Up of the Heart] 94:1-7}.

"Behold, God has bought of the believers their lives and their possessions, promising them paradise in return, [and so] they fight in God's cause, and slay, and are slain: a promise which in truth He has willed upon Himself in the Torah, and the Gospel, and the Qur'ān. And who could be more faithful to his covenant than God? Rejoice, then, in the bargain which you have made with Him; for this, this is the triumph supreme! [It is a triumph of] those who turn to God in repentance [whenever they have sinned], and who worship and praise [Him], and go on and on [seeking His goodly acceptance], and bow down [before Him] and prostrate themselves in adoration, and enjoin the doing of what is right and forbid the doing of what is wrong, and keep to the bounds set by God. And give thou [O Prophet] the glad tiding [of God's promise] to all believers" {Al-Tawbah [Repentance] 9:111-112}.

"Truly, to a happy state shall attain the believers: those who humble themselves in their prayer, and who turn away from all that is frivolous, and who are intent on inner purity, and who are mindful of their chastity, [not giving way to their desires] with any but their spouses—that is, those whom they rightfully possess [through wedlock]—: for then, behold, they are free of all blame, whereas such as seek to go beyond that [limit] are truly transgressors; and who are faithful to their trusts and to their pledges, and who guard their prayers [from all worldly] intent. It is they, they who shall be the inheritors that will inherit the paradise; [and] therein shall they abide" {Al-Mu'minūn [The Believers] 23:1-11}.

"Verily, for all men and women who have surrendered themselves unto God, and all believing men and believing women, and all truly devout men and truly devout women, and all men and women who are true to their word, and all men and women who are patient in adversity, and all men and women who humble themselves [before God], and all men and women who give in charity, all self-denying men and self-denying women, and all men and women who are mindful of their chastity, and all men and women who remember God unceasingly: for [all of] them has God readied forgiveness of sins and a mighty reward" {Al-Aḥzāb [The Confederates] 33:35}.

"Verily, man is born with a restless disposition. [As a rule,] whenever misfortune touches him, he is filled with self-pity, and whenever good fortune comes to him, he selfishly withholds it [from others]. Not so, however, those who consciously turn towards God in prayer, and who incessantly persevere in their prayer; and in whose possessions there is a due share, acknowledged [by them], for such as ask [for help] and such as are deprived [of what is good in life]; and who accept as true [the coming of] the Day of Judgment; and who stand in dread of their Sustainer's chastisement—for, behold, of their Sustainer's chastisement nonc may ever feel [wholly] secure; and who are mindful of their chastity, [got giving way to their desires] with any but their spouses—that is, those whom they rightfully possess [through wedlock]—: for then, behold, they are free of all blame, whereas such as seek to go beyond that [limit] are truly transgressors; and who are faithful to their trusts and their pledges; and who stand firm whenever they bear witness; and who guard their prayers [from all worldly intent]. These it is who in the gardens [of paradise] shall be honored!" {Al-Maᶜārij [The Ways of Ascent] 70:19-35}

O God, may fear [of Thee] be our companion, may longing [for Thee] pervade our beings, may our knowledge be enduring, and may our thoughts of Thee be unceasing. We ask Thee to grant us the mystery of mysteries by virtue of which we will never again persist in transgressions or faults. Choose us and guide us to act on the commands which Thou didst expound to us on the lips of Thy Messenger, through which Thou didst try Abraham Thy friend, and which he fulfilled. "[God] said, 'Behold I shall make thee a leader of men.' Abraham asked, 'And [wilt Thou make leaders] of my offspring as well?' [God] answered, 'My covenant does not embrace the evildoers.'" Therefore, cause us to be among those of Abraham's, Noah's and Adam's progeny who are doers of good, and enable us to walk the path of those who have been paragons of righteousness and fear of Thee.

In the name of God, through God, from God, and to God, let those who have placed their trust in God rely fully upon Him.

God is my sufficiency, I have believed in God, I have found my contentment in God, I have placed my trust in God, and there is no power save through God.

I bear witness that there is no god but God alone, Who has no partner, and I bear witness that Muḥammad is His servant and His messenger.

My Lord, forgive me, and forgive all believers, male and female. "All praise is due to God alone, the Sustainer of all the worlds, the Most Gracious, the Dispenser of Grace, Lord of the Day of Judgment! Thee alone do we worship, and unto Thee alone do we turn for aid. Guide us the straight way—the way of those upon whom Thou hast bestowed Thy blessings, not of those who have been condemned [by Thee], nor of those who go astray!"

Say: Praise be to God, and peace to His servants whom He has chosen.

My Lord, I have wronged myself greatly. Forgive me, and accept my repentance. There is no god but Thee; glory be to Thee. Indeed, I have been among the wrongdoers.

O God, Most High, Most Magnificent, Most Forbearing, Thou who knowest all, hearest all, and seest all, Thou whose will is incontrovertible, Thou who art infinite in Thy power, Ever-Living One, Self-Subsistent Fount of All Being, Most Gracious, Dispenser of Grace, Thou who art *huwa, huwa, huwa*, Thou who art First and Last, Manifest and Hidden! "Hallowed be thy Sustainer's name, full of majesty and glory!"

O God, unite me with Thy Name Supreme, in the presence of which nothing can bring harm on earth or in the heavens. Bestow upon me, out of this Name, a mystery in the presence of which transgressions can in no wise bring harm, and of this Name, grant me a portion out of which Thou supplieth the needs of heart, mind and spirit, inward being, soul and body. Likewise, O God, grant me a portion by virtue of which Thou dost lift burdens from heart and mind, inward being and spirit, body and soul. Embrace my names within Thy names, my attributes within Thy attributes, and my actions within Thy actions in such a way that I am rendered free of impurity and harm and delivered from reproach, and in such a way that Thy munificence descends through me and I am enabled to lead others in Thy worship and service. Fulfill, for me, the commands by which Thou hast tested the paragons of right guidance. Enrich me in order that, through me, Thou mightest enrich others; and bring me to life in order that, through me, Thou mightest bring to life whatsoever, and whomsoever, Thou willest of Thy creatures. Cause me to be a treasure-house of "the forty,"[14] embody within me the virtues of those who fear Thee, and forgive me, for Thy covenant does not embrace the doers of evil.

Ṭā sīn ḥā' mīm ᶜayn sīn qāf: "He has given freedom to the two great bodies of water, so that they might meet: [yet] between them is a barrier which they may not transgress" {Al-Raḥmān [The Most Gracious] 55:19}.

"All praise is due to God alone, the Sustainer of all the worlds, the Most Gracious, the Dispenser of Grace, Lord of the Day of Judgment! Thee alone do we worship, and unto Thee alone do we turn for aid. Guide us the straight way—the way of those upon whom Thou hast bestowed Thy blessings, not of those who have been condemned [by Thee], nor of those who go astray!"

"Say, 'He is the one God: God the Eternal, the Uncaused Cause of All That Exists. He begets not, and neither is He begotten; and there is nothing that could be compared with Him.'"

"Say, 'He is the one God: God the Eternal, the Uncaused Cause of All That Exists. He begets not, and neither is He begotten; and there is nothing that could be compared with Him.'"

"Say, 'He is the one God: God the Eternal, the Uncaused Cause of All That Exists. He begets not, and neither is He begotten; and there is nothing that could be compared with Him.'"

Herewith concludes the *ḥizb*, thanks be to God.

The mosque of al-Ḥakīm bi Amrillāh, built between 990 and 1013 C.E., in the Fatimid city of Cairo, before and after restoration (1980).

Conclusion

In conclusion:

When, ten years ago, I was in Cairo at the al-Ḥākim Mosque, I used to go to see the saint Abū ^{c}Abdullāh al-Ḥakīm al-Mursī. This man, who was loved and revered by the shaykh, said to me, "Once when I was aboard a ship I mentioned you, and one of the other passengers associated you with a particular shaykh. So I said, 'Rather, he is one of the companions of our shaykh Abū al-^{c}Abbās al-Mursī, may God be pleased with him.' Thus, if the matter is as I told them, write it down for me in your own handwriting." Hence, I wrote down for him at that time what I will mention here, God willing. Given that this book was written in extolment of the virtues of Shaykh Abū al-^{c}Abbās al-Mursī (may God be pleased with him)—and given that in what follows, we likewise speak in praise of him and the sublimity of his path—it was only fitting that this illuminating reminder should be a bangle for this book's forearm, as it were, and a sapphire with which we complete the "necklace" of these chapters. It is followed by words of counsel which I wrote to our brethren in Alexandria while I was in Cairo at the beginning of Rabī^{c} al-Awwal, 694 A.H. This, in turn, is followed by a poem containing exhortations and commands from the Truth, exalted be He, to His servant, which are concluded with a panegyric to the Messenger of God ﷺ. We hereby bring the book to a close, praying that this endeavor in its entirety might be an offering to God alone by His grace and bounty.

The first section of the conclusion consists of the following luminous reminder and precious pearl:

In the name of God, the Most Gracious, the Dispenser of Grace. May God's abundant blessings and peace rest upon our master Muḥammad, his household and his companions.

Praise be to God, whose praise is incumbent upon us, whose sublimity and glory are everlasting, whose signs are full of splendor, the evidences for Whose truth are unmistakable, Who has caused His light to shine in the hearts of His saints, illuminating the heavens of their spirits and the earth of their bodies and souls; God, who is the Light of the heavens and earth—the Light of their spirits' heavens through their witnessing of Him, and the Light of their souls' earth through their obedience and service to Him—has caused their hearts to be a mirror of His essence and His attributes. He has made them manifest in order Himself to be manifested in a manner most exceptional—He who is manifest in everything without exception. He has appeared in them through His mysteries and His light, just as He has appeared in them, as well as in others, through His power and might. His praise is ever upon their lips, and their hearts rejoice in His light. When they speak, they speak of Him, and when they listen, they listen to Him. How many a banner of sainthood flutters over them, and how many a decree of vicegerency has gone out to them! He has granted them entry into His presence by the gate of truth and honor through their annihilation to all that is other than Him, then brought them out, likewise through the gate of truth and honor: subsisting in His light and splendor, the *barzakhs* of lights,[1] the treasure-troves of secrets. When He severs their ties [with other entities], He unites them [with Himself], and once He has brought them into the station of union, He brings them once again into the station of separation.[2] He causes them to be absent from others, granting them knowledge of His mysteries; indeed, if the light possessed by one of them alone were divided among all Earth's inhabitants, it would be sufficient for them.

The vastness of their lights should be no cause for wonder, nor should the all-inclusive embrace of the mysteries to which they are privy. After all, the light in their hearts finds its source in the light of God. The Prophet ﷺ said, "Beware of the believer's insight, since he sees with the light of God."[3] As for the all-inclusive embrace of the saints' mysteries, it is reflected in God's declaration, "Behold, all who pledge their allegiance to thee pledge their allegiance to God: The hand of God is over their hands" {Al-Fatḥ [Victory] 48:10}. In keeping with what they have inherited from their Prophet, may God's blessings and peace be upon him, they have been realized in the station of uncompromised awareness of the divine uniqueness (*maqām al-fardāniyah*), and have been granted entrance into His presence in such a way that they see nothing but Him.

I have heard—may God be gracious unto you—that despite the varying degrees of your affection for us, we have the probe with which to plumb its depths, and we hold it in the place of esteem which it merits. Thus, others' hearts will incline toward you to the extent that you incline toward them, and if you experience an increase in divine spiritual provision through another servant, you will only do so to the extent that you have grown in your love for him. Thus has the All-Wise God, the Infinite in Power, the Knower of all, ordered [the affairs of the human spirit].

In general, the acts, attitudes and virtues required [of God's servants] in the realm of inward etiquette and obedience to outward precepts are included within the commands in a general way only; taken in their entirety, these two realms include:

- •Fear of God. As God, glory be to Him, has declared, "O Mankind! Reverence your Guardian-Lord" {Al-Nisā' [Women] 4:1}.[4]
- •Faithfulness to covenants. God declares, "O you who have attained to faith! Be true to your covenants!" {Al-Mā'idah [The Repast] 5:1}
- •Repentance. God, glory be to Him, commands us, "Turn unto God in repentance" {Al-Nūr [The Light] 24:31}.
- •Turning towards God and surrendering fully to Him: "Turn towards your Sustainer [alone] and surrender yourselves unto Him..." {Al-Zumar [The Throngs] 39:54}.
- •Responding to God. As He commands us, "Respond to your Sustainer" {Al-Shūrā [Consultation] 42:47}.
- •Being followers of God's Messenger ﷺ. As God, glory be to Him, has said, "Say [O Prophet], 'If you love God, follow me, [and] God will love you and forgive you your sins....'" {ĀL ᶜImrān [The House of Imran] 3:31}.
- •Bearing witness to every blessing as being from God. As God, glory be to Him, has declared, "For, whatever good thing comes to you, comes from God" {Al-Naḥl [The Bee] 16:53}.
- •Bearing witness to the guidance which comes from God. He declares, "All praise is due to God, who has guided us unto this; for we would certainly not have found the right path unless God had guided us" {Al-Aᶜrāf [The Faculty of Discernment] 7:43}.

May God not allow what we say and hear to become an argument against us. Rather, may He cause us, together with you, to be servants who are guided aright by His love, who continue in affectionate devotion to Him, and who are blessed with His nearness. May He shower both us and you with the light of His providential care and, by His grace and munificence, cause us to be worthy of His friendship. [It will thus come to pass] if He so wills, exalted be He. Praise be to God alone, and may God's abundant blessings and peace be upon our master Muḥammad, his household and his wives.

I heard our shaykh, Abū al-ᶜAbbās (may God be pleased with him) recite these lines:

> My heart sang, for me and from me,
> So I sang along.
>
> Wherever they were, so were we,
> And wherever we were, so were they.

The supreme manifestation, the most splendorous *barzakh*, the source from which all lights emerge, the treasure-trove of secrets, the one to whom the beginning and the end belong, he who has perfectly attained the highest of spiritual stations, the Messenger of the Lord of the Worlds and the master of those who have lived in both former and latter times—Muḥammad (may God's blessings and peace rest upon him, his household and his companions one and all)—he is the light of lights and the secret of secrets; to him descend the divine mysteries, and from him experiential knowledge of the Divine is received. Those possessing outward knowledge have taken their outward knowledge from him, just as those endowed with inward knowledge have received their inward knowledge from him. He has declared ﷺ, "The scholars are the heirs of the prophets."[5] Hence, what each [scholar] has is commensurate with what he has inherited; what he has inherited is commensurate with the light he possesses; the light he possesses is commensurate with the degree to which the truth has been laid open to him; the degree to which the truth has been laid open to him is commensurate with the purity of his heart; the purity of his heart is commensurate with his experiential knowledge of his Lord; and his experiential knowledge of his Lord is commensurate with the love [for Him] which God foreordained for him to have from time immemorial. Those who have pursued inward knowledge are more worthy of the inheritance, more closely related, as it were, and higher in rank. The reason for this is that their knowledge is always attended by reverent fear and awe, since the true nature of an inheritance is for the entity inherited to be passed on to its heir with the same qualities as those which characterized it when it was in the possession of the one who bequeathed it.

Every possessor of knowledge which is not attended by reverent fear is unworthy to be an heir. When the Prophet ﷺ stated that, "The scholars are the heirs of the prophets," what he meant by "scholars" was those endowed with the knowledge of God, since knowledge of God engenders reverent fear of Him. As God, exalted be He, has declared, "Of all His servants, only such as are endowed with knowledge stand [truly] in awe of God" {Fāṭir [The Originator] 35:28}.

The chain of righteous, martyrs, saints, men and women of truth, and poles has not been broken from the days of that supreme, all-encompassing *barzakh* ﷺ to the present day; nor will it be broken until God inherits the earth and all who dwell therein; indeed, He is the best of all to inherit.

Concerning God's declaration, "Any message which We annul or consign to oblivion We replace with a better or a similar one" {Al-Baqarah [The Cow] 2:106}, I heard our shaykh, Abū al-ᶜAbbās (may God be pleased with him) once say, "In other words, 'Any saint which We cause to pass away We replace with a better or similar one.'"

Whoever has no spiritual teacher to link him with the chain of followers and to disclose his heart to him is, in this respect, a foundling, a bastard with no lineage to claim. If such a person has light, he will most likely be someone who is dominated by his spiritual states and who relies upon that which proceeds from God to him, not content to be disciplined and refined, or to be led by the rein of education and training.

Our shaykh, our imam, our exemplar in this respect, was unique among those of his time, the sign of his age, the signpost of gnostics, the pole of the rightly guided, the manifestation of the truth's splendor, the one who pointed out the guideposts along the path, the one thoroughly versed in the [divine] names, the letters and the circles [of the saints] and who combined within himself knowledge of the manifest and the hidden: our master and lord Shihāb al-Dīn Abū al-ᶜAbbās Aḥmad Ibn ᶜUmar al-Anṣārī al-Mursī al-Shādhilī, may God sanctify his spirit and fill his tomb with light. It is his lights on which we have drawn, it is he in whose footsteps we have sought to tread; it is he who has hastened our spirits' advance until they came to share in [the knowledge of the greatest of saints], who loosened our tongues until they spoke [of the divine mysteries], and who planted experiential knowledge in our hearts until its fruits grew ripe and mellow and its blossoms gave off their fragrance.

It is he who, by God's grace, has promised us, and who by expounding in the two realms of knowledge, has beckoned us onward. With him only are we associated, and in matters of the spirit we rely upon him alone. Whoever traces our spiritual lineage through anyone but him is ignorant of who we truly are, or is someone whose own knowledge he disregards. After all, whoever traces a disciple's spiritual lineage to anyone but his true master is like someone who traces a child's lineage through someone other than his true father. Indeed, this fatherhood is the most worthy of recognition, and its foundation most deserving of being safeguarded and preserved. After all, fatherhood in the flesh is not complete without fatherhood in the spirit, whereas fatherhood in the spirit is complete in itself.

Your shaykh is not the one to whom you have listened; your shaykh is the one from whom you have received knowledge.

Your shaykh is not the one whose words have confronted you; your shaykh is the one whose silent reminders have coursed through your being.

Your shaykh is not the one who has invited you to the door; your shaykh is the one who has lifted the veil between you and him.

Your shaykh is not the one whose statements have challenged you; your shaykh is the one whose spiritual state has roused you to wakefulness.

Your shaykh is the one who brings you out of the prison of craving and ushers you into the presence of the Master.

Your shaykh is the one who goes on polishing the mirror of your heart until it reflects clearly the lights of your Lord. He lifts you up to God until you rise to greet Him. He marches forward with you until you have reached Him, and stays by your side until he has flung you into His arms. Casting you into the light of the Presence, he says, "Here you are with your Lord. Here is the seat of sainthood from God. Here are the places whence you receive spiritual sustenance from God; and here is the carpet, seated upon which, you will receive His truths." Thereupon, if He so chooses, He may leave you to drown in the sea of annihilation, and if He so chooses, He may return you to the shore of subsistence to live a life of spiritual realization and assist others in achieving the same blessed end.

The one in a state of annihilation receives from God, while the one in a state of subsistence sets forth to others what he has received from God.

The one in a state of subsistence stands in for God, while in the case of one in a state of annihilation, God stands in for him.

For one in a state of annihilation, the sphere of his perceptions has been obliterated and the holy sanctuary of the Divine has been opened to him; as for one in a state of subsistence, he remains, through his Lord, in that same holy sanctuary.

The one in a state of annihilation is called to God, while the one in a state of subsistence calls others to God; he serves as vicegerent and proxy for others with permission, assurance and stability and with firmly established inward certainty, calling others to God on the basis of divinely endowed spiritual insight. As God, glory be to Him, has declared, "Say [O Prophet], 'This is my way: Resting upon conscious insight accessible to reason, I am calling [you all] unto God—I and they who follow me'" {Yūsuf [Joseph] 12:108}. That is to say, the call he issues is founded upon direct vision, observation and witnessing. He does not call others to God while absent from God; rather, he calls others unto God while himself beholding Him.

This is the path of the prophets and messengers, the giants among men and women of truth; it is the most perfect spiritual station, the most excellent way. Those who trace our spiritual lineage to anyone other than this imam while knowing of our association with him are presumptuous and obstinate, while those who do so without knowing of our association with him have strayed from the path of integrity and good sense, violated God's commands, and failed to keep watch over their own hearts. Have you not heeded the words of the Sovereign, glory be to Him, "And never concern yourself with anything of which thou hast no knowledge: verily, [thy] hearing and sight and heart—all of them—will be called to account for it [on Judgment Day]" {Al-Isrā' [The Night Journey] 17:36}.

May God, glory be to Him, bring to full realization our kinship with this community; may He allow us to die still loving them; may He enable us to persevere in their ways; may He cause us to grow in our goodwill and affection for them; and may He, by His grace and kindness, forbid that we should be among those who break their covenant with them.

Praise be to God! May God grant protection and peace to His chosen servants, and may abundant blessings and peace be upon the chief of His messengers, the imam of the God-fearing, Muḥammad, seal of the prophets, and upon his household and his companions.

God is my sufficiency, and how excellent a guardian is He! There is no power or strength save through God, the Most Exalted, the Magnificent.

As for the Words of Counsel Written to Some of Our Brethren in Alexandria, They Are Presented Herewith

In the name of God, the Most Gracious, the Dispenser of Grace. May God's abundant blessings and peace be upon our master Muḥammad and upon his descendents and companions.

May the peace, mercy and blessings of God be upon the loving brethren, the beloved comrades. May God preserve and care for them, guard and nurture them, bestowing His grace upon them in ever-increasing abundance and showering them with His gifts and provisions. May God bring their hearts into a place of intimate communion, divinely bestowed understanding, disclosure and honor; may He bless them with obedience and [His goodly] acceptance, the ability to advance toward Him and to arrive, and permission to enter [His presence]. May He sanctify their spirits, granting them broad, open pasture in the realm of His unseen realities. May He transmit to them, of His light, that which will serve to guide them aright, and impart to them that which will preserve them from [attachment to] everything and everyone but Him both in this life and the life to come.

Know—may God be gracious unto you—that although divine providence is in the realm of the unseen, there is, even so, a witness which points to it and evidence which leads to it. You can perceive God's providential care for you through your observance of the limits which He has set for you and in your faithfulness to His covenants. Indeed, one sign of God's love for the servant is the servant's love for Him, and one sign of the servant's love for God is that he would never favor anything or anyone over Him. Moreover, a sign of the fact that the servant favors nothing and no one over God is that he looks upon this earthly existence with disdain, and created entities with heedful discretion.

Happy is the one to whom God has given a thinking heart, discerning vision, an ear which hears the Divine, and a soul eager to serve God. Of all God's rights over His servants, the one which they most tend to neglect is that of thanksgiving to Him. Thanksgiving to God, moreover, is of two types: outward and inward. Outward thanksgiving is expressed through living in accordance with His laws, while inward thanksgiving is expressed through the witnessing of His blessings. Thus, whoever fails to obey His commandments and observe His limits has not been thankful to Him, and whoever violates His covenants has not been mindful of Him. Therefore—may God be gracious to you—you must be thankful to God for His blessings to you.

I tell you truly: The heedless and the blind ask God to renew His blessings to them without being thankful for what He has already given them. Yet how is God to renew for you a blessing which you have sought, when you have neglected to give thanks for blessings which sought you out until they reached you? The first thing required of the person who seeks God's blessings is that he or she seek them with thanksgiving to God. For your grateful attitude conveys your request to the One to whom thanks is due even if you are silent; indeed, your spirit of thanksgiving petitions the One you have thanked even if you have made no audible request. God has guaranteed increased blessings to all who are thankful without exception, saying, "If you are grateful [to Me], I shall most certainly give you more and more" {Ibrāhīm [Abraham] 14:7}.

Now, if God has promised to increase what He has given people, how could He fail to allow them to keep what He has granted them already? I tell you truly: If someone wishes to keep what he has, he will do whatever is required to tie it down, as it were, for fear of losing it. Hence, "tie down" God's blessings to you with thanksgiving.

As an aid to a spirit of gratitude one need only look at the gifts of the Most Charitable One and the many things He has done, including the acts of grace He has performed in earlier times and later, the beginnings of His blessings and their conclusions. After all, never does one look with the eye of faith but that it falls upon a blessing, be it past or present. This will be confirmed to you if you examine your dealings with God, and His with you. For if you look at what has proceeded from Him to you, you will find nothing but bounty and goodness, whereas if you look at what has proceeded from you to Him, you will find nothing but heedlessness and disobedience.

The source of all things good, the treasure-trove of blessings, is to be found in acting in obedience to God and avoiding disobedience. You must ensure that your repentance is sound, for not only is what follows it founded upon it, but its blessings have a retroactive effect on what preceded it. There is no spiritual station but that it stands in need of it: One's spiritual states will not be purified, one's actions will not be acceptable to God, nor will what one has received from God be confirmed unless one's repentance is sound; and the truth of this on the communal level points to its truth on the individual level as well. Have you not heard the words of God, mighty and majestic is He, "And [always], O you believers—all of you—turn unto God in repentance, so that you might attain to a happy state!" {Al-Nūr [The Light] 24:31} God addresses all believers here concerning repentance, thereby indicating its grave importance. An aid to repentance is thought; an aid to thought is solitude, and an aid to solitude is awareness of the afflictions which result from mixing [with others].

One of the signs that you will reach your goal is that your beginning was sound, and for God to grant you soundness in the station of repentance is better for you than for Him to make you privy to 70,000 unseen realities, only then to take them away from you.

Invoke God's name with your tongue and observe Him in your heart. The good you have received from God, you have accepted, and what has come your way from the opposing realm you have warded off, in all of which you have sought refuge in Him. If you are troubled inwardly by some transgression or fault, or by pride in a good deed you have done or some pleasant spiritual state to which you have attained, then make haste to repent of it all and seek God's forgiveness. As for transgressions and faults, repentance of them is your duty in accordance with God's law, and as for good deeds or pleasant spiritual states, you should cast them aside.

In this respect, take a lesson from the Apostle's seeking of God's forgiveness after he received the glad tidings that God had forgiven him all his faults, past as well as future. For if this was the response of someone who had never committed any transgression whatsoever but, rather, had been granted infallibility, then how much more should it be the response of someone who is prone to transgress from time to time?

Know that God has placed the lights of [His] kingdom in the various types of obedience. Hence, whoever fails to perform a certain type of obedience or fails in some manner to surrender to His ways loses a commensurate degree of light. Therefore, neglect no sort of obedience, and do not dispense with your *awrād*[6] in favor of "inrushes" (*al-wāridāt*)[7] when they are your portion. Do not allow yourselves to be like those pretenders who pay lip service to the divine realities but whose hearts are devoid of their lights. In His wisdom, the Truth has caused His servants' ongoing obedience to be the knocker with which they knock on the door to the realm of the unseen; thus it is that the unseen will never be concealed from someone who perseveres in obedience and who relates to others with the courtesy which God has called upon us to observe. Rather, the veil which renders the world of the unseen inaccessible is the presence of faults; hence, it is by purifying yourself of faults and transgressions that it becomes possible for the door of the unseen to open to you.

Be not among those who make demands of God for themselves, yet make no demands of themselves for God; this is the habit of the ignorant who have understood nothing of God's ways, nor have they ever received spiritual treasures from Him. The believer, by contrast, is one who makes demands of himself for his Lord, and does not make demands of his Lord for himself. At all times the believer discerns the courtesy required of him, and never does he deem slow the answers to his petitions.

Permission to enter the kingdom of God is granted only to those who have been purged of the evils of human nature and who have devoted themselves to servanthood. One is purged of the evils of human nature by taking on the attributes of God and being annihilated to all but Him. As for realization in servanthood, it takes place through obedience to God's commands and surrender to His decrees. Once you have achieved this, you will have ample space for yourself in the realm of the unseen and a home in the kingdom, the divine spiritual provision will reach you continuously, and God will grant you ever increasing blessings.

You reach this objective by looking as little as possible at outward appearances and nurturing that which is inward. For one's inner being cannot be healed through outward proofs unless they are accompanied by a pure love which goes directly to the heart and a radiant light which banishes the darkness of transgressions. As for those who take a long time to reach their destination, it is because they have not followed a path based on truth, nor have they entered upon it in a manner true and sincere. For had they done so, what they seek would not be withheld from them; on the contrary, what they seek would come seeking them.

A Declaration, A Reflection, And an Emanation of Lights

Do not measure time's value by the appearance of "inrushes" (*wāridāt*), nor by the frequency with which you perform acts of obedience. Rather, examine your confidence in God, your reverence for God's commands and the degree to which you leave your choices to God. For if you find such virtues in yourself, and if none of them exists without being complemented by the others, then know that God has demonstrated providential care toward you, and that there are gifts which He has yet to reveal. Thank Him for what He has bestowed, praise Him for what He has given, and know—may God be gracious to you—that despite the varying degrees of your affection [for us], we have the probe with which to plumb its depths, and we hold it in the place of esteem which it merits. Thus, others' hearts will incline toward you to the extent that you incline toward them, and if you experience an increase in divine spiritual provision through another servant, you will only do so to the extent that you have grown in your love for him. Thus has the All-Wise God, the Infinite in Power, the Knower of all, ordered [the affairs of the human spirit].

In general, the actions, attitudes and virtues required [of God's servants] in the realm of inward etiquette and obedience to outward precepts are included within the commands in a general way only; taken in their entirety, these two realms include the fear of God: "O Mankind! Reverence your Guardian-Lord"; faithfulness to covenants: "O you who have attained to faith! Be true to your covenants!"; repentance: "Turn unto God in repentance"; turning towards

God and surrendering fully to Him: “Turn towards your Sustainer [alone] and surrender yourselves unto Him…”: responding to God: “Respond to your Sustainer”; following God’s Messenger ﷺ: “Say [O Prophet], ‘If you love God, follow me, [and] God will love you and forgive you your sins….”; bearing witness to every blessing as being from God: “For, whatever good thing comes to you, comes from God”; and bearing witness to the guidance which comes from God: “All praise is due to God, who has guided us unto this; for we would certainly not have found the right path unless God had guided us.”

May God not allow what we say and hear to become an argument against us. Rather, may He cause us, together with you, to be servants who are guided aright by His love, who continue in affectionate devotion to Him and who are blessed with His nearness. May He shower both us and you with the light of His providential care and, by His grace and munificence, cause us to be worthy of His friendship.

May all praise be to God alone, and may His abundant blessings rest upon our master and lord Muḥammad, His prophet, His beloved and His servant. There now follows the promised poem:

> Indeed, no life could possibly be sweet
> Anywhere but in the Beloved’s shadow.
>
> So choose no destination but Sa^{c}dā’s abode
> And bypass Ajāri^{c} and Kathīb.
>
> A lover knows no greater pain than the distance
> That renders the heart asunder,
>
> And one whose beloved is unattainable and elusive
> Never wearies of enduring trouble and sorrow.

Vie with the path before you to reach the heights,
And settle for nothing less than your full portion.

Ascend to a place of glory and honor, content with nothing less,
Aim your arrow at the goal like one who never misses his mark.

Muster the determination without which
You will dwell in a land of defeat and dejection.

Despair not, long though the nights may be,
For many a sun has risen after nightfall.

Never weary of striving,
Since glory and honor come through tireless effort.

Grieve not over the loss of the ephemeral,
For this, in the eyes of the discerning, is victory.

Be satisfied with none but God as your treasure,
A wondrous Sustainer, a Master who answers our every plea.

Complain of your sorrows to none but Him,
For none but He can deliver from distress.

Rely on none but God alone,
Lest you be denied the fragrant breezes of the Unseen.

How many an ordeal has loomed large
Only to reveal, within you, an imminent release?

Let no wrong committed rob you of hope,
For God is the Most Forgiving, the Pardoner of transgressions.

Lament not if you find yourself in sore straits
Lest you fail to attain the rank of the wise.

For many a kindness lies concealed in bare sufficiency,
Many are the mysteries hidden up the Divine sleeve!!

Many a deadly affliction comes disguised as ease
Only to prevent you from attaining your blessing in full.

Those who sport garments of abundance put on airs,
Too busy with themselves to notice the presence of the
Ever Watchful One.

Wonder of wonders that they should be blinded
By their wealth to the poverty that afflicts them!

Do you not know that God is the Incomparable One?
Do you not fear the power of the One Who knows all
things unseen?

Did He not create us from a lowly substance,
Lowly, that is, if we abandon the path of wisdom?

Did He not place us in wombs for a time,
Then bring us out of the grief of affliction?

Did He not sustain us from our mothers' breasts,
Then teach us how to claim our portion in life?

Did He not bless us with kindness in the cradle
And with hearts' love and tender care?

Indeed, this kindness never abandons us,
It follows us into old age.

He exempted us from moral responsibilities and commands
Until we had donned the robes of discernment.

But when we reached maturity we received a message from the Most Merciful
Warning us of a [Judgment Day] imminent.

You who were suckled on compassion and lovingkindness, do not forget My love,
A love once concealed deep in the Unknown.

Raised on Our bounty and a generosity that hastens to meet your needs,
Turn not away now to the glitter of appearances.

The subtle grace of Our Cosmos forgets not My covenant,
So remember, beloved one, the day of "Am I not…?"[8]

You have made a binding covenant with Me,
And faithfulness to covenants is a mark of the wise.

Have I not made you the secret of My existence,[9]
The point around which marvels revolve?

Have I not revealed My attributes in you for all to behold
While concealing that[10] in wondrous ways?

Have you not received My message and command?
If only you would respond to the One who has responded to you!

Our words came to you that you might apply yourself to the journey, so hasten
Into Our presence and strive with diligence.

Words without equal,
Their weightiness disquiets the heart,

While their gracious provisions for the spirit
are sweeter than the most delectable fruits.

When the oft-repeated verses[11] are recited, glasses of
lovingkindness
Are passed round from beneath the Beloved's wing.

Indeed, whatever verse is recited,
You see it as a beautiful bride being unveiled to a discerning heart,

And when you listen closely,
You perceive lights and mysteries.

When You call out saying, "Nay! O My servants,"
The mysteries rush to meet those who draw near.[12]

My response will not be mere words,
But the exertion of my utmost in obedience to the Beloved.

You sent the best of all humanity
That his light might wipe away hearts' impurities.

He brought the chosen path, inviting others
To the Most Merciful through the wondrous mystery.

When he came the earth was filled with darkness,
And all humankind were in a state of disquiet.

But he lifted the darkness and abolished injustice
With the sun of right guidance which never sets.

God set him apart for every grace and blessing
And gave him the love of people's hearts,

Declaring: "Whoever obeys the best of all mankind
Has thereby obeyed Me"—thus said the Beloved.

The words He spoke when they pledged him their allegiance
Revealed a glory visible to the wise and discerning.

He thus removed the *kāf*, the *kāf* of distinction,[13]
What more wonderful enigma could one desire?

He outruns all others to the loftiest heights,
He brings deliverance from the crises of affliction.

Words fail to describe his sublimity,
Sufficient alone is the praise bestowed by the Knower of
the Unseen.

May Your blessings and peace ever rest upon him,
O Lord, from dawn to the setting of the sun.

Upon the Prophet's household and his companions one
and all,
May prayers unceasing be offered up.

For they are the choicest of all generations, and
Through them has Our Sustainer guided us out of transgression.

Aḥmad's sole hope for the life to come
Is for the Prophet's intercession on behalf of the afflicted.

And his father, Muḥammad,[14]
Grant him Your pardon and surround him with
lovingkindness.

Be generous to Your servant, O Munificent One,
And enable him to attain his portion in full.

As for his father, ᶜAṭāʾAllāh, grant him
The finest reward, O Concealer of Transgressions.

Let me die in submission to You, free of blemishes
Thanks to Your having blotted out my sins.

Likewise, O God, bestow a most abundant portion
On all I have befriended and who have befriended me
in You.

Herein is the conclusion to this book.
All praise be to God, Lord of the worlds.
May God's abundant blessings and peace rest upon
our master Muḥammad, seal of the prophets,
and upon his household and companions one and all,
now and till the Day of Judgment.
God is our Sufficiency,
and what an excellent Guardian is He!

"EVERY VERSE HAS BOTH AN OUTWARD MEANING AND AN INWARD MEANING, A BEGINNING AND AN END."

Observation:

Know that this group's [the Sufis'] interpretation of God's word and the words of His Messenger ﷺ in such a way as to yield certain unexpected meanings—as reflected in the shaykh's statements to the effect that the words, "He bestows the gift of female offspring on whomever He wills" refer to good works, that the words, "He bestows the gift of male offspring on whomever He wills" refer to various types of knowledge, that the words, "...or He gives both male and female [to whomever He wills]" refer to God's granting knowledge and good works, and that the words, "and causes to be barren whomever He wills" refer to God's granting neither knowledge nor good works, as well as his interpretation of God's command "to sacrifice a cow" with the statement that "each person's 'cow' is himself, and God bids him to sacrifice it," and, as will be seen below, God willing, in his interpretation of Prophetic hadiths—know that this is not a denial of the outward or apparent meaning of such texts. Rather, the apparent meaning of each verse is a product of the situation in response to which it was revealed, and the message it yields based on people's customary use of the language. However, there are, in addition, hidden meanings of this or that verse or hadith which are disclosed to those whose hearts God has opened. Accordingly, the Prophet ﷺ declared, "Every verse has both an outward meaning and an inward meaning, a beginning and an end."

Ibn ᶜAṭaᵓ Allāh

Notes

Introduction

1. The term *awliyā'* (singular, *walī*) has traditionally been translated "saints"; however, I have chosen to combine this rendering with the use of "friends of God" (see William C. Chittick, *The Sufi Path of Knowledge: Ibn ᶜArabī's Metaphysics of Imagination*, Albany: State University of New York Press, 1989) since the latter conveys more fully the sense of intimacy between such servants and their Lord.

2. Literally, "in fulfilling the rights of His unity."

3. Chittick describes "poles" as "those friends of God around whom various realities of the universe turn" (*The Sufi Path of Knowledge*, p. 371).

4. This seems to be a reference, in part, to the discipline known in Arabic as *ḥisāb al-jummal*, which involves the use of letters of the alphabet according to their numerical values and the formation of circular diagrams representing such values which are believed to have the power to provide spiritual protection.

5. Literally, the domain of His holiness.

6. The editor notes that this is a reference to his having been stationed with other Muslim fighters on enemy frontiers, the era in which he lived having been that of the Crusades.

7. The editor interprets this as meaning "the path of worship, obedience and divine remembrance (*dhikr*)."

8. That is, his followers.

9. Narrated by al-Bukhārī in his "Book on Science," Section 10, by Abū Dāwūd in his *Sunan*, "Book on Science," Section 1, by Ibn Mājah in the introduction to his *Sunan*, Section 17, by al-Dārimī in the introduction to his *Sunan*, p. 32, and Aḥmad [Ibn Ḥanbal] in his *Musnad*, Vol. 5: 196. The remainder of the tradition reads, "...Indeed, the prophets bequeathed neither a dinar nor a dirham; rather, they bequeathed nothing but knowledge..."

10. A *ḥizb* is a special prayer of supplication which is committed to memory and recited on a daily basis.

11. That is, the Sufi community.

12. The editor points out that one of the meanings of the verb *kafara* is "to cover" or "to conceal"; hence, the connection drawn here between renouncing one's faith and the inability to see the divine realities.

13. To beseech God through the rank of glory and honor bestowed upon the Apostle ﷺ is to live by what he brought us from God, may He be exalted, that is, the Qur'an and the Sunnah. These are his glory and honor! As for those who do not live by the Qur'an and the Sunnah, they show contempt for the Prophet's glory and his honored rank.

14. That is, what it entails by way of knowledge, obedience, intimacy and love.

15. The word *barzakh* is defined by Chittick as "something that stands between and separates two other things, yet combines the attributes of both....In the hierarchy of worlds which makes up the cosmos the term *barzakh* refers to an intermediate world standing between the luminous or spiritual world and the dark or corporeal world" (*The Sufi Path of Knowledge*, p. 14). In the present context, the author is drawing attention to the role performed by God's prophets and messengers as intermediaries ("barzakhs") between different levels of spiritual awareness ("lights").

16. Muḥammad Asad, whose translation of the Qur'an I am using throughout, renders the word *raḥmah* as "grace," although it is more commonly rendered as "mercy." See Muhammad Asad, *The Message of the Qur'ān*, Gibraltar: Dār al-Andalus, 1980.

17. In his book, *Sharḥ al-Jāmiᶜ al-Ṣaghīr,* Al-ᶜAlamī states that this is a sound tradition. It is included by Aḥmad, by al-Bukhārī in his *Tārīkh*, by al-Baghawī, by Ibn Al-Sakan, and by Abū Naᶜīm in his *Al-Ḥilyah*, while al-Ḥākim classifies it as a sound tradition with the following wording, "I was a prophet when Adam was [still] between the spirit and the body." Al-Tirmidhī and others who narrate it on the authority of Abū Hurayrah record that he said to the Prophet ﷺ, "When were you, or when were you ordained to be, a prophet?" To which he replied, "I was a prophet when Adam was between the spirit and the body." Al-Tirmidhī states, "It is a good (*ḥasan*) and sound (*ṣaḥīḥ*) tradition, while it has been judged to be sound by al-Ḥākim as well."

18. Narrated by Aḥmad [Ibn Ḥanbal], al-Tirmidhī and Ibn Mājah, while Muslim and Abū Dāwūd narrate the same tradition on the authority of Abū Hurayrah without the addition of the phrase, "which I say without boasting."

19. Narrated by Aḥmad, al-Tirmidhī, and Ibn Mājah with the wording, "I am the master of Adam's son[s], which I say without boasting,

and I will be the first one to be revealed when the earth is split asunder, which I say without boasting. I am the first intercessor and the first intercessor whose pleas will be granted by God, which I say without boasting. And the banner of praise will be in my hand on the Day of Resurrection, which I say without boasting." [ed.]

20. That is, *al-ḥāfiẓ*, or one who has memorized the Qur'an from beginning to end.

21. A title of the descendents of Muḥammad ﷺ.

22. That is, the Muslim community.

23. Al-Anbiyā' [The Prophets] 21: 37.

24. The word rendered here as "gnostic sciences" (*al-ma*ᶜ*ārif*, singular, *ma*ᶜ*rifah*) refers to a kind of knowledge which, in contrast to the type of knowledge referred to in Arabic as ᶜ*ilm* (plural, ᶜ*ulūm*), is centered in the heart rather than in the mind, and is a fruit of direct spiritual experience. Sometimes translated as "gnosis," this type of knowledge, or *ma*ᶜ*rifah*, "is equivalent to the direct knowledge called unveiling, witnessing, and tasting...." Of equal importance, "it is a form of knowledge which can be achieved only through spiritual practice, not by book learning or study with a teacher. It is the knowledge to which the Koran refers when it says, 'Be god-fearing, and God will teach you' (2: 282)" (*The Sufi Path of Knowledge*, pp. 148, 149).

25. That is, with their ᶜ*ilm*.

26. That is, mercy.

27. Imam Aḥmad narrates the same tradition with the following wording, "I have left you on a clear path" [literally, on that which is like the white...., without direct reference to the entity being described] (Vol. 4: 126) and by Ibn Mājah in the Introduction to his *Sunan*, pp. 1 and 6. [ed.]

28. Narrated by al-Ṭabarānī in his *Al-Kabīr*, by al-Bazzār in his *Musnad,* and by Abū Yaᶜlā, who narrates several different wordings of the tradition. See al-Sakhāwī, *Al-Maqāṣid al-Ḥasanah*, Beirut: Dār al-Kitāb al-ᶜArabī, pp. 178–179. [ed.]

29. Narrated by al-Bukhārī and Muslim in their *Ṣaḥīḥs*, and by Abū Dāwūd, al-Tirmidhī and al-Nasā'ī in their *Sunan*. [ed.]

30. Narrated by the compiler of *Kanz al-*ᶜ*Ummāl*, No. 5750. [ed.]

31. Narrated by al-Bukhārī in his book on "Courtesy" (*Kitāb al-Adab*), 76, by al-Tirmidhī in his book on "Righteousness" (*Kitāb al-Birr*), 73, and by Aḥmad [Ibn Ḥanbal], Vol. 2: 175. [ed.]

32. Narrated by Aḥmad, Vol. 5: 196, by al-Tirmidhī, Vol. 3: 381, and by Abū Dāwūd, Vol. 3: 432. [ed.]

33. See previous note.

34. This tradition is groundless, and is nowhere to be found in any recognized *ḥadīth* collection. See al-Sakhāwī, *Al-Maqāṣid al-Ḥasanah*, p. 459. See also *Asnā al-Maṭālib*, p. 140 under the topic, "It has no foundation, as more than one memorizer [of *ḥadīth*] has affirmed." [ed.]

35. Narrated by al-Tirmidhī in his *Sunan*, "Book of Asceticism" (14), by Ibn Mājah in his *Sunan*, "Book of Asceticism" (3), and by al-Dārimī in the Introduction to his *Sunan*, p. 32. Al-Tirmidhī notes that it is a "good" tradition. [ed.] As for the word "cursed" as used here, it conveys the sense of being distant from God, may He be exalted, rather than being outside the pale of His mercy.

36. Narrated by Abū Dāwūd and al-Tirmidhī. [ed.] [These sources were not mentioned by al-^{c}Akk; rather, I derived them from another edition of *Laṭā'if al-Minan*, edited by Dr. ^{c}Abd al-Ḥalīm Maḥmūd, Cairo: Maṭbū^{c}āt al-Sha^{c}b, 1986—t.n.]

37. The remainder of the verse reads,"[for they alone comprehend that] verily, God is almighty, much-forgiving".

38. It is for this reason that the Apostle ﷺ used to say in one of his prayers of supplication (as narrated by Imam Aḥmad), "O God, I seek refuge in You from knowledge which holds no benefit, from a heart which is not submissive and humble, from a soul which is never satisfied, and from a supplication which goes unanswered." [ed.]

39. Narrated by al-Bukhārī, Vol. 4: 88, Vol. 5: 169 and Vol. 8: 155, by Muslim, "On Faith" (178) and by Aḥmad in his *Musnad*, Vol. 2: 309. [ed.]

40. The word I have rendered here as "signs" (Arabic, *āyāt*) is the same as that rendered by Asad in the verse quoted here as "messages"; hence, the saints are likened to the verses of the Qur'an, which were revealed in God's wisdom in a particular order and at appointed times for His servants' benefit.

41. This wording is found in none of the numerous recognized collections of prophetic traditions; hence, this saying must be judged to be inauthentic. [ed.]

42. Narrated by Abū Dāwūd in his *Sunan*, "On Fierce Battles" (17), by al-Tirmidhī in his *Sunan*, "On Exegesis: Sūrah 5: 18," and by Ibn Mājah in his *Sunan*, "On Uprisings" (21). [ed.]

43. Narrated by al-Bukhārī in his *Ṣaḥīḥ*, "On Seeking Refuge" (10) and "On Divine Unity" (29) and by Muslim in "On Faith" (247) and "On Governing Authority" (170–177). [ed.]

44. Narrated by al-Tirmidhī in his *Sunan*, "On Courtesy" (81) and by Imam Aḥmad in his *Musnad*, Vol. 3: 130, 143 and Vol. 4: 319. [ed.]

45. This saying is nowhere to be found in the recognized collections of prophetic traditions. [ed.]

46. Narrated by Ibn Abī Ḥātim in *Al-Tafsīr*. [ed.]

47. The relevant Qur'anic text reads in full: "He it is who has sent unto the unlettered people an apostle from among themselves, to convey unto them His messages, and to cause them to grow in purity, and to impart unto them the divine writ as well as wisdom—whereas before that they were indeed, most obviously, lost in error—and [to cause this message to spread] from them unto other people as soon as they come into contact with them; for He alone is almighty, truly wise!" {Al-Jum^cah [The Congregation] 62: 2–3}.

48. Narrated by al-Ḥakīm al-Tirmidhī in *Nawādir al-Uṣūl*, pp. 110 and 183. [ed.]

49. In other words, they are not attached to the merely temporal.

50. That is, by the troubles that attend temporal existence.

51. That is, the veil which conceals spiritual truth from one's heart.

52. Narrated by al-Ḥakīm al-Tirmidhī in his *Nawādir*, p. 431, with the wording, "God has servants whom He preserves from illness and infirmity, and whom He revives…." [ed.]

53. I have found this particular wording in none of the recognized collections of prophetic traditions. [ed.]

54. The version narrated by al-Bukhārī reads, "…I have declared war upon him." [ed.]

55. Narrated by al-Bukhārī in his *Tārīkh*, by al-Bazzār in his *Musnad* and by al-Bayhaqī in his *Shu^cab al-Īmān* from the tradition on the authority of ^cUmar Ibn al-Khaṭṭāb. [ed.]

56. Narrated by al-Bukhārī in "On Courtesy," by Muslim in "On Repentance," by Abū Dāwūd in "On Funerals," and by Ibn Mājah in "On Asceticism." [ed.]

57. Abdullah Yusuf Ali's rendering of this verse, namely, "God is the Protector of those who have faith," better demonstrates the relevance of this verse to the point at hand.

58. The Messenger of God ﷺ said, "If anyone reduces all of his concerns to one, namely, the life to come, God will spare him all other concerns. As for those whose concerns are scattered among the conditions of this world, God cares not in which of its valleys they perish" (*Saḥīḥ al-Jāmi^c al-Ṣaghīr* and its addition, Vol. 2: 1064–1065). [ed.]

59. Narrated by al-Quḍāʿī in his *Musnad al-Shihāb*, by Ibn ʿAsākir in his *Amālī* (where he classifies it as "unfamiliar" (*gharīb*) [that is, a tradition narrated by only two chains of narrators—t.n.], and al-Ṭabarānī in *al-Muʿjam al-Kabīr*. Al-Haythamī states, "All of the narrators in its chain of transmission are reliable with the exception of Ḥātim Ibn ʿAbbād Ibn Dīnār, for whom I have found no biographical sketch." Al-Munāwī states, "It [this tradition] has several chains of transmission, all of which require that it be deemed weak." [ed.]

60. From a tradition narrated by al-Bukhārī. [ed.]

61. Narrated by Abū Dāwūd, Ibn Mājah and al-Ḥākim on the authority of Tamīm al-Dārī with approximately the same wording, and judged to be sound by al-Suyūṭī. [ed.]

62. The intent of this statement must be that one's *intention* in performing the obligatory act of worship was sound, since according to the hadith quoted immediately before it, the performance of a voluntary prayer can, for example, serve to compensate for imperfections in one's performance of an obligatory prayer.

63. Muslim narrates the same tradition with the following wording: "The strong believer is better than and more beloved to God than the weak believer, though there is goodness in both. [Hence,] be keen to pursue that which is beneficial to you, rely upon God for aid, and be not helpless. Moreover, if some ill-fortune should befall you, say not, 'If only I had done such and such, such and such would have happened,' but rather say, 'God has decreed, and what He wills, He has done.' For the words 'if only' open the way for the work of Satan." [ed.]

64. Narrated by Aḥmad, al-Bukhārī and Abū Dāwūd. [ed.]

65. Narrated by al-Tirmidhī and by al-Ḥākim, who judges it to be sound. [ed.]

66. Narrated by Aḥmad, Abū Dāwūd and al-Nasā'ī, while Muslim and al-Bukhārī narrate a version similar to this. [ed.]

67. Narrated by al-Bukhārī. [ed.]

68. Narrated by Aḥmad on the authority of Anas; Aḥmad classifies the tradition as sound. [ed.]

69. I.e., whisper.

70. That is, allies Himself with them.

71. The imams being the recognized spiritual leaders of Islam over the ages.

72. That is, detachment from the created world.

73. In contrast to English, Arabic tends to convey general truths through the use of the past tense. The truths just cited by the author, for example, might be more literally translated, "He who believed was prosperous" and "He who denied the truth was disappointed," respectively.

74. By "this," Ibn [c]Aṭā Allāh must mean the way of the first type of saint mentioned here, that is, that of seeing nothing but God.

75. It may be that God is addressing the prophet as a representative member of this group, urging him simply to utter the divine name, while leaving others to their failure to perceive the divine reality in what God has revealed. The passage immediately prior to this reads, "For no true understanding of God have they when they say, 'Never has God revealed anything unto man.' Say: 'Who has bestowed from on high the divine writ which Moses brought unto men as a light and a guidance, [and] which you treat as [mere] leaves of paper, making a show of them the while you conceal [so] much—although you have been taught [by it] what neither you nor your forefathers had ever known?'" {Al-An[c]ām [Cattle] 6: 91}.

76. Asad translates the divine name *Ṣamad* as "the Eternal, the Uncaused Cause of all that exits." He states, "This rendering gives no more than an approximate meaning of the term *al-ṣamad*, which occurs in the Qur'ān only once, and is applied to God alone. It comprises the concepts of Primary Cause and eternal, independent Being, combined with the idea that everything existing or conceivable goes back to Him as its source and is, therefore, dependent on Him for its beginning as well as for its continued existence." See Note 1 on Al-Ikhlāṣ [The Declaration of God's Perfection] 112: 2.

77. I.e., a necessary outcome of one's vision of the truth.

78. Narrated [also] by al-Bukhārī and Muslim.

79. This is not a prophetic tradition; rather, it is a statement which was made by Yaḥyā Ibn Mu[c]ādh al-Rāzī. (See al-Sakhāwī, *al-Maqāṣid al-Ḥasanah*, p. 657, Dār al-Kitāb al-[c]Arabī.) [ed.]

80. The term *sālik*, rendered here as "spiritual wayfarer" has been defined as "one who is making his way to God, between a disciple (*murīd*) and one who has arrived at the full knowledge of God (*muntahī*)." See *Mu[c]jam Iṣṭilāḥāt al-Ṣūfiyah*, [c]Abd al-Razzāq al-Kāshānī (d. approximately 730 AH), edited, introduced and explained by Dr. [c]Abd al-[c]Āl Shāhīn, Cairo: Dār al-Manār, 1992, p. 119.

81. The Arabic term *majdhūb*, rendered here as "divinely possessed" is defined by al-Kāshānī as "someone who has been chosen by the Truth, may He be exalted, for Himself, i.e., for His intimate presence and

companionship; one whom [God] has purified with the water of His holiness such that he has attained gifts and graces which have ushered him into all spiritual stations and ranks without his being held accountable for earning his keep and exerting strenuous efforts (al-Kāshāni, p. 96).

82. This is an allusion to Al-Ḥijr 15: 16–18, where God says, "And indeed, We have set up in the heavens great constellations and endowed them with beauty for all to behold: and We have made them secure against every satanic force accursed so that anyone who seeks to learn [the unknowable] by stealth is pursued by a flame clear to see."

83. Al-Ḥāfiẓ al-ᶜIrāqī states, "I have found no origin for it…," and the same is stated by Ibn Taymiyah. It is mentioned in certain Judaica, but it has no known chain of transmission on the authority of the Prophet ﷺ (al-Sakhāwī, op. cit., p. 589). [ed.]

84. In other words, due to the reports that had reached the Prophet's enemies concerning his prowess in battle and the believers' valorous spirit of self-sacrifice, they would retreat from his approach in terror from distances an entire month's march away from him.

85. In other words, God refused to let the knowledge serve any but His own purposes.

86. That is, the association of any other entity with God in one's affections and allegiance.

87. Through, for example, the passing of gas or the excretion of bodily wastes, or any of the other events which, according to Islamic law, render one ritually impure.

88. Asad notes that this phrase could also be rendered, "He grants it unto whomever He wills." He states, "Both these formulations are syntactically correct; but since the bounty of God referred to in this passage relates to the divine guidance granted to man through the medium of the revelation bestowed upon God's Apostle, the construction chosen by me seems to be more appropriate, expressing as it does the idea that the bounty of God's guidance is always available to one who sincerely desires it" (*The Message of the Qur'ān*, p. 863, Note 3).

89. Narrated by Muslim in his *Ṣaḥīḥ*. [ed.]

An Interlude on…Miracles

1. In other words, the disintegration or disappearance of human attributes in the divine attributes, which is one of the marks of annihilation, and which comes about through actively combating and overcoming the soul's negative traits by divine grace.

2. At the time of Abū Bakr's death, he and his wife had four children: ᶜĀ'ishah, one other female, and their two brothers. By leaving ᶜĀ'ishah instructions to look after her two brothers and not one sister, but two, Abū Bakr was predicting that his wife, who was pregnant when he died, would bear a girl.

3. That is, Muᶜāwiyah.

4. Narrated by al-Bukhārī (in *al-Tārīkh*) and al-Tirmidhī on the authority of Abū Saᶜīd, by al-Ḥakīm al-Tirmidhī, al-Ṭabarānī and Ibn ᶜUdayy on the authority of Abū Umāmah, and by Ibn Jarīr on the authority of Ibn ᶜUmar. [ed.]

5. In accordance with the meaning of the term *karāmah*, the miracle performed is a sign of God's magnanimity toward the saint and the dignity which God has accorded him.

6. Literally, that which would be impossible for the person concerned (based on the word *muᶜjizah*'s derivation from the verb *aᶜjaza*, one meaning of which is "to be impossible [for someone]"). See Hans Wehr, *A Dictionary of Modern Written Arabic*, Ed. J. Milton Cowan, Beirut: Librairie du Liban, 1974.

7. In other words, they place God under no obligation to grant His light.

8. Narrated by al-Bukhārī, Muslim, Abū Dāwūd, al-Tirmidhī, al-Nasā'ī and Ibn Mājah. [ed.]

9. Maᶜrūf al-Karkhī, d. 200 AH/815 AD, an ascetic and Sufi of such renown for his righteousness that people, including even Imam Aḥmad Ibn Ḥanbal, used to come to receive his blessing.

10. Al-Sarī al-Saqaṭī, d. 253 AH/867 AD, was al-Junayd's maternal uncle, as well as his teacher along the Sufi path.

11. Al-Junayd al-Baghdādī, d. 297 AH/910 AD.

12. That is, they content themselves with the miracles rather than aspiring, beyond the miracles, to a greater knowledge of God.

Chapter One

1. The Arabic term rendered "wellspring" here, namely, *zamzam*, is the name of the well from which Hagar, upon her be peace, received water to revive herself and her son Ishmael during their trek in the wilderness after being sent away from Abraham's household at the behest of Abraham's wife Sarah. The Well of Zamzam is located within the precincts of the Sacred Mosque in Mecca.

2. I.e., the sciences pertaining to the external aspects of Islamic law and teachings, as opposed to those pertaining to the inward realities.

3. The Arabic term translated here as "substitute," namely, *badal*, refers to one of the ranks of saints, with the pole (*quṭb*) being the highest of all such ranks.

4. Al-Muddaththir [The Enfolded One] 74: 4.

5. Aḥmad was Abū al-ᶜAbbās's first name.

6. I haven't been able to verify the spelling of this location [t.n].

7. Approximately 58 kilos.

8. He appears to have bought the wheat on credit.

9. Referring to himself.

10. The Arab place name, *al-Maghrib*, can refer either to Tunisia or Algeria.

11. God declares, "Behold, in Thy Sustainer's sight, a day is like a thousand years of your reckoning" {Al-Ḥajj [The Pilgrimage] 22: 47}.

12. The Arabic term *samāᶜ*, which means "listening," is used in this context to refer to the singing of poetry during *dhikr* gatherings, that is, gatherings for the purpose of the remembrance of the divine name.

13. Recorded by Muslim and Abū Dāwūd. [ed.]

14. In other words, that which obscures the divine light in which the righteous dwells.

15. In other words, that which obscures God to the soul's view due to its attachments to "others," that is, entities other than God.

16. Possibly al-Barzanjī.

17. That is, with respect to the grace he has received.

Chapter Two

1. Qāf, in Islamic cosmology, is the name of the mountains surrounding the terrestrial world.

2. I haven't been able to identify this location on a map, but the context indicates that it is the name of a city.

3. The reference here appears to be to the divine reality which, when the awareness of it is withdrawn, causes the seeker to lament.

4. A reference to God's concealment of Abū al-ᶜAbbās's sainthood despite his profound influence on people's hearts..

5. "Pause" here being used in the sense of one's pausing, or standing (Arabic, *waqfah*) on Mt. ᶜArafah when one performs the hajj, or pilgrimage to Mecca.

6. Aḥmad being onc of the appellations of Muḥammad ﷺ.

7. My rendering of the phrase *ʿalā ḥīni fatrati* at the end of this line is based on the resemblance it bears to the Qur'anic phrase, *ʿalā fatratin min al-rusuli* in Al-Mā'idah 5: 19, which reads, "O followers of the Bible! Now, after a long time during which no apostles have appeared [*ʿalā fatratin min al-rusuli*], there has come unto you Our Apostle to make [the truth] clear to you...."

8. A *zāwiyah* is a center for Sufi worship and instruction which may also serve as a hostel for travelers and the needy.

9. The son of ʿAlī and Fāṭimah and the Prophet's grandson.

10. Arabic, *awtād* (singular, *watad*), an appellation for a rank of sainthood.

11. A *wird* is a series of Qur'anic verses, supplications, etc. which a disciple may be assigned by his shaykh to recite both morning and evening.

12. I.e., once your ego absents itself from your heart.

13. This may be a reference to the divine address which al-Tirmidhī reported hearing as he was reciting his *wird.*

14. The word for "prose" in Arabic is *nathr,* whereas what appears in the text is *nashr*; however, the context suggests that the word intended is, in fact, *nathr*.

Chapter Three

1. In other words, the mystic does not busy himself with the recording of worldly knowledge.

2. Through this reply, Abū al-ʿAbbās appears to be affirming, as is stressed repeatedly throughout this chapter, that the mystic may legitimately pursue both inward and outward knowledgc, and that his pursuit of outward knowledge does not taint his "heavenly records" with any sort of guilt.

3. In other words, Abū Bakr was so close to the Prophet ﷺ and so fully identified with the latter's spiritual states that, unlike others of the Prophet's Companions who concerned themselves with the transmission of his sayings and deeds, he concerned himself simply with living out the reality he had come to experience through his master ﷺ.

4. The Qur'ānic basis for the shaykh's statement may be seen in the fact that the Qur'ān declares concerning those "who repent and attain to faith and do righteous deeds" that "it is they whose [erstwhile] bad deeds God will transform into [*yubaddilu*, i.e., substitute with] good ones—seeing that God is indeed much-forgiving, a dispenser of grace,

and seeing that he who repents and [thenceforth] does what is right has truly turned unto God by [this very act of] repentance" {Al-Furqān [The Standard of True and False] 25:70–71}.

5. Most likely, a dictionary.

6. Since the pool of Kawthar is not an earthly reality, but something found in Paradise, Ḥājj Sulaymān's having drunk from it before he died is a miracle which was granted to him.

7. When the Messenger of God ﷺ suffered abuse and persecution at the hands of the inhabitants of al-Ṭā'if and uttered his well-known supplication, "O God, I complain to You of my weakness, my defenselessness, and my humiliation at others' hands," he was descended upon by Gabriel together with the angel of the mountains. Al-Bukhārī relates (with his particular chain of transmission) that ᶜĀ'ishah once asked the Prophet ﷺ, "Have you ever experienced anything more trying than the Battle of Uḥud?" He replied, "The treatment which I received at the hands of your people. The worst of all was the treatment I received on the day of al-ᶜAqabah, when I presented myself to ᶜAbd Yālayl Ibn Kalāl. When I failed to receive from him the response I had hoped for, I took off wandering, anxious and careworn, and I only regained my presence of mind when I reached Qarn al-Thaᶜālib. Looking up, I found myself overshadowed by a cloud. Peering into the cloud, who should I find but Gabriel, who called out to me saying, "God has heard what your people said to you and the manner in which they responded to you. I have sent you the angel of the mountains in order for you to instruct him however you choose concerning them." The angel of the mountains then called out to him ﷺ with a greeting and said, "O Muḥammad, let it be as you desire. If you wish, I will cause the two mountains of Mecca to close in upon them." The Prophet ﷺ replied, 'No. Rather, my hope is that God will bring forth from among their descendents those who worship God alone and associate no partners with Him." See *Al-Rawḍ al-Unuf* 4:56-57. [ed.}

8. Ibn ᶜAṭā' Allāh's grandfather had not been sympathetic toward the Sufis and their emphasis on both outward and inward knowledge.

9. That is, the Sufis.

Chapter Four

1. An interpretation of the Qur'ān.
2. A *whiba* is a dry measure equal to 33 liters in Egypt.
3. A dry measure equal to 198 liters in Egypt.

4. The Arabic word for "greed" consists of the letters *ṭā'*, *mīm*, and *ᶜayn*, each of which contains a circular or elliptical shape which is thus "hollow".

5. Literally, "it's all belly".

6. Namely, that of annihilation in the Divine.

7. That is, the knowledge which God discloses to His friends by virtue of their closeness to Him.

8. The two city names mentioned here are al-Qāhirah and Miṣr, both of which refer to Cairo; however, I have rendered one of the two as Alexandria given this city's importance in the context of the accounts here.

9. The term "discontiguous imagination" as used in the writings of Ibn ᶜArabī refers to "the intermediate world of imagination" which "exists independently of the viewer" (Chittick, p. 117). Ibn ᶜArabī states that this type of imagination is at work when God establishes something for one of His servants "as a sensory object after it had been imaginal" (Chittick, p. 198, quoting *Al-Futūḥāt al-Makkiyah* II, 544.16). Hence, through the discontiguous imagination, the disciple may experience his shaykh's presence on a sensory level despite his physical absence.

10. This is an allusion to a Qur'anic statement in which backbiting is likened to "eat[ing] the flesh of one's dead brother" (Al-Ḥujurāt [The Private Apartments] 49:12}. Hence, the message behind the words, "The flesh of the friends of God is poisoned" is that God comes to His friends' defense against those who would seek to do them harm.

11. Literally, "there is no veil between it and God".

12. That is, one of the ten Companions to whom the Prophet ﷺ announced that they would attain Paradise.

13. This is a reference to a poisoned meal which was served to the Prophet ﷺ by a Jewish woman in Khaybar.

14. In other words, if you do not share your God-given knowledge with others.

15. A *wird* is a spiritual discipline involving the repetition of certain phrases of divine remembrance and the like at specified times of the day, and which is generally assigned by the shaykh to the disciple.

16. The reason for this lies in the fact that someone like Abū al-ᶜAbbās, having reached the station of complete reliance on God (*maqām al-tawakkul*), resists the notion of storing up provisions for the morrow and seeks instead to live like "the birds of the air..." which "neither sow nor reap nor gather into barns" (Matthew 6:26).

17. There is a striking apothegm of Ibn ᶜAṭā'Allāh's in which he says, "Better a disobedience which begets humility and a sense of one's spiritual poverty than an obedience which begets self-sufficiency and pride!"

Chapter Five

1. Al-Fātiḥah, Verse 2. For this particular Qur'anic quotation, I have used Yusuf Ali's translation (*The Holy Qur'an: Text, Translation and Commentary*, Abdullah Yusuf Ali, Elmhurst, NY: Tahrike Tarsile Qur'an, Inc., Second US Edition, 1988).

2. The context of this statement is al-Khaḍir's explanation to Moses of various actions which he has taken but which have perplexed Moses, and which he concludes by saying, "And I did not do any of this of my own accord; this is the real meaning of all [these events] that thou wert unable to bear with patience" {Al-Kahf [The Cave] 18:82}.

3. I.e., the ship in which al-Khaḍir had made a hole, much to Moses's dismay (see 18:71).

4. Yusuf Ali's translation.

5. Yusuf Ali's translation.

6. That is, the idols of his worldly passions.

7. Yusuf Ali's translation.

8. As if, by not speaking of God, he suffers a sense of lack and longing which is likened here to a craving for water.

9. Muḥammad Asad translates this phrase as "will be…," whereas the Arabic text is, in fact, in the present tense.

10. See earlier note.

11. Yusuf Ali's translation.

12. Literally, "in annihilation from it" (*fanā'an ᶜanhā*); hence, not in the sense of physical death, but as a form of inward detachment from this world.

13. Zulaykha, wife of the nobleman in whose house Joseph was staying.

14. Yusuf Ali's translation.

15. The term rendered "God turned with favor to" (*tāba ᶜalā*) means, more precisely, that God accepted the repentance of those concerned.

16. This phrase refers to three of the Helpers, namely, Kaᶜb, Marār and Hilāl, who out of laxity and weakness failed to respond to the Prophet's summons to take part in the Battle of Tabūk, but who later repented of their dereliction. Hence, verse 118 tells us that God turned in mercy to them as well.

17. Asad renders the phrase, *rabbukum* as "your Sustainer," while Yusuf Ali renders it as "your Guardian-Lord".

18. In other words, this is not a time to be niggardly with oneself in receiving the blessings at hand.

19. From the context, it appears that these were not poor in the material sense, but in the sense of realizing their poverty toward God.

Chapter Six

1. That is, fasting.

2. In other words, let people exert themselves in expression of their faith rather than relying complacently on their verbal affirmation of belief.

3. Literally, "faith is tasted."

4. The hadith cited here, narrated by al-Bukhārī with a chain of transmission originating with ᶜImrān Ibn Ḥuṣayn, reads, "God was, and there was nothing with Him. His throne was upon the water, He recorded everything in the [Book of Remembrance] [i.e., the Qur'ān], and He created the heavens and the earth."

5. That is, the relationship of dependence between the creature and the Creator.

6. That is, those who neglect God's commands.

7. Literally, one's chest expands and become spacious.

8. In other words, the angels would grace you with their direct presence even in the midst of the most worldly preoccupations.

9. Among the Emigrants to Medina were certain individuals who were so poor that they had no homes, and who would thus find shelter in a certain shaded area of the mosque known as the *ṣuffah*; thus, their name, *ahl al-ṣuffah*.

Chapter Seven

1. In other words, rather than taking pride in the knowledge we have attained or the good works we have performed, we are urged to remember that were it not for God's pre-knowledge—and hence, decree—we would neither know what we know nor have been able to do what we have done.

2. That is, as someone who has experienced annihilation (*fanā'*).

3. The implication seems to be that the yogurt, or perhaps the goats which produced the milk for it, had been purchased with the money that the boy earned in this manner.

4. Yusuf Ali's translation.

5. *Kitāb al-Tanwīr fī Isqāṭ al Tadbīr*; *Kitāb al-Tanwīr* has been translated into English under the title *The Book of Illumination*, by Scott Kugle (Fons Vitae, 2005).

6. Junayd's uncle.

Chapter Eight

1. In other words, it is not you who decide, by an act of will, which station you will reach; rather, the basic attributes which you carry within you and with which God has endowed you cause you to tend toward this or that spiritual station.

2. The station of *ṣiddīqiyah*, or that of being "a person of truth," is the highest level of sainthood, or friendship with God (*walāyah*).

3. There are three basic circles of the friends of God, or saints (*dawā'ir al-awliyā'*): the circle of prophethood (*dā'irat al-nubūwah*), the circle of messengerhood (*dā'irat al-risālah*), and the circle of sainthood (*dā'irat al-walāyah*). According to Islamic teachings, the circles of prophethood and messengerhood have been discontinued, whereas the circle of sainthood is ongoing in the sense that even in the present day, sainthood is a realizable phenomenon. It was through the prophets and messengers that the law (*sharī*ᶜ*ah*) was revealed; and it is through the saints that the inner meaning, or truth of the law (*ḥaqīqah*) continues to be revealed. When those who concern themselves with the outward sciences (*al-*ᶜ*ulūm al-ẓāhirah*) enter into friendship with God, or sainthood, it is to them, and through them, that the divine realities or truths manifested through the divine attributes and names continue to be disclosed and clarified to others.

4. The pronoun "they" is often employed elliptically in Sufi poetry to refer to the Divine.

5. Narrated by Muslim in his *Ṣaḥīḥ*, and by al-Tirmidhī and Ibn Mājah in their *Sunan*. [ed.}

6. Yusuf Ali.

7. Arabic, *basaṭa... al-rizq*.

8. This statement by Shaykh Abū al-ᶜAbbās appears also in the Author's Introduction.

9. See Note 9, Chapter 6.

10. If the word Sufi were based on an attribution to the *ṣuffah* of the Prophet's mosque, it would, according to the usual rules for the formation of what are termed *nisbah* adjectives in Arabic, be *ṣuffī* rather than *ṣufī*.

11. A reference to the Gospel of John 3:3, "Truly, truly I say to you, unless one is born anew, he cannot see the kingdom of God." (Revised Standard Version)

12. "And then We said unto the angels, 'Prostrate yourselves before Adam!'—whereupon they all prostrated themselves, save Iblis; he was not among those who prostrated themselves. [And God] said, 'What has kept thee from prostrating thyself when I commanded thee?' Answered Iblis, 'I am better than he: Thou hast created me out of fire, whereas him Thou hast created him out of clay.' [God] said, 'Down with thee, then, from this [state]—for it is not meet for thee to show arrogance here!'" {Al-A^c^rāf [The Faculty of Discernment] 7:11–13}. There is an as-of-yet undisclosed mystery, or "meaning" within human beings which explains God's having commanded the angels to do obeisance to their forefather, Adam, and Iblis's transgression consisted in his unwillingness to humble himself before this mystery.

13. This line involves two plays on words, in that the name of the letter *alif* is also a verb in Arabic, namely, *alifa*, which means to love or to be on familiar or intimate terms with; while the name of the letter *lām* is similar to a syllable in the word *malāmah*, which means censure, blame or reproach.

14. The letter *hā'*, as indicated earlier, serves as a shortened form of the pronoun *huwa*, which refers to the Divine Essence.

15. In other words, it isn't simply a matter of an ascetic lifestyle.

16. The Arabic word for "state" (*ḥāl*) is derived from the verb *ḥāla*, which means to change or be transformed.

17. A *samā^c^* ceremony is a Sufi gathering which involves the recitation of poetry extolling the divine love and other divine attributes; such recitation commonly gives rise to spiritual states on the part of participants, some of whom may express their rapture through words or bodily movements.

18. Yusuf Ali's translation.

19. In other words, gnostics are those who realize that in the kindnesses which they receive from God in this life, there may be hidden adversity as, for example, in the form of the temptation to become complacent or proud; similarly, the goodness which God demonstrates toward them acts as a light which intensifies their awareness of their unworthiness and failures.

20. That is to say, when we focus on our negligence toward God, this reflects a subtle failure to recognize the totality of God's control

over all, including even those actions, or failures to act, for which we hold ourselves responsible.

21. Yusuf Ali.

22. I.e., the realm in which the foreknowledge and will of God are unknown to human beings.

23. That is, the Muslim community.

24. That is to say, the Prophet ﷺ was bearing witness to the divine will as something which is not predetermined but which, rather, remains unknown to human beings, while Abū Bakr (may God be pleased with him) was bearing witness to the manifest promise of victory which God had given them.

25. In other words, such individuals' focus on their own actions and responsibility prevents them from experiencing fully God's presence in their hearts.

26. Yusuf Ali.

27. That is, the Kacbah.

28. In other words, the shaykh did not make a show of the supernatural manifestations of sainthood which he had been granted.

29. Yusuf Ali.

Chapter Nine

1. That is, the station of union, in which they no longer experience any separation between Creator and created, themselves and the Beloved.

2. This is a reference to the Quranic passage which speaks of how God, after bringing Adam's descendents into existence in spirit form, made them testify concerning themselves saying, 'Am I not your Lord [who cherishes and sustains you]?'" Whereupon they replied "'Yea! We do testify!'" {Al-Acrāf [The Faculty of Discernment] 7:172, Yusuf Ali}. This encounter is generally understood to have taken place prior to God's creation of humankind in earthly form, and those who are faithful to this command—the command to acknowledge God as their Lord and Cherisher—are those who live in submission to their Creator and who thereby remind others of their own witness to God's lordship over them in the realm of pre-eternity.

3. In other words, the soul in its "descent" into the physical realm and its union with the body is likened to Adam's union with Eve.

4. In these verses the poet likens his heart to the Holy Kacbah in Mecca ("God's house") and his inward worship of the Divine to the pilgrimage rite of circumambulating the Kacbah, as well as the rite

which involves kissing or touching the Black Stone located near one of the Ka[c]bah's corners.

5. Imru' al-Qays, whose father, the King of Kindah, had been slain, went with a friend to request that Caesar grant him an army with which to reclaim his father's kingdom. In this line he seeks to reassure his companion that even if they die in the course of seeking to carry out their mission, they will have died honorably, and will therefore be pardoned by posterity.

6. In other words, the Sufi strives for spiritual "dominion" by seeking to attain to the station of subsistence (*baqā'*). Yet if the seeker should die before achieving this aim, he or she will at least have experienced the coveted station of annihilation (which is a necessary prerequisite for the attainment of subsistence) and, as such, find pardon, that is, liberation from the ego and its destructive bent.

7. These three lines contain allusions to the spiritually symbolic actions performed by Khaḍir in the presence of Moses, and which are recorded in The Cave [al-Kahf] 18:71–79.

8. The terms "sandals" and "both universes" are allegorical references to this earthly world and the world to come. Those who have experienced the Divine realities for themselves learn, by virtue of this experience, to relinquish their quest either for the rewards of this life or for those promised in the world to come; rather, their sole quest is for knowledge of and union with the Divine Himself/Herself.

9. There is a play on words here in that the Arabic word which refers to someone who has let down anchor (*al-mursī*) is identical to the name of his shaykh.

10. There is a possible play on words here in that the Arabic word for Thursday (*khamīs*) may also bear the sense of "an army." The writer might thus be suggesting that the shaykh is, to him, worth a thousand armies.

11. Shādhilah is the Moroccan town from which Shaykh Abu al-Ḥasan al-Shādhilī hailed, and Murcia (Arabic, Mursiyah) is the Andalusian hometown of Abū al-[c]Abbās al-Mursī.

12. The she-camel serves throughout as a symbol of the soul in its quest for the Divine Beloved; at this point in the poem, however, she becomes a symbol of the Muslim community as well. In keeping with this dual image, I've chosen to continue rendering all pronominal references to the she-camel as feminine singular despite the fact that the Muslim community might otherwise be referred to as "they."

Chapter Ten

1. A *hizb* (plural, *aḥzāb*) is a spiritual litany consisting of verses from the Qur'ān, prayers of supplication and other phrases in a set order, the recitation of which is believed to bring blessing to those who recite it (see Danner, *Miftāḥ al-Falāḥ*, pp. 11–12).

2. Based on its use in the writings of Shaykh Muhyī al-Dīn Ibn al-ᶜArabī, Chittick defines the term *barzakh* as "an intermediary realm between Being and nothingness" (p. 14), which is, in essence, what the entire created realm is.

3. That these letters make up a set of symbols familiar to those who deal in the science of letters (*ᶜilm al-ḥurūf*).

4. For the definition of a *wird*, see Chapter 4, Note 15.

5. A veil can either be a form of protection or something which, by constituting a barrier between the perceiver and that which is perceived, prevents us from seeing reality as it is. Hence, the writer seeks both protection from harm and transgression through the veils of God's honor, and protection from those veils which would hinder him from perceiving truth fully.

6. The "increase" referred to here is God's promise to His servants of seeing His blessed countenance.

7. The person referred to here may be the angel Gabriel.

8. We often fail to realize where our true interests lie, as a result of which we do not know how to be truly merciful to ourselves; God, on the other hand, knows best what our souls genuinely need.

9. This concluding prayer for the Prophet appears in the Cairo edition, but not in the Damascus edition.

10. God's "initial, consummate act of goodness" was the act of bringing the creation into existence.

11. This may be a reference to the Angel Gabriel, upon him be peace.

12. The number seventy may be a reference to the 70 Muslim fighters who went into battle on the Day of Badr, while the number eight may refer to the Companions of the Cave, about whom some have said, "[They were] seven, the eighth of them being their dog" {Al-Kahf [The Cave] 18:22}.

13. In other words, God's relationship to the creation goes beyond mere immanence, in which case He would be coterminous with the universe, as well as mere transcendence, in which He would be inaccessible to created beings. Rather, He is both immanent and transcendent, within us and beyond us.

14. "The forty" may be a reference to the forty days which Moses spent with God on Mt. Sinai and during which he received guidance to be passed on to the people of Israel, as well as the forty days which Jesus spent fasting in the wilderness before embarking on his ministry. Based on the resultant significance of the number forty, Sufi practices include a forty-day retreat, at the conclusion of which there is the anticipation that God will open up a storehouse of experiential knowledge, light and wisdom to the person who has undergone this discipline.

Conclusion

1. For commentary on the meaning of the term *barzakh* in this context, see the Author's Introduction, Note 15.

2. In other words, after bringing His friends into union with Himself (*jam*[c]) through annihilation (*fanā'*), God brings them back into the world through the station of subsistence (*baqā'*), as a result of which they experience separation (*farq*) once again, only this time for the sake of bringing others into the union they themselves have experienced.

3. Narrated by al-Bukhārī in *al-Tārīkh*, as well as by al-Tirmidhī and Ibn Mājah. [ed.]

4. Yusuf Ali.

5. Narrated by Aḥmad, Abū Dāwūd, al-Tirmidhī and others on the authority of Abū al-Dardā' with a chain of transmission originating with the Prophet ﷺ. [ed.]

6. Plural of *wird*; for the definition of the term *wird*, see Chapter Four, Note 15.

7. Ibn al-[c]Arabī defines the term 'inrush' (*wārid*) as 'every praiseworthy incoming thought (*khāṭir*) which arrives at the heart without self-exertion; or, any affair which enters in upon the heart from any divine name'" (Chittick, p. 266, quoting from *Meccan Revelations* II 132.26).

8. See Note 2, Chapter 9.

9. God declares here that human beings bear within them a "secret" pertaining to the Divine Existence itself. This statement reflects the Sufi teaching that the human being is a microcosm of the universe and that as such, if one were to unlock the secrets of the human spirit, one would unlock the mysteries of existence itself.

10. This indeterminate "that" may refer to the "secret" mentioned in the previous verse. Similarly, it may refer to the human spirit, which

can never be observed directly, but only indirectly through the phe-nomena which point to its existence and nature.

11. The Arabic word rendered "oft-repeated verses," namely, *mathānī*, is commonly taken to refer to the Fātihah, or the opening chapter of the Qur'ān.

12. The word, "Nay!" (Arabic, *kallā*) as an expression of emphatic negation and/or affirmation appears upwards of twenty times in the Qur'ān in the context of God's address to His servants. When the Divine "Nay!" is uttered, those who have striven to draw near to God will find spiritual mysteries hastening to unfold before them.

13. In other words, when God declared that obedience to the Prophet was tantamount to obedience to Him, He was, in effect, erasing the distinction between Himself and the Prophet ﷺ. In so doing, He was removing the *kāf* which marks the "I-Thou" distinction (the letter *kāf* being the pronominal suffix in Arabic which would be rendered in English as "you," as in, "I see you"—*arāka*).

14. According to Ibn al-Mulaqqan, *Ṭabaqāt al-Awliyā'*, pp. 418–419, Muḥammad was not the name of Abū al-Abbās's father, but that of his grandfather; his father was named ᶜUmar.

APPENDIX

THE HELP OF WOMEN

Fons Vitae is ever grateful to Nancy Roberts of Amman, Jordan, for bringing these *Subtle Blessings* before the English-speaking world. It is indeed touching that so many ladies participated in the effort of translation, photography, publishing, and funding of this important work of classical Sufism.

Beyond the work at hand is the very shrine of Abū al-Ḥasan al-Shādhilī (d. 1258) located in Ḥumaythirā (Upper Egypt) whose establishment and maintenance has been well served by women. Most notable of these was Hagga Zakiyya who founded a rest house there for pilgrims and is buried (d. 1982) near this great saint. Hagga Zakiyya, herself, came to be recognized as a saint and *mawlids* are celebrated for her there in Ḥumaythirā as well.

In order to give the reader an "up-date," as it were, of this timeless mystical tradition and lineage as it endures today, we include the following offerings. Following Nancy's description of her experience in translating this work, we have a wonderful account of Hagga Zakiyya's life by Professor Valerie Hoffman, whose time in Egypt with Hagga Zakiyya's family, and those who knew her well, was deeply moving for her. One of Hagga Zakiyya's "spiritual daughters" has shared with us her intimate impression of this saintly woman, among other contributions. Leslie Cadavid, translator of *Two Who Attained* (which includes the autobiography of Sayyida Fatma al-Yashrutiyya, a renown woman Sufi), describes her recent visit to the site in Ḥumaythirā, and Noura Durkee relates her husband's personal account of this blessed place for us. We thank the many ladies who sent in their photography to embellish this volume—Haajar Gouverneur, Caroline Williams, Catherine Goddard, Leila Fitzcharles, Safina Habib, Noha Abou-Khatwa, and several gentlemen including Arin McNamara and Nurideen Durkee.

And so, from 1258 until today, we embrace all these dear friends who have preserved and transmitted so much for us all.

This appendix to *Subtle Blessings* concludes with an account of how the body of Ibn ᶜAṭa' Allāh al-Iskandari (d.1309), the author of the *Subtle Blessings* himself, was found and this site commemorated (his place of burial had been unknown until the twentieth century).

The Publisher

"May God love you as you have loved me," he replied, whereupon I complained to him of my cares and sorrows.

Then he said, may God be pleased with him, "There are only four states in which the servant of God will find himself: blessing, affliction, obedience and disobedience. If you are in a state of blessing, what the Truth requires of you is that you be thankful. If you are in a state of affliction, what the Truth requires of you is that you bear it patiently. If you are in a state of obedience, what the Truth requires of you is that you bear witness to His grace towards you; and if you are in a state of disobedience, what the Truth requires of you is that you seek forgiveness."

Ibn ᶜAṭa' Allāh al-Iskandari

The Translation

I would not be exaggerating if I said that the translation of this book felt like entering into a sacrament, day after day after day. From my first reading of its opening pages, I knew it had something profoundly special to offer me, and that I would be a fortunate woman indeed if I could convey it in English to others with a spiritual hunger in their hearts. For those who seek a better understanding of what it means to walk the Sufi path, Ibn ᶜAṭā' Allāh offers a marvelous entry, not by giving them a list of how-tos but, rather, simply by introducing his readers to his beloved shaykh, Abū al-ᶜAbbās al-Mursī and his shaykh's shaykh, Abū al-Ḥasan al-Shādhilī. As I entered their world—their actions, their words, and the formative influence they exerted on the author—I felt myself unwittingly receiving their blessing and wanting more than ever to experience something of the immediacy of the Divine which was so vivid for them. For those who struggle with crippling guilt, Ibn ᶜAṭā' Allāh brings assurance of the depth of the Divine mercy, and for those complacent in their righteousness, a reminder that even the most virtuous of our actions are nothing but gifts of grace. Whether in commenting on words from the Qur'ān or prophetic hadiths, relating incidents from his life and the lives of his spiritual masters, or transmitting the words of their prayers and spiritual litanies, this man of faith has a way of addressing spiritual truths to his reader's situation and infusing life with a sense of hope and Divine purpose, sometimes with a touch of humor, sometimes in a way that forces one to stop and puzzle, but never without the profoundest compassion and wisdom. Whoever reads Ibn ᶜAṭā' Allāh's words with an open heart will find both challenge and solace, a mirror reflecting his or her own frailties and a potion that offers renewed strength for the journey.

Nancy Roberts

Hagga Zakiyya in the early and later years of her lifetime, 1899–1982

Hagga Zakiyya ʻAbd Al-Muṭṭalib Badawī (1899-1982) of Cairo was a Sufi ascetic who combined a life of devotion with a life of hospitality, who taught mainly in an indirect fashion but exerted enormous influence, a miracle worker and "one whose prayers are answered." One of her followers mentions among her virtues *muru'ah*, which could mean valor or generosity but which literally means "manliness."[1] Yet the epithet most often bestowed upon her is "mother of compassion." Her compassion is almost always the first quality people mention in describing her. It is difficult to know whether this particular quality was cultivated so carefully, or perceived to be so dominant, because it is valued so highly in women. Surely Aḥmad Raḍwān (another recognized Sufi saint) could be characterized as compassionate in his care for his neighbors during the malaria and typhoid epidemic of 1944, yet he is more apt to be described as noble, generous, and righteous. People saw Hagga Zakiyya as a motherly figure, and it would appear that she also saw herself as a "mother" to many "children." She administered no oaths and gave no formal lessons, but the bonds she had with her spiritual children were often intense, and the transformations she effected in their lives were often profound.

Zakiyya ʻAbd al-Muṭṭalib Badawī came from the village of Mt. Muragga' Salsil in the Delta province of Mansura. Descendants of Husayn, her family is said to have been pious and exemplary. She married the son of her maternal aunt, Muḥammad al-Mahdī ʻAssasa, who, according to those who knew him, was a great scholar of Al-Azhar [2] as well as a Sufi. He followed, as his parents had before him, a Shadhili *shaykh* named ʿAbd al-Raḥīm al-Sabʾ (d. 1947), who lived by the shrine of Husayn in Cairo. Through her husband, Zakiyya also came to follow this shaykh and to assume the life of a devotee of the *ahl al-bayt*.[3] She would come to Cairo and visit all the shrines of the *ahl al-bayt* in a single day, beginning and ending with the shrine of Husayn, and on Friday evenings would attend the *ḥaḍrah*[4] of Shaykh ʿAbd al-Raḥīm, the only woman present, doing *dhikr* separately on a balcony overlooking the men.

From her marriage she had only one child, her daughter, Nafisa, who was conceived after a number of childless years. When Nafisa was only four years old, she told her father, "Divorce my mother!" Her father was astonished, because they were very happy together. But he consulted Shaykh ʿAbd al-Raḥīm, who advised him that the counsel was from God. He divorced Zakiyya, and both of them remarried. Zakiyya married another cousin from her village, a merchant who had no strong religious inclinations, but the marriage was not happy, and she eventually left him. One of Hagga Zakiyya's spiritual daughters testifies, "And I saw with my own eyes how much she loved her first husband's second wife." She speculates that perhaps God wanted her to experience life with an irreligious man so she would be able to empathize with the troubled people who were to come to her.

Hagga Zakiyya was, to all appearances, blind—since childhood, according to one follower. "But no one ever felt that she had lost her sight. She could see colors and would comment on them. She would see by the light of God." A young medical doctor, however, said, "People said she was blind, but she wasn't really blind. I was there personally when the medical doctors examined her and said there was

Hung in the *ṣaḥḥah* are these two likenesses.

On the left, the daughter, Sayyida Nafisa.

Below, the mother, Hagga Zakiyya.

"If created entities do lead [us] to God, they do so not out of some capacity which they possess in and of themselves. Rather, God is the One who has assigned them this function and they, accordingly, perform it. For nothing can lead to Him but His own divinity."

Abū al-ᶜAbbās al-Mursī

The entrance to Hagga Zakiyya's *ṣaḥḥah* in the Gamaliyya area near the Hussein mosque.

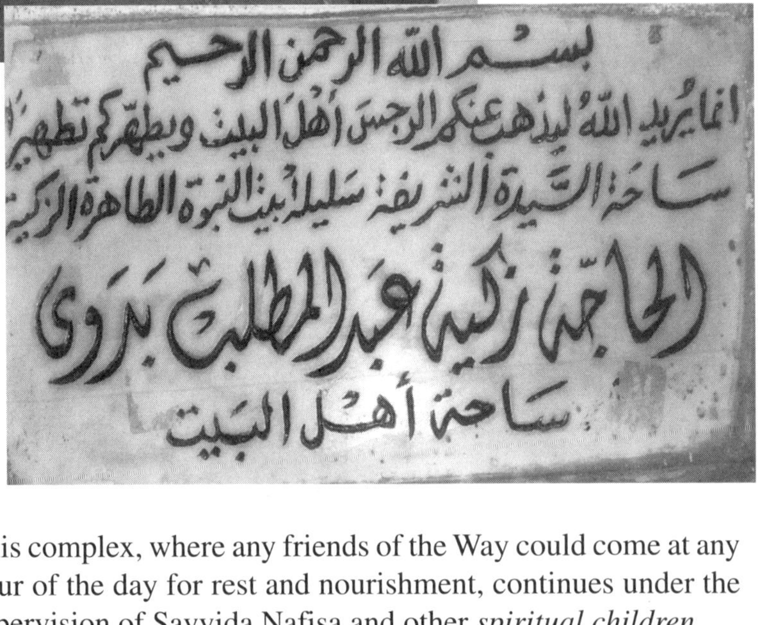

This complex, where any friends of the Way could come at any hour of the day for rest and nourishment, continues under the supervision of Sayyida Nafisa and other *spiritual children*.

nothing wrong with her eyes. But she didn't use her eyes, because she moved by inner vision (*baṣīrah*), not physical vision (*baṣar*)." Her spiritual devotions included much *dhikr* and recitations of praise, and a daily litany of prayers for blessings on the Prophet. She spent many nights in devotion and rarely needed to sleep at all. After her move to Cairo, she prayed the dawn prayer every morning in the mosque of Husayn.

According to one of Hagga Zakiyya's spiritual sons, "She was overcome by lights, and the *ahl al-bayt* (in a moment of intense spiritual connection) ordered her to come to Cairo." She took an apartment in the Darrasa district, near the shrine of Husayn, where she began her life's ministry of offering hospitality, kindness, and spiritual guidance to "children of the Way." Her spiritual son continued, "She solved their problems, gave kindness to the needy, and prayed for those in distress. God, may He be exalted, did not disappoint her hopes but met needs at her hands, and she solved the problems of all who came to her. If a rebellious person came to her, God changed him into something good, both women and men. Many repented at her hands and became saints of God, having shrines and being visited by the pious." Later, when her father died, she used her inheritance to buy a piece of land in the Gamaliyya area even closer to the Husayn mosque, where she built a *ṣaḥḥah*[5] complex that includes three buildings with a number of bedrooms, a kitchen, and a mosque, in the words of a follower, "to honor those who love the *ahl al-bayt*."

Her method was a spiritual discernment and influence by simple association. "God gave her a light in her heart by which she knew the needs of those who came to her and those who needed her kindness," says one of her followers. She would welcome anyone into her presence, and kept her *ṣaḥḥah* open and her kitchen operative twenty-four hours a day. Although she spent a good deal of time in solitary devotion, emerging, according to one follower, only on Fridays to sit with her followers and circulate among all the rooms of the *ṣaḥḥah*, anyone could knock on her door at any time. She would become angry if anyone were refused an audience with her. "She welcomed everyone," said one of her spiritual daughters. "Each one felt that she loved him more than anyone else. She would be interested in your problem, and you would feel able to bear it after being with her." She would not correct people openly but would test people secretly to determine their character. She offered her children words of counsel and exhortations to be patient, generous, open-minded, striving for what is good, and obedient to God and His Messenger. Little by little those around her would change for the better. One of her spiritual daughters said this was God's grace to her, that she always obtained the desired moral effect on people without making them feel it.

Other stories tell of dramatic healings from moral defects, mental illness, or spirit possession. One woman who suffered from association with a man whose spiritual power was derived from jinn came to Hagga Zakiyya in great fear of the man's power. He had threatened to harm her and her family if she ever left him, and when she realized that his power was derived not from God but from jinn, she did not know where to turn. But Hagga Zakiyya paralyzed him and stripped him of his power shortly after she first came to know her, and soon the man died. Like so many people healed by Hagga Zakiyya, she became a close follower, visiting her several times each week despite the distance of her home from Hagga Zakiyya's *ṣaḥḥah*.

One man tells of his attachment to Hagga Zakiyya: "On a Friday after the death of my mother, I went to the mosque of our lord Imam Husayn, where I saw a man who was one of the leading followers of the Gnostic, Hagga Zakiyya. He asked me, 'What is wrong?' I told him, 'I am terribly depressed over the death of my mother.' He said, 'I will show you a mother who has kindness, compassion, and mercy.' I went with him to the *ṣaḥḥah* of this virtuous lady. When I saw her I began to weep. She motioned to me to sit next to her. I did, and said nothing, but wept. She felt sorry for me and patted me without saying anything. Then she said to me, 'You are thinking of your mother. I have more compassion for you than your mother of whom you are thinking. I belong to you in this world and the next. Any time you are troubled, remember me with the *Fātiḥah*[6], and your troubles will vanish.' I have lived my whole life with her since 1952, until she passed to the mercy of God, in compassion and in contentment."

His attachment to her became profound, and he developed the habit of visiting her and dining with her every day after work. He says, "I have only had troubles in my life since her death." He accompanied her on the pilgrimage four times. He says, "After the morning prayer in the Prophet's mosque, she would stand for a long time. I became tired, but I said, 'It is better that she is with her grandfather, the Messenger of God,' and I was afraid to talk with her [to tell her of my fatigue]. But she [sensed it and] said, 'Visitation is over, Hagg 'Abduh.'

"When she went to the Meccan sanctuary, I saw that the path in front of her was wide open [despite the density of the crowds during the pilgrimage]. When she entered the Kaaba, people made way for her, and no one touched her. She kissed the Black Stone[7] for a long time."

Both Hagga Zakiyya's sensitivity to Hagg 'Abduh's fatigue ("everyone felt that she could feel what they felt," said another follower) and the unobstructed path before her during the pilgrimage are seen as miraculous. Most pilgrims are lucky if they get a chance to touch the Black Stone, but she kissed it a long time, following the example of the Prophet. The fact that no one in the crowd touched her implies not only her spiritual power but also the preservation of her female modesty and dignity.

Nonetheless, her female modesty and dignity did not prevent her from embracing men or enjoying emotional intimacy with them. A mother, after all, may do so with her sons. As we have seen, Shaykh 'Izz says she used to have him lay his head in her lap, and called him her daughter, not her son, to indicate that fleshly labels had become meaningless. Shaykh 'Izz at that time was a young man, and she was already an elderly woman with an aura of compassion and holiness. I commented to 'Izz that her appearance in her photographs is formidable, swathed in heavy cloths up to her mouth or even her nose, her eyes covered by sunglasses, her features sharp, her body thin. Such things suggested aloofness to me, not the warmth and openness I heard from those who knew her. 'Izz agreed that her appearance was formidably dignified and that when he first met her he was afraid of her. But gradually he came to see her as the warm, loving person everyone described.

"Hagga" (or "*ḥājjah*") is a title given to a woman who has performed the pilgrimage (*ḥajj*) to Mecca, just as "Hagg" (or "*ḥajj*") is given to a man. There could scarcely be a woman more deserving of the title than Hagga Zakiyya, who performed the pilgrimage twenty-six times and performed the lesser pilgrimage (*'umra*) more than fifty times. Many of her miracles occurred during the pilgrimage. She

The daughter and grandson of Hagga Zakiyya,
Cairo, 2005.

Her bedroom in the *ṣaḥḥah* as she left it.

I was told by Shaykh Shihāb al-Dīn al-Abarqūhī, "I went in to see Shaykh Abū al-Ḥasan al-Shādhilī (may God be pleased with him) and heard him say, 'God, almighty and majestic is He, says, "O My servant, make Me your supreme concern and I will guard you from that which causes you concern. O My servant, so long as you belong to yourself, you are in the place of remoteness, and so long as you live through Me, you are in the place of nearness. So choose for yourself."'"

Shaykh Abū al-ʿAbbās al-Mursī

invited a woman to accompany her on the pilgrimage at the last minute, although the woman had neither a passport nor a plane ticket. The woman boarded the plane with her, and although the flight crew and authorities in Saudi Arabia were alerted that an unauthorized woman had boarded the plane, the number of passengers was always correct, and the woman was never detected. On one of her pilgrimages with Hagg 'Abduh, Hagga Zakiyya pulled fish out of the sand and told him to cook it for the pilgrims. He fried some of it and made soup with the rest, and though many pilgrims ate, the food did not run out. In fact, it lasted for five days in that hot climate un-refrigerated before the supply was finally exhausted, and always remained fresh.

On one of her pilgrimages performed with a young woman, Hagga Zakiyya instructed the young woman to go on ahead of her at the Kaaba and find a Hagga Zaynab from Ḥusayn, whom she described as a dark woman wearing a green dress. The young woman did as she was told, confident that despite the crowd, the saint's *baraka* (transmission of blessing) would enable her to find Hagga Zaynab. Soon she saw a woman of this description. Furthermore, the woman ran to her immediately and, hearing that Hagga Zakiyya was there, rushed to find her. The two women embraced and talked at length, head to head. But when the woman had gone, Hagga Zakiyya said to her young companion, "It is not her." The young woman was puzzled but went and found another woman of the same description, spoke to her, and confirmed that she was indeed Hagga Zaynab from Husayn, and went with her to Hagga Zakiyya. After that woman had gone, the young woman asked Hagga Zakiyya about the first woman. Zakiyya replied, "She doesn't speak Arabic." "And this," exclaimed the young woman who told me the story, "after they had talked with their heads close together for a long time! She didn't openly admit it, but she could understand all the languages. Once when I was talking with an American visitor I misunderstood something he said, and Hagga Zakiyya gently and subtly corrected me, saying, 'He meant such-and-such,' although she allegedly knew no foreign languages at all! Although Hagga Zakiyya didn't perform miracles openly, she could have turned a wall into gold if she'd so desired!"

Her miracles were many: miracles of knowledge and healing and the ability to transcend spatial limitations and appear in more than one place at a time. Shaykh 'Izz said that Ahmad Radwan had said that she was one of the *abdāl*, that category of saints who could produce replicas of themselves, and appear and disappear at will. A woman said that one time she placed her hand on top of Hagga Zakiyya's, and found that there was nothing there at all.

She also visited the tomb of Sidi Abū al-Ḥasan al-Shādhilī, in the remote mountainous region of Ḥumaythirā, near the Red Sea, three or four times a year toward the end of her life. According to one of her followers, Hagga Zaynab, she was the first woman to visit the tomb, in the early 1920s, before she was even married. At that time the way to Sidi Shādhilī was a dangerous desert journey without any proper road to a place that had no electricity or water and was inhabited only by poverty-stricken Bedouins who were ignored by the government and who in turn shunned the rest of society. Later, when Shaykh 'Abd al-Ḥalīm Maḥmūd was head of the Islamic University of al-Azhar in the 1970s, he had a beautiful white shrine and mosque complex built in honor of Sidi Shādhilī. Hagga Zakiyya returned, bringing with her a group of women. A woman who was among the group says, "We found that by merely visiting the shrine, everything changed for us: colors changed, we were able to keep from anger, from passions, our spiritual senses were heightened."

When Hagga Zakiyya saw the poverty of the Bedouins of the region around Sidi Shadhili, she decided to build a *ṣaḥḥah* to serve them. This *ṣaḥḥah* was completed only in the last year of her life, but her generous hospitality became well known among the local people long before that. Says one of her followers, "The government itself showed no interest in them until after the 1967 war. They had no social services whatsoever, and no conscription. She is the one who brought electricity there and arranged for trucks to bring in water and food every day. The governor went and visited her because he heard there was a seventy-year-old woman in that harsh climate who had no education and was blind...The Bedouin women never used to let any strange person see them at all. They would go to Hagga Zakiyya, where she sat on her bed, and they would call her 'Mama.' She would give them sweet things and money."

Today, the *ṣaḥḥah* built by Hagga Zakiyya is one of several in the area around Sidi Shadhili, which, thanks to paved roads and daily public buses, is visited by pilgrims year-round. Among the *ṣaḥḥahs* in the area, however, only that of Hagga Zakiyya is constantly open and serving meals to visitors, who also sleep in one of the bedrooms of the *ṣaḥḥah* or on the benches on its veranda. Her spiritual children who service the *ṣaḥḥah* continue to pay special attention to any of the Bedouin who come for a meal. Indeed, the more ragged and poverty-stricken the visitor, the more he is treated with honor, because these were the ones Hagga Zakiyya especially loved.

It is said that Sidi Shādhilī informed Hagga Zakiyya that she would die near him, and indeed this transpired. Hagga Zakiyya was aware of the date of her death seven months before it occurred. Ibrahim Ramadan 'Ali, the "Shaykh Faris" who wrote a book on the virtues of the *ahl al-bayt*, tells in this book that he visited her at the Shādhilī shrine during the feast of the great sacrifice (*'Īd al-Aḍḥā*) shortly before she died, and she requested that he remain twenty days after the feast. He asked why, and she said, "So you can wish me farewell, for I am traveling soon." He excused himself because of prior commitments, and they tearfully embraced before his departure. True to her word, she died twenty days after the feast, on December 24, 1982. She is buried in a shrine adjacent to her *ṣaḥḥah* in Ḥumaythirā.

This selection is excerpted from *Sufism, Mystics, and Saints in Modern Egypt*, by Valerie J. Hoffman (Columbia: University of South Carolina Press, 1995), pp. 291–99., reprinted in *Women of Sufism, A Hidden Treasure*, selected and introduced by Camille Helminski, Shambhala, 2003.

1. See Sachiko Murata, *The Tao of Islam*, for a discussion of gender.

2. Al-Azhar is the oldest university in the world. Founded in 969 C.E., it remains today the primary center of Islamic learning in the world.

3. *Ahl al-bayt*, "the people of the house," refers especially to the family of Muḥammad (may peace and blessings be upon them all): the Prophet; his daughter Fāṭimah and her husband, 'Ali; their children, Ḥasan and Ḥusayn; and their descendants. Ḥusayn and many of his descendants are buried in Cairo.

4. *Ḥaḍrah* is the word for "presence," used to refer to the Divine Presence; it has also come to be used as a title of respect (*hazrat*). In Egypt it is the term often used to refer to *zhikr* gatherings.

5. A *ṣaḥḥah* is a center for receiving the friends of the Way.

6. *Fātiḥah*: See note 14 of the selection by Annemarie Schimmel, on p. 106.

7. The Black Stone is the cornerstone of the Kaaba. See note 7 in the chapter "Those Who Weep," p. 42.

When I first met Hagga Zakiyya, she appeared to be quite elderly. When she entered the room she looked at me. Shortly thereafter she tapped me on my back and said "Mabruk" (which can mean both "congratulations" and "a blessed state" of being). I thought to myself, "Why is she saying 'Mabruk' to me?" At that time I was suffering in myself because I found it too difficult to keep up the regular five daily prayers. But when I parted company with Hagga Zakiyya I found myself making the full ablution and from that time forward I have never stopped praying.

When I asked her what she "does," she replied, "I move people from the Left to the Right." We are like transparent glasses to her and she is able to see the dust inside us. I found that although she was present to me in this world, she dwelled in *upper spheres*. And although she was blind, she could *see*.

She often took the illnesses of people onto herself. Once when visiting a person with cancer in the hospital she pulled the malady upon herself, leaving the patient cured. She became very sick for a period of time.

I noted that she was able to be in two places at once—that while she was in Cairo, she could also be in Jeddah with me.

She was a very great soul who changed the lives of many people whether they were judges, lawyers, police or army officers. Such spiritual luminaries of the time as Shaykh 'Abd al-Haleem Mahmoud and Shaykh Sharawi were frequent visitors. Shaykh 'Abd al-Haleem Mahmoud was the Rector of the Islamic University of al-Azhar (founded 969) and later became "Shaykh al-Islam."

Shaykh Abd al-Haleem Mahmoud

Doctora Zahira Abdeen

Some of the great religious personages who visited Hagga Zakiyya included Shaykh Salih al-Jaffari, the imam of the Azhar mosque. His photograph hangs on the wall of her *ṣaḥḥah*.

Shaykh Salih as a younger man. His *maqam* is located in Darasa, near al-Azhar (founded 969 C.E.) in the district of the mosque of Sayyidina Hussein, where he is known for several *karamat*.

Shaykh Salih al-Jaffari al-Tariqa al-Ja'fariyya al-Ahmadiyya al-Muhammadiyya

I called her "Amma"—which means mother. Once I told her of an occurrence which happened to me when I was fifteen years of age living in New York City. I was taken to a renowned Hindu Guru who did not speak. He signaled me to draw closer.

When I looked into his eyes, I began to weep most profoundly. I explained to Amma that I had been greatly moved by a Hindu although he was not from among the People of the Book (those from Judaism, Christianity and Islam). She explained, "Yes, you *recognized* a high soul." When I asked what she meant by this, she discretely replied, "My daughter, you *recognized*."

When my father died I went to the mosque of Sayyidina Hussein and prayed to Hussein, asking him to care for my father. Later in the day I went to Zakiyya's home and she mentioned, "Your father came (to me) and thanks you for what you did this morning." Hagga Zakiyya herself never mourned for those who died, as she saw death as a door that simply opened onto another room—death was an entrance. And Hagga Zakiyya, though blind, could actually see.

In anticipation of her own death to this world, Hagga Zakiyya was actually the first Cairene who had been able to obtain permission to be buried in her own home (as was the Prophet Mohammad) located near the Hussein mosque, where she nourished and fed those in need.

For many years however, she had been making the arduous journey to Ḥumaythirā, a place in the desert in the southern part of Egypt, east from Luxor, nearing the Red Sea where the great saint Sidi Abū al-Ḥasan al-Shādhilī was buried. She found many poor Bedouins there for whom she had a rest house constructed. She regularly took them clothes and food. A small room was built for her to stay in during these visits.

In 1982, Hagga Zakiyya was preparing to travel again to Arabia to visit the sanctuary of the Kaaba at Mecca and the mosque in Medina whose precincts include the home—and grave within—of the Prophet Mūḥammad, peace be upon him. She stopped in Ḥumaythirā.

While there, the Prophet Muḥammad came to Amma and said that Sidi Abū al-Ḥasan al-Shādhilī had asked his permission that she stay and be buried near him in Egypt. You have to understand that Amma was spiritually in touch with Shaykh Abū al-Ḥasan, Seyyed Ahmad al-Badawi and Abū al-ᶜAbbās al-Mursī.

She asked some of the people of Ḥumaythirā to inform the shaykh of the mosque that preparations would be needed for her death on the following day. She commented, "I died fifty years ago—it's just a formality to be put in a tomb." To each of those sitting around her she inquired, "Are you in need of anything?" They replied no. Her last words to them were, "*As-salamu aleikum wa Rahmatallah wa Barakatuh* (The peace and blessings of God be upon you, and His mercy)."

Reflections shared with us by a lady from Arabia who prefers anonymity.

The Prophet Muhammad ﷺ was buried in his home, which a green dome now covers in Medina.

How the Road Was Built

This story is paraphrased from a lesson given by Shaykh Abdullah Nooruddeen Durkee to a gathering of students as part of an introduction to the Way of the Shadhdhuliyya. He knows all the people involved, and has traveled that road many times with them in visits to Shaykh Abū al-Ḥasan al-Shādhilī. They always go to pay their respects at Hajjah Zakiyyah's house there, and to lie on her bed. In that house is a telephone which she used, long before the days of cordless phones, to call Cairo; it has no connection to any phone line whatsoever.

Abd al-Haleem Mahmoud, was the Shaykh of Azhar, his title being both a recognition of his scholarship and denoting a very high position in the Egyptian government. He was on a political visit to the Red Sea Province as the guest of its governor Ma'dawi Az-Zirr. He told Ma'dawi of his deep wish to visit Abū al-Ḥasan's *maqam* in Ḥumaythirā. His host ordered up the helicopter that had brought him, there being no other way to get there, and they flew from the seat of governance to Ḥumaythirā, which is in a very inhospitable place in the middle of a very bleak desert. The only redeeming thing about it is that there is a sweet spring there that used to be brackish and undrinkable. It is sweet because one time on a visit Sidi Abū al-Ḥasan spit into it; now the water is delightful. There are many miracles like that from the *awliyya* (saints) of Allah. In any case, they went by helicopter, accompanied by Shaykh Dr. Ibrahim al-Battawi. Hajjah Zakiyyah was living there, as she wanted to be close to Sidi Abū al-Ḥasan at the end of her life, and they were all sitting around, talking, and somebody said to her, 'You know, Hajjah, it would be great if there were a

Hanging on the chamber wall above the tomb of Ibn ᶜAṭāʾ Allāh, is this photograph taken beside Abū al-Ḥasan al-Shādhilī. From left to right are Shaykh Ibrahim al-Battawi, Shaykh Abd al-Haleem Mahmoud, and Abd al-Haleem al-Mujahid.

road to get here.' She said, 'Why, that's a very good idea!' She had known the governor for a long time, as she was also from a very well known and well-connected established family. So she told him, 'Look, Ma'adawi, you build the road - here!' And she reached into her bag, and pulled out five piasters, which is about the smallest amount of money you can think of. Everybody laughed and said, "Ya, Hajjah, you know these people, lovers of Allah, they're crazy people, and like that." But Ma'dawi took the five piasters.

Now, shortly after that time President Sadat went and made peace in Al Quds (Jerusalem), at the insistance of a man by the name of General Hasan al-Tahami, who used to be the vice president of Egypt under Nasser. Nasser wanted to get rid of him for a while at one point, so when there was a delegation of shaykhs and other people that came from the Maghrib, he said to Hasan al-Tahami, 'Go, take these people down to visit Abū al-Ḥasan.' General Tahami was a very straight guy; he had fought in all the wars, and he was a real hero, having fought bare-handed and single-handed. He was a real man among men. He was from Ahl-i-Beit, but he was not involved in Sufism or anything like that. So he went there, and he fell so in love with Sidi Abū al-Ḥasan that he slept there for three months. He never came back to his old state, and he resigned his vice-presidency and everything, just to stay in the company of Abū al-Ḥasan. Of course, Abū al-Ḥasan had passed away many centuries before, but as Allah says, "And do not say that those who are slain in the Way of Allah are dead. Rather, they are living, but you do not know [in what way]" {Q 2:154}.

So, when Sadat made his famous journey north, and when peace came between Egypt and Israel, one of the negotiations concerned some islands south of Sinai that produce oil. Israel had been pumping that oil, but in the terms of the peace accord, it reverted to Egypt. And on that oil there was a five piaster tax, which was to be used for what? Road building. The Americans liked this idea, and they said, "Every five piasters that you take off the top of this, we will match with another five piasters, and we will give you engineers from America to help build the roads." So the Egyptians and the Americans thought among themselves about what would be the most difficult place to try out their new skills. There was an existing road from Edfu to Marsa 'Alam between the Nile and the Red Sea. About half way across it, they decided to build a road through the desolate desert south to: Abū al-Ḥasan.

Nowadays, this is a four or five hour trip from Edfu by road, a road entirely paid for by the five piaster tax on the oil, which was then matched by the United States government with their five piasters to build a road to Abū al-Ḥasan. It doesn't go anyplace else. It stops at his tomb.

Hajjah Noura Durkee

In the winter of 2004, my husband and I along with two friends decided to visit the tomb of the great saint and founder of the Shadhili Sufi Order, Abū al-Ḥasan al-Shādhilī, who is buried in a village called Ḥumaythirā in Upper Egypt, between the Nile and the Red Sea. We knew that many pilgrims visited this desert sanctuary every year, and that the place was inhabited originally only by a few Bedouin. The presence of the great Shadhili master had made it become a community of *Khanqahs*, or Sufi rest-houses. We were told by a friend that the best rest-house to stay in was that of the Shaykha Zakkiya, and that we should ask when we arrived, for the caretaker, one Muḥammad Abdul Latif. We thought it interesting that a Shaykha had lived there, or was at least buried there, and set off eagerly on our journey.

We arrived in the late afternoon to the small town of simple dwellings, and before arriving at the tomb of the great Shaykh, stopped at another tomb and rest-house, that of the Shaykha Zakkiya. Muḥammad Abdul Latif greeted us, and gave us permission to stay overnight there. As we entered the courtyard, we saw a beautiful structure that housed the remains of the Shaykha. When we asked about her, Muḥammad Abdul Latif told us that she was a very great saint, and showed us a photograph of her that hangs in the outer corridor. She was very beautiful, clearly an aristocrat with most luminous eyes. He recounted to us that she had come very often on pilgrimage to visit "Sidi Abū al-Ḥasan" and then had a vision ordering her to move there. This she did, and lived in a room in the rest-house compound until her death. We were invited to visit her room, and immediately felt an enormous *barakah*, like a wave of sweetness and mercy from above. Later, after visiting the tomb of Sidi Abū al-Ḥasan, just a few minutes' walk away, we retired to our rooms in the rest-house, but there were many cats in our room, and my husband, who is very allergic to cats, could not sleep. We tried to chase the cats away, and Muḥammad Abdul Latif heard us. We had to explain why we were awake, and much to our surprise and delight, we were given permission to sleep in the blessed room of the Shaykha! My husband told me in the morning that he had never had such a blissful sleep, and I could almost touch her luminous presence that night.

After returning from Ḥumaythirā, we found out much more about this great and most generous saint—of how she fed many in the area of Sayyidna Hussein in Cairo, of how she helped the ill and those in difficulties. We feel very fortunate to have felt the unexpected grace of her presence.

Leslie Cadavid

"My heart was enlightened one day and I saw the kingdom of the seven heavens and the seven earths. I then committed a minor sin, after which the vision was concealed from me. I was astonished that such a trifling occurrence could conceal from me something so momentous. Just then someone said to me, '[Spiritual] insight is like [physical] sight: The tiniest thing that gets in the eye can obstruct one's vision.'"

Abū al-Ḥasan al-Shādhilī

أبوبكر عمر

بسم الله الرحمن الرحيم

(رحمت الله وبركاته عليكم أهل البيت إنه حميد مجيد)

صدق الله العظيم

اللهم صلى على سيدنا محمد الفاتح لما أغلق و الخاتم لما سبق
ناصر الحق بالحق و الهادى إلى صراطك المستقيم وعلى آله.
حق قدره ومقداره العظيم

السيد / ....

نتشرف بدعوة سيادتكم لحضور الإحتفال الدينى بمولد

السيدة زكيه عبد المطلب بدوى

(رضى الله عنها)

برحاب سيدى أبا الحسن الشاذلى رضى الله عنه بحميثرا - بمحافظة البحر الأحمر

. وإفتتاح المولد ١٤ صفر ١٤٢٦ هـ الموافق ٢٤ / ٣ / ٢٠٠٥ م

و الليلة الختامية ٢٨ صفر ١٤٢٦ هـ الموافق ٧ / ٤ / ٢٠٠٥ م

أعاده الله عليكم بالخير و السعادة و الدعوة عامة

الداعية الحاجة /

نفيسة محمد المهدى

عثمان على

An invitation to attend events (2005) in honor of Hagga Zakiyya at Ḥumaythirā, including a *moulid* celebrating her birth.

Pilgrims visiting the shrine of Hagga Zakiyya.

Shaykh [c]Abd al-Haleem Mahmoud,
Rector of Al-Azhar University and *Shaykh al-Islam*.

The tomb of [c]Alī al-Wafā[ɔ] (d. 1405) within the confines of a mosque standing within view of the place where Ibn [c]Aṭa[ɔ] Allāh's (d. 1309) body was discovered.

In 1969, Shaykh Abd al-Haleem Mahmoud (may God be pleased with him) was the Director of the Islamic Research Academy of al-Azhar University (built in 969 C.E. Cairo) and was soon to be appointed Shaykh al-Azhar, making him the "intellectual director" of the Islamic World, as it were. Shaykh Abd al-Haleem, a graduate of the Sorbonne, was a saintly man, and a spiritual master of the Shadhili Sufi order, whose lineage goes back to Ibn ᶜAṭaᵓ Allāh al-Iskandari, and his master Abū al-ᶜAbbās al-Mursī who succeeded Abū al-Ḥasan al-Shādhilī.

In the early 1970s, Dr. Abd al-Haleem asked a friend of ours, and some others, to try to locate the site where Ibn ᶜAṭaᵓ Allāh had been buried so that the place could be properly marked and acknowledged. This company of friends set about digging in the appropriate vicinity, near to the shrine of ᶜAlī al-Wafāᵓ, who followed in the spiritual lineage of Ibn ᶜAṭaᵓ Allāh. There arose from the excavation the smell of perfume—which those digging described as a "perfume not of this world" but paradisal. Soon they came upon the actual body of Ibn ᶜAṭaᵓ Allāh which was unchanged. The bodies of some saints do not seem to be subject to time or decay, but remain as they were before death.

Over this hallowed spot a small prayer room was constructed which included a *mushrabiyya* (wooden lattice) screen surrounding the cenotaph indicating the place of burial below. In this chamber hangs a wonderful photograph of Shaykh Abdul Haleem next to the grave of Shaykh Abū al-Ḥasan al-Shādhilī. Later it was decided that a mosque should be built and attached to this small shrine.

The completed mosque and *maqam* built in the 1970s, made possible by the generosity of Abdul Haleem Mujahid.

On July 23, 1973, the new mosque was opened.

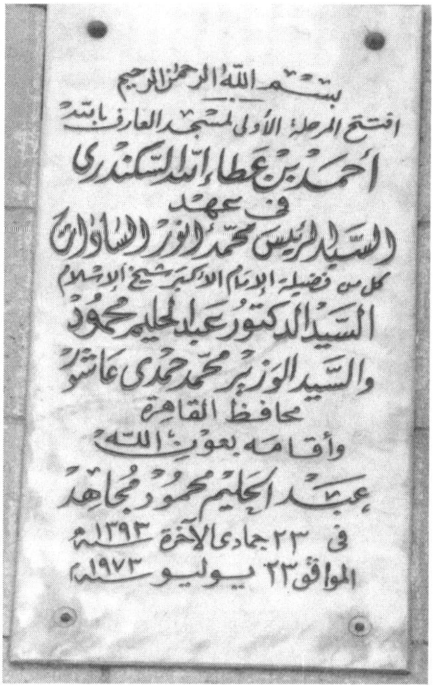

The patron, who saw to the finances of this undertaking, noticed that each time he went to remove needed funds from his safe, the original amount miraculously never diminished. Surprised, he mentioned this to Shaykh Abd al-Haleem, who then explained that once he had mentioned this occurrence to anyone, the funds would begin depletion when drawn upon.

When the beautiful mosque, with its geometric designs painted on the ceiling, was completed—there beside the cliffs of the Muqattam Hills with a view far off of the pyramids on the distant west bank of the Nile, friends assembled. Shaykh Abd al-Haleem climbed up the *mimbar* (pulpit) and spoke to us. Among those present was Hawa (Eva) de Vitray Meyerovitch who had translated Rumi's work into French and was preparing to make the pilgrimage.

I wanted to commit this account, as I recall it, to paper lest it be unknown in subsequent generations.

Aisha Gouverneur

The view from the tombs of Ibn ᶜAṭaᵓ Allāh and ᶜUmar Ibn al-Faarid of the pyramids on the far west bank of the Nile.

Shaykh Muḥyī al-Dīn Ibn ᶜArabī, may God be pleased with him, said, "We were once invited by some of the poor to a meal in Ziqāq al-Qanādīl in Cairo, where a number of shaykhs gathered. There was so much food that the vessels in which it was served could hardly hold it all. Among these was a new glass pot which had been acquired for use as a urinal but which had not yet been put to use. The host was dipping the food out of it, and as the group ate, it said, "Now that God has honored me by allowing such noble souls to eat from me, never will I allow myself to be a place of offense," whereupon it broke in two.

"Did you hear what the pot said?" I asked them.

"Yes, we did," they replied.

"What did you hear?" I asked.

In reply, they repeated the words above.

"It [also] said something else," I told them.

"What is that?" they queried.

I replied, "It said, 'So it is with your hearts: Now that God has honored them with faith, never again allow them to be the site of the impurity of disobedience and love of the world. God has given you and us understanding from Him and the ability to receive His disclosures thanks to His grace and bounty.'"

Ibn ᶜAṭaᵓ Allāh

Index

A

ᶜAbd Allāh al-Jībī 113
ᶜAbd al-Raḥmān al-Madanī 114
ᶜAbd al-Salām Ibn Mashīsh 66, 96, 114, 134
Abraham 13, 16, 191, 192, 197, 198, 272, 273, 345, 349, 350, 354, 361, 376
abstinence 151, 155, 156, 157, 158, 292. *See waraᶜ*
Abū al-ᶜAbbās Ibn al-ᶜArīf 131
Abū al-ᶜAbbās al-Bujā'ī, 128
Abū al-ᶜAbbās al-Damanhūrī 127
Abū Bakr 60, 75, 96, 111, 134, 154, 224, 225, 230, 232, 234, 242, 243, 284, 287, 290, 291, 295
Adam 5, 11, 12, 105, 235, 244, 285, 288, 307, 309, 340, 350, 390, 405
Aden 157
ahl al-ṣuffah 236, 403
Alexandria 93, 94, 95, 98, 105, 121, 125, 127, 138, 139, 140, 143, 145, 153, 156, 166, 183, 184, 277, 289, 293, 301, 365, 374, 401
ᶜAlī Ibn Abī Ṭālib 25, 89, 114
Allāh 12, 27, 29, 43, 90, 91, 96, 97, 112, 113, 114, 121, 124, 125, 126, 142, 143, 265, 270, 271, 272, 387, 395
Allāh Ibn al-Nuᶜmān 129
Anas Ibn Mālik 12, 15, 16
annihilation 38, 39, 40, 42, 48, 71, 226, 265, 269, 283, 291, 307, 312, 314, 333, 366, 373, 396, 401, 402, 403, 407, 409. *See fanā'*
Ashmūm 128, 139
asrār 151, 249. *See* mysteries
assurance 255, 373. *See tamkīn*
Aswān 127

B

badal 398. *See* substitute
Baghdad 156, 210
Bahansā 119, 129
baqā' 38, 283, 407, 409. *See* permanence
basṭ 258, 259. *See* gaiety
Battle of Badr 284

C

Cairo 92, 98, 128, 129, 166, 212, 301, 365, 392, 395, 401, 408
certainty 3, 6, 27, 28, 43, 45, 47, 53, 56, 64, 65, 71, 74, 75, 79, 85, 152, 197, 220, 223, 224, 241, 250, 254, 255, 256, 270, 289, 339, 342, 354, 373. *See yaqīn*
communion 49, 64, 212, 216, 217, 253, 312, 320, 342, 375. *See* muwāṣalah
contentment 45, 64, 70, 75, 80, 108, 162, 251, 268, 276, 351, 361
courtesy 17, 57, 58, 86, 116, 275, 277, 378, 379, 391, 393